# A CENTURY OF AMERICAN POPULAR MUSIC

D0169239

# A CENTURY OF
# AMERICAN POPULAR MUSIC

2000 BEST-LOVED

AND REMEMBERED SONGS

(1899–1999)

## DAVID A. JASEN

ROUTLEDGE

NEW YORK   LONDON

Published in 2002 by
Routledge
29 West 35th Street
New York, NY 10001

Published in Great Britain by
Routledge
11 New Fetter Lane
London EC4P 4EE

Copyright © 2002 by David A. Jasen

Routledge is an imprint of the Taylor & Francis Group.

Printed in the United States of America on acid-free paper.

All rights reserved. No part of this book may be reprinted or reproduced or utilized in
any form or by any electronic, mechanical, or other means, now known or hereafter invented, including photocopying and recording, or in any information storage or retrieval
system, without permission in writing from the publisher.

Library of Congress Cataloging-in-Publication Data
Jasen, David A.
       A century of American popular music (1899–1999) :
       2000 best-loved and remembered songs / David A. Jasen.
          p.  cm.
       Includes indexes.
       ISBN 0-415-93700-0
       1. Popular music—United States—Bibliography.
       I. Title.

    ML128.P63 J37 2002
    016.78242164—dc21                              2001043112

Ref.
ML
128
.P63
J37
2002

*TO GENE JONES*
*MY DEAR FRIEND AND COLLABORATOR*
*WHO ALSO LOVES THESE SONGS*

7/14/04 RSR #47658890

# CONTENTS

# INTRODUCTION

In the twentieth century, American popular music became the dominant world musical style. Running the gamut from Victorian sentimental songs through blues and jazz and swing to rock, R&B, country, and soul, this music has defined an entire era of cultural history. This book attempts to index the best of this music. It is hoped that all of this pertinent information, gathered together for the first time in one easy-to-use volume, will appeal to the casual reader, the fan, the music critic, the archivist, the academician, and the professional musician.

The book is organized in several parts. The main section of the book lists songs alphabetically by title, giving full annotations and information. Following that are indexes of Academy Award–winning songs; indexes by composer and by publisher (giving song title); and a chronological list.

Determining the "best" is a difficult job. In this book, we've used several different criteria:

1. *Most popular.* Determining which songs were most popular in their day is more difficult than you might first expect. Prior to the mid-1930s, there were no "charts" of greatest hits, and sales information is not always available for sheet music or recordings. Sales figures are often reported that can't be verified. After the charts came in, they themselves were open to manipulation by recording executives and others, so that it's difficult to say whether a "number 1 hit" really was more popular than a number 5 or number 10 hit. When Soundscan was introduced in the mid-1980s—a service that recorded actual sales of records at major retailers—many people were surprised to see songs reaching number 1 on the pop charts that previously would have been considered only country hits.

At one time, a number 1 song was the one that was covered by the most artists and/or sold the most copies of sheet music; after recordings came in, this changed gradually to the best-selling record. In the future, it may be the "most downloaded" song off the Internet; who knows? Measures of popularity are subjective, despite the impressive compendia available of "biggest hits," but we've tried to minimize the subjectivity in this book.

For the pop songs from 1935 on, we have used the *Billboard* charts as compiled by Joel Whitburn for the single recording's ranking and number of weeks it charted. During the sixty-four years covered, the pop music scene has changed dramatically, and this is reflected by Whitburn in his *Top 40 Hits* (Billboard Books, 7th edition, 2000), by including such additional charts as airplay on the radio, best-selling sheet music, most popular records on jukeboxes, and the Hot 100 chart, reflecting regional favorites before they got to be national hits. Donald Stubblebine's *Cinema Sheet Music* (McFarland, 1991), provided most of the film information. Facts and stories about the pop songs came from this author's *Tin Pan Alley* (Donald I. Fine, 1988). The rest came from the sheet music itself in the author's archive.

2. *Best remembered.* You'll notice that not every number 1 song is listed in this book. Today's number 1 song may be tomorrow's forgotten relic. Because this reference is intended for those seeking information on songs that they're likely to have heard (or want to learn), it seemed important to include primarily those songs that are best remembered. And, sometimes a nonhit can be more popular than a hit. For example, John Hartford's "Gentle on My Mind" is second only to the Beatles's "Yesterday" in number of airplays

and recordings since it was written in 1967; but it was never a number 1 or even a Top 10 hit.

3. *Historically important.* Many of the best-remembered songs of the 1960s were never pop hits; Bob Dylan's entire songbook is a perfect example. While he produced hits for others, his own recordings only charted briefly during the 1960s and early '70s, and were never chart toppers. But who can think of popular songs of the 1960s—or indeed of the second half of the twentieth century—without including Bob Dylan? Similarly, songs that defined their era may never have been major hits.

4. *Interesting or unusual.* Finally, there are some songs that hold interest because they appeal to me. Although I've tried not to allow personal prejudice influence this selection, some of my favorites have probably crept in along with those that are universally recognized as important.

This book is a collection of popular music. *Popular* describes rather loosely those songs that were sung, played, or loved by a large portion of the American population. In the pre–World War II era, popular music was pretty well defined; since then, numerous subgenres have arisen, including R&B, country, easy listening, and so on. Although there are some hits drawn from these genres, I have tried to select only those that transcended their genre and became truly popular. Some may question this bias, but again an attempt was made to chronicle those songs that the reader/researcher was most likely to be searching for. I have also used the original names for each genre or style; thus, although offensive to today's ears, the term *coon song* was widely used at the turn of the century to describe pop songs that were written, by black and white composers alike, with either African-American subject matter or in a ragtime-influenced style.

The annotations include, where possible, the best or most popular recordings and piano rolls with their labels and numbers, the origin of the song if not strictly a pop song (Broadway shows, movie musicals, television music), as well as performers who introduced the numbers and those who made them famous. Full information is provided with song title; composer; lyricist; publisher and place of publication; year of published copyright; if from a Broadway show, the first performer; and if from a film, the production company and year of distribution.

Note that songs are listed by year of published copyright, which may differ from actual year of composition (or the year when the song was a hit). Similarly, composer information is as registered for copyright; where there has been controversy over these listings, I've tried to make a note of it in the annotation. In the early part of the century, it was not unusual for performers and publishers to demand "a cut" in order to ensure that they would popularize a song; once recordings became dominant after World War II, producers, managers, and others would shamelessly take partial or full credit for others' work. On the other hand, songwriters often happily sold all rights to their material in return for a quick buck, so the system cut both ways.

Sometimes the same composer will appear under different names on different published sheets; William "Smokey" Robinson is sometimes credited as Bill "Smokey" Robinson" or just as William Robinson. The credit information in the text is given as it appears on the original sheet; for the purposes of the index by composer, I have chosen to use one standard version of the name to avoid too many "see also" cross-references.

Note that by *publisher* I mean the actual firm that published the sheet music. During at least the first half of the century, an item wasn't "published" if it didn't appear in this form. As popular music is changing, fewer songs are now published in this traditional sense. This is particularly true of rap music. However, I have decided to select only music published in this traditional sense for inclusion in this book. I leave it to scholars of twenty-first century popular music to wrestle further with this problem.

In the main index by song, the full publishing information is given as it appeared on the original sheet music. Sometimes the same publishing company would operate under various names at different times, as well as from offices in different cities. Also, in later years, many of these publishing companies were subsumed by other companies. To avoid confusion in the publishers' index, publications by the same company are grouped together as much as possible. Either ASCAP or BMI should be able to pro-vide information as to the current owners of each company's back catalog; these catalogs change hands so frequently that it would be pointless to give current owner information here.

Popular music reflects the history of its time. Entire eras are remembered by their musical sound-tracks: the turn of the century for ragtime; the "roarin' twenties" for its jazz and blues; the Depression for its topical songs; the 1950s for rock and roll; the 1960s for social-protest songs; the 1970s for disco; the 1990s for rap. This book attempts to give an overview of the best songs of each era.

# THE SONGS: A to Z

## "A"—YOU'RE ADORABLE
Sid Lippman/Buddy Kaye/Fred Wise
Laurel Music—New York
1948
Perry Como, with the Fontane Sisters, had the number 1 hit that charted for fifteen weeks (Victor 20-3381).

## ABA DABA HONEYMOON
Arthur Fields and Walter Donovan
Leo Feist—New York
1914
Arthur Collins and Byron Harlan had the first hit recording (Victor 17620). Debbie Reynolds and Carlton Carpenter revived it in the film *Two Weeks With Love* (MGM, 1950). Their soundtrack recording became the number 3 hit in 1951 and sold over one million copies (MGM 30282). It was revived again in 1960 by Joe "Fingers" Carr and Ira Ironstrings on their LP *Together for the Last Time, Volume 1* (Warner Bros. 1389).

## ABRAHAM, MARTIN & JOHN
Dick Holler (w & m)
Regent Music—New York
1968
Former doo-wop star Dion DiMucci made a big comeback with this 1968 song in honor of the assassinated heroes Abraham Lincoln, Martin Luther King Jr., and John F. Kennedy. It was a number 4 hit, remaining on the charts for twelve weeks (Laurie 3464). The song was also covered by comedian Moms Mabley (Mercury 72935) and the Miracles (Tamla 54184), both in 1969.

## ABSENCE MAKES THE HEART GROW FONDER
Herbert Dillea (w: Arthur Gillespie)
M. Witmark and Sons—New York
1900
Tearjerker sung in vaudeville by Fred Gladdish. Harry MacDonough made the best-selling disc in 1901 (Victor 907).

## ABSINTHE FRAPPE
Victor Herbert (w: Glen MacDonough)
M. Witmark and Sons—New York
1904
**Show**: *It Happened in Nordland*
Sung by Harry Davenport in the show. Sung in the film *The Great Victor Herbert* (Paramount, 1939) by Allan Jones.

## AC-CENT-TCHU-ATE THE POSITIVE
Harold Arlen (w: Johnny Mercer)
Edwin H. Morris—New York
1944
**Film**: *Here Come the Waves* (Paramount)
Bing Crosby and Sonny Tufts sang it in the film. Crosby, with the Andrews Sisters, had a number 2 hit that charted for nine weeks (Decca 23379). Lyricist Johnny Mercer had the number 1 hit, which charted for sixteen weeks (Capitol 180).

## ACHIN' HEARTED BLUES
Clarence Williams/Clarence Johnson/
Spencer Williams
Clarence Williams Music—New York
1922
Introduced in vaudeville by Johnny Wiesser and Cora Reeser. Leona Williams and Her Dixie Band (actually the Original Memphis Five) made the first recording (Columbia A-3599), followed by Clarence Williams's Blue Five (Okeh 4966). Jazzbo's Carolina Serenaders also had a fine version (Cameo 269).

## ADDICTED TO LOVE
Robert Palmer (w & m)
Ackee Music
1986
British rock-pop singer Robert Palmer's biggest hit, which held the number 1 spot for one out of fourteen weeks on the charts (Island 99570) in 1986.

## AFFAIR TO REMEMBER, AN
Harry Warren (w: Harold Adamson and
Leo McCarey)
Leo Feist—New York
1957
**Film**: *An Affair to Remember* (20th Century Fox)
Vic Damone sang it in the film and had the number 16 hit (Columbia 40945).

## AFRICA
David Paich and Jeff Porcaro

Hudmar Publishing

1982

Pop-rock band Toto had the number 1 hit in 1983 that charted for sixteen weeks (Columbia 03335). Paich and Porcaro were band members. It sold over one million copies.

## AFRICAN 400, THE

Charles J. Roberts

Carl Fischer Inc.—New York

1909

Arthur Pryor's Band (Victor 16444) and the Zonophone Concert Band (Zonophone 5531) had fine versions.

## AFTER YOU GET WHAT YOU WANT, YOU DON'T WANT IT

Irving Berlin (w & m)

Irving Berlin Inc.—New York

1920

Hit recording by Van and Schenck (Columbia A-2966). Revived by Marilyn Monroe in the movie *There's No Business like Show Business* (20th Century Fox, 1954).

## AFTER YOU'VE GONE

John Turner Layton (w: Henry Creamer)

Broadway Music—New York

1918

Sophie Tucker first made it a hit in vaudeville, then on recordings. Al Jolson popularized it on the Broadway stage. The Coon-Sanders Original Nighthawks made a hit record in 1929 (Victor 22342), while the Benny Goodman Quartet played it in Disney's film *Make Mine Music* (1946). Shirley MacLaine revived it in the film *Some Came Running* (MGM, 1959).

## AFTERNOON DELIGHT

Bill Danoff (w & m)

Cherry Lane Music

1976

The Starland Vocal Band was a one-hit wonder, and this number 1 hit charted for fourteen weeks (Windsong 10588). It sold over one million copies.

## AGAINST ALL ODDS (TAKE A LOOK AT ME NOW)

Phil Collins (w & m)

Golden Torch Music

Film: *Against All Odds* (Columbia)

1984

Theme song from the film of the same name; Phil Collins's first number 1 hit, which held the top spot for three out of sixteen weeks on the charts (Atlantic 89700).

## AGGRAVATIN' PAPA

J. Russel Robinson/Roy Turk/Addy Britt

Waterson, Berlin and Snyder—New York

1922

The Virginians, a contingent from Paul Whiteman and His Orchestra, recorded it as a splendid syncopated dance tune (Victor 19021), which contrasts nicely with Bessie Smith's very bluesy interpretation (Columbia A-3877).

## AH! SWEET MYSTERY OF LIFE

Victor Herbert (w: Rida Johnson Young)

M. Witmark and Sons—New York

1910

**Show**: *Naughty Marietta*

Introduced by Orville Harrold in the operetta. In the MGM movie, it was sung by Jeanette MacDonald and Nelson Eddy (1935), and later by Allan Jones in *The Great Victor Herbert* (Paramount, 1939). The song was revived in the Mel Brooks comedy *Young Frankenstein* (20th Century Fox, 1974), where it was sung by Madeline Kahn as she was ravished by the monster.

## AH-HA!

James V. Monaco (w: Sidney Clare)

Shapiro, Bernstein and Co.—New York

1925

Introduced in vaudeville by Ted Lewis. Two hit recordings, by Paul Whiteman and His Orchestra (Victor 19666) and the Oriole Orchestra (Brunswick 2874). Zez Confrey made an outstanding piano roll (Ampico 206411).

## AIN'T DAT A SHAME

Walter Wilson (w: John Queen)

Howley, Haviland and Dresser—New York

1901

Classic coon song made famous in vaudeville by Jack Gardner. Minstrel and lyricist John Queen served as inspiration to Hughie Cannon for "Bill Bailey, Won't You Please Come Home?"

## AIN'T MISBEHAVIN'

Thomas Waller and Harry Brooks (w: Andy Razaf)
Mills Music—New York

1929

**Show**: *Hot Chocolates*

Sung in the show by Louis Armstrong, making his Broadway debut; his performance brought the house down. He subsequently recorded the song (Okeh 8714). But it was Fats Waller's own piano solo that is seen as the classic performance (Victor 22108). Fats and Ada Brown sang it in the film *Stormy Weather* (20th Century Fox, 1943).

## AIN'T NO MOUNTAIN HIGH ENOUGH

Nicholas Ashford and Valerie Simpson
Belwin Mills

1967, 1970

Diana Ross had her first number 1 hit as a solo performer (she had been the lead singer with the Supremes) with this song; it held the number 1 position for three out of thirteen weeks on the chart (Motown 1169). It had previously been recorded by Marvin Gaye and Tami Terrell for a minor pop hit in 1967.

## AIN'T SHE SWEET?

Milton Ager (w: Jack Yellen)
Ager, Yellen and Bornstein—New York

1927

A million seller in sheet music. Ben Bernie and His Orchestra with vocal by Scrappy Lambert and Billy Hillpot had the hit record (Brunswick 3444). It was featured in the film *You Were Meant for Me* (20th Century Fox, 1948).

## AIN'T THAT A SHAME!

Antoine "Fats" Domino and Dave Bartholomew
Commodore Music—Hollywood

1955

Fats Domino, the song's cowriter, had his first major pop hit with this rocking ballad. Domino's version reached number 10 and charted for thirteen weeks, selling over one million copies (Imperial 5348). Bartholomew, given cowriter credit, was the song's

producer and arranged the session. As was typical in the late 1950s, it took a white "cover artist," Pat Boone, to make the song a number 1 hit. Boone's rather tepid version charted for twenty weeks and outsold the original (Dot 15377). The Four Seasons revived it in 1963 with a number 22 hit (Vee-Jay 512). Cheap Trick revived it again in 1979 with a number 35 hit (Epic 50743).

## AIN'T WE GOT FUN?

Richard A. Whiting (w: Ray Egan and Gus Kahn)
Jerome H. Remick and Co.—New York

1921

**Show**: *Satires of 1920*

Sung by Arthur West in the show and popularized by Ruth Roye in vaudeville. Gus Van and Joe Schenck made a hit recording (Columbia A-3412). It was revived in the Gus Kahn biopic *I'll See You in My Dreams* (Warner Bros., 1951), and featured in *By The Light of the Silvery Moon* (Warner Bros., 1953). Eddie Cantor sang it on the soundtrack of *The Eddie Cantor Story* (Warner Bros., 1953). In the mid-1990s, the song was revived as a theme song for Carnival Cruise Lines commercials.

## AIN'T YOU ASHAMED

Seymour Simons (w: Sid Mitchell and Lew Brown)
Broadway Music Corp.—New York

1923

Introduced by the Coon-Sanders Night Hawks in vaudeville. Paul Whiteman (Victor 19284) and the Arcadia Peacock Orchestra (Okeh 40052) had the hit recordings.

## ALABAMA JUBILEE

George L. Cobb (w: Jack Yellen)
Jerome H. Remick—New York

1915

Great syncopated song recorded by the great singing comedians Arthur Collins and Byron Harlan (Victor 17825). It was introduced in vaudeville by Elizabeth Murray and revived in 1955 by the Ferko String Band as a number 14 instrumental hit (Media 1010).

## ALABAMY BOUND

Ray Henderson (w: Bud DeSylva and Bud Green)
Shapiro, Bernstein and Co.—New York

1925

Introduced by Al Jolson. Blossom Seeley and Eddie Cantor also featured it in vaudeville. Isham Jones and His Orchestra made a fine recording (Brunswick 2789). Sheet music sales exceeded one million copies. It was revived by the Ink Spots in the film *The Great American Broadcast* (20th Century Fox, 1941).

## ALCOHOLIC BLUES
Albert Von Tilzer (w: Edward Laska)
Broadway Music—New York
1919
Billy Murray had the vocal hit (Columbia A-2702) and the Louisiana Five had the hit instrumental (Columbia A-2768).

## ALEXANDER, DON'T YOU LOVE YOUR BABY NO MORE?
Harry Von Tilzer (w: Andrew B. Sterling)
Harry Von Tilzer—New York
1904
Great syncopated comedy dialect song made famous by Walter Stock and other minstrels. The man's name when said with a rising inflection produced hilarity. A forerunner of Irving Berlin's hit "Alexander's Ragtime Band." Alexander was a stock name on the minstrel stage for a black character.

## ALEXANDER'S GOT A JAZZ BAND NOW
Chris Schonberg (w: Bud DeSylva)
Deely, DeSylva and Schonberg—Los Angeles
1917
Introduced in vaudeville by Sophie Tucker. Gene Greene had the hit vocal recording (Columbia A-2472).

## ALEXANDER'S RAGTIME BAND
Irving Berlin (w & m)
Ted Snyder Co.—New York
1911
Introduced in vaudeville by Emma Carus. It is the best-known song about ragtime, although it is not a "ragtime" piece. It quickly became a million-seller in sheet music, with sixty-five individual performers with their photos on separate sheet covers. Collins and Harlan had the vocal hit (Victor 16908), while the Victor Military Band had the instrumental hit (Victor 17006). Alice Faye sang it in the film of the same name (20th

Century Fox, 1938). The song has become a classic and the entire cast of the film sang it in *There's No Business Like Show Business* (20th Century Fox, 1954). Jazz pianist Monia Liter made the most unusual piano recording (English Brunswick 01814).

## ALICE BLUE GOWN
Harry Tierney (w: Joseph McCarthy)
Leo Feist—New York
1919
**Show:** *Irene*
Named for Alice Roosevelt, it was sung in the show by Edith Day in what became the longest-running Broadway musical up to that time (675 performances), a record held for the next twenty-eight years! Anna Neagle sang it in the film *Irene* (RKO, 1940) and Debbie Reynolds sang it in the 1973 Broadway revival.

## ALICE'S RESTAURANT
Arlo Guthrie (w & m)
Appleseed Music—New York
1966–69
**Film:** *Alice's Restaurant* (United Artists)
A half-spoken, half-sung tragicomic tale that won great popularity in the late 1960s. It was based on Guthrie's life in Stockbridge, Massachusetts, where there really was an Alice's Restaurant, a local hippie hangout. The song became the basis of a popular film, directed by Arthur Penn, and featuring Guthrie in the title role. Guthrie continues to regularly perform it at his annual New York Thanksgiving concert.

## ALL ABOARD FOR DIXIE LAND
George L. Cobb (w: Jack Yellen)
Jerome H. Remick and Co.—New York
1913
**Show:** *High Jinks*
Interpolated by Elizabeth Murray into the Broadway show, this syncopated song became a hit in vaudeville as well. It was given a fine recording by Ada Jones with the Peerless Quartet (Columbia A-1481).

## ALL ALONE
Irving Berlin (w & m)
Irving Berlin—New York
1924

**Show:** *Music Box Revue*
Sung in the show by Grace Moore and Oscar Shaw. Vincent Lopez and Orchestra made a hit recording (Okeh 40226). Alice Faye sang it in the film *Alexander's Ragtime Band* (20th Century Fox, 1938).

## ALL ALONE MONDAY
Harry Ruby (w: Bert Kalmar)
Harms Inc.—New York
1926
**Show:** *The Ramblers*
Sung in the show by Marie Saxon and Jack Whiting. The Colonial Club Orchestra made a fine recording (Brunswick 3380). Gale Robbins sang it in the biopic *Three Little Words* (MGM, 1950).

## ALL BY MYSELF
Irving Berlin (w & m)
Irving Berlin—New York
1921
Introduced by Charles King in vaudeville. A million selling success in sheet music. Ted Lewis had the hit recording (Columbia A-3434). Bennie Krueger and His Orchestra also had a popular recording (Brunswick 2130). It was revived in the film *Blue Skies* (Paramount, 1946).

## ALL FOUR LOVE
Color Me Badd and Howard Thompson
Me Good Publishing
1991
R&B vocal quartet Color Me Badd had this number 1 hit that charted for twenty-five weeks (Giant 19236). It sold over half a million copies.

## ALL FOR LOVE
Bryan Adams/Robert Lange/Michael Kamen
Almo Music
1993
Bryan Adams, Rod Stewart, and Sting had this number 1 hit that charted on the Top 40 for twenty weeks (A&M 0476). It sold over one million copies.

## ALL I DO IS DREAM OF YOU
Nacio Herb Brown (w: Arthur Freed)
Robbins Music—New York
1934

**Film:** *Sadie McKee* (MGM)
Gene Raymond sang it in the film. Jan Garber and His Orchestra had the hit recording (Victor 24629). It was revived in the film *Singin' in the Rain* (MGM, 1952), sung by Debbie Reynolds.

## ALL I HAVE TO DO IS DREAM
Felice and Boudeleaux Bryant
Acuff-Rose
1958
Number 1 hit for the Everly Brothers, holding that position for five out of sixteen weeks on the charts (Cadence 1348). Also a number 1 country hit, it was later covered by actor Richard Chamberlin (MGM 13121, 1963), and Bobbie Gentry and Glen Campbell as a duet (Capitol 2745, 1970).

## ALL I WANNA DO (IS HAVE SOME FUN)
Sheryl Crow/Wyn Cooper/Bill Bottrell/
David Baerwald/Kevin Gilbert
Warner-Tamerlane
1993
Number 2 hit in 1994 that launched the career of pop-rock singer Sheryl Crow (A&M 0702). It held this position for six out of its twenty-seven weeks on the charts and was also a number 1 adult-contemporary hit (eight weeks).

## ALL IN, DOWN AND OUT
Chris Smith/Billy Johnson/Elmer Bowman
(w: Cecil Mack)
Gotham-Attucks Music Co.—New York
1906
Introduced in vaudeville by Bert Williams, who also recorded it (Columbia 30039). Clarice Vance also sang it in vaudeville.

## ALL MUDDLED UP
Percy Wenrich (w & m)
Leo Feist—New York
1922
A marvelously syncopated song by a ragtime composer. Many orchestra recordings were made but the outstanding version was done by Zez Confrey, who played an extended piano solo with his orchestra (Victor 18973).

## ALL NIGHT BLUES
Richard Jones (w & m)
Melrose Bros.——Chicago
1923
Hit record by Callie Vassar, accompanied on the piano
by the composer (Gennett 5172).

## ALL NIGHT LONG (ALL NIGHT)
Lionel Richie (w & m)
Brockman Music
1983
Lionel Richie wrote and sang this number 1 hit that
lasted seventeen weeks on the Top 40 charts (Motown
1698). It sold over one million copies.

## ALL OF ME
Gerald Marks (w: Seymour Simons)
Irving Berlin——New York
1931
A standard made famous in vaudeville by Belle Baker.
Paul Whiteman and His Orchestra, with vocal by Mil-
dred Bailey, had the hit recording (Victor 22879).
Louis Armstrong also had a hit (Columbia 2606-D).
Through the years, Russ Columbo, Billie Holiday,
Frank Sinatra, Louis Jordan, and Willie Nelson enjoyed
reviving it. It was the title theme song for a Steve Mar-
tin/Lily Tomlin comic film in 1984 (Universal).

## ALL OR NOTHING AT ALL
Jack Lawrence and Arthur Altman
Leeds Music——New York
1940
Frank Sinatra with Harry James and His Orchestra
recorded the song in 1939. It was not released, however, until 1943, when it was a number 1 hit that
charted for twenty-one weeks and sold over one million copies (Columbia 35587).

## ALL OVER NOTHING AT ALL
James Rule (w: J. Keirn Brennan and
Paul Cunningham)
M. Witmark and Sons——New York
1922
Introduced in vaudeville by the Watson Sisters. Nora
Bayes had the hit vocal recording (Columbia A-3601),

while the Great White Way Orchestra (Victor 18963)
had the instrumental hit.

## ALL SHE'D SAY WAS UMH HUM
Mac Emery/King Zany/Van and Schenck
Harry Von Tilzer——New York
1920
**Show:** *Ziegfeld Follies of 1920*
Sung in the show by Van and Schenck. They also had
the hit vocal recording (Columbia A-3319). Isham
Jones and His Orchestra had the instrumental hit
(Brunswick 5052).

## ALL SHOOK UP!
Otis Blackwell and Elvis Presley
Shalimar Music——New York
1957
Elvis Presley had the number 1 hit, which charted for
twenty-two weeks and sold more than four million
copies (RCA Victor 47-6870). It was the best-selling
single of the year.

## ALL THE QUAKERS ARE SHOULDER SHAKERS DOWN IN QUAKER TOWN
Pete Wendling (w: Bert Kalmar and Edgar Leslie)
Waterson, Berlin and Snyder——New York
1919
Sold over three-quarters of a million copies of sheet
music. The All Star Trio had the hit recording (Victor
18626).

## ALL THE THINGS YOU ARE
Jerome Kern (w: Oscar Hammerstein)
Chappell——New York
1939
**Show:** *Very Warm For May*
Hiram Sherman, Frances Mercer, Hollace Shaw, and
Ralph Stuart sang it in the show. It is now not only a
standard, but the most admired song by other song-
writers. When the Broadway show was adapted for
films, it was renamed *Broadway Rhythm* (MGM, 1944),
where the song was sung by Ginny Simms. Tommy
Dorsey and His Orchestra, with vocal by Jack
Leonard, had the number 1 hit that charted for thir-
teen weeks (Victor 26401). It was featured in the Kern

biopic *Till the Clouds Roll By* (MGM, 1946), where it was sung by Tony Martin, and in the film *Because You're Mine* (MGM, 1952), where it was sung by Mario Lanza.

## ALL THE WAY
James Van Heusen (w: Sammy Cahn)
Barton Music—New York
1957
**Film:** *The Joker is Wild* (Paramount)
Academy Award winner for Best Song. Frank Sinatra, who starred in the film, had the number 2 hit, which charted for seventeen weeks (Capitol 3793).

## ALL THROUGH THE NIGHT
Cole Porter (w & m)
Harms—New York
1934
**Show:** *Anything Goes*
William Gaxton and Bettina Hall sang it in the show. It was also featured in both versions of the film (Paramount, 1936 and 1956). Paul Whiteman and His Orchestra, with vocal by Bob Lawrence, had the number 8 hit (Victor 24770).

## ALL YOU NEED IS LOVE
John Lennon and Paul McCartney
Maclen Music—New York
1967
The Beatles had the number 1 hit, which charted for nine weeks and sold over a million copies (Capitol 5964). The song was premiered on the first worldwide, simultaneous television broadcast. The song opens with a quotation from "La Marsailaise" and closes with a brief quotation from the Beatles's early hit "She Loves You."

## ALLIGATOR CRAWL
Thomas "Fats" Waller (w: Andy Razaf and Joe Davis)
Joe Davis Inc.—New York
1937
The composer had the hit piano solo (Victor 24830) and Fess Williams and His Orchestra had the hit instrumental (Brunswick 3589).

## ALMOST LIKE BEING IN LOVE
Frederick Loewe (w: Alan Jay Lerner)

Sam Fox—New York
1947
**Show:** *Brigadoon*
David Brooks and Marion Bell sang it in the show. Frank Sinatra had a number 20 hit that charted for five weeks (Columbia 37382). Michael Johnson revived it in 1978, when it reached number 32 in the charts (EMI America 8004).

## ALONE
Billy Steinberg and Tom Kelly
Billy Steinberg Music
1987
Number 1 hit for the heavy metal/pop group Heart (Capitol 44002). It held this position for three out of fifteen weeks on the charts.

## ALONE AGAIN (NATURALLY)
Raymond O'Sullivan (w & m)
Management Agency and Music Pub.—New York
1972
Gilbert O'Sullivan had his only number 1 hit with this weepy pop ballad, which stayed at that position for six of the fifteen weeks on the chart (MAM 3619). It sold over one million copies.

## ALONE AT LAST
Ted Fiorito (w: Gus Kahn)
Irving Berlin—New York
1925
One of the great tunes composed by the Chicago bandleader. It was when the Kansas City based Coon-Sanders Original Nighthawks came to Chicago to perform that they discovered this song and recorded it (Victor 19728).

## ALWAYS
Irving Berlin (w & m)
Irving Berlin—New York
1925
One of the all-time favorites including that of the composer, it was a hit as soon as it was released. Berlin wrote it for his new wife, Ellin MacKay; as she was the daughter of a wealthy, patrician family, their romance and marriage made tabloid headlines. George Olsen

and His Orchestra had the hit recording (Victor 19955). It was revived by Deanna Durbin in the film *Christmas Holiday* (Universal, 1944). The others of Berlin's own personal favorites are "Easter Parade," "God Bless America," "There's No Business like Show Business," and "White Christmas." Is it merely a coincidence that all five of his favorite songs are multimillion sellers?

## ALWAYS
Jonathan Lewis/David Lewis/Wayne Lewis
Jodway Music
1983
Number 1 pop hit in 1987 for soul vocal group Atlantic Starr (Warner 28455), remaining on the charts for fourteen weeks. It was also number 1 on the R&B and Adult-contemporary charts.

## ALWAYS TRUE TO YOU IN MY FASHION
Cole Porter (w & m)
T. B. Harms Co.—New York
1948
**Show:** *Kiss Me Kate*
Sung by Lisa Kirk in the show.

## AM I BLUE?
Harry Akst (w: Grant Clarke)
M. Witmark and Sons—New York
1929
**Film:** *On With the Show* (Warner Bros.)
Ethel Waters sang it in the film and she had a hit recording (Columbia 1837-D). Barbra Streisand revived it in the film *Funny Lady* (Columbia, 1975).

## AMERICAN WOMAN
Randy Bachman/Burton Cummings/
Jim Kale/Garry Peterson
Cirrus Music-Toronto
1969
Number 1 hit in 1970 for Guess Who, holding the top slot for three out of fourteen weeks on the charts (RCA 0325).

## AMERICAN PIE
Don McLean (w & m)
Mayday Music—New York
1972
Don McLean had this number 1 hit, which charted for seventeen weeks and sold more than one million copies (United Artists 50856). The song immortalized the death of late 1950s rock and roll with the plane crash of Buddy Holly, as "the day the music died."

## AND ALL THAT JAZZ
John Kander (w: Fred Ebb)
Chappell and Co.—New York
1973, 1975
Show: *Chicago*
Chita Rivera sang it in the show. When the show was revived in 1996, it was sung by Bebe Neuwirth.

## AND I AM ALL ALONE
Jerome Kern (w: P. G. Wodehouse and
Jerome Kern)
T. B. Harms—New York
1916
**Show:** *Have a Heart*
One of Kern's most beautiful ballads, it was introduced in the show by Eileen Van Biene and Thurston Hall. It was recorded by Henry Burr, the most famous ballad singer of the first two decades of the twentieth century (Pathe 20141).

## AND THEY CALLED IT DIXIELAND (THEY MADE IT TWICE AS NICE AS PARADISE)
Richard A. Whiting (w: Raymond Egan)
Jerome H. Remick and Co.—New York
1916
Geoffrey O'Hara was responsible for making this a hit in vaudeville and on disc (Victor 18051).

## ANGEL CHILD
Abner Silver/George Price/Benny Davis
M. Witmark and Sons—New York
1922
**Show:** *Spice of 1922*
Georgie Price sang it in the show, but Al Jolson made it famous (Columbia A-3568). The Benson Orchestra had a popular version (Victor 18870).

## ANGIE
Mick Jagger and Keith Richards

Promo Publishing

1973

Number 1 hit for the Rolling Stones, a pop-rock ballad inspired by David Bowie's then wife, Angela Bowie. It held the number 1 position only one out of the thirteen weeks it charted, and sold over a million copies (Rolling Stones 19105).

## ANGRY

Henry and Merritt Brunies and Jules Cassard (w: Dudley Mecum)

Ted Browne — Chicago

1925

Art Gillham, the "whispering pianist," had the hit record (Columbia 411-D). Ray Miller and His Orchestra (Brunswick 4224) and Johnny Hamp's Kentucky Serenaders (Victor 19786) also had great versions.

## ANOTHER BRICK IN THE WALL (PART II)

Roger Waters (w & m)

Pink Floyd Music

1979

Pink Floyd anthem from their concept album *The Wall*. Features a choir of angry school children on the chorus. Their only number 1 hit, and only their second charting single; it held the top spot for four out of nineteen weeks on the charts in 1980, and sold over a million copies (Columbia 11187).

## ANOTHER DAY IN PARADISE

Phil Collins (w & m)

Philip Collins Ltd.

1989

Phil Collins had this number 1 hit for fourteen weeks (Atlantic 88774). It sold over half a million copies. Unlike Collins's other hits, light love ballads, this song offered social commentary on homelessness and poverty.

## ANOTHER ONE BITES THE DUST

John Deacon (w & m)

Queen Music

1980

John Deacon, bassist for Queen, wrote this number 1 hit that charted for twenty-one weeks (Elektra 47031). It sold over two million copies. It is marked by its catchy bass riff — not surprisingly, since that was Deacon's

instrument. "Weird" Al Jankovic cleverly parodied it as "Another One Rides the Bus."

## ANTI RAG-TIME GIRL

Elsie Janis (w & m)

Jerome H. Remick and Co. — New York

1913

A lively, syncopated number introduced and made popular by the composer in vaudeville.

## ANY ICE TODAY, LADY?

Pat Ballard (w & m)

Skidmore Music Co. — New York

1926

Hit recording was by Fred Waring's Pennsylvanians (Victor 20083).

## ANY RAGS

Thomas S. Allen (w & m)

George M. Krey Co. — Boston

1902

Introduced in vaudeville by Gladys Fisher, the hit recording was by the Columbia Band (Columbia A-64).

## ANY TIME BLUES

Herbert Happy Lawson (w & m)

Lawson Music — Cincinnati

1921

A personal hit for the composer in vaudeville. It was revived by Eddie Fisher in 1952 with a number 2 hit that charted for thirty weeks and sold over one million copies (his first of eight million-sellers; RCA Victor 20-4359).

## ANYTHING FOR YOU

Gloria Estefan (w & m)

Foreign Imported Productions

1987

First number 1 hit for Gloria Estefan and Miami Sound Machine, holding the top position for two out of fourteen weeks on the charts in 1988 (Epic 07759). It was also a number 1 adult-contemporary hit.

## ANYTHING GOES

Cole Porter (w & m)

Harms — New York

1934

**Show:** *Anything Goes*
Ethel Merman and the Foursome sang it in the show. Paul Whiteman and His Orchestra, with vocal by Bob Lawrence, had the number 5 hit recording that charted for eight weeks (Victor 24770). It was sung in both of the film versions of the show (Paramount, 1936 and 1956).

## ANYTHING YOU CAN DO
Irving Berlin (w & m)
Irving Berlin—New York
1946
**Show:** *Annie Get Your Gun*
Ethel Merman and Ray Middleton sang this in the show. Its playful, back-and-forth exchange between male and female protagonists made it a favorite on variety TV programs of the 1950s and 1960s.

## ANYTIME ANYDAY ANYWHERE
Max Kortlander (w: Louis Weslyn)
Richmond Music—New York
1920
One of the great tunes of the 1920s. Piano roll composer-arranger-pianist Kortlander wrote this gem, which Paul Whiteman and His Orchestra made famous (Victor 18694). San Franciscan bandleader Art Hickman also had a fine version (Columbia A-3325), as did the All Star Trio (Brunswick 2052).

## APRIL IN PARIS
Vernon Duke (w: E. Y. Harburg)
Harms—New York
1932
**Show:** *Walk a Little Faster*
Evelyn Hoey sang it in the show. Freddy Martin and His Orchestra had the number 5 hit in 1934 (Brunswick 6717). Doris Day and Claude Dauphin sang it in the film of the same name (Warner Bros., 1952).

## APRIL LOVE
Sammy Fain (w: Paul Webster)
Leo Feist—New York
1957
**Film:** *April Love* (20th Century Fox)
Pat Boone sang it in the film and had the number 1 hit, which charted for nineteen weeks and sold over one million copies (Dot 15660).

## APRIL SHOWERS
Louis Silvers (w: Buddy DeSylva)
Sunshine Music—New York
1921
**Show:** *Bombo*
Al Jolson sang it in the show and had a hit record (Columbia A-3500), and it became a standard and part of his act from then on. When he revived it on the soundtrack of his biopic *The Jolson Story* (Columbia, 1946), and issued a single (Decca 23470), it sold over a million copies. Others had hit recordings such as Paul Whiteman and His Orchestra (Victor 18825) and Gene Rodemich and His Orchestra (Brunswick 2169). Jack Carson sang it in the film of the same name (Warner Bros., 1948).

## AQUARIUS/LET THE SUNSHINE IN
Galt MacDermot (w: James Rado and Gerome Ragni)
United Artists Music—New York
1966, 1970
**Show:** *Hair*
The 5th Dimension had the number 1 hit in 1969 of this medley of two hits from the show. It charted number 1 for six of the sixteen weeks (Soul City 772), and it sold over two million copies.

## ARE YOU FROM DIXIE?
George L. Cobb (w: Jack Yellen)
M. Witmark and Sons—New York
1915
A great hit in vaudeville with comedy teams. Billy Murray and Irving Kaufman sang it as a hit the following year (Victor 17942).

## ARE YOU HAPPY?
Milton Ager (w: Jack Yellen)
Ager, Yellen and Bornstein—New York
1921
Introduced in vaudeville by Van and Schenck. The Ipana Troubadours had a hit recording (Columbia 1098-D).

## ARE YOU HAVIN' ANY FUN?
Sammy Fain (w: Jack Yellen)
Crawford Music—New York
1939

**Show:** *George White's Scandals*: 1939–40 edition
Ella Logan sang it in the show. Tommy Dorsey and His Orchestra, with vocal by Edythe Wright, had the number 6 hit that charted for twelve weeks (Victor 26335).

## ARE YOU LONESOME TONIGHT?
Lou Handman (w: Roy Turk)
Irving Berlin—New York
1927
Introduced by Frank Cornwell in vaudeville. Little Jack Little had a hit record (Columbia 1173-D). Revived in 1960 by Elvis Presley, who had a number 1 hit that charted for fourteen weeks and sold over four million copies (RCA 47-7810).

## ARGENTINES, THE PORTUGUESE, AND THE GREEKS, THE
Carey Morgan and Arthur Swanstrom
Jos. W. Stern—New York
1920
Hit recordings were made by Nora Bayes (Columbia A-2980) and Eddie Cantor (Emerson 10200).

## ARKANSAS BLUES
Anton Lada and Spencer Williams
Frances Clifford Music—Chicago
1921
Introduced in vaudeville by Lada's Louisiana Five and on record by Noble Sissle, accompanied by pianist Eubie Blake (Emerson 10443). Lanin's Southern Serenaders had the hit instrumental (Regal 9164).

## ARTHUR'S THEME
Burt Bacharach/Carole Sager/
Christopher Cross/Peter Allen
Warner Bros. Publications—New York
1981
**Film:** *Arthur* (Orion)
Academy Award winner for Best Song. Christopher Cross had the number 1 hit that charted for seventeen weeks (Warner 49787). It sold over one million copies.

## AS LONG AS I LIVE
Harold Arlen (w: Ted Koehler)
Mills Music—New York
1934

**Show:** *Cotton Club Parade*: 24th edition.
Lena Horne and Avon Long sang it in the show. Benny Goodman and His Orchestra, with a swinging vocal by Jack Teagarden, had the number 24 hit (Columbia 2923-D).

## AS TIME GOES BY
Herman Hupfeld (w & m)
Harms—New York
1931
**Show:** *Everybody's Welcome*
Frances Williams sang it in the show. Rudy Vallee made it popular on radio and had a number 15 hit (Victor 22773). Immortalized by Dooley Wilson, who sang it in the film *Casablanca* (Warner Bros., 1942); after the film opened, Victor rereleased Vallee's recording, which became a number 1 hit in 1943 (Victor 20-1526). It established the song as a standard. Ray Anthony and His Orchestra revived it in 1952, having a number 10 hit (Capitol 2104). In 1994, a British television situation comedy, starring Judi Dench and Geoffrey Palmer, used the song as the show's title and theme song.

## AT SUNDOWN
Walter Donaldson (w & m)
Leo Feist—New York
1927
A million-seller in sheet music and over two million in record sales. George Olsen and His Orchestra had the biggest recording (Victor 20476), and Jimmy Andrews had the nicest piano solo (Banner 6066). It was featured in the biopic *The Fabulous Dorseys* (United Artists, 1947), and Doris Day sang it in *Love Me or Leave Me* (MGM, 1955).

## AT THE BALL, THAT'S ALL
J. Leubrie Hill (w & m)
Lafayette—New York
1913
**Show:** *Darktown Follies*
When Florenz Ziegfeld saw the show, he immediately bought this song to include in his *Follies of 1913*. It then became a favorite in vaudeville.

## AT THE DEVIL'S BALL
Irving Berlin (w & m)

Waterson, Berlin and Snyder—New York

1913

This syncopated number was a favorite in vaudeville, the hit recording belonging to the Peerless Quartet with Henry Burr singing lead tenor (Victor 17315).

## AT THE HIGH BROWN BABIES' BALL

Ernie and Sid Erdman (w: Benny Davis)

Leo Feist—New York

1919

A favorite in vaudeville. Yerke's Novelty Five had a hit record (Lyric 4207).

## AT THE HOP

Artie Singer/John Medora/David White

ARC Music—New York

1957

Danny and the Juniors had the number 1 hit, which charted for eighteen weeks and sold over one million copies (ABC-Paramount 9871). The song was originally titled "At the Bop," but changed when Dick Clark suggested that the "bop" was already fading in popularity. Clark heavily promoted it on his *American Bandstand* TV show.

## AT THE MISSISSIPPI CABARET

Albert Gumble (w: A. Seymour Brown)

Jerome H. Remick and Co.—New York

1914

Popular in vaudeville and with barbershop quartets. The hit recording was by the American Quartet, featuring Billy Murray (Victor 17650).

## AUNT HAGAR'S CHILDREN BLUES

W. C. Handy (w: J. Tim Brymn)

Handy Bros. Music—New York

1921

When published by Richmond-Robbins the same year, it was revised and called "Aunt Hagar's Blues." It is a blues standard. Isham Jones and His Orchestra's recording became famous (Brunswick 2358). The Virginians (Victor 19021) and the Original Memphis Five (Pathe 020900) also had fine versions. It was revived in 1941 by Lena Horne and the Chamber Music Society of Lower Basin Street (Victor 27544) and was featured in the Handy biopic *St. Louis Blues* (Paramount, 1958).

## AUNTIE SKINNER'S CHICKEN DINNER

Theodore Morse (w: Arthur Fields and Earl Carroll)

M. Witmark and Sons—New York

1915

Introduced in vaudeville by Ruth Roye, the Princess of Ragtime. Collins and Harlan had the hit recording (Victor 17755).

## AUTUMN IN NEW YORK

Vernon Duke (w & m)

Harms—New York

1934

**Show:** *Thumbs Up!*

J. Harold Murray sang it in the show. It took a while before the song achieved the status of a standard, because of its unusual melody and harmonies. It was revived by Frank Sinatra as a number 27 hit in 1949 (Columbia 38316).

## AUTUMN LEAVES

Joseph Kosma (w: Johnny Mercer)

Ardmore Music—New York

1950

Number 1 hit in 1955 for Roger Williams, holding that position for four out of twenty-six weeks on the charts (Kapp 116). It was based on a 1947 French song, "Les Feuilles Mortes."

## AVALON

Vincent Rose and Al Jolson

Jerome H. Remick and Co.—New York

1920

Vincent Rose and Buddy DeSylva wrote this standard, which Puccini's publishers claim was stolen from his aria "E lucevan le stelle" from *Tosca;* a judge agreed! Al Jolson demanded a cut for his participation in making it a hit (Columbia A-2995), but DeSylva lost his credit. Jolson revived it in his biopic *The Jolson Story* (Columbia, 1946); Benny Goodman played it in his biopic *The Benny Goodman Story* (Universal, 1956).

## BABY BABY

Amy Grant and Keith Thomas

Age to Age Music

1991

Number 1 pop hit for Christian rocker Amy Grant, holding that position for two out of sixteen weeks on the charts (A&M 1549). It was also a number 1 Adult-Contemporary song. Written for Grant's newly born daughter Millie.

## BABY FACE
Harry Akst (w: Benny Davis)
Jerome H. Remick—New York
1926
A standard introduced by bandleader Jan Garber who recorded it with lyricist Davis as vocalist (Victor 20105). The Ipana Troubadours also had a hit (Columbia 696-D) as did the Buffalodians (Banner 1776). It was revived in 1948 when Art Mooney and His Orchestra had a number 3 hit that charted for fifteen weeks and sold over one million copies (MGM 10156). It was revived again in 1975 by the Wing and a Prayer Fife and Drum Corp., who had a number 14 hit that charted for twelve weeks (Wing and Prayer 103). Julie Andrews sang it in the film *Thoroughly Modern Millie* (Universal, 1967).

## BABY GOT BACK
Sir Mix-A-Lot (w & m)
Songs of PolyGram International
1992
Sir Mix-A-Lot, a one-hit wonder, scored big on this number 1 for five of the twenty-four weeks on the chart (Def American 18947). It sold over three million copies.

## BABY, IT'S COLD OUTSIDE
Frank Loesser (w & m)
Frank Music Co.—New York
1948
**Film:** *Neptune's Daughter* (MGM)
Academy Award winner for Best Song of 1949. Johnny Mercer and Margaret Whiting had the number 3 hit (Capitol 567), and Dinah Shore and Buddy Clark had the number 4 hit (Columbia 38463), both of which charted for nineteen weeks.

## BABY LOVE
Brian Holland/Lamont Dozier/Eddy Holland
Jobete Music—Detroit
1964

Number 1 pop and R&B hit for the Supremes, holding the top pop slot for four out of twelve weeks on the charts (Motown 1066). A classic girl-group song.

## ... BABY ONE MORE TIME
Max Martin (w & m)
Grantsville
1998
Britney Spears began her career at the end of the 1990s with this number 1 hit, which charted twenty-nine weeks (Jive 42545). It sold over one million copies.

## BABY, WON'T YOU PLEASE COME HOME
Charles Warfield and Clarence Williams
Clarence Williams Music—New York
1923
Eva Taylor introduced this jazz standard in vaudeville and on the radio. Bessie Smith had a best-selling disc (Columbia A-3888). It was revived in 1939 in a stunning arrangement by Sy Oliver for Jimmie Lunceford's band (Vocalion 4667). It was sung by Jo Stafford and Nat "King" Cole in the film *That's the Spirit* (Universal, 1945).

## BACK IN MY ARMS AGAIN
Brian Holland/Lamont Dozier/Eddy Holland
Jobete Music—Detroit
1965
A Motown classic, and number 1 pop and R&B hit for the Supremes, remaining on the pop charts for ten weeks (Motown 1075).

## BACK IN YOUR OWN BACKYARD
Dave Dreyer/Billy Rose/Al Jolson
Irving Berlin—New York
1927
Al Jolson made it famous in vaudeville, on radio, and in the film *Say It With Songs* (Warner Bros., 1929). Ruth Etting had the big hit recording (Columbia 1288-D). Jolson revived it in his biopic *Jolson Sings Again* (Columbia, 1949).

## BACK O'TOWN BLUES
L. M. Bowen and Herbie Herbedeaux
Leo Feist—New York
1923

Two great jazz renditions by The Cotton Pickers (Brunswick 2486) and the Black Dominoes (Gennett 5347).

## BAD
Michael Jackson (w & m)
Mijac Music
1987
Jackson toughened up his image with this number 1 hit from the album of the same name (Epic 07418). It held the top position for two out of eleven weeks on the charts. The video was directed by well-known film-maker Martin Scorcese.

## BAD, BAD LEROY BROWN
Jim Croce (w & m)
Blendingwell Music—New York
1972, 1973
Jim Croce had this number 1 hit, which charted for sixteen weeks (ABC 11359). It sold over one million copies.

## BAD GIRLS
Bruce Sudano/Joe Esposito/Eddie Hokenson
(w: Donna Summer)
Starrin Music
1978
Donna Summer had this number 1 hit in the same position for five of the fifteen weeks on the Top 40 chart (Casablanca 988). It sold over two million copies and became a disco standard.

## BAD MOON RISING
John C. Fogerty (w & m)
Jondora Music—Oakland
1969
Number 2 hit for roots rockers Creedence Clearwater Revival, selling over a million copies (Fantasy 622). Endlessly parodied, the words are often sung (in jest) as "There's a bathroom on the right," even by the song's composer. Revived by Fogerty during his later 1990s tours.

## BAKE DAT CHICKEN PIE
Frank Dumont (w & m)
M. Witmark and Sons—New York
1906

Hit recording by Collins and Harlan (Victor 17221). It was popular in the 1920s among country artists, including banjoist Uncle Dave Macon.

## BALLAD OF DAVY CROCKETT, THE
George Bruns (w: Tom Blackburn)
Wonderland Music—New York
1954
**TV Show:** *Davy Crockett Indian Fighter* (ABC-TV)
Fess Parker starred as Crockett and had the number 5 hit, which charted for seventeen weeks (Columbia 40449). Bill Hayes had the number 1 hit, which charted for twenty weeks and sold over one million copies (Cadence 1256). The song and show also spurred fashion fads, including the famous Crockett coonskin cap.

## BALLAD OF THE GREEN BERETS, THE
Barry Sadler and Robin Moore
Music Music Music—New York
1966
Staff Sergeant Barry Sadler, who served with the Green Berets in Vietnam, had the number 1 hit which held its top position for five of the eleven weeks charted (RCA Victor 8739). It sold over one million copies. The song was a conservative answer to many of the anti-Vietnam demonstrations (and songs) of the era.

## BALLIN' THE JACK
Chris Smith (w: Jim Burris)
Jos. W. Stern—New York
1913
Introduced in vaudeville by Eddie Cantor, who made it famous. Dancers Billy Kent and Jeanette Warner also made it popular in vaudeville. It was interpolated into the show *The Girl from Utah* for star Donald Brian. It became the most famous fox-trot of the decade, with the Victor Military Band making a superb dance record (Victor 35405). It was revived in the films *For Me and My Gal* (MGM, 1942), *On the Riviera* (20th Century Fox, 1951) as a specialty for Danny Kaye, and in Dean Martin and Jerry Lewis's *That's My Boy* (Paramount, 1951).

## BAMBALINA
Vincent Youmans (w: Otto Harbach and
Oscar Hammerstein)

Harms—New York

1923

**Show:** *The Wildflower*

Edith Day sang it in the show. Paul Whiteman and His Orchestra had the hit recording (Victor 19035).

## BAND ON THE RUN

Paul McCartney (w & m)

MPL Communications

1974

Paul McCartney and Wings had this number 1 hit, which charted for thirteen weeks (Apple 1873). It sold over one million copies. The song served as the title of the Wings album, recorded in Lagos, Nigeria; many feel this album included the group's best work.

## BANDANA DAYS

Eubie Blake (w: Noble Sissle)

M. Witmark and Sons—New York

1921

**Show:** *Shuffle Along*

Arthur Porter sang it in the show. Eubie Blake and His Shuffle Along Orchestra had the hit recording (Victor 18791).

## BARBARA ANN

Fred Fassert (w & m)

Shoestring Music—New York

1961

A number 13 hit for the vocal group the Regents in 1961 (Gee 1065/Cousins 1002), successfully revived for a number 2 hit by the Beach Boys in 1966 (Capitol 5561). The original version was made as a demo in 1958, but went unreleased until 1961, by which time the group was no more. A classic doo-wop/teen harmony number.

## BARNEY GOOGLE

Con Conrad (w: Billy Rose)

Jerome H. Remick and Co.—New York

1923

Radio favorites Ernie Hare and Billy Jones had the hit recording of this comic song (Columbia A-3876). It was taken from a Billy DeBeck newspaper comic strip (this team followed up with "Come On, Spark Plug"), which also featured cast members of Barney's strip.

Billy Rose devised an act for the zany newcomers Olsen and Johnson to use in vaudeville. They became so identified with this song that they became full-fledged headliners.

## BASIN STREET BLUES

Spencer Williams (w & m)

Joe Davis—New York

1933

Louis Armstrong has been strongly identified with this song, having first recorded it in 1928 (Okeh 8690), then in 1933 (Victor 24351). He sang it in three films, *New Orleans* (United Artists, 1947), *The Strip* (MGM, 1951) where he sang it with Jack Teagarden, and *The Glenn Miller Story* (Universal, 1954).

## BAT DANCE

Prince (w & m)

Controversy Music

1989

**Film:** *Batman* (Warner Bros.)

A number 1 hit for Prince, selling over a million copies, and remaining on the charts for eleven weeks (Warner 22924).

## BATTLE OF NEW ORLEANS, THE

Jimmy Driftwood (w & m)

Warden Music—Nashville

1957, 1959

Johnny Horton had the number 1 hit, which charted for eighteen weeks and sold over one million copies (Columbia 41339). Driftwood had previously recorded it on an album of "folksongs" that he wrote in traditional style. This one borrowed the traditional fiddle tune "The Eighth of January" for its melody.

## BAUBLES, BANGLES AND BEADS

Robert Wright and George Forrest

Frank Music—New York

1953

**Show:** *Kismet*

Doretta Morrow sang it in the show. Peggy Lee had the number 30 hit (Decca 28890). The Kirby Stone Four revived it in 1958 with a number 25 hit (Columbia 41183).

## BE MY LIFE'S COMPANION

Bob Hilliard and Milton DeLugg

Edwin H. Morris—New York

1951

The Mills Brothers had the number 7 hit in 1952, which charted for twelve weeks (Decca 27889).

## BE MY LITTLE BABY
## BUMBLE BEE

Henry I. Marshall (w: Stanley Murphy)

Jerome H. Remick—New York

1912

**Show:** *A Winsome Widow*

The Dolly Sisters sang it in the show. It was revived in the biopic *Irish Eyes Are Smiling* (20th Century Fox, 1944), where it was sung by June Haver. It was also sung by Doris Day and Russell Arms in the film *By the Light of the Silvery Moon* (Warner Bros., 1953), and Eddie Cantor sang it in his biopic *The Eddie Cantor Story* (Warner Bros., 1953).

## BE MY LOVE

Nicholas Brodszky (w: Sammy Cahn)

Miller Music—New York

1950

**Film:** *The Toast of New Orleans* (MGM)

Mario Lanza and Kathryn Grayson sang it in the film. Lanza had the number 1 hit that charted for thirty-four weeks and sold over two million copies (RCA Victor 20-1561).

## BE-BOP BABY

Pearl Lendhurst (w & m)

Travis Music—Hollywood

1957

Ricky Nelson had the number 3 hit, which charted for eighteen weeks and sold over one million copies (Imperial 5463). The title was a play on Gene Vincent's hit, "Be-Bop-a-Lula."

## BE-BOP-A-LULA

Gene Vincent and Sheriff Tex Davis

Lowery Music—New York

1956

Gene Vincent had the number 7 hit, which charted for fifteen weeks (Capitol 3450). The song was a favorite of teenage Paul McCartney, who sang it in the early Beatles' repertoire.

## BEALE STREET

W. C. Handy (w & m)

Pace and Handy Music—Memphis

1917

A classic blues favorite with singers and dance bands in vaudeville, radio, and on many recordings, including Herb Wiedoeft and His Orchestra (Brunswick 2795), Jack Linx and His Orchestra (Okeh 40803), Jack Teagarden (Columbia 35323), and Lena Horne (Victor 27543).

## BEALE STREET MAMA

J. Russel Robinson (w: Roy Turk)

Waterson, Berlin and Snyder—New York

1923

Introduced on record by Lucille Hegamin and Her Blue Flame Syncopators (Cameo 270). Hit instrumental recording by Arthur Gibbs and His Gang (Victor 19070).

## BEAT IT

Michael Jackson (w & m)

Mijac Music

1982, 1983

Michael Jackson had the number 1 hit, which charted for eighteen weeks (Epic 03759). It sold over two million copies. The song was strongly promoted by a video that recalled the famous gang dance numbers in *West Side Story*. "Weird" Al Yankovic recorded a wonderful parody, "Eat It" (including a clever parody video), which reached number 12 in 1984.

## BEAUTIFUL OHIO

Mary Earl (pseudonym of Robert King) (w: Ballard MacDonald)

Shapiro, Bernstein—New York

1918

Its five-million sheet-music sales made it the biggest seller in the publisher's history. The waltz started in vaudeville, featured by a variety of singers, and the tune was also used as background music for acrobats. Henry Burr's recording (Columbia A-2701) helped make it the official state song of Ohio. A year later, the composer turned it into "Beautiful Ohio Blues"; the successful recording was by the Columbia Saxophone Quartette (Columbia A-2784).

## BEAUTY AND THE BEAST
Alan Menken (w: Howard Ashman)
Walt Disney Music
1991
**Film:** *Beauty and the Beast* (Disney)
Academy Award winner for Best Song. Celine Dion and Peabo Bryson had the number 9 hit, which charted for fourteen weeks (Epic 74090). It sold over one million copies.

## BEBE
Abner Silver (w: Sam Coslow)
M. Witmark and Sons—New York
1923
Dedicated to silent film star Bebe Daniels. Introduced in vaudeville by Moss and Frye. Hit recordings by Gene Rodemich and His Orchestra (Brunswick 2454) and Markel's Orchestra (Okeh 4883).

## BECAUSE MY BABY DON'T MEAN MAYBE NOW
Walter Donaldson (w & m)
Donaldson, Douglas and Gumble—New York
1928
Ruth Etting had the best-selling vocal disc (Columbia 1420-D) and Lanin's Arcadians had the instrumental hit (Perfect 15008).

## BECAUSE OF YOU
Arthur Hammerstein and Dudley Wilkinson
BMI—New York
1940
Larry Clinton and His Orchestra, with vocal by Peggy Mann, had the number 23 hit in 1941 (Bluebird 11094). It was revived in the film *I Was an American Spy* (Allied Artists, 1951). Tony Bennett had the number 1 hit in 1951 that charted for thirty-two weeks and sold over one million copies (Columbia 39362)

## BECAUSE YOU LOVED ME
Diane Warren (w & m)
Realsongs
1996

**Film:** *Up Close and Personal* (Touchstone)
Celine Dion's biggest number 1 hit, which charted for thirty weeks (500 Music/Epic 78237). It sold over one million copies. Her version was also featured on the film soundtrack.

## BEDELIA
Jean Schwartz (w: William Jerome)
Shapiro, Bernstein—New York
1903
Sold over three million copies. Introduced in *The Jersey Lily* by Blanche Ring in her first starring role on Broadway. Revived in the film *The Eddie Cantor Story* (Warner Bros. 1953).

## BEE'S KNEES
Ray Lopez and Ted Lewis (w: Leo Wood)
Leo Feist—New York
1922
Ted Lewis cut himself in on this one and his band had the best-selling disc (Columbia A-3730). The Virginians weren't too far behind with theirs (Victor 19000), and the Bostonian Syncopators had the best jazz version (Grey Gull 1138).

## BEER BARREL POLKA
Wladimir Timm/Jaromir Vejvoda/
Lew Brown
Shapiro, Bernstein—New York
1939
Will Glahe and the Glahe Musette Orchestra had the number 1 hit, which charted for twenty-one weeks and sold over one million copies (Victor V-70). It was revived in 1975 by Bobby Vinton, who had a number 33 hit (ABC 12056). The song has become a standard among polka bands, both as a vocal and instrumental, with its theme being parodied and quoted in dozens of recordings.

## BEFORE I MET YOU
Jerome Kern (w: P. G. Wodehouse)
T. B. Harms—New York
1918
**Show:** *Oh Lady! Lady!!*
A peppy, cheerful number introduced in the Princess Theatre show by Vivienne Segal and Carl Randall.

## BEGIN THE BEGUINE

Cole Porter (w & m)

Harms Inc.—New York

1935

**Show:** *Jubilee*

June Knight sang it in the show. Xavier Cugat and His Waldorf-Astoria Orchestra had the first recording at number 13 (Victor 25133). It wasn't until Artie Shaw and His Orchestra had the number 1 hit in 1938—which charted for eighteen weeks and sold over two million copies (Bluebird 7746)—that the song became a standard. This recording was voted by the *Billboard* Disc Jockey poll in 1990 as the number 3 all-time record and number 5 all-time song.

## BEHIND YOUR SILKEN VEIL

Vincent Rose and Earl Burtnett

(w: Richard Coburn)

Sherman, Clay—San Francisco

1919

A fine recording by the Happy Six (Columbia A-2758) features a piano in the last chorus.

## BEING ALIVE

Stephen Sondheim (w & m)

Valando Music—New York

1970

**Show:** *Company*

Dean Jones sang it in the show.

## BELIEVE

Brian Higgins/Stuart McLennan/

Paul Barry/Stephen Torch/Matt Gray/Tim Powell

Xenomania Music

1998

Cher had the number 1 hit in 1999, which charted for twenty-five weeks (Warner 17119). It sold over one million copies. The song was a top hit worldwide, and helped revive disco rhythms in popular music as it renewed Cher's career. She is one of the few artists to have number 1 hits in four decades (from the 1960s to the 1990s).

## BESIDE A BABBLING BROOK

Walter Donaldson (w: Gus Kahn)

Jerome H. Remick—New York

1923

Marion Harris had the hit vocal (Brunswick 2421). The Great White Way Orchestra had the hit instrumental (Victor 19058).

## BESSIE COULDN'T HELP IT

Byron H. Warner/J.L. Richmond/Charles Bayha

Shapiro, Bernstein—New York

1925

Introduced in vaudeville by the Diplomats. Warner's Seven Aces had the hit recording (Okeh 40198). It has become a standard with jazz bands.

## BEST I GET IS MUCH OBLIGED TO YOU, THE

Benjamin Hapgood Burt (w & m)

Jerome H. Remick—New York

1907

The best comic number of the year. Introduced by Louise Dresser in the show *The Girl behind the Counter*, who greatly contributed to its success. This is in the "Nobody" vein of Bert Williams; the point of the lyric is that no one ever said, "Sylvester you keep the change."

## BEST OF MY LOVE

Don Henley/Glenn Frey/John Souther

WB Music

1974

The Eagles had a number 1 hit with this soft-rock ballad in 1975, which charted for fourteen weeks (Asylum 45218).

## BEST OF MY LOVE

Maurice White and Al Mc Kay

Saggifire Music

1977

The Emotions, a vocal trio of sisters from Chicago, had this number 1 hit, which charted for seventeen weeks (Columbia 10544). It sold over one million copies.

## BEST THINGS IN LIFE ARE FREE, THE

Ray Henderson (w: Bud DeSylva and Lew Brown)

DeSylva, Brown and Henderson—New York

1927

**Show:** *Good News*

Mary Lawlor and John Price Jones sang it in the show. George Olsen and His Orchestra had a hit version (Victor 20872), as did Frank Black's Orchestra (Brunswick 3657). June Allyson revived it in the film version of the show (MGM, 1947), and it was revived once again in the DeSylva, Brown, and Henderson biopic *The Best Things In Life Are Free* by Gordon MacRae, Dan Dailey, Ernest Borgnine, and Sheree North (20th Century Fox, 1956).

## BETTE DAVIS EYES

Jackie DeShannon (w: Donna Weiss)

Plain and Simple Music

1975, 1981

Kim Carnes had this number 1 hit, which held this position for nine out of twenty weeks on the chart (EMI America 8077). It sold over one million copies. It was the most successful hit for Carnes, whose raspy voice recalled that of another 1970s hit maker, Rod Stewart.

## BETTY CO-ED

J. Paul Fogarty and Rudy Vallee

Carl Fischer—New York

1930

Rudy Vallee and His Connecticut Yankees had a number 4 hit, which charted for seven weeks (Victor 22473). It was associated with Vallee, because he sang it on his radio show for quite a while and his picture appeared on the sheet music cover.

## BETWEEN THE DEVIL AND THE DEEP BLUE SEA

Harold Arlen (w: Ted Koehler)

Mills Music Inc.—New York

1931

**Show:** *Rhythmania*

Aida Ward sang it in the show. Louis Armstrong had the number 12 hit (Okeh 41550).

## BEWITCHED

Richard Rodgers (w: Lorenz Hart)

Chappell—New York

1941

**Show:** *Pal Joey*

Sung in show by Vivienne Segal. Leo Reisman and His Orchestra, with vocal by Anita Boyer, had the first recording (Victor 27344). It was revived in 1950 by the Bill Snyder Orchestra, whose number 3 recording sold over one million copies (Tower 1473).

## BEYOND THE BLUE HORIZON

Richard Whiting and Franke Harling

(w: Leo Robin)

Famous Music—New York

1930

**Film:** *Monte Carlo* (Paramount)

Jeanette MacDonald sang it in the film. She had the number 9 hit, which charted for four weeks (Victor 22514). Hugo Winterhalter and His Orchestra revived it in 1951 with a number 23 hit (RCA Victor 20-4288).

## BIG BAD BILL (IS SWEET WILLIAM NOW)

Milton Ager (w: Jack Yellen)

Ager, Yellen and Bornstein—New York

1924

Introduced in vaudeville by Healy and Cross. Margaret Young, accompanied by pianist Rube Bloom, had the hit vocal record (Brunswick 2736), while the Don Clark Orchestra had the hit instrumental (Victor 19622).

## BIG BAD JOHN

Jimmy Dean (w & m)

Acuff-Rose-Opryland Music—Nashville

1961

Jimmy Dean (later of sausage-making fame) had the number 1 hit, which held this position for five of the thirteen weeks it charted (Columbia 42175). It sold over one million copies.

## BIG BOY

Milton Ager (w: Jack Yellen)

Ager, Yellen and Bornstein—New York

1924

Introduced in vaudeville by Jack Sidney. A favorite of dance bands especially after Ted Weems and His Orchestra (Victor 19344) and the Lanin Orchestra (Okeh 40111) recorded it. Jazz bands loved it after the Wolverine Orchestra released their version with Bix Beiderbecke playing cornet lead and taking a chorus on piano (Gennett 5565).

## BIG GIRLS DON'T CRY

Bob Gaudio (w: Bob Crewe)

BoBob Music—New York

1962

The Four Seasons had the number 1 hit; it held this position for five of the fourteen weeks charted (Vee-Jay 465), and sold more than one million copies. Noteworthy for Frankie Valli's high-pitched "Cry-yi-yi" harmony.

## BIG HUNK O' LOVE, A
Aaron Schroeder and Sid Wyche
Elvis Presley Music—New York
1959
Number 1 hit for Elvis, charting for ten weeks and selling over a million copies (RCA 47-7600). It was one of four songs recorded and released while Elvis was in the service.

## BILL
Jerome Kern (w: P. G. Wodehouse and
Oscar Hammerstein)
T. B. Harms—New York
1927
**Show:** *Show Boat*
Originally written for the Princess Theatre show *Oh, Lady! Lady!!* (1918), it was dropped during tryouts. Helen Morgan sang it in the show and her 1928 disc was a best seller (Victor 21238). This famed torch singer also sang it in the film versions (Universal, 1929 and 1936). Gogi Grant revived it when she sang it on the soundtrack of the third version of *Show Boat* (MGM, 1951).

## BILL BAILEY, WON'T YOU PLEASE COME HOME?
Hughie Cannon (w & m)
Howley, Haviland and Dresser—New York
1902
A syncopated classic leading to other Bill Bailey songs, it was introduced by minstrel/songwriter John Queen. Several people claimed to be the original Bill Bailey. Jimmy Durante and his sidekick Eddie Jackson often used it in their act and finally recorded it (MGM 30255). Arthur Collins had the hit recording in 1902 (Columbia A-872), and Bobby Darin revived it in 1960 with a number 19 hit that charted for five weeks (ATCO 6167). A favorite of Dixieland jazz bands. A source of numerous parodies, including Tom Lehrer's "(Won't You Come Home) Disraeli?"

## BILLIE JEAN
Michael Jackson (w & m)
Mijac Music
1982, 1983
Michael Jackson was the top-selling artist in the 1980s, largely thanks to this and other top singles drawn from his *Thriller* album. This number 1 hit stayed at that position for seven out of seventeen weeks on the chart (Epic 03509). It sold over two million copies.

## BILLY
James Kendis and Herman Paley (w: Joe Goodwin)
Kendis and Paley—New York
1911
Vaudeville favorite introduced by Billy Clifford. Revived by Bonnie Baker with a number 10 hit in 1939 (Vocalion 4914).

## BIRD DOG
Felice and Boudeleaux Bryant
Acuff-Rose—Nashville
1958
Number 1 hit for the Everly Brothers, charting for fifteen weeks; also a number 1 country hit (Cadence 1350).

## BIRD IN A GILDED CAGE, A
Harry Von Tilzer (w: Arthur J. Lamb)
Shapiro, Bernstein and Von Tilzer—New York
1900
First two million-selling song by Von Tilzer, the most prolific composer of this decade. This tearjerker appeared soon after he was made a partner in this well-established publishing firm. It was used in the film *Ringside Maisie* (MGM 1941) and in the musical *Coney Island* (20th Century Fox, 1943).

## BIRD ON NELLIE'S HAT, THE
Alfred Solman (w: Arthur J. Lamb)
Jos. W. Stern—New York
1906
Comic song introduced in vaudeville by May Ward. Helen Trix recorded it in 1907. (Victor 4904).

## BIRMINGHAM BLUES
Charles McCord and Matthews

Perry Bradford Music—New York

1922

Introduced on record by Fats Waller—his first record—a piano solo (Okeh 4757).

## BIRTH OF THE BLUES, THE
Ray Henderson (w: Bud DeSylva and Lew Brown)

Harms—New York

1926

**Show:** *George White's Scandals*: 8th edition

Harry Richman sang it in the show and had a hit recording (Vocalion 15412). Pianist Francis J. Carter made a fabulous solo recording (Okeh 40693). It has become one of the outstanding standards of all time. Bing Crosby sang it in the film of the same name (Paramount, 1941), and Gordon MacRae sang it while sexpot Sheree North danced in the DeSylva, Brown and Henderson biopic *The Best Things in Life Are Free* (20th Century Fox, 1956).

## BLACK AND WHITE
Earl Robinson (w: David Arkin)

Shawnee Press

1956, 1972

Three Dog Night, a vocal trio, had this last number 1 hit, which charted for nine weeks (Dunhill/ABC 4317). It sold over one million copies.

## BLACK AND WHITE RAG
George Botsford

Jerome H. Remick—New York

1908

One of the all-time great rags. A million-seller using three consecutive notes in a four-beat measure, it has been a winner with audiences. The first recording on disc was by the Victor Orchestra (Victor 16350) and was a resounding hit. El Cota, a xylophonist, had another in 1911 (Columbia A-1118). It was revived in 1941 by Wally Rose (Jazz Man 1), and again in 1951 by Winifred Atwell (English Decca F-9790).

## BLACK BOTTOM
Ray Henderson (w: Bud DeSylva and Lew Brown)

Harms Inc.—New York

1926

**Show:** *George White's Scandals*: 8th edition

Introduced in the show by Ann Pennington. Johnny Hamp and His Kentucky Serenaders had the hit recording (Victor 20101), although recordings by Howard Lanin (Columbia 689-D) and Ohman and Arden with their orchestra (Brunswick 3242) sold well, too. Far from Charleston-like, the dance step resembled dragging the feet as though through mud. It is an extremely lively number, as seen in the biopic *The Best Things in Life Are Free* (20th Century Fox, 1956).

## BLACK OR WHITE
Michael Jackson (w & m)

Mijac Music

1991

A number 1 hit that lasted fifteen weeks on the charts (Epic 74100). It sold over one million copies. A paen for cross-racial understanding, the video for the song, directed by Jon Landis, was controversial because of a coda sequence in which Jackson smashed the windows of a parked car; it was quickly withdrawn and the offending passage edited out before rerelease.

## BLACK WATER
Patrick Simmons (w & m)

WB Music

1974

Number 1 hit in 1975 for the pop-rock group the Doobie Brothers, charting for twelve weeks (Warner 8062). It was their only major hit before singer/pianist Michael McDonald joined the band.

## BLINDED BY THE LIGHT
Bruce Springsteen (w & m)

Laurel Canyon Music—New York

1972

Manfred Mann's Earth Band had this number 1 hit in 1977 that charted for fifteen weeks (Warner 8252). It sold over one million copies.

## BLOWIN' IN THE WIND
Bob Dylan (w & m)

M. Witmark and Sons—New York

1963

Peter, Paul and Mary had the number 2 hit that charted for twelve weeks (Warner 5368). It became Dylan's most famous song.

## BLUE (AND BROKEN HEARTED)

Lou Handman (w: Grant Clarke and Edgar Leslie)

Stark and Cowan—New York

1922

Marion Harris had the hit vocal recording (Brunswick 2310), and Bennie Krueger (Brunswick 2315) and the Virginians (Victor 18933) had the hit dance records.

## BLUE BELL

Theodore Morse (w: Edward Madden)

F. B. Haviland—New York

1904

A hit in vaudeville, it was featured by Madeline Burdette, among many others. It was used in the film *The Jolson Story* (Columbia 1946).

## BLUE DANUBE BLUES

Jerome Kern (w: Anne Caldwell)

T. B. Harms—New York

1921

**Show:** *Good Morning, Dearie*

Introduced in the show by Louise Groody and Oscar Shaw. Among the popular recordings were those by Carl Fenton's Orchestra (Brunswick 2170), the Knickerbocker Orchestra (Columbia A-3516), and the Yerkes S.S. Flotilla Orchestra (Vocalion 14261).

## BLUE GRASS BLUES

Elmer Schoebel (w: Billy Meyers)

Jack Mills—New York

1923

Introduced by Abe Lyman and His Orchestra. Hit records were by Gene Rodemich and His Orchestra (Brunswick 2527), David H. Silverman and His Orchestra (Victor 19237), and the Original Memphis Five (Pathe 036072).

## BLUE HOOSIER BLUES

Abel Baer/Cliff Friend/Jack Meskill

Leo Feist—New York

1923

Introduced in vaudeville by Rose and Mae Wilton. Several great arrangements were recorded by Isham Jones and His Orchestra (Brunswick 2456), Sam Lanin's Orchestra (Regal 9486), and Vincent Lopez and His Orchestra (Okeh 4869).

## BLUE MOON

Richard Rodgers (w: Lorenz Hart)

Robbins Music—New York

1934

Glen Gray and the Casa Loma Orchestra had the number 1 hit, which charted for eight weeks in 1935 (Decca 312). The Benny Goodman Orchestra, with singer Helen Ward, had the number 2 hit the same year (Columbia 3003). It was revived in the biopic film *Words and Music* (MGM, 1948) by Mel Torme, whose 1949 number 20 hit charted for five weeks (Capitol 15428). It was used in many films, including *With a Song in My Heart* (20th Century Fox, 1952); *This Could Be the Night* (MGM, 1957); and *New York, New York* (UA, 1977). It was revived yet again by the vocal group the Marcels, who had the number 1 hit in 1961 that charted for eleven weeks (Colpix 186). It has become both a supper-club and doo-wop standard.

## BLUE RIVER

Joseph Meyer (w: Alfred Bryan)

Jerome H. Remick—New York

1927

Sophie Tucker, accompanied by Ted Shapiro on piano, had the hit vocal recording (Okeh 40895). Jean Goldkette and His Orchestra had the hit instrumental (Victor 20981).

## BLUE ROOM, THE

Richard Rodgers (w: Lorenz Hart)

Harms—New York

1926

**Show:** *The Girl Friend*

Eva Puck and Sammy White sang it in the show. Phil Ohman and Victor Arden with their Orchestra had a hit recording (Brunswick 3197). Perry Como sang it in the Rodgers and Hart biopic *Words and Music* (MGM, 1948), followed by his number 18 hit in 1949 (RCA Victor 20-3329).

## BLUE SKIES

Irving Berlin (w & m)

Irving Berlin—New York

1927

**Show:** *Betsy*

Belle Baker sang it in the show. Although the rest of

BLUE SUEDE SHOES • BLUIN' THE BLUES

this musical was scored by Rodgers and Hart, she asked Berlin to write this song to feature her. The Knicker-bockers had a splendid recording (Columbia 860-D), as did Vaughn Deleath (Okeh 40750). Count Basie and His Orchestra, with vocal by Jimmy Rushing, revived it with a number 8 hit in 1946 (Columbia 37070). Benny Goodman and His Orchestra, with vocal by Art Lund, had the number 9 hit (Columbia 37053). Ethel Merman and Alice Faye sang it in the film *Alexander's Ragtime Band* (20th Century Fox, 1938), and Bing Crosby sang it in *Blue Skies* (Paramount, 1946) and again in *White Christmas* (Paramount, 1954). It is a jazz standard.

## BLUE SUEDE SHOES
Carl Lee Perkins (w & m)
Hill and Range Songs—New York
1956
Carl Perkins introduced this rock and roll favorite and had a number 2 hit that charted for seventeen weeks (Sun 234). Perkins claims to have scribbled the lyrics on an old potato sack in a moment of sudden inspiration. It was Perkins's biggest hit, and became closely associated with him throughout his career. Elvis Presley subsequently recorded it, and had a number 20 hit that came out on an extended-play 45 rpm disc and sold over one million copies (RCA Victor EPA-747). Johnny Rivers revived it in 1973 with a number 38 hit (United Artists 198).

## BLUE VELVET
Bernie Wayne and Lee Morris
Vogue Music—Santa Monica
1951, 1963
Bobby Vinton had the number 1 hit, which charted for twelve weeks (Epic 9614). Vinton's recording was used as the theme song for the creepy David Lynch film of the same name (De Laurentis, 1986).

## BLUEBERRY HILL
Vincent Rose (w: Al Lewis and Larry Stock)
Chappell—New York
1940
Glenn Miller and His Orchestra had the number 1 hit, which charted for twenty weeks (Bluebird 10768). Fats Domino revived it in 1957 with a number 2 hit that charted for twenty-one weeks and sold over one million copies (Imperial 5407).

## BLUE-EYED SALLY
J. Russel Robinson (w: Al Bernard)
Waterson—New York
1924
Introduced in vaudeville and recorded by the composers under the name the Dixie Stars (Brunswick 2689). Ted Weems and His Orchestra helped popularize it (Victor 19547).

## BLUES IN THE NIGHT
Harold Arlen (w: Johnny Mercer)
Remick Music—New York
1941
**Film:** *Blues in the Night* (Warner Bros.)
William Gillespie sang it in the film. Woody Herman and His Orchestra had the number 1 hit that charted for eighteen weeks (Decca 4030). Dinah Shore had a number 4 hit in 1942 that sold over one million copies (Bluebird 11436).

## BLUES MY NAUGHTY SWEETIE GIVES TO ME
Arthur Swanstone/Chas. McCarron/Carey Morgan
Jos. W. Stern—New York
1919
Ted Lewis and His Band made this popular in vaudeville and on disc (Columbia A-2798). It was revived in the film *Atlantic City* (Republic, 1944). The first record of the Dixieland revival in 1949 was this song, performed by the Firehouse Five Plus Two (Good Time Jazz L-12010). It has become a standard for Dixieland jazz bands.

## BLUIN' THE BLUES
Henry W. Ragas
Leo Feist—New York
1918
Introduced in vaudeville, cabaret, and on records by the Original Dixieland Jazz Band, whose pianist was the composer (Victor 18483). J. Russel Robinson made a fine piano roll arrangement (QRS 754). The following year Sidney Mitchell added lyrics. A standard for Dixieland bands, it was revived in 1940 by Sherry Magee and His Dixielanders (Vocalion 5436) and again in 1946 by Pete Daily and his Chicagoans (Jump 14).

## BO LA BO
George Fairman (w & m)
M. Witmark and Sons—New York
1919
Introduced in vaudeville by Ted Lewis and his Band, who also recorded it (Columbia A-2895). A popular recording was made by Biese Novelty Orchestra (Vocalion 14002). Charley Straight did the interesting piano roll (Imperial 9992).

## BODY AND SOUL
John Green (w: Edward Heyman)
Harms—New York
1930
**Show:** *Three's a Crowd*
Libby Holman sang it in the show and had the number 3 hit that charted for seven weeks (Brunswick 4910). Paul Whiteman and His Orchestra, with vocal by Jack Fulton, had the number 1 hit, which charted for fifteen weeks (Columbia 2297-D). Coleman Hawkins, the great tenor saxophonist, revived it in his number 13 hit in 1939, and it became one of the most important jazz recordings of all time (Bluebird 10523).

## BON BON BUDDY
Will Marion Cook (w: Alex Rogers)
Gotham-Attucks Music—New York
1907
**Show:** *Bandanna Land*
Written for George Walker—of Williams and Walker —who personified the dandy in his presentation in the show. He was forever identified with this song.

## BONGO ON THE CONGO
Jerome Kern (w: P. G. Wodehouse)
Harms—New York
1924
**Show:** *Sitting Pretty*
Introduced in the show by Eugene Revere, Dwight Frye, and Frank McIntyre. Ira Gershwin admired Wodehouse's ability to create a true comic lyric, something he felt he himself had been unable to do.

## BOO HOO HOO (YOU'RE GONNA CRY WHEN I'M GONE)
Bob Nelson/Harry Link/Al Lentz/Irving Aaronson

Broadway Music—New York
1922
Introduced in vaudeville by Adele Rowland. Sissle and Blake (Emerson 10512) and Aileen Stanley and Billy Murray (Victor 18855) had the popular vocal recordings, while the Bar Harbor Society Orchestra (Vocalion 14302) had the instrumental.

## BOOGIE OOGIE OOGIE
Janice Marie Johnson and Perry Kibble
Conducive Music
1978
Number 1 disco hit for A Taste of Honey, holding the top position for three out of seventeen weeks on the charts (Capitol 4565).

## BOOGIE WOOGIE
Clarence "Pine-Top" Smith
Melrose Music—New York
1939
Pine Top's recording (Vocalion 1245) was the first boogie woogie piano solo (1929). It was first published in sheet music ten years later. Tommy Dorsey and His Orchestra, featuring pianist Howard Smith, sold over a million copies in 1938 (Victor 26054). Also known as "Pine-top's Boogie Woogie" for obvious reasons.

## BOOK OF LOVE
Warren Davis/George Malone/Charles Patrick
ARC Music—New York
1957
The Monotones had the number 5 hit in 1958, which charted for twelve weeks (Argo 5290).

## BORN FREE
John Barry (w: Don Black)
Screen Gems-Columbia Music—New York
1966
**Film:** *Born Free* (Columbia)
Academy Award winner for Best Song. Roger Williams had the number 7 hit, which charted for fourteen weeks (Kapp 767).

## BORN TO BE WILD
Mars Bonfire (w & m)

Duchess Music—New York

1968

Steppenwolf had the number 2 hit, which charted for twelve weeks and sold over one million copies (Dunhill/ABC 4138). It was the group's most popular number.

## BOW WOW BLUES

Cliff Friend and Nat Osborne

Irving Berlin—New York

1922

Introduced on disc by Bennie Krueger and His Orchestra (Brunswick 2174). He also appears playing this number on his alto sax on the Original Dixieland Jazz Band's last recording session (Victor 18850). It is a marvelous novelty number.

## BOY IS MINE, THE

Lashawn Daniels/Rodney and Fred Jerkins/Brandy Norwood/Japhe Tejeda

EMI April Music

1998

Brandy and Monica joined forces to create the number 1 hit that held its top position for thirteen out of the twenty-seven weeks charted (Atlantic 84089). It sold over three million copies.

## BREAKING UP IS HARD TO DO

Neil Sedaka and Howard Greenfield

Aldon Music—New York

1962

Neil Sedaka had the number 1 hit, which charted for twelve weeks (RCA Victor 8046). He revived it in 1975, when it was number 8 for eleven weeks (Rocket 40500).

## BREEZE BLOW MY BABY BACK TO ME

James F. Hanley (w: Ballard MacDonald and Joe Goodwin)

Shapiro, Bernstein—New York

1919

Introduced in vaudeville by Owsley and O'Day. The Synco Jazz Band had the popular recording (Columbia A-2783), and it has been a favorite of Dixieland-styled jazz bands ever since.

## BREEZIN' ALONG WITH THE BREEZE

Richard Whiting/Seymour Simons/Haven Gillespie

Jerome H. Remick—New York

1926

Johnny Marvin had this hit recording (Columbia 699-D), as did Abe Lyman and His California Orchestra (Brunswick 3240). The Seattle Harmony Kings had the first jazz band version (Victor 20142). It was revived in the Nora Bayes biopic *Shine On, Harvest Moon* (Warner Bros., 1944).

## BRIDGE OVER TROUBLED WATER

Paul Simon (w & m)

Charing Cross Music—New York

1969, 1970

Simon and Garfunkel had this number 1 hit for thirteen weeks (Columbia 45133). It sold over one million copies.

## BROADWAY BLUES

Carey Morgan (w: Arthur Swanstrom)

Irving Berlin—New York

1920

Sissle and Blake had the hit recording (Emerson 10296), and vaudeville star Nora Bayes also had a hit (Columbia A-3311).

## BROADWAY MELODY

Nacio Herb Brown (w: Arthur Freed)

Robbins Music—New York

1929

**Film:** *The Broadway Melody* (MGM)

Charles King sang it in the film and also recorded it (Victor 21964). Ted White's Collegians made a nice version (Oriole 1507). It was revived in the film *Singin' in the Rain* (MGM, 1952).

## BROKEN HEARTED

Ray Henderson (w: Bud DeSylva and Lew Brown)

DeSylva, Brown and Henderson—New York

1927

Belle Baker introduced it in vaudeville. Paul Whiteman and His Orchestra had the hit recording (Victor 20757). Johnny Ray revived it with a number 8 hit in 1952 that charted for fifteen weeks (Columbia 39636).

## BROTHER, CAN YOU SPARE A DIME?

Jay Gorney (w: E. Y. Harburg)

Harms Inc.—New York

1932

**Show:** *Americana*

Rex Weber sang it in the show. Probably the song most associated with the Great Depression, its two number 1 hits were by the most outstanding male vocalists of the time: Bing Crosby (Brunswick 6414) and Rudy Vallee (Columbia 2725-D). Each version charted for eight weeks.

## BROTHERHOOD OF MAN

Frank Loesser (w & m)

Frank Music—New York

1961

**Show:** *How To Succeed in Business without Really Trying*

Robert Morse, Sammy Smith, and Ruth Kobart sang it in the show.

## BROWN EYES, WHY ARE YOU BLUE?

George W. Meyer (w: Alfred Bryan)

Henry Waterson—New York

1925

Favorite on radio and in vaudeville. Nick Lucas had a hit recording (Brunswick 2961) and so did the Majestic Dance Orchestra (Banner 1600).

## BROWN SKIN, WHO YOU FOR?

Clarence Williams and Armand J. Piron

Williams and Piron—New Orleans

1916

Introduced on disc by the Victor Military Band (Victor 18203).

## BROWN SUGAR

Harry Barris

Larry Conley—St. Louis

1926

Great jazz tune composed by one of Paul Whiteman's Rhythm Boys. The Dixie Jazz Band (Oriole 748), Doc Cook and His Orchestra (Columbia 813-D), and the Piccadilly Revels Band, with Donald Thorne taking a piano solo (E-Columbia 4249), have the best versions.

## BROWN SUGAR

Mick Jagger and Keith Richards

Abkco

1971

Number 1 hit for the Rolling Stones, a position it held for two out of the twelve weeks it charted (Rolling Stones 19100). Famous for its opening cowbell rhythm.

## BUGLE CALL RAG

Jack Pettis/Billy Meyers/Elmer Schoebel

Mills Music—New York

1923

Abe Lyman and His Ambassador Orchestra introduced it in vaudeville. It soon became a jazz standard, with Ted Lewis and His Band (Columbia 826-D) and the Missouri Jazz Band (Regal 9514) having the initial successes. The Mills Brothers revived it in 1932 with a number 2 hit (Brunswick 6357). Benny Goodman and His Orchestra had a number 5 hit in 1934 (Columbia 2958-D) and again with a number 13 hit in 1936 (Victor 25467). The Goodman band performed it in the film *The Big Broadcast of 1937* (Paramount, 1936). It was revived again in the biopic *The Benny Goodman Story* (Universal, 1956).

## BULL FROG BLUES

Tom Brown and Gus Shrigley

Will Rossiter—Chicago

1916

**Show:** *Chin Chin*

Introduced in the show by the Six Brown Brothers, who made the hit recording (Victor 18097).

## BULL FROG PATROL

Jerome Kern (w: Anne Caldwell)

T. B. Harms—New York

1919

**Show:** *She's a Good Fellow*

Introduced in the show by the Duncan Sisters, who also recorded it accompanied by Edna Fisher (Victor 19352).

## BUNGALOW IN QUOGUE, THE

Jerome Kern (w: P. G. Wodehouse)

T. B. Harms—New York

1917

**Show:** *The Riviera Girl*
Introduced in the show by Sam Hardy and Juliette Day. The hit recording was by Billy Murray and Gladys Rice (Edison 80381).

## BUSHEL AND A PECK, A
Frank Loesser (w & m)
Susan—New York
1950
**Show:** *Guys and Dolls*
Vivian Blaine sang it in the show. Perry Como and Betty Hutton had the number 3 hit, which charted for eighteen weeks (RCA Victor 20-3930).

## BUT NOT FOR ME
George and Ira Gershwin
New World Music—New York
1930
**Show:** *Girl Crazy*
Ginger Rogers sang it in the show. Judy Garland sang it in the 1943 film version (MGM). Harry James and His Orchestra had the number 12 hit in 1942 (Columbia 36599).

## BUTTON UP YOUR OVERCOAT
Ray Henderson (w: Bud DeSylva and Lew Brown)
DeSylva, Brown and Henderson—New York
1928
**Show:** *Follow Thru*
Zelma O'Neal and Jack Haley sang it in the show. They also performed it in the film version (Paramount, 1930). Helen Kane had one of the hit recordings (Victor 21863) and Fred Waring's Pennsylvanians had another (Victor 21861). It was revived in 1954 by the Glenn Brown Trio (Coronet 550). Gordon MacRae, Dan Dailey, Ernest Borgnine and Sheree North sang it in the biopic *The Best Things in Life Are Free* (20th Century Fox, 1956). It has remained a popular melody, revived on occasion in advertising jingles in the 1960s and 1970s (at one point, it was used to promote Alka-Seltzer). Also known as "Take Good Care of Yourself."

## BUTTONS AND BOWS
Jay Livingston and Ray Evans
Famous Music—New York
1948

**Film:** *Paleface* (Paramount)
Academy Award winner for Best Song. Bob Hope sang it in the film. Dinah Shore had the number 1 hit, which held that position for ten of twenty-five weeks on the charts, and sold over one million copies (Columbia 38284). It was long associated with Shore, who continued to perform it for decades.

## BUZZIN' THE BEE
Jack Wells (w & m)
Waterson, Berlin and Snyder—New York
1916
**Show:** *No. 33 Washington Square*
Introduced in the show by May Irwin. Gene Greene popularized it on disc (Columbia A-2276).

## BY THE BEAUTIFUL SEA
Harry Carroll (w: Harold Atteridge)
Shapiro, Bernstein—New York
1914
The Stanford Four introduced it in vaudeville. It was revived in the following films: *The Story of Vernon and Irene Castle* (RKO, 1939), *Coney Island* (20th Century Fox, 1943), *Atlantic City* (Republic, 1944), and *Some Like It Hot* (United Artists, 1959).

## BY THE LIGHT OF THE SILVERY MOON
Gus Edwards (w: Edward Madden)
Gus Edwards Music—New York
1909
A huge hit in vaudeville, originally sung by Georgie Price in the Gus Edwards revue *School Boys and Girls*. A film of the same name starred Doris Day and Gordon MacRae, who also sang it (Warner Bros., 1953).

## BY THE WATERMELON VINE LINDY LOU
Thomas S. Allen (w & m)
Walter Jacobs—Boston
1904
A lovely ballad featured in minstrel and vaudeville shows. Bob Roberts had the hit recording (Columbia 1882). Revived in 1928 by the Dixie Stars (Brunswick 4121), and again in the film *Hello, Frisco, Hello* (20th Century Fox, 1943).

## BYE BYE BLACKBIRD
Ray Henderson (w: Mort Dixon)
Jerome H. Remick—New York
1926
Introduced in vaudeville by Eddie Cantor. Gene Austin had the hit recording (Victor 20044). Revived by Russ Morgan (Decca 24319) in 1948. Eddie Cantor sang it on the soundtrack of his biopic *The Eddie Cantor Story* (Warner Bros., 1953).

## BYE BYE BLUES
Fred Hamm and Dave Bennett
Irving Berlin—New York
1925
Introduced by composer/bandleader Fred Hamm and His Orchestra (Victor 19662). In 1930, bandleader Bert Lown and Chauncey Grey got cut in when Lown used it as his theme song and made a hit record (Columbia 2258-D). Revived in 1953 by Les Paul and Mary Ford with a number 5 hit (Capitol 2316).

## BYE BYE LOVE
Felice and Boudleaux Bryant
Acuff-Rose—Nashville
1957
First number 1 hit for the Everly Brothers, holding that position for four of the twenty-two weeks it was on the chart (Cadence 1315). It was also their first release on the Cadence label, and established them as rock and country hit makers.

## BYE BYE PRETTY BABY
Jack Gardner and Spike Hamilton
Shapiro, Bernstein—New York
1927
Introduced by Abe Lyman and His Orchestra (Brunswick 3615), but Jan Garber shared the success (Victor 20833). Vocal soloists Peggy Britton (Cameo 1213) and Freddie Rose (Brunswick 3616) helped make it a hit.

## CABARET
John Kander (w: Fred Ebb)
Sunbeam Music—New York
1966
**Show:** *Cabaret*

Jill Haworth sang it in the show; Liza Minelli sang it in the film version (Allied Artists, 1972).

## CAKEWALK IN THE SKY, THE
Ben Harney
M. Witmark and Sons—New York
1899
A cakewalk made popular in vaudeville by the composer. The Victor Dance Orchestra made the famous recording first in 1905, then again in 1909 (Victor 35088).

## CAKEWALKING BABIES FROM HOME
Chris Smith/Henry Troy/Clarence Williams
Clarence Williams—New York
1924
A Jazz standard introduced in vaudeville, on radio, and on records by the composer/publisher/pianist/music director Clarence Williams and his wife Eva Taylor (Okeh 40321). On that recording can be heard Louis Armstrong and Sidney Bechet in Clarence's group the Blue Five. Every Dixieland jazz band has it in its repertory.

## CALIFORNIA DREAMIN'
John and Michelle Phillips
Wingate Music—Hollywood
1965, 1966
The Mamas and The Papas had the number 4 hit, which charted for thirteen weeks and sold over one million copies (Dunhill 4020). The song was composed by the Phillipses while they were living in New York City. This song—along with Brian Wilson's many popular numbers for the Beach Boys—made California a prime destination for young people in the 1960s.

## CALIFORNIA GIRLS
Brian Wilson (w & m)
Sea of Tunes—Whittier, California
1965
Although only a number 3 hit when it was first issued (Capitol 5464), it has become one of the most famous songs performed by sun-in-the-fun vocal group the Beach Boys. The song opens with a mini-instrumental introduction that sets the stage for amusement-park-

style organ and an incredibly complex harmony arrangement. The song was covered twenty years later by rocker David Lee Roth, again reaching number 3 (Warner 29102). It remains one of the best-loved of all 1960s rock songs.

## CALIFORNIA, HERE I COME
Joseph Meyer/Bud DeSylva/Al Jolson
M. Witmark and Sons—New York
1924
**Show:** *Bombo*
Introduced in the show by Al Jolson whose recording helped make it a hit (Brunswick 2569). Paul Whiteman's version was also important (Victor 19267). Jolson revived it in the film *Rose of Washington Square* (20th Century Fox, 1939) and in his two biopics *The Jolson Story* (Columbia, 1946) and *Jolson Sings Again* (Columbia, 1949).

## CALL ME
Deborah Harry and Giorgio Moroder
Ensign Music—Los Angeles
1980
**Film:** *American Gigolo* (Paramount)
The new-wave group Blondie had three number 1 hits, this being the most popular, staying in this position for six out of nineteen weeks on the chart (Chrysalis 2414). Debbie Harry was the vocalist in the group; Moroder was a noted producer of disco hits (primarily for Donna Summer). It sold over one million copies.

## CALL ME IRRESPONSIBLE
James Van Heusen (w: Sammy Cahn)
Paramount Music—New York
1963
**Film:** *Papa's Delicate Condition* (Paramount)
Academy Award winner for Best Song. Jackie Gleason sang the song in the film. It has since become a cabaret standard.

## CAMELOT
Frederick Loewe (w: Alan Jay Lerner)
Chappell—New York
1960
**Show:** *Camelot*

Richard Burton sang it in the show. Richard Harris sang it in the film version (Warner Bros., 1967). The song and show were both associated with the Kennedy presidency, known informally as the "Camelot years" in Washington.

## CAN THIS BE LOVE?
Kay Swift (w: Paul James)
Harms—New York
1930
**Show:** *Fine and Dandy*
Alice Boulden sang it in the show. The Arden-Ohman Orchestra had the number 11 hit (Victor 22552).

## CAN YOU FEEL THE LOVE TONIGHT?
Elton John (w: Tim Rice)
Wonderland Music
1994
**Film:** *The Lion King* (Disney)
Academy Award winner for Best Song. Elton John had the number 4 hit, which charted for twenty-three weeks (Hollywood 64543). It sold over half a million copies. The song was also included in the successful Broadway show based on the film.

## CAN'T BUY ME LOVE
John Lennon and Paul McCartney
Northern Songs—London
1964
The Beatles had the number 1 hit, which held its top position for five of the nine weeks charted (Capitol 5150). It sold over one million copies. The song was featured on the soundtrack of their first film, *A Hard Day's Night* (United Artists, 1964).

## CAN'T HELP FALLING IN LOVE
Hugo Peretti/Luigi Creatore/George David Weiss
Gladys Music
1961
Elvis Presley had this number 2 hit in 1962 (RCA Victor 47-7968), which sold over two million copies. UB40, a name taken from the British Unemployment form, revived it in 1993. Their version went to number 1 and stayed there for seven weeks out of the twenty-three it was on the Top 40 chart and sold over a million copies (Virgin 12653); it was featured in the

Sharon Stone thriller *Sliver* (20th Century Fox, 1993). Hugo Peretti and Luigi Creatore were well-known producers and also performers; as Hugo and Luigi they created some classics of what is now called "lounge music."

## CAN'T HELP LOVIN' DAT MAN
Jerome Kern (w: Oscar Hammerstein)
T. B. Harms—New York
1927
**Show:** *Show Boat*
Helen Morgan sang it in the show and also in the first two film versions (Universal, 1929 and Universal, 1936). She also had a hit recording (Victor 21238). Annette Warren sang it in the third film version (MGM, 1951). Lena Horne sang it in the Kern biopic *Till the Clouds Roll By* (MGM, 1946) and Gogi Grant sang it in the Morgan biopic *The Helen Morgan Story* (Warner Bros., 1957). It has become a cabaret standard.

## CAN'T WE BE FRIENDS?
Kay Swift (w: Paul James)
Harms—New York
1929
**Show:** *The Little Show*
Libby Holman sang it in the show. Harry James and His Orchestra revived it in the film *Young Man with A Horn* (Warner Bros., 1950).

## CAN'T WE TALK IT OVER?
Victor Young (w: Ned Washington)
Remick Music—New York
1931
Bing Crosby and the Mills Brothers had the number 10 hit in 1932 (Brunswick 6240). Vincent Rose and His Orchestra had the instrumental version (Oriole 2423). The Andrews Sisters revived it in 1950 with a number 22 hit (Decca 27115).

## CANADIAN CAPERS
Gus Chandler/Bert White/
Henry Cohen
Roger Graham—Chicago
1915
Although it has been a standard for years, this rag went unrecorded until 1921 when Paul Whiteman and His

Orchestra first cut it (Victor 18824). It led to many other recordings. Interest was sustained throughout the 1930s, notably with a piano duet by Arthur Schutt and Jack Cornell in 1931 (English Brunswick 01134) and the 1937 swing band arrangement by Tommy Dorsey and His Orchestra (Victor 25887). It was revived again in 1950 by Sid Phillips and His Orchestra (HMV B-10015).

## CANDLE IN THE WIND 1997
Elton John (w: Bernie Taupin)
Polygram Music Publishing
1973, 1997
Elton John originally wrote this about Marilyn Monroe in 1973, but it was rewritten in 1997 to honor England's Princess Diana, who had died in a car crash less than two months earlier. It was a number 1 hit that charted for twenty-eight weeks (Rocket 568108), selling over twelve million copies.

## CANDY
Alex Kramer / Joan Whitney / Mack David
Leo Feist—New York
1944
Johnny Mercer, Jo Stafford, and the Pied Pipers had the number 1 hit, which charted for eighteen weeks (Capitol 183).

## CANDY MAN, THE
Leslie Bricusse and Anthony Newley
Taradam Music—Los Angeles
1970, 1971
**Film:** *Willy Wonka and The Chocolate Factory*
(Paramount)
Sammy Davis Jr. had the number 1 hit, which charted for sixteen weeks (MGM 14320). It sold over one million copies.

## CANNON BALL
Jos. C. Northup
Victor Kremer—Chicago
1905
This classic rag had surprisingly few recordings. The first was by the Home Guards Band in 1908 (English Zonophone 74). It was revived in 1928 by Guy Lombardo and His Orchestra (Columbia 1451-D) and Ben

Bernie and His Orchestra (Brunswick 4042), and again, in 1949, by Marvin Ash (Capitol 15435).

## CARELESS WHISPER
George Michael and Andrew Ridgeley
Morrison-Leahy Music
1984
Wham! featuring George Michael scored their biggest success when this number 1 hit topped the charts for three out of seventeen weeks (Columbia 04691). It sold over two million copies.

## CARIBBEAN QUEEN
Keith Diamond and Billy Ocean
Willesden Music
1984
Billy Ocean had this most successful number 1 hit, which stayed on the chart for fifteen weeks (Jive 9199). It sold over one million copies.

## CARIOCA
Vincent Youmans (w: Gus Kahn and Edward Eliscu)
T. B. Harms—NY
1933
**Film:** *Flying Down to Rio* (RKO)
Etta Moten sang it in the film and Fred Astaire and Ginger Rogers danced to it. The RKO Studio Orchestra issued the soundtrack recording, which became a number 13 hit in 1934 (Victor 24515). Enric Madriguera and His Orchestra had the number 1 hit, which charted for ten weeks (Columbia 2885).

## CAROL
Chuck Berry (w & m)
ARC Music—New York
1958
Chuck Berry had the number 18 hit, which charted for five weeks (Chess 1700).

## CAROLINA IN THE MORNING
Walter Donaldson (w: Gus Kahn)
Jerome H. Remick—New York
1922
**Show:** *Passing Show of 1922*
Willie and Eugene Howard sang it in the show. Van and Schenck had a hit recording (Columbia A-3712), as did Marion Harris (Brunswick 2329) and Paul Whiteman and His Orchestra (Victor 18962). It was revived in the Gus Kahn biopic *I'll See You in My Dreams* (Warner Bros., 1951).

## CAROLINA SHOUT
James P. Johnson
Clarence Williams Music—New York
1926
Introduced on disc by the composer in 1921 (Okeh 4495). His piano roll version (QRS 100999) established this classic as the stride-cutting contest selection. The composer rerecorded it in 1944 (Decca 24885). There have been many other recordings through the years.

## CASEY JONES
Eddie Newton (w: T. Lawrence Seibert)
Southern California Music—Los Angeles
1909
Named after train engineer John Luther Jones (1864-1900), the lyric describes his tragic death. Popularized by the vaudeville team of the Leighton Brothers, it became the most notable railroad song ever. Gene Autry sang it in the film *Sunset in Wyoming* (Republic 1941).

## CASTLE WALK, THE
James Reese Europe and Ford Dabney
Jos. W. Stern—New York
1914
Introduced in vaudeville by Irene and Vernon Castle, for whom it was composed. Europe's Society Orchestra (Victor 17553) had the first recording. Europe, a black bandleader, was an important force among black musicians in New York, active in the Clef Club; he was also the official bandleader for the popular Castles, who had their own dance studios and helped introduce modern jazz-era dances to the greater public as performers and teachers.

## CAT'S IN THE CRADLE
Harry and Sandy Chapin
Story Songs
1974
Harry Chapin's only number 1 hit, which charted for twelve weeks, sold over one million copies (Elektra

45203). It was revived in 1993 by Ugly Kid Joe, who had a number 6 hit, which charted for thirteen weeks and sold half a million copies (Stardog 864888).

## CATCH A FALLING STAR
Paul Vance and Lee Pockriss
Fred Fisher Music—New York
1957
Perry Como had the number 1 hit in 1958 that charted for sixteen weeks and sold over one million copies (RCA Victor 47-7128).

## CATHY'S CLOWN
Don and Phil Everly
Acuff-Rose—Nashville
1960
The Everly Brothers had the number 1 hit, which held its top position for five of the thirteen weeks (Warner 5151). It sold over one million copies. It was the first song the Everlys cut after leaving Cadence Records, where they had scored their initial hits, mostly written by Felice and Boudleaux Bryant.

## CECILIA
Dave Dreyer (w: Herman Ruby)
Irving Berlin—New York
1925
Introduced on disc by Johnny Hamp and His Orchestra (Victor 19756), and Whispering Jack Smith had the vocal hit (Victor 19787). Revived in 1951 by Joe "Fingers" Carr and Candy Candido (Capitol 1847).

## CELEBRATION
Ronald Bell and Kool and The Gang
Delightful Music
1980
Kool and the Gang had this number 1 hit on the Top 40 chart for twenty-one weeks (De-Lite 807). It sold over two million copies. This has since become a wedding/bar mitzvah standard.

## CENTERFOLD
Seth Justman (w & m)
Center City Music
1981
The composer was the keyboardist for the J. Geils

Band, which had their only number 1 hit with this song, remaining on the Top 40 chart for twenty weeks (EMI America 8102). It sold over one million copies.

## CHAIN GANG
Sam Cooke (w & m)
Kags Music—Hollywood
1960
Sam Cooke had the number 2 hit, which charted for thirteen weeks (RCA Victor 7783).

## CHANCES ARE
Robert Allen (w: Al Stillman)
Korwin Music—New York
1957
Johnny Mathis had the number 1 hit, which charted for twenty-two weeks and sold one million copies (Columbia 40993). Mathis kept it in his repertory for over four decades.

## CHANGES
Walter Donaldson (w & m)
Leo Feist—New York
1927
Hit recording by Paul Whiteman and His Orchestra, with vocal by the Rhythm Boys, and featuring hot solos by Bix Beiderbecke (Victor 21103). A great novelty piano treatment on piano roll by Vee Lawnhurst (Welte Y-75333).

## CHANSONETTE
Rudolf Friml (w: Dailey Paskman, Sigmund Spaeth, Irving Caesar)
Harms—New York
1923
Originally published as a piano solo, it became famous with Paul Whiteman and His Orchestra's recording (Victor 19145).

## CHANTILLY LACE
J. P. Richardson (w & m)
Glad Music—Houston, Texas
1958
The Big Bopper (J. P. Richardson) had the number 6 hit, which charted for twenty-two weeks (Mercury 71343). Richardson was originally a deejay, taking on

the personality of the Big Bopper. This novelty disc remains one of the classics of early rock and roll.

## CHARIOTS OF FIRE
Vangelis
Spheric B.V.
1981
**Film:** *Chariots of Fire* (Warner Bros.)
Vangelis had the number 1 hit in 1982, which charted for fifteen weeks (Polydor 2189).

## CHARLESTON
James P. Johnson (w: Cecil Mack)
Harms—New York
1923
**Show:** *Runnin' Wild*
Introduced in the show by Elizabeth Welch. It became the defining tune of the 1920s. Two great recordings are those by Isham Jones and His Orchestra (Brunswick 2970) and the Tennessee Tooters (Vocalion 15086). It was used in the film *Tea for Two* (Warner Bros., 1950). Johnson was raised on the west side of New York (near where Lincoln Center now stands); many South Carolinians had settled there, and performed a version of this dance, which Johnson often accompanied. He created this piece for the dance, which went on to be the archetypical dance of the 1920s.

## CHARLESTON BABY OF MINE
Dan Dougherty (w: Bernie Grossman)
Stark and Cowan—New York
1925
Hit recording by Don Bestor and His Orchestra (Victor 19751), obviously an attempt to cash in on the Charleston dance craze.

## CHARLESTON CHARLEY
Gene Austin/Emmet O'Hara/
Irving Mills
Jack Mills—New York
1924
Introduced in vaudeville and on record by Marion Harris (Brunswick 2735). A great instrumental disc was recorded by the Wilshire Dance Orchestra (Sunset 1088).

## CHARLEY, MY BOY
Ted Fiorito (w: Gus Kahn)
Irving Berlin—New York
1924
Standard pop song originally featured by Eddie Cantor (Columbia 182-D). It was subsequently covered by the fine dance orchestras of Bennie Krueger (Brunswick 2667), Okeh Syncopators (Okeh 40166), and Fletcher Henderson (Regal 9680), and revived when Charles Lindbergh made the first transatlantic flight.

## CHARLIE BROWN
Mike Stoller (w: Jerry Leiber)
Tiger Music—New York
1959
The Coasters had the number 2 hit, which charted for twelve weeks and sold over one million copies (Atco 6132). It was famous for the bass singer's lament, "Why's everybody always pickin' on me?"

## CHARMAINE
Erno Rapee and Lew Pollack
Sherman, Clay—San Francisco
1926
**Film:** *What Price Glory?* (Fox)
Started the vogue in the late 1920s for movie theme songs. Guy Lombardo and His Royal Canadians had the big hit (Columbia 1048-D). It was revived in 1951 by Mantovani with a number 10 hit that charted for nineteen weeks and sold over one million copies (London 1020).

## CHATTANOOGA CHOO CHOO
Harry Warren (w: Mack Gordon)
Leo Feist—New York
1941
**Film:** *Sun Valley Serenade* (20th Century Fox)
Glenn Miller and His Orchestra played and starred in the film. They also had the number 1 hit, which held that position for nine of twenty-five weeks on the charts, and sold over one million copies (Bluebird 11230). It was revived in 1962 by Floyd Cramer who had a number 36 hit (RCA Victor 7978), and was again revived in 1978 by female disco quartet Tuxedo Junction, who had a number 32 hit (Butterfly 1205). It remains a vocal-group standard.

## CHEATIN' ON ME
Lew Pollack (w: Jack Yellen)
Ager, Yellen and Bornstein—New York
1925
Ben Bernie and His Orchestra had the hit recording (Vocalion 15027), but Eddie Frazier and His Orchestra had the most interesting arrangement (Sunset 1100).

## CHEEK TO CHEEK
Irving Berlin (w & m)
Irving Berlin—New York
1935
**Film:** *Top Hat* (RKO)
Fred Astaire sang and danced it in the film with Ginger Rogers. Astaire also had the number 1 hit, which charted for eighteen weeks (Brunswick 7486).

## CHERISH
Terry Kirkman (w & m)
Beechwood Music—Hollywood
1966
The Association, for whom Terry Kirkman played keyboards, had the number 1 hit, which charted for twelve weeks and sold more than one million copies (Valiant 747). It was revived by David Cassidy with a number 9 hit in 1971 that charted for eleven weeks and again sold more than one million copies (Bell 45,150). The song was quoted in Madonna's "Cherish," a number 2 hit for the singer in 1989 (Sire 22883).

## CHERRY PINK AND APPLE BLOSSOM WHITE
Louiguy (w: Mack David)
Chappell—New York
1955
**Film:** *Underwater!* (RKO Radio)
Perez Prado had the number 1 hit, which charted for twenty-six weeks and sold over one million copies (RCA Victor 20-5965).

## CHICAGO
Fred Fisher (w & m)
Fred Fisher—New York
1922
Paul Whiteman had the hit recording (Victor 18946), though the Bar Harbor Society Orchestra (Vocalion 14412), Markels Orchestra (Okeh 4671), and Jazzbo's Carolina Serenaders (Cameo 284) have fine arrangements. It was revived for Fred Fisher's biopic *Oh, You Beautiful Doll* (20th Century Fox, 1949).

## CHICKEN REEL
Joseph M. Daly (w & m)
Joseph M. Daly—Boston
1910
Although recorded by Arthur Collins in 1911 (Victor 16897), it became well-known in vaudeville as a great accompaniment for soft-shoe dancers. It also has become a standard number among novelty fiddlers.

## CHIM CHIM CHER-EE
Richard and Robert Sherman
Wonderland Music—Burbank
1963
**Film:** *Mary Poppins* (Disney)
Academy Award winner for Best Song of 1964. Dick Van Dyke, Julie Andrews, Karen Dotrice, and Matthew Garber sang it in the film.

## CHINA BOY
Phil Boutelje (w: Dick Winfree)
Leo Feist—New York
1922
Introduced in vaudeville by Henry E. Murtagh. Arnold Johnson and His Orchestra had the hit record (Brunswick 2355). It was revived in 1936 by the Benny Goodman Trio (Victor 25333). Teddy Wilson made a great piano solo recording in 1941 (Columbia 36634). It was revived again in 1952 by Pete Daily and His Dixieland Band (Capitol 2041).

## CHINATOWN, MY CHINATOWN
Jean Schwartz (w: William Jerome)
Jerome H. Remick—New York
1910
It was introduced in the Broadway musical *Up and Down Broadway*. The American Quartet had a number 1 hit in 1915 (Victor 17684). Louis Armstrong and His Orchestra revived it in 1932 with a number 5 hit, which charted for seven weeks (Okeh 41534). Bobby Maxwell and His Swinging Harps revived it again in 1952 with a number 24 hit (Mercury 5773).

## CHIRPIN' THE BLUES

Alberta Hunter and Lovie Austin

Jack Mills—New York

1923

Introduced by Bessie Smith in vaudeville. Alberta Hunter had the hit recording, accompanied by Fletcher Henderson on piano (Paramount 12017).

## CHLOE

Neil Moret (w: Gus Kahn)

Villa Moret—San Francisco

1927

**Show:** *Africana*

Ethel Waters sang it in the show. Paul Whiteman had the hit recording, with vocal by Austin Young (Victor 35921). It was revived in 1945 by Spike Jones and His City Slickers, with vocal by Red Ingle (Victor 20-1654), who also featured it in the film *Bring On the Girls* (Paramount, 1945).

## CHRISTMAS SONG, THE

Mel Torme (w: Robert Wells)

Burke and Van Heusen—New York

1946

The King Cole Trio had the number 3 hit, which charted for seven weeks and sold over one million copies (Capitol 311). It was revived every season until Nat "King" Cole rerecorded it, backed by Nelson Riddle's Orchestra in the number 29 hit (Capitol 2955, 1954). It remains a perennial holiday favorite.

## CHURCH STREET SOBBIN' BLUES

Anton Lada/Jos. Cawley/Al Nunez

Leo Feist—New York

1919

Introduced in vaudeville and on record by the Louisiana Five, who composed it (Emerson 7517). The Plantation Dance Orchestra revived it in 1921 (Emerson 10368).

## CLAP HANDS! HERE COMES CHARLEY!

Joseph Meyer (w: Billy Rose and Ballard MacDonald)

Ager, Yellen and Bornstein—New York

1925

Introduced in vaudeville by Johnny Marvin, who also recorded it (Okeh 40558). The Dixie Stompers (Har-mony 70-H) and Jack Shilkret's Orchestra (Victor 19859) also had fine versions. In a historic pairing, Capitol Records joined their two biggest recording artists in ragtime and dixieland when Pee Wee Hunt and Joe "Fingers" Carr made their first LP together (Capitol T-783) and revived this song.

## CLAP YO' HANDS

George and Ira Gershwin

Harms—New York

1926

**Show:** *Oh, Kay!*

Introduced in the show by dancer Harlan Dixon (it was written as a dance number). Roger Wolfe Kahn and His Orchestra had the hit record (Victor 20327) and George Gershwin made a piano solo recording (Columbia 809-D). The curious thing about these recordings is that no matter which company released this song or who performed it, the flip side was always "Do-Do-Do."

## CLARINET MARMALADE

Larry Shields and Henry Ragas

Leo Feist—New York

1918

Introduced on disc by the Original Dixieland Jazz Band (Victor 18513), it has become a standard and must-play for all Dixieland jazz bands. While such unlikely musicians as Jim Europe (Pathe 22167), Fletcher Henderson (Brunswick 3406), and Jimmy Joy (Okeh 40329) enjoyed success with this number, it was revived in 1927 by Frankie Trumbauer and His Orchestra, featuring Bix Beiderbecke (Okeh 40772).

## CLEMENTINE (FROM NEW ORLEANS)

Harry Warren (w: Henry Creamer)

Shapiro, Bernstein—New York

1927

Introduced in vaudeville by Blossom Seeley. Jean Gold-kette and His Orchestra had the hit recording, featuring Bix Beiderbecke on cornet (Victor 20994). The Original Indiana Five had a nice version (Harmony 510-H).

## CLEOPATTERER

Jerome Kern (w: P. G. Wodehouse)

T. B. Harms—New York

1917

**Show:** *Leave It to Jane*

One of the cleverest of Wodehouse's historical comic numbers, it was introduced in the show by Georgia O'Ramey. In the Off-Broadway revival (1959), which ran a record-breaking 927 performances, Dorothy Greener performed it hilariously (CD-DRG 15017). Revived in the Kern biopic *Till the Clouds Roll By* (MGM, 1946) by June Allison.

## COCKTAILS FOR TWO

Arthur Johnston and Sam Coslow

Famous Music—New York

1934

**Film:** *Murder at the Vanities* (Paramount)

Carl Brisson sang it in the film. Duke Ellington and His Famous Orchestra had the number 1 hit, which charted for fifteen weeks (Victor 24617). Spike Jones and His City Slickers had the number 4 hit in 1945, with vocal by Carl Grayson, and it sold over one million copies (RCA Victor 20-1628). After Jones's parody was released, the song was never again thought of as a love ballad.

## COLD HEARTED

Elliott Wolff (w & m)

Virgin Music

1988

Number 1 hit in 1989 for singer/dancer Paula Abdul, the third hit from her first album (Virgin 99196). It charted for fifteen weeks, and was originally issued as a B-side to her first single, "Straight Up." The video was an homage to choreographer Bob Fosse.

## COLLEGIATE

Moe Jaffe and Nat Bonx

Shapiro, Bernstein—New York

1925

Introduced in vaudeville by Fred Waring's Pennsylvanians, who also had the hit record (Victor 19648). It was heard in the Marx Brothers film *Horse Feathers* (Paramount, 1932) and revived in *Margie* (20th Century Fox, 1946).

## COLORS OF THE WIND

Alan Menken (w: Stephen Schwartz)

Wonderland Music

1995

**Film:** *Pocahontas* (Disney)

Academy Award winner for Best Song. Vanessa Williams had the number 4 hit, which charted for nineteen weeks (Hollywood 64001). It sold over half a million copies.

## COME AFTER BREAKFAST, BRING 'LONG YOUR LUNCH AND LEAVE 'FORE SUPPER TIME

Chris Smith/James Burris/J. Tim Brymn

Jos. W. Stern—New York

1909

**Show:** *His Honor the Barber*

Sung by S. H. Dudley, it became the hit of the show. Passed into the repertoire of traditional blues performers, including the Reverand Gary Davis, who featured it in his concerts in the 1960s and 1970s.

## COME DOWN MA EVENIN' STAR

John Stromberg (w: Robert B. Smith)

M. Witmark and Sons—New York

1902

**Show:** *Twirly Whirly*

Sung in the show by Lillian Russell, it was the last song written by its musical director before he committed suicide. It was featured in the Chauncey Olcott biopic *My Wild Irish Rose* (Warner Bros., 1947).

## COME, JOSEPHINE, IN MY FLYING MACHINE

Fred Fisher (w: Alfred Bryan)

Shapiro, Bernstein—New York

1910

Introduced in vaudeville by Blanche Ring, who had a number 1 hit (Victor 60032). Fred Astaire sang and danced to it in the film *The Story of Vernon and Irene Castle* (RKO, 1939). It was revived in the Fred Fisher biopic *Oh, You Beautiful Doll* (20th Century Fox, 1949).

## COME ON EILEEN

Kevin Rowland/Kevin Adams/Jim Patterson

EMI Music

1982

Dexy's Midnight Runners, an English pop-rock group, had the number 1 hit in 1983 that charted for fourteen weeks (Mercury 76189).

## COME RAIN OR COME SHINE
Harold Arlen (w: Johnny Mercer)
A-M Music—New York
1946
**Show:** *St. Louis Woman*
Ruby Hill and Harold Nicholas sang it in the show. Margaret Whiting had the number 17 hit (Capitol 247).

## COME SEE ABOUT ME
Brian Holland/Lamont Dozier/Eddy Holland
Jobete Music—Detroit
1964
The Supremes had the number 1 hit, which charted for thirteen weeks (Motown 1068). Holland-Dozier-Holland were staff writers for Motown, who helped create the label's distinctive sound. They often worked with the Supremes, crafting songs specifically for their image.

## COME TAKE A TRIP IN MY AIRSHIP
George Evans (w: Ren Shields)
Chas. K. Harris—New York
1904
The first hit song about airplanes, it was introduced in vaudeville by Ethel Robinson. Billy Murray had the hit record (Victor 2986).

## COME TOGETHER
John Lennon and Paul McCartney
Maclen Music—New York
1969
The Beatles had the number 1 hit, which charted for sixteen weeks and sold over four million copies (Apple 2654). John Lennon originally envisioned it as a campaign song for Abbie Hoffman's Youth International party (the yippies).

## COMING OUT OF THE DARK
Gloria Estefan/John Estefan/Jon Secada
Foreign Imported Productions
1990
Number 1 hit in 1991 for singer Gloria Estefan, holding the top spot for two out of fourteen weeks on the charts (Epic 73666). Recorded after Estefan recovered from injuries in a bus accident, the song, which had a gospel flavor, announced Estefan's return to performing and recording.

## COMING UP
Paul McCartney (w & m)
MPL Communications
1980
Paul McCartney and Wings had this number 1 hit, which stayed on the chart for sixteen weeks (Columbia 11263). It sold over one million copies. The video featured McCartney playing a number of characters in various makeups and costumes.

## CONEY ISLAND WASHBOARD
Hampton Durand and Jerry Adams (w: Ned Nestor and Claude Shugart)
Lewis Music—New York
1926
It became a favorite with jazz bands during the dixieland revival of the forties and has become a standard. The big recording came from Bob Scobey's Frisco Band in 1950 (Good Time Jazz 49). It was popular during the jug band revival of the 1960s.

## CONFESSIN' THAT I LOVE YOU
Doc Daugherty and Ellis Reynolds (w: Al Neiburg)
Irving Berlin—New York
1930
Guy Lombardo and His Royal Canadians had the number 2 hit (Columbia 2259-D). Perry Como revived it in 1945 with a number 12 hit (Victor 20-1629). It was revived again by Les Paul and Mary Ford in 1952, when they had the number 13 hit (Capitol 2080).

## CONTINENTAL, THE
Con Conrad (w: Herb Magidson)
Harms—New York
1934
**Film:** *Gay Divorcee* (RKO)
First Academy Award winner for Best Song. Sung and danced to in the film by Fred Astaire, Ginger Rogers, Erik Rhodes, and Lillian Miles. Leo Reisman and His

Orchestra had the number 1 instrumental hit, which charted for seven weeks (Brunswick 6973).

## CONVOY
C. W. McCall/Bill Fries/Chip Davis
American Gramaphone
1975
Number 1 truck driver anthem by country singer C. W. McCall in 1976, cashing in on the then-current craze for CB radios. It charted for eleven weeks, and was also a number 1 country hit (MGM 14839).

## COPENHAGEN
Charlie Davis (w: Walter Melrose)
Melrose Bros.—Chicago
1924
A standard with jazz bands mostly because of the Wolverines' recording (Gennett 5453). The Benson Orchestra had the hit popular recording (Victor 19470).

## COQUETTE
Carmen Lombardo and John Green (w: Gus Kahn)
Leo Feist—New York
1928
Introduced in vaudeville by Johnny and Gus Stambecks. Introduced on disc by Guy Lombardo and his Royal Canadians (Columbia 1345-D). Paul Whiteman and His Orchestra (Victor 21301) also had a nice version.

## COTTON
Albert Von Tilzer
York Music—New York
1907
Popularized on disc by Arthur Pryor's Band (Victor 16044).

## COTTON BELT BLUES
Spencer Williams (w & m)
Spencer Williams Music—New York
1923
Popularized on disc by Lizzie Miles (Victor 19124).

## COULD I? I CERTAINLY COULD
Milton Ager (w: Jack Yellen)
Ager, Yellen and Bornstein—New York
1926

Sophie Tucker introduced it in vaudeville and the Oriole Dance Orchestra (Oriole 605) had the snappiest arrangement. Other fine versions include those of Sid Sydney (Victor 20029) and Bob Haring (Cameo 926).

## CRACKLIN' ROSIE
Neil Diamond ( w & m)
Prophet Music—Los Angeles
1970
Neil Diamond, a prolific songwriter, gave his own career as a singer a boost with this number 1 hit, which charted for fourteen weeks (Uni 55250). It sold more than two million copies.

## CRAZY BLUES
Perry Bradford (w & m)
Perry Bradford Music—New York
1920
This was the first blues ever recorded. On disc by Mamie Smith and her Jazz Hounds (Okeh 4169) it sold three-quarter million copies. The Original Dixieland Jazz Band also had a hit recording (Victor 18729), as did Bennie Krueger and His Orchestra with a vocal by Al Bernard (Brunswick 2077).

## CRAZY FOR YOU
Jon Lind and John Bettis
WB Music
1983, 1985
**Film:** *Vision Quest* (Warner Bros.)
Madonna had this number 1 hit, which remained on the chart for fourteen weeks (Geffen 29051). It sold over one million copies.

## CRAZY LITTLE THING CALLED LOVE
Freddie Mercury (w & m)
Queen Music Ltd.
1979
Number 1 hit in 1980 for heavy-metal rockers Queen, holding the top spot for four out of seventeen weeks on the charts and selling over a million copies (Elektra 46579). Recorded in a pseudo-rockabilly style.

## CRAZY QUILT
Paul F. Van Loan

Denton and Haskins Music—New York

1926

A marvelous tune for jazz bands exemplified by recordings by Charles Creath's Jazz-O-Maniacs (Okeh 8477) and the Tennessee Tooters (Brunswick 3332).

## CRAZY RHYTHM

Joseph Meyer and Roger Wolfe Kahn

(w: Irving Caesar)

Harms—New York

1928

**Show:** *Here's Howe!*

Introduced in the show by Ben Bernie, who also recorded it (Brunswick 3913). Roger Wolfe Kahn had the hit recording (Victor 21368).

## CRAZY WORDS—CRAZY TUNE

Milton Ager (w: Jack Yellen)

Ager, Yellen and Bornstein—New York

1927

Great comic song recorded by Irving Aaronson's Orchestra (Victor 20473) and revived by comedian Jerry Lewis in 1952 (Capitol F-2141).

## CREAM

Prince (w & m)

Controversy Music

1991

Prince and the New Power Generation had a number 1 hit, which charted for sixteen weeks (Paisley Park 19175). It sold over half a million copies.

## CREOLE BELLES

J. Bodewalt Lampe

Lampe Music—Buffalo

1900

One of the greatest cakewalks ever composed. Recorded by five-string banjoist Vess L. Ossman for both Columbia and Victor, it was the Sousa Band recording of 1912 (Victor 17252) that helped make it a perennial. Lu Watters's Yerba Buena Jazz Band revived it in 1946 (West Coast 102) and thus secured its top rank of Dixieland tunes.

## CRICKETS ARE CALLING, THE

Jerome Kern (w: P. G. Wodehouse)

T. B. Harms—New York

1917

**Show:** *Leave It To Jane*

This charming song was introduced in the show by Edith Hallor and Robert Pitkin. When it was revived Off-Broadway in 1959, it was sung by Kathleen Murray and Art Matthews (CD-DRG 15017).

## CRIMSON AND CLOVER

Tommy James and Peter Lucia

Big Seven Music—New York

1968

Number 1 hit in 1969 for Tommy James and the Shondells, holding the top position for two out of fifteen weeks on the charts (Roulette 7028). It is very much in the psychedelic style of the era. It was covered in 1982 by Joan Jett and the Blackhearts for a number 7 hit.

## CRINOLINE DAYS

Irving Berlin (w & m)

Irving Berlin—New York

1922

**Show:** *Music Box Revue*

Grace LaRue sang it in the show. Paul Whiteman had the hit recording (Victor 18983).

## CROCODILE ROCK

Elton John (w: Bernie Taupin)

Dick James Music—New York

1972

Elton John had this number 1 hit, which charted for fourteen weeks (MCA 40000). It sold more than two million copies.

## CROSS WORDS BETWEEN SWEETIE AND ME

Billy Heagney and Bert Reed (w: Bob Schafer and Fred Steele)

Broadway Music—New York

1925

Popularized by Jan Garber and His Orchestra (Victor 19708).

## CRUISING DOWN THE RIVER

Eily Beadell and Nell Tollerton

Henry Spitzer Music—New York

1945

A number 1 hit, four years after it was written, for two different bands: Blue Barron and His Orchestra (MGM 10346), who enjoyed a 20-week chart run, and Russ Morgan and His Orchestra (Decca 24568), whose version charted for twenty-two weeks. Both sold over a million copies.

## CRY
Churchill Kohlman (w & m)

Mellow Music—New York

1951

Johnny Ray had the number 1 hit, which charted for twenty-seven weeks and sold over two million copies (Okeh 6840). Ronnie Dove revived it in 1966 with a number 18 hit (Diamond 214).

## CRY BABY BLUES
George W. Meyer (w: Sam Lewis and Joe Young)

Irving Berlin—New York

1921

A big hit with Gene Rodemich and His Orchestra (Brunswick 2159). James P. Johnson made an outstanding piano roll (QRS 1673).

## CRYIN'
Roy Orbison (w & m)

Acuff-Rose—Nashville

1961

Operatic rock ballad, that was a number 2 hit for Orbison, charting for fourteen weeks (Monument 438) in 1961. It was revived in 1981 by Don McLean for a number 5 hit, with fifteen weeks on the charts (Millennium 11799).

## CUBAN MOON
Norman Spencer (w: Joe McKiernan)

Jack Mills—New York

1920

Carl Fenton and His Orchestra (Brunswick 2048) and Art Hickman's Orchestra (Columbia A-2982) had splendid arrangements for this lovely song.

## CUBANOLA GLIDE, THE
Harry Von Tilzer (w: Vincent P. Bryan)

Harry Von Tilzer—New York

1909

One of the great syncopated songs of the age, made famous in vaudeville by Sophie Tucker. Collins and Harlan had a hit vocal recording (Columbia A-800), as did Prince's Band, instrumentally (Columbia A-811). Alice Faye revived it in the film *Fallen Angel* (20th Century Fox, 1945). Max Morath revived it in the 1960s (Epic BN 26106).

## CUDDLE UP A LITTLE CLOSER
Karl Hoschna (w: Otto Harbach)

M. Witmark and Sons—New York

1908

**Show:** *The Three Twins*

Tremendous hit sung by Alice Yorke in Harbach's first operetta. Subsequently used in film musicals by Fred Astaire and Ginger Rogers in *The Story of Vernon and Irene Castle* (RKO, 1939), Mary Martin in *Birth of the Blues* (Paramount, 1941), Bob Haymes in *Is Everybody Happy?* (Columbia, 1943), Betty Grable in *Coney Island* (20th Century Fox, 1943), and Gordon MacRae in *On Moonlight Bay* (Warner Bros., 1951); also used as background in *Tall Story* (Warner Bros., 1960).

## CUP OF COFFEE, A SANDWICH AND YOU, A
Joseph Meyer (w: Al Dubin and Billy Rose)

Harms—New York

1925

**Show:** *Charlot's Revue of 1926*

Gertrude Lawrence and Jack Buchanan sang it in the show. They also had the hit recording (Columbia 512-D).

## CURSE OF AN ACHING HEART, THE
Al Piantadosi (w: Henry Fink)

Leo Feist—New York

1913

This throwback tearjerker was introduced in vaudeville by Emma Carus, who made it a hit. It was revived in 1936 by Fats Waller (Victor 25394) and again by Eddie Cantor in the film *Show Business* (RKO, 1944).

## DA DOO RON RON
Ellie Greenwich/Jeff Barry/
Phil Spector

Trio Music—New York

1963

Number 3 hit for the Crystals, charting for ten weeks (Philles 112). A classic production by Phil Spector, who also gave himself a cut of the songwriters' credit. Sean Cassidy revived it as a number 1 hit in 1977 (Warner/Curb 8365), when it sold over a million copies and charted for twelve weeks. The song has become a vocal group standard.

## DA YA THINK I'M SEXY

Rod Stewart and Carmine Appice

Warner Bros. Music

1978

Number 1 hit in 1979 for big-lunged rock singer Rod Stewart. It held that position for four out of eighteen weeks on the charts and sold over a million copies (Warner 8724). Stewart took a lot of flack at the time for recording this disco-flavored number, but it nonetheless helped relaunch his career.

## DAINTY MISS

Bernard Barnes

Sherman, Clay—San Francisco

1924

Popularized by Nat Shilkret and His Orchestra (Victor 21037).

## DAISIES WON'T TELL

Anita Owens (w & m)

Jerome H. Remick and Co.—New York

1908

A throwback to the sentimental ballads of a decade earlier, it won favor in vaudeville particularly with Arthur Clough, who also had a hit recording in 1910 (Columbia A-792).

## DALLAS BLUES

Hart A. Wand

Wand Publishing Co.—Oklahoma City

1912

Probably the first published blues number. Words were added (by Lloyd Garrett in 1918). Although a favorite of dance and jazz bands, Ted Lewis and His Band had the number 7 hit in 1931, with Fats Waller as vocalist (Columbia 2527-D).

## DANCE, BALLERINA, DANCE

Carl Sigman (w: Bob Russell)

Jefferson Music—New York

1947

Vaughn Monroe had the number 1 hit, which charted for twenty-two weeks and sold more than one million copies (RCA Victor 20-2433). Nat "King" Cole revived it in 1957 with a number 18 hit (Capitol 3619).

## DANCE OF THE GRIZZLY BEAR

George Botsford (w: Irving Berlin)

Ted Snyder Co.—New York

1910

**Show:** *Ziegfeld Follies of 1910*

Introduced in vaudeville by Sophie Tucker and interpolated into the Follies. Started the trend in animal dances (the bunny hug, turkey trot, fox-trot). Revived by Alice Faye in the film *Hello, Frisco, Hello* (20th Century Fox, 1943).

## DANCE WITH A DOLLY

Terry Shand (w: Jimmy Eaton and Mickey Leader)

Shapiro, Bernstein—New York

1940

Adapted from the Ethiopian Serenaders' 1848 hit "Buffalo Gals." Russ Morgan and His Orchestra had the number 3 hit in 1944 (Decca 18625).

## DANCIN' DAN

Jack Stanley (w: William Tracey)

Irving Berlin—New York

1923

Popularized on disc by the Original Memphis Five (Banner 1292), the Black Dominoes (Gennett 5347), Fred Waring's Pennsylvanians (Victor 19257), and Bennie Krueger and his Orchestra (Brunswick 2551). Margaret Young (Brunswick 2583) made the hit vocal recording.

## DANCING FOOL

Ted Snyder (w: Harry B. Smith and Francis Wheeler)

Waterson, Berlin and Snyder—New York

1922

The Bar Harbor Society Orchestra, with piano interlude by Frank Banta and Cliff Hess had the most interesting recording (Vocalion 14394).

## DANCING IN THE DARK

Arthur Schwartz (w: Howard Dietz)

Harms—New York

1931

**Show:** *The Band Wagon*

John Barker sang it and Tillie Losch danced to it in the show. Fred Waring's Pennsylvanians had the number 3 hit, which charted for eleven weeks (Victor 22708). Artie Shaw and His Orchestra had the number 9 hit in a revival in 1941 that charted for three weeks and yet sold over one million copies (Victor 27335). When the show was made into a film, Fred Astaire and Cyd Charisse danced to the song (MGM, 1953).

## DANCING IN THE DARK

Bruce Springsteen (w & m)

Bruce Springsteen

1984

Bruce Springsteen's biggest hit (to date) reached number 2 and stayed on the chart for fifteen weeks (Columbia 04463). It sold over two million copies. It was the first single from his highly successful *Born in the U.S.A.* album.

## DANCING QUEEN

Benny Andersson/Stig Anderson/Bjorn Ulvaeus

Countless Songs—New York

1976

ABBA, the Swedish vocal pop group, had an eight-year career on the Top 40 charts, but this is their only number 1 hit (in 1977), and it charted for fifteen weeks (Atlantic 3372). It sold over one million copies.

## DANGEROUS BLUES

Billie Brown (w: Anna Welker Brown)

J. W. Jenkins' Sons Music—Kansas City, Mo.

1921

Popularized on disc by Bennie Krueger and His Orchestra (Brunswick 2109). Mamie Smith had the hit vocal (Okeh 4351). There is an outstanding piano roll version by Clarence Jones (US 40522).

## DANIEL

Elton John (w: Bernie Taupin)

Dick James Music—New York

1972

Soft pop-rock ballad that has been a long-time favorite in John's repertoire. The original recording sold over a million copies, reaching number 2 on the charts in 1973 (MCA 40046). It enjoyed a twelve-week chart run.

## DARDANELLA

Johnny S. Black and Felix Bernard

McCarthy and Fisher—New York

1919

Unlike any other popular song, this one stands out for its continuous bass line. It became an instant hit with Ben Selvin and His Orchestra having a number 1 hit that sold over six-and-a-half million copies (Victor 18633). It was revived in the Fred Fisher biopic *Oh, You Beautiful Doll* (20th Century Fox, 1949).

## DARKTOWN STRUTTERS' BALL, THE

Shelton Brooks (w & m)

Will Rossiter—Chicago

1917

This catchy standard was introduced by the Original Dixieland Jazz Band, whose recording was never imitated (Columbia A-2297). Collins and Harlan had the vocal hit (Columbia A-2478). It was revived in 1929 by the Coon-Sanders Orchestra (Victor 22342). Lou Monte had a number 7 hit in 1954 that charted for eleven weeks (RCA Victor 20-5611).

## DARN THAT DREAM

Jimmy Van Heusen (w: Eddie DeLange)

Bregman, Vocco and Conn—New York

1939

**Show:** *Swingin' the Dream*

Louis Armstrong, Maxine Sullivan, Bill Bailey, the Dandridge Sisters, the Rhythmetts, and the Deep River Boys sang it in the show. Benny Goodman, who was also in the show, had the number 1 hit, which charted for eleven weeks (Columbia 35331). The show was a modern musicalization of Shakespeare's *A Midsummer Night's Dream*.

## DAUGHTER OF ROSIE O'GRADY, THE

Walter Donaldson (w: Monte Brice)

M. Witmark and Sons—New York

1918

Introduced in vaudeville by Pat Rooney Jr., it became his trademark while he did a clog dance to it. It was used in the film of the same name, where it was sung by Gordon MacRae (Warner Bros., 1950).

## DAY BY DAY
Paul Weston/Axel Stordahl/Sammy Cahn
Barton Music—New York
1945
Frank Sinatra, accompanied by Axel Stordahl's Orchestra, had the number 5 hit in 1946 that charted for ten weeks (Columbia 36905).

## DAY BY DAY
Stephen Schwartz (w & m)
Valando Music—New York
1971
**Show:** *Godspell*
Robin Lamont sang it in the show. The *Godspell* company had the number 13 hit in 1972 (Bell 45,210). Lamont and company sang it in the film (Columbia, 1973).

## DAYDREAM BELIEVER
John Stewart (w & m)
Screen Gems-Columbia Music—New York
1967
Number 1 hit hit for the Monkees, holding that position for four out of twelve weeks on the charts (Colgems 1012).

## DAYS OF WINE AND ROSES
Henry Mancini (w: Johnny Mercer)
M. Witmark and Sons—New York
1962
**Film:** *Days of Wine and Roses* (Warner Bros.)
Academy Award winner for Best Song. Andy Williams had the number 26 hit (Columbia 42674). Composer Mancini also had a recording, which charted at number 33 for ten weeks (RCA Victor 8120)

## DEAR HEARTS AND GENTLE PEOPLE
Sammy Fain (w: Bob Hilliard)
Edwin H. Morris—New York
1949

Bing Crosby, with Jud Conlon's Rhythmaires, had a number 2 hit, which charted for seventeen weeks and sold over one million copies (Decca 24798).

## DEAR LITTLE BOY OF MINE
Ernest R. Ball (w: J. Keirn Brennan)
M. Witmark and Sons—New York
1918
A favorite of tenors in vaudeville, Charles Harrison made the hit recording (Columbia A-2613). Opera star Blanche Thebom sang it in the Ball biopic *Irish Eyes Are Smiling* (20th Century Fox, 1944).

## DEARIE
Bob Hilliard and Dave Mann
Laurel Music—New York
1950
Guy Lombardo and His Royal Canadians had the number 5 hit, which charted for fourteen weeks (Decca 24899).

## DECATUR STREET BLUES
Clarence Williams and T. A. Hammed
(w: Mercedes Gilbert)
Clarence Williams Music—New York
1922
Introduced in vaudeville and on records by Leona Williams and Her Dixie Band (actually the Original Memphis Five; Columbia A-3565).

## DEDE DINAH
Pete DeAngelis (w: Bob Marcucci)
Debmar—New York
1957
Frankie Avalon had the number 7 hit in 1958 that charted for eleven weeks (Chancellor 1011).

## 'DEED I DO
Fred Rose (w: Walter Hirsch)
Ted Browne Music—Chicago
1926
Introduced in vaudeville by S. L. Stambaugh. Ruth Etting had the hit recording (Columbia 865-D). Revived in 1948 by Lena Horne (MGM 10165).

## DEEP HENDERSON
Fred Rose (w & m)

Melrose Bros.—Chicago

1926

A jazz standard introduced by Charley Straight and His Orchestra (Brunswick 3224). The Coon Sanders Original Nighthawks had a hit recording (Victor 20081). Mike Markel's Orchestra (Okeh 40625) and the Original Indiana Five (Harmony 217-H) had fine versions.

## DEEP IN MY HEART, DEAR

Sigmund Romberg (w: Dorothy Donnelly)

Harms—New York

1924

**Show:** *The Student Prince*

Howard Marsh and Ilse Marvenga sang it in the show. Franklin Bauer, the original "Voice of Firestone" on radio, had the hit recording (Victor 19378). Mario Lanza sang it in the film version (MGM, 1954). It was also featured in the Romberg biopic *Deep In My Heart* (MGM, 1954).

## DEEP PURPLE

Peter DeRose (w: Mitchell Parish)

Robbins Music—New York

1934, 1939

This perennial favorite was originally a piano solo. Mitchell Parish turned it into a song in 1939. Larry Clinton and His Orchestra had the number 1 hit, with Bea Wain as vocalist; it remained in the top spot for nine of the thirteen weeks that it charted (Victor 26141). Jimmy Dorsey, Guy Lombardo, Bing Crosby, and Artie Shaw all covered it in 1939. Ten years later, Paul Weston arranged it as an instrumental (Capitol 15294). Billy Ward and His Dominoes revived it in 1957, and it charted for eight weeks (Liberty 55099). It was again revived in 1963 by Nino Tempo and April Stevens with their number 1 hit, which charted for twelve weeks (Atco 6273). Donny and Marie Osmond had another hit with it in 1976 that charted for thirteen weeks (MGM/Kolob 14840).

## DESERT SONG, THE

Sigmund Romberg (w: Otto Harbach and Oscar Hammerstein)

Harms—New York

1926

**Show:** *The Desert Song*

Robert Halliday and Vivienne Segal sang it in the show. Warner Brothers produced three films based on the popular musical drama in 1929, 1943, and 1953.

## DIAMONDS ARE A GIRL'S BEST FRIEND

Jule Styne (w: Leo Robin)

J. J. Robbins—New York

1949

**Show:** *Gentlemen Prefer Blondes*

Carol Channing sang it in the show. Jo Stafford with the Starlighters had the number 30 hit in 1950 (Capitol 824). Marilyn Monroe sang it in a lavish production number in the film version (20th Century Fox, 1953), and the song became associated with her. Madonna parodied this production number in her video for "Material Girl" (1985).

## DIANE

Erno Rapee and Lew Pollack

Sherman, Clay—San Francisco

1927

**Film:** *Seventh Heaven* (Fox)

As the theme song for the film, it sold over one million copies of sheet music. Nat Shilkret and His Orchestra, with vocal by the Troubadours, had the hit recording (Victor 21000). The Hurtado Brothers Marimba Orchestra had an unusually nice version (Columbia 1161-D). The Bachelors revived it in 1964 with a number 10 hit, which charted for eight weeks (London 9639).

## DID YOU MEAN IT?

Abe Lyman/Phil Baker/Sid Silvers

Shapiro, Bernstein—New York

1927

**Show:** *A Night in Spain*

Introduced by Marion Harris, who had the hit recording (Victor 21116).

## DIDN'T WE ALMOST HAVE IT ALL

Michael Masser and Will Jennings

Prince Street Music

1986

Whitney Houston had the number 1 hit in 1987 that charted for thirteen weeks (Arista 9616).

## DIGGA-DIGGA-DO

Jimmy McHugh (w: Dorothy Fields)

Jack Mills—New York

1928

**Show:** *Lew Leslie's Blackbirds of 1928*

Adelaide Hall sang it in the show. Duke Ellington and His Famous Orchestra had the hit (Okeh 8602). Lena Horne revived it in the film *Stormy Weather* (20th Century Fox, 1943).

## DILL PICKLES

Charles L. Johnson

Carl Hoffman Music—Kansas City

1906

The first million-selling rag after Scott Joplin's "Maple Leaf Rag" of 1899, it was notable for featuring three notes in a four beat measure. Xylophonist Chris Chapman's 1908 acoustic recording (Victor 16678) was selling continuously until electric recordings came in 1926. Arthur Pryor's Band had a hit disc in 1909 (Victor 16482), and Pee Wee Hunt and His Dixieland Band had a hit in 1949 (Capitol 57-773). It is a ragtime staple.

## DINAH

Harry Akst (w: Sam Lewis and Joe Young)

Henry Waterson—New York

1925

**Show:** *The New Plantation*

Ethel Waters sang it in the show and also had a hit recording (Columbia 487-D). Jean Goldkette and His Orchestra had a nice version (Victor 19947). Eddie Cantor interpolated it into the show *Kid Boots,* which helped make it a standard. Bing Crosby and the Mills Brothers revived it in 1932 with a hit (Brunswick 6240), and Crosby sang it in the film *The Big Broadcast* (Paramount, 1932). Eddie Cantor and Joan Davis sang it in the film *Show Business* (RKO, 1944). It was the first song sung on radio by Frances Rose Shore, who thereafter took the title for her first name.

## DIXIE MOON

Eubie Blake (w: Noble Sissle)

Harms—New York

1924

**Show:** *The Chocolate Dandies*

Introduced in the show by Sissle and Blake. It was their favorite song of their own composing, and they recorded it (Victor 19494).

## DIZZY

Tommy Roe and F. Weller

Low-TWI Music—Atlanta

1968

Tommy Roe had the number 1 hit in 1969 that charted for thirteen weeks and sold over one million copies (ABC 11164).

## DIZZY FINGERS

Zez Confrey

Jack Mills—New York

1923

One of Confrey's classic novelty rags. Although his name is on the hit recording with orchestra (Victor 20777) he did not ever record this number, which sold over a million copies of sheet music. Willie Eckstein (Okeh 40076) made the outstanding piano solo and Muriel Pollock and Vee Lawnhurst the outstanding duet in 1934 (Decca 164).

## DO IT AGAIN

George Gershwin (w: Bud DeSylva)

Harms—New York

1922

**Show:** *The French Doll*

Introduced in the show by Irene Bordoni. This song became a standard despite being banned on the airwaves for its suggestive lyrics. Lanin's Roseland Orchestra made a nice recording (Federal 5186).

## DO SOMETHING

Sam Stept (w: Bud Green)

Green and Stept—New York

1929

**Film:** *Nothing But the Truth* (Paramount)

Helen Kane had the hit recording (Victor 21917).

## DO THAT TO ME ONE MORE TIME

Toni Tennille (w & m)

Moonlight and Magnolias

1979

The Captain and Tennille had their last number 1 hit in 1980 that charted for twenty-two weeks (Casablanca 2215). It sold over one million copies. The title and lyrics were changed from the original, more suggestive "Do It to Me One More Time."

## DO WAH DIDDY DIDDY
Jeff Barry and Ellie Greenwich
Trio Music—New York
1963
Number 1 hit in 1964 for British-invasion popster Manfred Mann, holding that spot for two out of twelve weeks on the charts (Ascot 2157). The only top hit from Mann's 1960s lineup.

## DO YOU KNOW WHAT IT MEANS TO MISS NEW ORLEANS?
Louis Alter (w: Eddie DeLange)
Edwin H. Morris—New York
1946
**Film:** *New Orleans* (United Artists)
Louis Armstrong and his All-Stars, Billie Holiday, Woody Herman, and Dorothy Patrick sang and played it in the film.

## DO YOU WANT TO DANCE?
Robert Freeman (w & m)
Clockus Music—Tarzana, California
1958
Originally a number 5 hit for Bobby Freeman (Josie 835), charting for twelve weeks, this teen pop classic was covered by the Beach Boys for a number 12 hit in 1965 (Capitol 5372) and again in 1973 by Bette Midler (Atlantic 2928). Sometimes called "Do You Wanna Dance?" which is the actual lyric but not as grammatically correct as the official title.

## DO-DO-DO
George and Ira Gershwin
Harms—New York
1926
**Show:** *Oh, Kay!*
Introduced in the show by Gertrude Lawrence. The hit recording was by George Olsen and His Orchestra (Victor 20327), and the composer made a piano solo (Columbia 809-D). It was revived by Doris Day and Gordon MacRae in the film *Tea for Two* (Warner Bros., 1950). Gogi Grant sang it in the biopic *The Helen Morgan Story* (Warner Bros., 1957) while Julie Andrews sang it in the film *Star!* (20th Century Fox, 1968).

## DOCTOR JAZZ
Joseph Oliver (w: Walter Melrose)
Melrose Bros.—Chicago
1927
A jazz classic made famous by Jelly Roll Morton's Red Hot Peppers (Victor 20415). It was revived in 1950 by Lu Watters and his Yerba Buena Jazz Band (Clef 89055), and today it remains in every Dixieland jazz band's repertory.

## DOES THE SPEARMINT LOSE ITS FLAVOR ON THE BEDPOST OVERNIGHT?
Ernest Breuer (w: Marty Bloom and Billy Rose)
Waterson, Berlin and Snyder—New York
1924
Ernie Hare and Billy Jones, the "Happiness Boys" on radio, had this comedy hit (Cameo 504). Lonnie Donegan and His Skiffle Group revived it in 1961 with a number 5 hit, which charted for nine weeks (Dot 15911).

## DOIN' THE NEW LOW-DOWN
Jimmy McHugh (w: Dorothy Fields)
Jack Mills—New York
1928
**Show:** *Blackbirds of 1928*
Introduced in the show by Bill "Bojangles" Robinson, who also recorded it (Brunswick 4535). Jack Pettis and His Pets had a nice version (Victor 21559).

## DOIN' WHAT COMES NATUR'LLY
Irving Berlin (w & m)
Irving Berlin—New York
1946
**Show:** *Annie Get Your Gun*
Ethel Merman sang it in the show. Freddy Martin and His Orchestra had the number 2 hit, which charted for thirteen weeks (RCA Victor 20-1878).

## DOLL DANCE, THE
Nacio Herb Brown

Sherman, Clay—San Francisco

1926

A ragtime classic that sold a million copies of sheet music. Recorded piano solos include Frank Banta recording as "Jimmy Andrews" (Banner 6116), Pauline Alpert (Victor 21252), and Rube Bloom (Okeh 40842). Orchestral versions include the Nat Shilkret Orchestra (Victor 20503), Imperial Dance Orchestra (Banner 1981) and Carl Fenton Orchestra (Brunswick 3519).

## DOMINIQUE

Soeur Sourire (w: Randy Sparks)

General Music—New York

1966

**Film:** *The Singing Nun* (MGM)

The Singing Nun, Sister Luc Gabrielle, had the number 1 hit that charted for twelve weeks (Philips 40152).

## DON'T BE CRUEL

Otis Blackwell and Elvis Presley

Shalimar Music—New York

1956

Elvis Presley had the number 1 hit, which stayed in that position for eleven of twenty-three weeks charted and sold over six million copies (RCA Victor 47-6604). It was the top-selling single of the 1950s. It is a prototypical rockabilly song, characterized by a heavy, rhythmic bass line. Cheap Trick revived it in 1988 with a number 4 hit, which charted for twelve weeks (Epic 07965).

## DON'T BRING LULU

Ray Henderson (w: Billy Rose and Lew Brown)

Jerome H. Remick—New York

1925

Introduced in vaudeville by the Avon Comedy Four. Hit vocal recording by Ernest Hare and Billy Jones (Okeh 40354). Popularized instrumentals include Jan Garber and His Orchestra (Victor 19661), Bennie Krueger and His Orchestra (Brunswick 2859), and the Varsity Eight (Cameo 714).

## DON'T CRY FOR ME ARGENTINA

Andrew Lloyd Webber (w: Tim Rice)

Leeds Music

1976, 1977

**Show:** *Evita*

Patti LuPone sang it in the show. Madonna, who starred in the film (Cinergi, 1997), had the number 8 hit in 1997 that charted for seven weeks (Warner 43809).

## DON'T FENCE ME IN

Cole Porter (w & m)

T. B. Harms—New York

1944

**Film:** *Hollywood Canteen* (Warner Bros.)

The Andrews Sisters sang it in the film. Bing Crosby and the Andrews Sisters had the number 1 hit, which charted in that position for eight of the twenty-one weeks and sold over one million copies (Decca 23364).

## DON'T GET AROUND MUCH ANYMORE

Duke Ellington (w: Bob Russell)

Robbins Music—New York

1942

Duke Ellington and His Famous Orchestra recorded it in 1940 as "Never No Lament." It was reissued under this new title in 1942. A year later, the Ellington band's rerecording was a number 8 hit that charted for fourteen weeks (Victor 26610), while the Ink Spots' version reached number 2 and charted for 28 weeks (Decca 18503).

## DON'T GO BREAKING MY HEART

Carte Blanche and Ann Orson

Leeds Music

1976

Elton John and Kiki Dee achieved their number 1 hit, charting for fifteen weeks (Rocket 40585). It sold more than one million copies.

## DON'T LET THE STARS GET IN YOUR EYES

Slim Willet (w & m)

Four Star Sales—New York

1952

Perry Como had the number 1 hit that charted for twenty-one weeks and sold over one million copies (RCA Victor 5064).

## DON'T SIT UNDER THE APPLE TREE

Sam Stept/Charlie Tobias/Lew Brown

Robbins Music—New York

1942

Glenn Miller and His Orchestra had the number 1 hit, which charted for seventeen weeks and featured Marion Hutton, Tex Beneke, and the Modernaires on vocals (Bluebird 11474).

## DON'T STOP

Christine McVie (w & m)

Gentoo Music

1977

Number 3 hit for Fleetwood Mac, charting for fourteen weeks (Warner 8413). The song was revived in 1992 as a campaign anthem for then presidential candidate Bill Clinton.

## DON'T THINK TWICE, IT'S ALL RIGHT

Bob Dylan (w & m)

M. Witmark & Sons—New York

1963

A number 9 hit for Peter, Paul, and Mary in 1963 (Warner 5385). Notable as one of Dylan's first personal love songs, as opposed to his social-protest work of the same era.

## DON'T WORRY BE HAPPY

Bobby McFerrin (w & m)

Prob Noblem Music

1988

Number 1 vocal novelty by jazz-flavored vocalist Bobby McFerrin, holding the top position for two out of thirteen weeks on the charts, and selling over a million copies (EMI-Manhattan 50146). Promoted by a clever video, the song is one of few pop hits that is created entirely by a singer's overtracked vocals; there is no instrumental accompaniment.

## DONKEY SERENADE, THE

Rudolf Friml and Herbert Stothart (w: Bob White and Chet Forrest)

G. Schirmer—New York

1937

**Film:** *The Firefly* (MGM)

Allan Jones sang it in the film and also had the number 8 hit in 1938 (Victor 4380).

## DOO WACKA DOO

Clarence Gaskill/Will Donaldson/George Horther

Leo Feist—New York

1924

Introduced and popularized on disc by Paul Whiteman and His Orchestra (Victor 19462). Isham Jones (Brunswick 2767), Marion McKay (Gennett 5615), and the Georgia Melodians (Edison 51420) also had fine versions.

## DOODLE-DOO-DOO

Art Kassel and Mel Stitzel

Leo Feist—New York

1924

Eddie Cantor had the hit vocal recording (Columbia 213-D) with hit dance band recordings by Ray Miller (Brunswick 2724), the Benson Orchestra of Chicago (Victor 19318) and the Jack Linx Orchestra (Okeh 40188). It was the theme song for Art Kassel and his Kassels in the Air.

## DOWN AMONG THE SHELTERING PALMS

Abe Olman (w: James Brockman)

LaSalle Music—Chicago

1914

The song was a favorite in vaudeville, and the Lyric Quartet had the hit recording (Victor 17778). Sammy Kaye and His Orchestra revived it in 1948 with a number 14 hit that charted for six weeks and had a vocal by Don Cornell (RCA Victor 20-3100). It was sung in the film of the same name by Mitzi Gaynor (20th Century Fox, 1950).

## DOWN AMONG THE SUGAR CANE

Chris Smith and Cecil Mack (w: Avery and Hart)

Gotham-Attucks Music—New York

1908

This was sung by Clara Morton in vaudeville, while Arthur Collins and Byron Harlan had the hit recording (Victor 5670). It was the prolific Chris Smith's biggest hit up to that time. Bennie Kreuger and His Orchestra revived it in 1929 (Victor 21903).

## DOWN BY THE OLD MILL STREAM

Tell Taylor (w & m)

Tell Taylor—Chicago

1910

A song that sold six million copies of sheet music and became a favorite with barbershop quartets. Pioneer recording tenor Harry MacDonough made the hit disc (Victor 17000). Revived for the film *Her Master's Voice* (Paramount, 1936).

## DOWN HEARTED BLUES
Lovie Austin (w: Alberta Hunter)
Jack Mills—New York
1923
Hit recording by Bessie Smith (Columbia A-3844) that sold over a million copies. Noble Sissle accompanied on piano by Eubie Blake also had a popular vocal (Victor 19086). The Tennessee Ten had a hit instrumental (Victor 19094).

## DOWN HOME RAG
Wilbur C. S. Sweatman
Will Rossiter—Chicago
1911
Introduced on disc by the Victor Military Band (Victor 17340). Revived in 1915 by the Six Brown Brothers (Victor 17834).

## DOWN IN GEORGIA ON CAMP MEETING DAY
Nathan Bivins (w: John Madison Reed)
Enterprise Music—New York
1907
Popularized on disc by Collins and Harlan (Zonophone 5162).

## DOWN IN HONKY TONKY TOWN
Chris Smith (w: Chas. McCarron)
Broadway Music—New York
1916
A popular hit in vaudeville, not associated with any one group or person. In the instrumental one-step version "Honky Tonky," the Victor Military Band had the hit recording (Victor 18039).

## DOWN IN JUNGLE TOWN
Theodore F. Morse (w: Edward Madden)

F. B. Haviland—New York
1908
Made famous by the comedy/singing team of Arthur Collins and Byron Harlan (Victor 5484). A favorite with barbershop quartets, it was revived in 1947 by Spike Jones and His City Slickers (Victor 20-2820).

## DOWN ON THE CORNER
John Fogerty (w & m)
Jondora Music—Oakland
1969
Number 3 hit for Creedence Clearwater Revival, selling over a million copies (Fantasy 634). The lyrics provided the title for their album, *Willie and the Poor Boys*. A celebration of amateur music-making everywhere, and a garage-rock favorite.

## DOWN SOUTH BLUES
Fletcher Henderson/Ethel Waters/
Alberta Hunter
Down South Music—New York
1923
Popularized on disc by the Virginians (Victor 19175) and Fletcher Henderson and His Orchestra (Vocalion 14691).

## DOWN UNDER
Colin Hay and Ron Strykert
Impulsive Music
1982
Men At Work, an Australian group, had the number 1 hit in 1983 that charted for nineteen weeks (Columbia 03303). It sold over one million copies.

## DOWN WHERE THE WURZBURGER FLOWS
Harry Von Tilzer (w: Vincent P. Bryan)
Harry Von Tilzer—New York
1902
Vaudeville singer Nora Bayes was so identified with this drinking song that she was known for years as "The Wurzburger girl." It started the trend for name-brand beer songs.

## DOWN YONDER
L. Wolfe Gilbert (w & m)

L. Wolfe Gilbert—New York

1921

Ernest Hare and Billy Jones had the hit vocal record
(Okeh 4347), and the Happy Six had the instrumental
hit (Columbia A-3423). Del Wood revived it in 1951
with a number 4 hit that charted for twenty-five weeks
and sold over one million copies (Tennessee 775). Joe
"Fingers" Carr had a number 14 hit, which charted for
seventeen weeks (Capitol 1777). It has become a standard among bluegrass and contest fiddlers.

## DOWNTOWN

Tony Hatch (w & m)

Leeds Music—New York

1964

Petula Clark had the number 1 hit in 1965 that charted
for thirteen weeks and sold over one million copies
(Warner 5494).

## DREAM

Johnny Mercer (w & m)

Capitol Songs—New York

1945

Closing theme for *Johnny Mercer's Music Shop*, his radio
show. The Pied Pipers had the number 1 hit, which
charted for eighteen weeks and sold over one million
copies (Capitol 185). The Voices of Walter Schumann
made a magnificent arrangement (Capitol 1505) in
1952. The Four Aces revived it in 1954 with a number
17 hit (Decca 29217). Betty Johnson revived it again in
1958 with her number 19 hit (Atlantic 1186). Not to
be confused with the Everly Brothers's 1958 hit, "All I
Have To Do Is Dream."

## DREAM A LITTLE DREAM OF ME

W. Schwandt and F. Andree (w: Gus Kahn)

Davis, Coots and Engel—New York

1931

Wayne King and His Orchestra had the number 1 hit
which charted for twelve weeks (Victor 22643). Jack
Owens, featured singer on Don McNeill's "Breakfast
Club" radio show on ABC, had the number 14 hit in his
1950 revival (Decca 27096). "Mama" Cass Elliot of the
Mamas and Papas revived it again in 1968 with her
number 12 hit (Dunhill 4145).

## DREAM ALONG WITH ME

Carl Sigman (w & m)

Roncom Music—New York

1955

Perry Como used it as the opening theme song for his
television show.

## DREAM IS A WISH YOUR HEART MAKES, A

Jerry Livingston/Mack David/Al Hoffman

Walt Disney—Burbank

1949

**Film:** *Cinderella* (Disney)

Ilene Woods sang it in the film.

## DREAMLOVER

Mariah Carey and Dave Hall

Sony Songs

1993

Mariah Carey had the number 1 hit for eight of the
twenty-six weeks it charted (Columbia 77080). It sold
over one million copies.

## DREAMS

Stevie Nicks (w & m)

Screen Gems-EMI Music

1977

First number 1 hit for British pop-rock group Fleetwood Mac, charting for thirteen weeks (Warner 8371)
and selling over half a million copies.

## DUCK'S QUACK, THE

Hannibal Maguire (w & m)

Leo Feist—New York

1923

Fine early jazz tune with a great recorded version by
the Cotton Pickers (Brunswick 2461).

## DUKE OF EARL

Earl Edwards/Eugene Dixon/Bernice Williams

Conrad Publishing—Chicago

1961

Gene Chandler had the number 1 hit in 1962 that
charted for eleven weeks and sold over one million
copies (Vee-Jay 416). A rock and roll classic.

## DUMBELL
Zez Confrey (w & m)
Leo Feist—New York
1922
Introduced by the composer and his orchestra (Victor 19009). It was a great hit in vaudeville and on discs. Joseph Samuels and His Orchestra scored well (Banner 1145) as did Bennie Krueger and His Orchestra (Brunswick 2354). The composer also made a fabulous piano roll (QRS 2357).

## DUSKY STEVEDORE
J. C. Johnson (w: Andy Razaf)
Triangle Music—New York
1928
Theme song for Nat Shilkret and His Orchestra, who had the hit recording (Victor 21515). Famous jazz version recorded by Frankie Trumbauer and His Orchestra, with cornet by Bix Beiderbecke (Okeh 41100).

## EARLY IN THE MORNING BLUES
Ray Brown and Ray Klages
Irving Berlin—New York
1922
Popularized by the Virginians (Victor 18946) and Markel's Orchestra (Okeh 4691). A very fine song.

## EARTH ANGEL
Curtis Williams (w & m)
Dootsie Williams—New York
1954
The Penguins originated the song, and had the number 8 hit, which charted for fifteen weeks and sold over one million copies (DooTone 348). The Crew Cuts, a white cover group, picked it up for a number 3 hit, which charted for thirteen weeks (Mercury 70529). New Edition revived it in 1986 with the number 21 hit that charted for six weeks (MCA 52905). A doo-wop standard.

## EASTER PARADE
Irving Berlin (w & m)
Irving Berlin—New York
1933
**Show:** *As Thousands Cheer*

Marilyn Miller and Clifton Webb sang it in the show. The melody originally came from Berlin's 1917 song "Smile and Show Your Dimple." Clifton Webb with Leo Reisman's Orchestra had the number 5 hit, which charted for twelve weeks (Victor 24418). Guy Lombardo and His Royal Canadians revived it in 1939 with a number 11 hit (Decca 2345). Bing Crosby sang it in the film *Holiday Inn* (Paramount, 1942). Judy Garland and Fred Astaire sang it in the film *Easter Parade* (MGM, 1948). It has become a holiday standard.

## EBONY AND IVORY
Paul McCartney (w & m)
MPL Communications
1982
Paul McCartney collaborated vocally with Stevie Wonder in this number 1 hit, holding this position for seven out of fifteen weeks (Columbia 02860). It sold over one million copies.

## EIGHT DAYS A WEEK
John Lennon and Paul McCartney
Maclen Music—New York
1964
The Beatles had the number 1 hit, which charted for nine weeks and sold more than one million copies (Capitol 5371).

## EL PASO
Marty Robbins (w & m)
Marty's Music—Nashville
1959
Marty Robbins had the number 1 hit in 1960, which charted for sixteen weeks (Columbia 41511).

## ELMER'S TUNE
Elmer Albrecht/Sammy Gallop/Dick Jurgens
Robbins Music—New York
1941
Glenn Miller and His Orchestra had the number 1 hit, which charted for twenty weeks and had Ray Eberle and the Modernaires on vocals (Bluebird 11274). Bandleader/composer Dick Jurgens had an instrumental number 8 hit, which charted for eighteen weeks (Okeh 6209).

## EMBRACEABLE YOU
George Gershwin (w: Ira Gershwin)
New World Music—New York
1930
**Show:** *Girl Crazy*
Ginger Rogers and Allen Kearns sang it in the show. It became one of the Gershwins' all-time classics. Red Nichols and His Five Pennies, who were the pit band in the show, had the number 2 hit, which charted for nine weeks (Brunswick 4957). Judy Garland sang it in the film version (MGM, 1943). Joan Leslie sang it in the Gershwin biopic *Rhapsody in Blue* (Warner Bros., 1945). Leslie Caron danced to it in the film *An American in Paris* (MGM, 1951).

## END OF THE ROAD
Babyface/L. A. Reid/Daryl Simmons
Ensign Music
1992
**Film:** *Boomerang* (Paramount)
Boyz II Men had the hit record (Motown 2178) from this film starring Eddie Murphy. It was number 1 for thirteen of the twenty-eight weeks charted and sold over one million copies.

## ENDLESS LOVE
Lionel Richie (w & m)
PGP Music
1981
**Film:** *Endless Love* (Polygram Pictures)
Diana Ross and Lionel Richie combined their voices to produce their biggest success. This number 1 hit stayed in that position for nine of the nineteen weeks on the chart and sold over two million copies (Motown 1519). Luther Vandross and Mariah Carey had a number 2 hit with it in 1994 that charted for thirteen weeks and sold over half a million copies (Columbia 77629).

## ENJOY YOURSELF
Carl Sigman (w: Herb Magidson)
Edwin H. Morris—New York
1949
Guy Lombardo had the number 10 hit, which charted for nineteen weeks and featured Kenny Gardner on vocals (Decca 24839).

## ENTERTAINER, THE
Scott Joplin
John Stark and Son—St. Louis
1902
This tune created a Joplin and ragtime revival—one that is still going strong—when it was featured in the film *The Sting* (Universal, 1974). The Marvin Hamlisch recording from the film's score sold over two million copies (MCA 40174).

## ETIQUETTE BLUES
Gayle Grubb (w & m)
Bibo-Lang—New York
1928
Introduced in vaudeville by Happy Stanley. There is a great recording by the Six Jumping Jacks (Brunswick 3940).

## EVE OF DESTRUCTION
P. F. Sloan (w & m)
Trousadle Music—Beverly Hills
1965
Barry McGuire had the number 1 hit, which charted for ten weeks (Dunhill 4009).

## EVERGREEN
Barbra Streisand (w: Paul Williams)
Warner Bros. Publications—New York
1976
**Film:** *A Star Is Born* (Warner Bros.)
Academy Award winner for Best Song. Barbra Streisand starred in the film and recorded this number 1 hit, which charted for eighteen weeks (Columbia 10450). It sold over two million copies.

## EVERY BREATH YOU TAKE
Sting (w & m)
G. M. Sumner
1983
Police featured songwriter/singer Gordon "Sting" Sumner in this giant number 1 hit, which held that position for eight out of twenty weeks on the chart (A&M 2542). It sold over one million copies. Oddly, this story of a somewhat obsessed lover has become a favorite at weddings.

## EVERY DAY IS LADIES' DAY TO ME
Victor Herbert (w: Henry Blossom)
M. Witmark and Sons—New York
1906
**Show:** *The Red Mill*
A popular operetta featured Neil McCay singing this most famous song from the score. The show was revived successfully in 1945, starring Dorothy Stone, daughter of Fred Stone, who himself starred in the original production.

## EVERY LITTLE MOVEMENT
Karl Hoschna (w: Otto Hauerbach)
M. Witmark and Sons—New York
1910
**Show:** *Madame Sherry*
Florence Mackie and Jack Reinhard sang it in the show. Harry MacDonough and Lucy Isabelle Marsh had the hit recording (Victor 5784). It was revived in the Nora Bayes biopic *Shine On, Harvest Moon* (Warner Bros., 1944). Jack Smith sang it in the film *On Moonlight Bay* (Warner Bros., 1951).

## EVERYBODY LOVES MY BABY
Jack Palmer and Spencer Williams
Clarence Williams Music—New York
1924
Introduced by Aileen Stanley, who had the hit recording (Victor 19486), it has become a jazz standard. Dance band versions include those of George Olsen (Victor 19610), Gene Rodcemich (Brunswick 2843), and the Georgians (Columbia 252-D).

## EVERYBODY LOVES SOMEBODY
Ken Lane (w: Irving Taylor)
Sinatra Songs—New York
1948
Frank Sinatra introduced this and had a number 25 hit (Columbia 38225), but it is best remembered from the 1964 recording by Dean Martin, who had a number 1 hit that charted for thirteen weeks and sold more than one million copies (Reprise 0281). The song became one of Martin's theme songs.

## EVERYBODY STEP
Irving Berlin (w & m)

Irving Berlin—New York
1921
**Show:** *Music Box Revue*
Introduced by the Brox Sisters. Paul Whiteman had the hit recording (Victor 18826). It was revived in the film *Alexander's Ragtime Band* (20th Century Fox, 1938) and in *Blue Skies* (MGM, 1946).

## EVERYBODY TWO-STEP
Wallie Herzer
Jerome H. Remick—New York
1910, 1911
Mike Bernard made the first piano rag on disc in 1912 (Columbia A-1266). The Victor Military Band had the first orchestra hit (Victor 17271). The song version was issued a year later with a lyric by Earl Jones. It was hugely popular in vaudeville. Billy Murray had the vocal hit accompanied by the American Quartet (Victor 17171).

## EVERYBODY WANTS TO RULE THE WORLD
Roland Orzabal/Ian Stanley/Chris Hughes
Virgin Music
1985
First number 1 hit for British new wavers Tears for Fears and also their debut single, holding the top spot for two out of fourteen weeks on the charts (Mercury 880659).

## EVERYBODY WORKS BUT FATHER
Jean Havez (w & m)
Helf and Hager—New York
1905
This was originally an English music-hall tune for which Havez wrote new words (he took credit for the tune, too, although he did not write it). It was a feature for Lew Dockstader in his minstrel shows.

## EVERYBODY'S CRAZY 'BOUT THE DOGGONE BLUES BUT I'M HAPPY
Turner Layton and Henry Creamer
Broadway Music Corp.—New York
1917
Hit recording by Marion Harris (Victor 18443).

## EVERYBODY'S DOIN' IT NOW
Irving Berlin (w & m)

Ted Snyder—New York

1911

This song was identified with the dance the turkey trot. It was introduced in vaudeville by Claire Maynard. Arthur Pryor and His Band had the instrumental hit (Victor 17091). It was revived by Alice Faye, Dixie Dunbar, and Wally Vernon in the film *Alexander's Ragtime Band* (20th Century Fox, 1938).

## EVERYBODY'S SOMEBODY'S FOOL

Howard Greenfield (w: Jack Keller)

Screen Gems-Columbia Music—New York

1960

Connie Francis had the number 1 hit, which charted for sixteen weeks and sold over one million copies (MGM 12899).

## (EVERYTHING I DO) I DO IT FOR YOU

Bryan Adams/Robert Lange/Michael Kanen

Zachary Creek Music

1991

**Film:** *Robin Hood: Prince of Thieves* (Warner Bros.)

Bryan Adams had this number 1 hit for seven out of seventeen weeks on the chart (A&M 1567). It sold over four million copies.

## EVERYTHING I HAVE IS YOURS

Burton Lane (w: Harold Adamson)

Robbins Music—New York

1933

**Film:** *Dancing Lady* (MGM)

Joan Crawford and Art Jarrett sang it in the film. Rudy Vallee and his Connecticut Yankees had the number 3 hit in 1934 that charted for seven weeks (Victor 24458). Monica Lewis sang it in the film of the same name (MGM, 1952). Eddie Fisher had the number 23 hit in 1952 (RCA Victor 20-4841).

## EVERYTHING IS BEAUTIFUL

Ray Stevens (w & m)

Ahab Music—Nashville

1970

Ray Stevens had this number 1 hit, which charted for thirteen weeks (Barnaby 2011). It sold over one million copies. It has remained one of Stevens's best-loved songs, despite the fact that he specialized in novelty and comic numbers rather than inspirational songs.

## EVERYTHING IS HOTSY TOTSY NOW

Jimmy McHugh (w: Irving Mills)

Jack Mills—New York

1925

A favorite with dance bands and jazz bands, with major recordings by Eddie Frazier (Sunset 1100), Herb Wiedoeft (Brunswick 2916), the Keystone Serenaders (Vocalion 15122), the Original Indiana Five (Gennett 3060), and the California Ramblers (Columbia 380-D).

## EVERYTHING IS PEACHES DOWN IN GEORGIA

Milton Ager and George W. Meyer

(w: Grant Clarke)

Leo Feist—New York

1918

Introduced in vaudeville by Al Jolson. The American Quartet, with lead vocalist Billy Murray, made the hit recording (Victor 18497).

## EVERYTHING'S COMING UP ROSES

Jule Styne (w: Stephen Sondheim)

Williamson Music—New York

1959

**Show:** *Gypsy*

Ethel Merman sang it in the show, and the song became closely associated with her.

## EVERYTHING'S GONNA BE ALL RIGHT

Harry Akst (w: Benny Davis)

Henry Waterson—New York

1926

Introduced in vaudeville by lyricist Benny Davis. Hit recordings came from the Coon-Sanders Nighthawks (Victor 20003) and Jane Gray (Harmony 128-H).

## EVERYWHERE YOU GO

Joe Goodwin/Mark Fisher/Larry Shay

Milton Weil Music—Chicago

1927

Introduced on radio by Mac Sattley. Popularized on disc by Bubbles Reeber (Paramount 20594) and Charley Straight and His Orchestra (Brunswick 3797).

Revived in 1949 by Guy Lombardo and His Orchestra (Decca 24549).

## EYE OF THE TIGER
Frankie Sullivan and Jim Peterik
Holey Moley Music
1982
The only number 1 hit for Survivor, a Chicago-based pop-rock outfit. It held that position for six out of eighteen weeks on the chart (Scotti Brothers 02912) and sold over four million copies.

## EXHALE (SHOOP, SHOOP)
Babyface (Kenny Edmonds) (w & m)
Ecaf Music
**Film:** *Waiting to Exhale* (20th Century Fox)
1995
Number 1 film theme song for Whitney Houston, who also appeared in the film. It charted for twenty weeks on the pop charts, was also a number 1 R&B hit (Arista 12885), and sold over a million copies.

## FAITH
George Michael (w & m)
Chappell and Co.
1987
George Michael had this number 1 stay on the chart for fifteen weeks (Columbia 07623). It sold over one million copies. His first major hit after leaving the pop duo Wham!

## FALLIN' IN LOVE
Dan Hamilton (w & m)
Spitfire Music—Beverly Hills
1974, 1975
Hamilton, Joe Frank, and Reynolds had this number 1 hit that charted for twelve weeks (Playboy 6024). It sold over one million copies.

## FALLING IN LOVE WITH LOVE
Richard Rodgers (w: Lorenz Hart)
Chappell—New York
1938
**Show:** *The Boys from Syracuse*
Muriel Angelus sang it in the show. In the film version (Universal, 1940) it was sung by Allan Jones and Rose-

mary Lane. Frances Langford had the number 18 hit in 1939 (Decca 2247).

## FAME
Michael Gore (w: Dean Pitchford)
Warner Bros. Publications—New York
1980
**Film:** *Fame* (MGM)
Academy Award winner for Best Song. Irene Cara had the number 4 hit, which charted for twelve weeks (RSO 1034).

## FANNY
Harold Rome (w & m)
Chappell—New York
1954
**Show:** *Fanny*
William Tabbert sang it in the show. Eddie Fisher had the number 29 hit (RCA Victor 20-5871).

## FANTASY
Mariah Carey/Tina Weymouth/Chris Frantz/
Dave Hall/Adrian Belew/Stephen Stanley
Sony Songs
1995
Mariah Carey had this number 1 hit on the charts for twenty-three weeks. It remained on top for eight weeks (Columbia 78043). It sold over three million copies.

## FAR AWAY PLACES
Joan Whitney and Alex Kramer
Laurel Music—New York
1948
Bing Crosby had the number 2 hit in 1949 that charted for nineteen weeks and featured the Ken Darby Singers (Decca 24532).

## FAREWELL BLUES
Elmer Schoebel/Paul Mares/Leon Rappolo
Jack Mills—New York
1923
A jazz standard introduced by the Friars Society Orchestra (Gennett 4966), among whose members are the composers. Isham Jones and His Orchestra had a hit recording (Brunswick 2406), as did the Original Memphis Five (Perfect 14104).

## FASCINATING RHYTHM
George and Ira Gershwin
Harms—New York
1924
**Show:** *Lady, Be Good*
Introduced in the show by Cliff Edwards (aka Ukulele Ike) and Fred and Adele Astaire. Paul Whiteman had the hit recording (Victor 19551). In the film version, Eleanor Powell sang and danced it (MGM, 1941).

## FEEL LIKE MAKIN' LOVE
Eugene McDaniels (w & m)
Skyforest Music—New York
1973, 1974
Roberta Flack had this number 1 hit, which charted for thirteen weeks (Atlantic 3025). It sold over one million copies.

## FIDGETY FEET
James D. LaRocca and Larry Shields
Leo Feist—New York
1918
A jazz standard, one of the Original Dixieland Jazz Band favorites, and introduced by them (Victor 18564). Other fine versions through the years include those by the Arcadian Serenaders (Okeh 40272), Bob Crosby's Bob Cats (Decca1593), Benny Strickler with the Yerba Buena Jazz Band (Good Time Jazz 22), and Irving Fazola and His Orchestra (Victor 40-0143). It remains in the Dixieland jazz band repertoire.

## FIFTH OF BEETHOVEN, A
Walter Murphy
RFT Music—New York
1976
Number 1 hit for Walter Murphy and the Big Apple Band, based on—what else?—Beethoven's Fifth Symphony (Private St. 45073). It spent twenty-two weeks on the charts, and sold over a million copies. Murphy is a former *Tonight Show* arranger.

## FIFTY WAYS TO LEAVE YOUR LOVER
Paul Simon (w & m)
Paul Simon
1975

Paul Simon had this number 1 hit, which charted for thirteen weeks (Columbia 10270). It sold over one million copies.

## FINE AND DANDY
Kay Swift (w: Paul James)
Harms—New York
1930
**Show:** *Fine and Dandy*
Joe Cook and Alice Boulden sang it in the show. The Arden-Ohman Orchestra had the number 10 hit (Victor 22552).

## FINE ROMANCE, A
Jerome Kern (w: Dorothy Fields)
Chappell—New York
1936
**Film:** *Swing Time* (RKO)
Ginger Rogers and Fred Astaire sang it in the film. Fred Astaire had the number 1 hit, which charted for twelve weeks (Brunswick 7716). Virginia O'Brien sang it in the Kern biopic *Till the Clouds Roll By* (MGM, 1946).

## FINGERTIPS, PT. 2
Henry Cosby & Clarence Paul
Jobete Music—Detroit
1963
Thirteen-year-old "Little" Stevie Wonder's first release, a number 1 hit that held that position for three of its twelve weeks on the pop charts; also a number 1 R&B hit (Tamla 54080). A harmonica tour de force, the cut was recorded live and featured Wonder on both harmonica and bongos.

## FIRE
Bruce Springsteen (w & m)
WB Music—New York
1978
Number 2 hit for the Pointer Sisters, which held that spot for two out of sixteen weeks on the charts and sold over one million copies (Planet 45901). It launched a decade-long period of hits for the vocal trio.

## FIRST NIGHT, THE
Tamara Savage/Jermaine Dupri/
Marilyn McLeod/Pamela Sawyer

EMI April Music

1998

Monica started her career in Atlanta, Georgia when she was fifteen, in 1995; that same year, she scored her first of seven number 1 hits that she would have over the next five years. This one was number 1 for five of its twenty-five weeks on the Top 40 chart (Arista 13522). It sold over one million copies.

## FIRST TIME EVER I SAW YOUR FACE, THE

Ewan MacCall (w & m)

Stormking Music

1962, 1972

Roberta Flack had the number 1 hit with it staying in that position for six of the fifteen weeks on the chart (Atlantic 2864). It sold over one million copies.

## FIVE FOOT TWO

Ray Henderson (w: Sam Lewis and Joe Young)

Leo Feist—New York

1925

Perennial favorite from the 1920s. Jane Gray, accompanied by Rube Bloom on piano, had one of the better recordings (Harmony 114-H). Art Landry and His Orchestra also had a fine recording (Victor 19850). It has been revived since the 1940s in film and on disc. It was featured in the film *Has Anybody Seen My Gal?* (Universal, 1952).

## FLASHDANCE . . . WHAT A FEELING

Giorgio Moroder (w: Keith Forsey and Irene Cara)

Chappell—New York

1983

**Film:** *Flashdance* (Paramount)

Academy Award winner for Best Song. Irene Cara had the number 1 hit, which held that position for six of the twenty weeks charted (Casablanca 811440). It sold over one million copies.

## FLY ME TO THE MOON

Bart Howard (w & m)

Almanac Music—New York

1954

It was originally titled "In Other Words," but quickly became known by the opening words of the chorus. It

became a standard through many radio and television performances through the 1950s and '60s, though no recordings made the Top 40 chart. Joe Harnell and His Orchestra recorded it in 1963 as a bossa nova, attaining the number 14 position (Kapp 497).

## FOLLOW THE SWALLOW

Ray Henderson (w: Billy Rose and Mort Dixon)

Jerome H. Remick—New York

1924

**Show:** *The Greenwich Village Follies*: 6th edition

Introduced in the show by Brooks and Ross. Introduced on disc by Al Jolson (Brunswick 2671). The hit recording was by George Olsen and His Music (Victor 19428).

## FOOLS RUSH IN

Rube Bloom (w: Johnny Mercer)

Bregman, Vocco and Conn—New York

1940

Glenn Miller and His Orchestra, with vocal by Ray Eberle, had the number 1 hit that charted for thirteen weeks (Bluebird 10728). Rick Nelson revived it in 1963 with a number 12 hit (Decca 31533).

## FOOTLOOSE

Kenny Loggins and Dean Pitchford

Famous Music

1984

**Film:** *Footloose* (Paramount)

Kenny Loggins had the number 1 hit—also featured in the film—that charted for sixteen weeks (Columbia 04310). It sold over two million copies.

## FOR ALL WE KNOW

J. Fred Coots (w: Sam Lewis)

Leo Feist—New York

1934

Hal Kemp and His Orchestra, with vocal by Bob Allen, had the number 3 hit, which charted for eight weeks (Brunswick 6947).

## FOR ALL WE KNOW

Fred Karlin (w: Robb Wilson and Arthur James)

Pamco Music—Los Angeles

1970

**Film:** *Lovers and Other Strangers* (Cinerama)
Academy Award winner for Best Song. The Carpenters, brother and sister Richard and Karen, had the number 3 hit for twelve weeks on the charts (A&M 1243). It sold over one million copies.

## FOR ME AND MY GAL
George W. Meyer (w: Edgar Leslie and
E. Ray Goetz)
Waterson, Berlin and Snyder—New York
1917
Belle Baker, Eddie Cantor, and Al Jolson each featured it in vaudeville. The sheet music sold over three million copies. Pete Wendling had an outstanding piano roll (QRS 249). Judy Garland and Gene Kelly sang it in the film of the same name (MGM, 1942). They recorded it and had the number 3 hit that year with backing by Garland's then husband David Rose and His Orchestra (Decca 18480). It charted for twenty-one weeks.

## FOR ONCE IN MY LIFE
Orlando Murden (w: Ronald Miller)
Stein and Van Stock—Detroit
1967
Number 2 pop ballad hit for Stevie Wonder in 1968, holding that spot for two of its thirteen weeks on the charts (Tamla 54174). Covered by many mainstream pop singers, it has become a pop standard.

## FOREVER YOUR GIRL
Oliver Leiber (w & m)
Virgin Music
1988
Paula Abdul had this number 1 hit on the chart for fourteen weeks (Virgin 99230). It sold over half a million copies.

## FORGIVE ME
Milton Ager (w: Jack Yellen)
Ager, Yellen and Bornstein—New York
1927
Introduced in vaudeville by Lillian Roth. Gene Austin had the hit vocal record (Victor 20561), and Nat Shilkret and His Orchestra had the hit instrumental (Victor 20514). Revived in 1952 by Eddie Fisher, with a number 7 hit (RCA Victor 20-4574).

## FORTY-FIVE MINUTES FROM BROADWAY
George M. Cohan (w & m)
F. A. Mills—New York
1905
**Show:** *Forty-Five Minutes from Broadway*
Victor Moore sang it in the show. It became one of three song hits from the show. James Cagney sang it in the biopic *Yankee Doodle Dandy* (Warner Bros., 1942). Joel Grey sang it with Loni Ackerman in the 1968 show *George M!*

## FORTY-SECOND STREET
Harry Warren
(w: Al Dubin)
M. Witmark and Sons—New York
1932
**Film:** *Forty-Second Street* (Warner Bros.)
Dick Powell and Ruby Keeler sang it in the film. Don Bestor and His Orchestra had the number 1 hit, which charted for twelve weeks (Victor 24253). When it was turned into a Broadway musical in 1980, Lee Roy Reams and Wanda Richert sang it. The Broadway version was revived in 2001.

## FOUR OR FIVE TIMES
Byron Gay (w: Marco Hellman)
Sherman, Clay—San Francisco
1927
Introduced on disc by Jimmy Noone's Apex Club Orchestra, it became their theme song (Vocalion 1185). Don Redman made a special arrangement for McKinney's Cotton Pickers (Victor 21583). Woody Herman and His Band That Plays the Blues had a number 14 hit recording in 1943 (Decca 18526).

## FRENESI
Albert Dominguez (w: Ray Charles and
S. K. Russell)
Southern Music—New York
1939
Artie Shaw and His Orchestra had the number 1 hit in 1940 that maintained that position for thirteen of the thirty weeks charted, and sold over one million copies (Victor 26542). It helped popularize Brazilian rhythms in jazz and pop music.

## FRIENDSHIP
Cole Porter (w & m)
Chappell—New York
1939
**Show:** *DuBarry Was a Lady*
Ethel Merman and Bert Lahr sang it in the show. Kay Kyser and His Orchestra had the number 11 hit in 1940 (Columbia 35368). When the show was turned into a film (MGM, 1943), the song was sung by Gene Kelly, Lucille Ball, Red Skelton, Margaret O'Brien, Zero Mostel, and Rags Ragland, accompanied by Tommy Dorsey and His Orchestra.

## FROM A DISTANCE
Julie Gold (w & m)
Irving Music
1987
Number 2 hit for Bette Midler in 1990, charting for nineteen weeks and selling over a million copies; a number 1 adult-contemporary hit (Atlantic 87820). A powerful pop ballad, it was also recorded by country/pop singer Nanci Griffith, among many others.

## FROM THIS MOMENT ON
Cole Porter (w & m)
Buxton Hill—New York
1950
**Show:** *Out of This World*
This song was dropped from the show but added to the film version of *Kiss Me Kate* (MGM, 1953). Subsequently, it was also added to the stage version.

## FROSTY THE SNOW MAN
Steve Nelson and Jack Rollins
Hill and Range Songs—New York
1950
Gene Autry had the number 7 hit in 1951, which only charted for six weeks yet sold over one million copies (Columbia 38907). It has become a perennial Christmas favorite.

## FUNKY TOWN
Steve Greenberg (w & m)
Rick's Music
1980
Number 1 pop/dance hit for Lipps, Inc., holding the top spot for four of fifteen weeks on the charts and selling over a million copies (Casablanca 2233). The "group" was the brainchild of producer Steven Greenberg, who also played many of the synthesizers and other instruments on the track. Australian pop group Pseudo Echo covered the song in 1987, for a number 6 hit (RCA 5217).

## FUNNY FACE
George Gershwin (w: Ira Gershwin)
New World Music—New York
1927
**Show:** *Funny Face*
Introduced in the show by Adele and Fred Astaire. Arden and Ohman and their orchestra made the hit recording (Victor 21114). Revived in the film of the same name by Fred Astaire (Paramount, 1957). Revived again in the 1983 Broadway show *My One and Only*.

## GABY GLIDE, THE
Louis A. Hirsch (w: Harry Pilcer)
Shapiro Music Co.—New York
1911
**Show:** *Vera Violetta*
Introduced by Gaby Deslys and lyricist/dancer Harry Pilcer in the show. Arthur Pryor's Band's version was made for dancing (Victor 17063).

## GANG THAT SANG "HEART OF MY HEART," THE
Ben Ryan (w & m)
Robbins Music—New York
1926
A favorite of barbershop quartets. The title was shortened to "Heart of My Heart" by Don Cornell, Alan Dale, and Johnny Desmond. Their version was a number 10 hit in 1953 that charted for ten weeks (Coral 61076). A year later, the Four Aces had a number 7 hit that charted for eighteen weeks (Decca 28927).

## GANGSTA'S PARADISE
Artis Ivey Jr./Larry Sanders/Doug Rasheed/
Stevie Wonder
Jobette Music
1995

Film: *Dangerous Minds* (20th Century Fox)
Number 1 hit for rap star Coolio, holding that position for three out of thirty-five weeks on the charts and selling over three million copies (MCA 55104). It was based on the Stevie Wonder track "Pastime Paradise," drawn from his *Songs in the Key of Life* album (Tamla [2] 340, 1976). Parodied by "Weird" Al Yankovic as "Amish Paradise."

## GEE, I LIKE THE MUSIC WITH MY MEALS
Nat D. Ayers (w: Seymour Brown)
Jerome H. Remick—New York
1911
**Show:** *A Million*
A marvelous raggy tune introduced by William Burress in the show.

## GENIE IN A BOTTLE
Steve Kipner/David Frank/Pam Sheyne
EMI April Music
1998
Christina Aguilera scored a great hit in the number 1 position for five out of twenty-three weeks on the charts (RCA 65692). It sold over one million copies. The song was controversial because of its sexual imagery and provocative video, featuring the teenage Aguilera.

## GENTLE ON MY MIND
John Hartford (w & m)
Glaser—Nashville, Tennessee
1967
Although not a top hit, the song became closely associated with pop-country singer Glen Campbell (Capitol 5939); it was the theme song for his television variety show (1968–72). BMI states that the song is one of the most recorded standards of all time, with over three hundred versions ranging from those of Elvis Presley to Frank Sinatra.

## GEORGIA
Walter Donaldson (w: Howard Johnson)
Leo Feist—New York
1922
A wonderful song that was adopted as the official state song of Georgia (later, "Georgia On My Mind"

replaced it). Paul Whiteman had the hit recording (Victor 18899), and Carl Fenton's Orchestra also had a fine version (Brunswick 2259). Pete Wendling made a great piano roll (QRS 1897).

## GEORGIA ON MY MIND
Hoagy Carmichael
(w: Stuart Gorrell)
Southern Music—New York
1930
Mildred Bailey was firmly associated with this standard when she recorded it in 1931 and used it extensively on radio. It was revived in 1960 by Ray Charles, who had a number 1 hit that charted for ten weeks (ABC-Paramount 10135). Willie Nelson revived it again in 1978 (Columbia 10704). Charles sang the song in the Georgia State Legislature when the song was made the official state song in 1979.

## GET A JOB
The Silhouettes (w & m)
Wildcat Music—New York
1957
The Silhouettes had the number 1 hit in 1958 that charted for thirteen weeks and sold over one million copies (Ember 1029). It inspired many answer songs, including "Got A Job."

## GET BACK
John Lennon and Paul McCartney
Maclen Music—New York
1969
The Beatles, with Billy Preston on keyboards, had the number 1 hit, which held its top position for five of the twelve weeks charted (Apple 2490). It sold over four million copies.

## GET HAPPY
Harold Arlen (w: Ted Koehler)
Remick Music—New York
1930
**Show:** *Nine-Fifteen Revue*
Ruth Etting sang it in the show. Nat Shilkret and the Victor Orchestra had the number 6 hit, which charted for seven weeks (Victor 22444). It has become a perennial nightclub and cabaret favorite.

## GET OFF OF MY CLOUD

Mick Jagger and Keith Richards

Gideon Music

1965

Number 1 hit for the Rolling Stones in autumn 1965, a position it held for two out of the eleven weeks it charted (London 9792).

## GET OUT OF TOWN

Cole Porter (w & m)

Chappell—New York

1938

**Show:** Leave It to Me

Tamara sang it in the show. Eddie Duchin and His Orchestra had the number 7 hit in 1939 (Brunswick 8252).

## GETTING TO KNOW YOU

Richard Rodgers (w: Oscar Hammerstein)

Williamson Music—New York

1951

**Show:** *The King and I*

Gertrude Lawrence sang it in the show. Deborah Kerr sang it in the film version (MGM, 1956).

## GET TOGETHER

Chet Powers (w & m)

Irving Music—Hollywood

1963

Originally recorded as a number 3 hit in 1965 by the We Five as "Let's Get Together" (A&M 770), and as a number 5 hit for the folk-rock group the Youngbloods in 1969, whose version was first released on a single in 1967 (RCA 9752). The song became something of a hippie anthem in the late 1960s, and at one time was discussed as a possible replacement for the national anthem!

## GHOST OF THE SAXOPHONE, THE

F. Henri Klickmann (w: Jack Frost)

Frank K. Root—Chicago

1917

Introduced in vaudeville and on disc by the Six Brown Brothers (Victor 18309). Collins and Harlan made the hit vocal record (Victor 18354).

## GHOST OF THE VIOLIN, THE

Ted Snyder (w: Bert Kalmar)

Ted Snyder—New York

1912

Introduced in vaudeville by the Courtney Sisters. The Peerless Quartet had the hit vocal recording (Columbia A-1244) while Prince's Orchestra had the instrumental hit (Columbia A-1292).

## GHOSTBUSTERS

Ray Parker Jr. (w & m)

Golden Torch Music—Burbank

1984

Film: *Ghostbusters* (Columbia)

Number 1 hit for Ray Parker Jr., holding that spot for three out of fourteen weeks on the charts (Arista 9212); the theme song for the very successful film comedy of the same name. The funky hit sold over one million copies.

## GIANNINA MIA

Rudolf Friml (w: Otto Hauerbach)

G. Schirmer—New York

1912

**Show:** *The Firefly*

Emma Trentini sang it in the show. Jeanette MacDonald sang it in the film version (MGM, 1937).

## GIGI

Frederick Loewe (w: Alan Jay Lerner)

Lowal Corp.—New York

1958

**Film:** *Gigi* (MGM)

Academy Award Winner for Best Song. Louis Jourdan sang it in the film.

## GIMME A LITTLE KISS, WILL YA HUH?

Maceo Pinkard/Roy Turk/Jack Smith

Irving Berlin—New York

1926

Jean Goldkette and His Orchestra had a hit with this song (Victor 20031), and Phil Hughes and His High Hatters had the comic recording (Pathe 36423). It was revived in 1951 by April Stevens (RCA Victor 20-4208) and as a result of her number 10 hit, the song was included in the film *Has Anybody Seen My Gal?* (Universal, 1952).

## GIRL FRIEND, THE
Richard Rodgers (w: Lorenz Hart)
Harms—New York
1926
**Show:** *The Girl Friend*
Introduced in the show by Eva Puck and Sam White. Hit recordings by George Olsen (Victor 20029) and Ohman and Arden with their orchestra (Brunswick 3197). It was revived in the Rodgers and Hart biopic *Words and Music* (MGM, 1948).

## GIRL OF MY DREAMS
Sunny Clapp (w & m)
Jack Mills—New York
1927
Introduced in vaudeville by Blue Steele and His Orchestra on disc (Victor 20971). Gene Austin made the vocal hit (Victor 21334). Armand Hug revived it in a 1949 recording (Capitol 987). The song has become a standard.

## GIRL ON THE MAGAZINE, THE
Irving Berlin (w & m)
Irving Berlin—New York
1915
**Show:** *Stop! Look! Listen!*
Joseph Santley sang it in the show. Dick Beavers sang it in the film *Easter Parade* (MGM, 1948).

## GIRL THAT I MARRY, THE
Irving Berlin (w & m)
Irving Berlin—New York
1946
**Show:** *Annie Get Your Gun*
Ray Middleton sang it in the show. Frank Sinatra had the number 11 hit, which charted for two weeks (Columbia 36975). Tom Wopat sang it in the 1999 Broadway revival.

## GIRLS JUST WANT TO HAVE FUN
Robert Hazard (w & m)
Heroic Music
1983
Number 2 hit for pop singer Cyndi Lauper in 1984, and it held that position for two out of fourteen weeks on the charts and sold over a million copies (Portrait 04120). The song was written in a pseudo-1950s style, and was cleverly promoted with a video featuring Lauper and her mother. Lauper's first major hit, which launched her brief pop career.

## GIVE ME LOVE (GIVE ME PEACE ON EARTH)
George Harrison (w & m)
Harrisongs
1973
Number 1 hit for the ex-Beatle, then deep in his religious phase. It spent eleven weeks on the charts (Apple 1862).

## GIVE ME THE SIMPLE LIFE
Rube Bloom (w: Harry Ruby)
Triangle Music—New York
1945
**Film:** *Wake Up and Dream* (20th Century Fox)
John Payne and June Haver sang it in the film. Benny Goodman and His Orchestra, with vocalist Lisa Morrow, had the number 13 hit (Columbia 36908).

## GIVE ME THE SULTAN'S HAREM
Abner Silver (w: Alex Gerber)
M. Witmark and Sons—New York
1919
Henry Lewis introduced it in vaudeville. A. Hyland made a great piano roll (Connorized 6641). It has become a great favorite with Dixieland bands, with a remarkable version recorded by the St. Louis Ragtimers in 1968 (Paseo DF-102).

## GIVE MY REGARDS TO BROADWAY
George M. Cohan (w & m)
F. A. Mills—New York
1904
**Show:** *Little Johnny Jones*
Introduced by the composer in the show, in which he also wrote, directed, produced, acted in, and danced in. James Cagney sang it in the Cohan biopic *Yankee Doodle Dandy* (Warner Bros.,1942). Al Jolson sang it in *Jolson Sings Again* (Columbia, 1949) and it served as the title of a film (20th Century Fox, 1948). Joel Grey sang it in the Broadway musical *George M!* (1968). It has become a standard.

## GIVE PEACE A CHANCE
John Lennon and Paul McCartney
Northern Songs—London
1969
The Plastic Ono Band had the number 14 hit, which charted for six weeks (Apple 1809). This version was recorded live in Toronto during a "bed-in" for peace staged by John Lennon and Yoko Ono. It became an anthem for the antiwar movement.

## GLAD RAG DOLL
Milton Ager and Dan Dougherty (w: Jack Yellen)
Ager, Yellen and Bornstein—New York
1929
**Film:** *Glad Rag Doll* (Warner Bros.)
Introduced in the film by Dolores Costello. Ruth Etting had the hit vocal (Columbia 1733-D), and Ben Bernie and His Orchestra had the instrumental hit (Brunswick 4168). Earl Hines made a fancy piano solo (Bluebird 10555).

## GLOW-WORM, THE
Paul Lincke (w: Lilla Cayley Robinson)
Jos. W. Stern—New York
1907
May Naudain sang it in the Broadway musical *The Girl behind the Counter*. It became the biggest hit for the publisher to that date, selling over three million copies. Prince's Orchestra had the hit recording (Columbia A-711). Johnny Mercer rewrote the lyrics in 1952, giving the Mills Brothers a million-selling disc (Decca 28384).

## GO AWAY, LITTLE GIRL
Gerry Goffin and Carole King
Aldon Music—New York
1962
Steve Lawrence had the number 1 hit in 1963, which charted for twelve weeks and sold more than one million copies (Columbia 42601). It was revived by Donny Osmond in 1971 with a number 1 hit that charted for thirteen weeks and sold more than one million copies (MGM 14285).

## GOING UP
Louis A. Hirsch (w: Otto Harbach)
M. Witmark and Sons—New York
1917
**Show:** *Going Up*
Delightful title song from the hit show, the first musical about aviation.

## GOLD DIGGER'S SONG, THE
Harry Warren (w: Al Dubin)
Remick Music—New York
1933
**Film:** *The Gold Diggers of 1933* (Warner Bros.)
Ginger Rogers sang it in the film. Ted Lewis and His Band had the number 5 hit, which charted for seven weeks (Columbia 2775-D). It was better known as "We're In the Money," taken from the opening line lyric.

## GONNA MAKE YOU SWEAT (EVERYBODY DANCE NOW)
Robert Clivilles & Frederick Williams
Virgin Music
1990
Number 1 hit in 1991 for disco-funk group C & C Music Factory, holding the top spot for two out of seventeen weeks on the charts, and selling over one million copies (Columbia 73604). The song has become a wedding and bar mitzvah band favorite to get people "up on the dance floor."

## GOOD BYE, MY LADY LOVE
Joseph E. Howard (w & m)
Chas. K. Harris—New York
1904
A sequel to his "Hello, My Baby," the music appears to have been taken from W. H. Myddleton's "Down South." It was interpolated into the Broadway musical *Show Boat* (1927). Featured in the Howard biopic *I Wonder Who's Kissing Her Now* (20th Century Fox, 1947).

## GOOD MAN IS HARD TO FIND, A
Eddie Green (w & m)
Pace and Handy Music—New York
1918
Made famous in vaudeville by Sophie Tucker. Marion Harris made a hit recording (Victor 18535). Revived in the film *Meet Danny Wilson* (Universal, 1952). Also used as a short story title by Flannery O'Connor.

## GOOD MORNING, CARRIE

Chris Smith and Elmer Bowman

(w: R. C. McPherson)

Windsor Music—Chicago

1901

Sung by Bert Williams and George Walker in their first recording (Victor 997). Eubie Blake and Noble Sissle revived it on their 1958 LP *The Wizard of Ragtime* (Fox 3003).

## GOOD NEWS

Ray Henderson (w: Bud DeSylva and Lew Brown)

DeSylva, Brown and Henderson—New York

1927

**Show:** *Good News*

Zelma O'Neal sang it in the show. Fred Rich and His Orchestra had a hit recording (Columbia 1108-D). Dorothy McNulty, who later changed her name to Penny Singleton, sang it in the first film version (MGM, 1930), and Joan McCracken sang it in the second film version (MGM, 1947). Gordon MacRae, Ernest Borgnine, and Dan Dailey sang it in the songwriters' biopic *The Best Things in Life Are Free* (20th Century Fox, 1956).

## GOOD TIMES

Bernard Edwards and Nile Rodgers

Chic Music

1979

Number 1 hit for disco duo Bernard Edwards and Nile Rodgers, aka Chic, charting for fourteen weeks and selling over one million copies (Atlantic 3584). A favorite backing track for rappers, it served as the basis for the first major rap hit, "Rapper's Delight." Edwards and Rodgers have gone on to be important pop producers, working with Madonna and many other artists.

## GOOD VIBRATIONS

Brian Wilson and Mike Love

Sea of Tunes—Whittier, Calif.

1966

The Beach Boys had the number 1 hit, which charted for twelve weeks and sold over one million copies (Capitol 5676). The recording is noteworthy for featuring a version of the Theremin, an electronic instrument used to create the song's distinctive "whoo-ee-yoo" sound. It is also claimed that the total recording cost was over a million dollars because of the many months of sessions that Wilson did before settling on the final version.

## GOOD-BYE, DOLLY GRAY

Paul Barnes (w: Will D. Cobb)

Howley Haviland—New York

1900

First popularized during the Spanish-American War; when it was published two years later, it sold over a million copies of sheet music, thanks to vaudevillian Hamilton Hill. It was revived in the film *Wait Till the Sun Shines, Nellie* (20th Century Fox, 1952).

## GOODBYE BLUES

Jimmy McHugh (w: Arnold Johnson)

Robbins Music—New York

1932

The Mills Brothers had the number 4 hit, which charted for seven weeks (Brunswick 6278). They also sang it in the film *The Big Broadcast* (Paramount, 1932) later that year. They subsequently used it as their theme song.

## GOODBYE YELLOW BRICK ROAD

Elton John (w: Bernie Taupin)

Dick James Music—New York

1973

Inspired by the *Wizard of Oz*. A perennial Elton John favorite, the original recording remained at number 2 for three out of fourteen chart weeks (MCA 40148). It sold over two million copies.

## GOODNIGHT, ANGELINE

Eubie Blake/Noble Sissle/Jim Europe

M. Witmark and Sons—New York

1919

Introduced by Ivan Harold Browning in the smash Broadway musical *Shuffle Along* (1921), he finally recorded it with Eubie Blake accompanying him at the piano in 1971 (Eubie Blake Music 1). He was part of the Four Harmony Kings, who initially recorded it on a 78 rpm disc (Black Swan 2016).

## GOODNIGHT, IRENE

Huddie Ledbetter and John Lomax

Spencer Music—New York

1950

The Weavers had the number 1 hit, which charted for twenty-five weeks and sold over two million copies (Decca 27077). Ironically, Ledbetter (better known as Leadbelly) died a year before his song became a major hit. Lomax "discovered" Leadbelly in a Mississippi prison, and took cocomposer credit. Charles Wolfe and Kip Lornell, in their book *The Life and Legend of Leadbelly*, trace the song to Gussie Davis's song, "Irene, Goodnight," published in 1886 in Cincinnati, and then again in New York in 1892. Both are waltz songs, and there are similarities in the lyrics, but Davis's words are far more floridly written. It is likely that the Davis sheet passed into the traditional song repertoire in Leadbelly's native Texas, and he learned it second- or thirdhand in that way.

## GOODNIGHT SWEETHEART
Ray Noble/James Campbell/Reg Connelly
Robbins Music—New York
1931
**Show:** *Earl Carroll's Vanities*
Milton Watson and Woods Miller sang it in the show. Guy Lombardo and His Royal Canadians had the number 1 hit, which charted for eleven weeks (Columbia 2547-D). It became the favorite closing number of dance bands.

## GOT MY MIND SET ON YOU
Rudy Clark (w & m)
Carbert Music
1962, 1987
It was originally recorded by James Roy in 1962 (Dynamic Sound 503), but failed to chart. George Harrison revived it in 1987, scoring a number 1 hit, that charted for fifteen weeks (Dark Horse 28178).

## GOT TO COOL MY DOGGIES NOW
Bob Schafer/Babe Thompson/
Spencer Williams
Clarence Williams Music—New York
1922
**Show:** *The Passing Show of 1922*
Jazz classic first recorded by Lucille Hegamin (Paramount 20151). Two other fine jazz recordings are by

the Cotton Pickers (Brunswick 2338) and the Original Memphis Five (Perfect 14051).

## GREASE
Barry Gibb (w & m)
Stigwood Music
1978
**Film:** *Grease* (Paramount)
Frankie Valli, who was the lead vocalist of the four Seasons (1962–76), had this number 1 hit, which charted for fifteen weeks and sold more than two million copies (RSO 897). John Travolta sang it in the film.

## GREAT BALLS OF FIRE
Jack Hammer and Otis Blackwell
Hill and Range Songs—New York
1957
Jerry Lee Lewis had the number 2 hit, which charted for thirteen weeks and sold over one million copies (Sun 281). The song introduced Lewis's manic performance style, and became his signature number.

## GREAT DAY
Vincent Youmans (w: Billy Rose and
Edward Eliscu)
Vincent Youmans—New York
1929
**Show:** *Great Day*
Lois Deppe and His Jubilee Singers sang it in the show. Paul Whiteman and His Orchestra had the hit recording (Columbia 2023-D). Barbra Streisand sang it in the film *Funny Lady* (Columbia, 1975).

## GREAT PRETENDER, THE
Buck Ram (w & m)
Panther Music—New York
1955
The Platters had the number 1 hit, which charted for nineteen weeks and sold over one million copies (Mercury 70753). A doo wop classic.

## GREAT WHITE WAY BLUES
Phil Napoleon and Frank Signorelli
Jack Mills—New York
1923

Introduced by the Original Memphis Five in a splendid recording (Vocalion 14527). The Cotton Pickers also had a fine version (Brunswick 2380).

## GREATEST LOVE OF ALL
Michael Masser (w: Linda Creed)
Gold Horizon Music
1977
Film: *The Greatest* (Columbia)
Whitney Houston had this number 1 hit in 1986, which charted for fourteen weeks (Arista 9466). It sold over one million copies. The original 1977 version was cut by jazz-guitarist-turned-soul-vocalist George Benson (Arista 0251).

## GREEN TAMBOURINE
Shelly Pinz and Paul Leka
Kama Sutra Music—New York
1967
Psychedelic/pop group the Lemon Pipers had the number 1 hit in 1968, which charted for twelve weeks and sold over one million copies (Buddah 23).

## GRIEVING FOR YOU
Joe Gibson/Joe Ribaud/Joe Gold
Leo Feist—New York
1920
Despite all of the "Joes" who were given credit for it, this song was the solo effort of Sam Coslow, who became a professional composer/lyricist/publisher. Al Jolson and Eddie Cantor made a hit of it in vaudeville, and Marion Harris had the hit vocal recording (Columbia A-3353). The Green Bros. Novelty Band (Brunswick 2056), Selvin's Dance Orchestra (Vocalion 14127), and the Happy Six (Columbia A-3345) had fine recordings. Zez Confrey made the finest piano roll version (QRS 1262).

## GRIZZLY BEAR, THE
George Botsford (w: Irving Berlin)
Ted Snyder—New York
1910
Introduced in vaudeville by Sophie Tucker. Hit instrumental record was by Arthur Pryor and His Band (Victor 5802). The vocal hit was by Billy Murray and the American Quartet (Victor 16681). It was revived in

1951 by Teresa Brewer (London 794). It was a favorite among 1960s-era revival jug bands.

## GROOVIN'
Felix Cavaliere and Eddie Brigati
Slacsar Publishing—New York
1967
The Young Rascals had this number 1 hit, which charted for eleven weeks and sold over one million copies (Atlantic 2401).

## GROOVY KIND OF LOVE, A
Toni Wine and Carole Bayer
Screen Gems-Columbia Music
1966
British Invasion group the Mindbenders had the number 2 hit, which charted for ten weeks (Fontana 1541). It was revived in 1988 by Phil Collins, for the soundtrack of his first starring film *Buster* (MGM/UA). The film was not much of a hit, but the song went number 1, and charted for thirteen weeks (Atlantic 89017). Collins's version sold over one million copies.

## GULF COAST BLUES
Clarence Williams (w & m)
Clarence Williams Music—New York
1923
Bessie Smith had the hit recording, accompanied by the composer at the piano (Columbia A-3844). The Tennessee Ten had an instrumental hit (Victor 19094).

## GYPSIES, TRAMPS AND THIEVES
Bob Stone (w & m)
Peso Music—Hollywood
1971
Cher had the number 1 hit, which charted for fourteen weeks (Kapp 2146). It sold over one million copies.

## GYPSY BLUES
Eubie Blake (w: Noble Sissle)
M. Witmark and Sons—New York
1921
**Show:** *Shuffle Along*
Introduced in the show by Lottie Gee, Gertrude Saunders, and Roger Matthews. Paul Whiteman and His Orchestra had the big recording (Victor 18839), and

Irving Weiss and His Orchestra had a lovely version (Banner 1021).

## HAIL, HAIL THE GANG'S ALL HERE
Theodore Morse and Arthur Sullivan
(w: D.A. Esrom)
Leo Feist—New York
1917
The melody comes from the song "With Catlike Tread" from the *Pirates of Penzance* (which is why Arthur Sullivan gets a composer credit). But why doesn't Giuseppe Verdi get a piece of the action for his *Anvil Chorus?* Irving Kaufman and the Columbia Quartet had the hit record (Columbia A-2443). The song is a perennial favorite among campers, club members, and other places where "the gang" congregates.

## HALLELUJAH!
Vincent Youmans (w: Clifford Grey and Leo Robin)
Harms—New York
1927
**Show:** *Hit the Deck*
Originally composed ten years earlier, while Youmans was in the Navy, it was featured by John Philip Sousa during World War I. Stella Mayhew sang it in the show. Marguerite Padula sang it in the first film version (RKO, 1930), while Tony Martin, Russ Tamblyn, and Vic Damone sang it in the second film version (MGM, 1955).

## HALLS OF IVY, THE
Henry Russell and Vic Knight
Ivy Music—New York
1950
Radio theme song for the show of the same name. Popularized on disc by the Voices of Walter Schumann (Capitol 1505).

## HANDFUL OF KEYS
Thomas "Fats" Waller
Southern Music—New York
1933
Introduced on disc by the composer in 1929 (Victor 38508). It has become a test piece for stride pianists. The Benny Goodman Quartet revived it in 1937 (Victor 25705).

## HANDY MAN
Otis Blackwell & Jimmy Jones
United Artists Music—Los Angeles
1959
Number 2 hit for Jimmy Jones in 1960, charting for fourteen weeks (Cub 9049). Revived in 1964 by Del Shannon for a number 22 hit (Amy 905), and then again in 1977 by James Taylor for a number 4 hit (Columbia 10557). A relaxed, soulful ballad.

## HANGIN' AROUND
Fred Hamm and Jack Gardner (w: Harry Harris)
Melrose Bros. Music—Chicago
1926
Introduced in vaudeville by Ray Allen. Popularized by Warner's Seven Aces (Columbia 752-D) and a great jazz version by the Original Indiana Five (Harmony 267-H).

## HANKY PANKY
Jeff Barry & Ellie Greenwich
T. M. Music—New York
1962, 1966
Number 1 hit in 1966 for Tommy James and the Shondells, holding that spot for two out of ten weeks on the charts, and selling over a million copies (Roulette 4686). A garage-rock classic.

## HAPPY DAYS AND LONELY NIGHTS
Fred Fisher (w: Billy Rose)
Ager, Yellen and Bornstein—New York
1928
Ruth Etting had a hit recording (Columbia 1454-D). The Fontane Sisters revived it in 1954 with a number 18 hit (Dot 15171).

## HAPPY DAYS ARE HERE AGAIN
Milton Ager (w: Jack Yellen)
Ager, Yellen and Bornstein—New York
1929
**Film:** *Chasing Rainbows* (MGM)
Charles King and Bessie Love sang it in the film. Ben Selvin and His Orchestra had the first hit recording (Columbia 2116-D). Franklin D. Roosevelt used it as a campaign theme song and to promote his New Deal in 1932. It has become the standard Depression-era number.

## HAPPY, HAPPY BIRTHDAY, BABY
Margo Sylvia and Gilbert Lopez
ARC Music—New York
1956, 1957
The Tune Weavers, half of whom wrote this number 5 hit that charted for fourteen weeks (Checker 872), are responsible for this soulful takeoff on the perennial "Happy Birthday to You."

## HAPPY TOGETHER
Garry Bonner and Alan Gordon
Chardon Music—New York
1966, 1967
The Turtles had the number 1 hit, which charted for twelve weeks and sold more than one million copies (White Whale 244). It was the group's first (and only) number 1 hit and perhaps their best-known song. Mark Volman and Howard Kaplan, the original leaders of the band, have revived it through their constant touring, under the name of Flo and Eddie and also in various revival Turtles bands.

## HARD DAY'S NIGHT, A
John Lennon and Paul McCartney
Maclen Music—New York
1964
**Film:** *A Hard Day's Night* (United Artists)
The Beatles had the number 1 hit, which charted for twelve weeks and sold more than one million copies (Capitol 5222). The title was said to be taken from an expression used by drummer Ringo Starr.

## HARD HEARTED HANNAH
Milton Ager (w: Jack Yellen/Bob Bigelow/Charles Bates)
Ager, Yellen and Bornstein—New York
1924
**Show:** *Innocent Eyes*
Frances William sang it in the show. Hit vocal recordings were by Dolly Kay (Columbia 151-D) and Margaret Young (Brunswick 2652). Herb Wiedoeft and His Orchestra had the instrumental hit (Brunswick 2751). Ella Fitzgerald revived it in the film *Pete Kelly's Blues* (Warner Bros., 1955). It was also a favorite of the 1960s-era jug band revival.

## HARD-TO-GET GERTIE
Milton Ager (w: Jack Yellen)
Ager, Yellen and Bornstein—New York
1926
Irving Aaronson and His Commanders had a hit recording (Victor 20100). The Original Indiana Five had a fine jazz recording (Perfect 14609).

## HARD TO SAY I'M SORRY
David Foster and Peter Cetera
Double Virgo Music
1982
**Film:** *Summer Lovers* (Orion)
The pop-rock group Chicago had this number 1 hit, written by one of its vocalists (Cetera) along with the record's producer, and it was on the chart for eighteen weeks (Full Moon 29979). It sold over one million copies.

## HARPER VALLEY P.T.A.
Tom T. Hall (w & m)
Newkeys Music—Nashville
1967
Jeannie C. Riley had the number 1 hit in 1968, which charted for twelve weeks and sold over one million copies (Plantation 3).

## HARRIGAN
George M. Cohan (w & m)
F. A. Mills—New York
1907
**Show:** *Fifty Miles From Boston*
One of several successful spelling songs, it was sung in the show by James C. Marlowe. James Cagney sang it in the Cohan biopic *Yankee Doodle Dandy* (Warner Bros., 1942). Joel Grey revived it on Broadway in *George M!* (1968). Alan Sherman parodied it as "Horowitz."

## HAS ANYBODY HERE SEEN KELLY?
C. W. Murphy and Will Letters
T. B. Harms—New York
1909
**Show:** *The Jolly Bachelors*
An Irish song adapted by William McKenna for Nora Bayes to sing in the show. With her recording (Victor 60013), it became a smash hit. A great comic song.

## HAVE YOU EVER REALLY LOVED A WOMAN?
Michael Kamen (w: Bryan Adams and
Robert Lange)
Badams Music Limited
1995
**Film:** *Don Juan DeMarco*
Pop-rock songster Bryan Adams had this number 1 hit,
a position it held for five of its twenty weeks on the
chart (A&M 1028).

## HAVE YOU EVER SEEN THE RAIN?
John C. Fogerty (w & m)
Jondora Music—Berkeley
1970, 1971
Number 8 hit for Creedence Clearwater Revival, selling over one million records (Fantasy 655). Widely
interpreted as an anti-Vietnam war song.

## HAVE YOU NEVER BEEN MELLOW?
John Farrar (w & m)
ATV Music—Los Angeles
1974, 1975
Olivia Newton-John had this number 1 hit for eleven
weeks on the chart (MCA 40349). It sold over one
million copies. A very mellow disc, indeed.

## HAVE YOURSELF A MERRY LITTLE CHRISTMAS
Ralph Blane (w: Hugh Martin)
Leo Feist—New York
1944
**Film:** *Meet Me In St. Louis* (MGM)
Judy Garland sang it in the film. Her record (Decca
23362) did well at Christmas time, and the song has
since become a holiday perennial.

## HE AIN'T HEAVY . . . HE'S MY BROTHER
Bobby Scott (w: Bob Russell)
Cyril Shane Music—London
1969
The Hollies had the number 7 hit in 1970, which
charted for eleven weeks (Epic 10532). The song's
title entered into the pop vocabulary.

## HE LOVES AND SHE LOVES
George and Ira Gershwin
Harms—New York
1927
**Show:** *Funny Face*
Adele Astaire and Allen Kearns sang it in the show.
Fred Astaire sang it in the film version (Paramount,
1957). Tommy Tune and Twiggy sang and danced it in
the all-Gershwin Broadway musical *My One and Only*
(1984). Like many Gershwin numbers, this remains a
favorite of cabaret and nightclub singers everywhere,
as well with jazz musicians as a basis for instrumental
improvisation.

## HE MAY BE YOUR MAN BUT HE COMES TO SEE ME SOMETIMES
Lemuel Fowler (w & m)
Ted Browne Music—Chicago
1922
Introduced in vaudeville by Lucille Hegamin, accom-
panied by her Blue Flame Snycopators (Arto 9129).
The Cotton Pickers (Brunswick 2380), the Original
Memphis Five (Pathe 020855), and the Virginians
(Victor 19018) also had fine versions. A standard
blues.

## HE'D HAVE TO GET UNDER, GET OUT, AND GET UNDER
Maurice Abrahams (w: Grant Clarke and
Edgar Leslie)
Maurice Abrahams Music Co.—New York
1913
Introduced in vaudeville by Adele Ritchie and sung by
Billy Murray (Victor 17491), this was a hit automobile
song.

## HE'S A COUSIN OF MINE
Chris Smith and Silvio Hein (w: Cecil Mack)
Gotham-Attucks Music—New York
1906
**Show:** *Marrying Mary*
A comic hit introduced in the show by Marie Cahill. Bert
Williams's disc (Columbia 3536) made it a hit in 1907.

## HE'S A REBEL
Gene Pitney (w & m)

January Music—New York

1962

The Crystals had the number 1 hit, which charted for twelve weeks (Philles 106). The song was given a classic Phil Spector "wall of sound" production in the group's recording.

## HE'S GOT THE WHOLE WORLD IN HIS HANDS

Adapted by Geoff Love

Chappell—New York

1957

Laurie London had the number 1 hit in 1958, which charted for fourteen weeks and sold over one million copies (Capitol 3891). The song, preaching world brotherhood, became popular around campfires and among boy and girl scout troups.

## HE'S SO FINE

Ronald Mack (w & m)

Bright Tunes Music—Brooklyn

1962, 1963

The Chiffons had the number 1 hit, which charted for twelve weeks (Laurie 3152). George Harrison used the same melody for his 1970 number 1 hit, "My Sweet Lord." In 1976, he was found guilty of "unconcious plagiarism" and settled with the original publisher.

## HE'S THE LAST WORD

Walter Donaldson (w: Gus Kahn)

Leo Feist—New York

1927

Jane Gray, accompanied by Rube Bloom on piano, made a hit recording (Harmony 329-H), as did Art Kahn and His Orchestra (Columbia 830-D).

## HEART OF GLASS

Deborah Harry and Chris Stein

Rare Blue Music

1978

Number 1 disco hit for new-wave pop group Blondie in 1979—their first big hit—charting for fourteen weeks (Chrysalis 2295).

## HEART OF GOLD

Neil Young (w & m)

Silver Fiddle

1972

Number 1 hit for nasal-voiced Neil Young—his only top hit—charting for thirteen weeks (Reprise 1065). An early dip into country-flavored rock for the songster.

## HEARTACHE TONIGHT

Don Henley/Glenn Frey/Bob Seger/J. D. Souther

Cass County Music

1979

The Eagles had this number 1 hit, which charted for thirteen weeks (Asylum 46545). It sold over one million copies.

## HEARTACHES

Al Hoffman (w: John Klenner)

Olman Music—New York

1931

Ted Weems and His Orchestra originally recorded the song, with whistling chorus by Elmo Tanner in 1933 (Bluebird 5131). It bombed until a disc jockey in North Carolina discovered it over a decade later and played it on his show endlessly. It caught on, and RCA Victor reissued the original recording in 1947; it became a number 1 hit, maintaining that position for thirteen of the twenty weeks charted (RCA Victor 20-2175). It sold over two million copies. The Marcels covered the song for a number 7 hit in 1961 that charted for eight weeks (Colpix 612).

## HEARTBREAK HOTEL

Mae Axton/Tommy Durden/Elvis Presley

Tree Publishing—New York

1956

Elvis Presley had his first number 1 hit, which charted for twenty-two weeks and sold over four million copies (RCA Victor 47-6420). Mae Axton was the sole author of the song (although Durden and Presley were "cut in"); she wrote a number of country and pop hits, and was the mother of singer/songwriter Hoyt Axton.

## HEAT WAVE

Irving Berlin (w & m)

Irving Berlin—New York

1933

**Show:** *As Thousands Cheer*

Ethel Waters sang it in the show. She also had the number 7 hit (Columbia 2826-D). Ethel Merman sang it in the film *Alexander's Ragtime Band* (20th Century Fox, 1938) as did Marilyn Monroe in *There's No Business like Show Business* (20th Century Fox, 1954). Not to be confused with Martha and the Vandellas' 1963 R&B hit of the same name.

## HEAVEN IS A PLACE ON EARTH
Rick Nowels and Ellen Shipley
Future Furniture Music
1987
Belinda Carlisle had the number 1 hit, which charted for fifteen weeks (MCA 53181).

## HEAVEN WILL PROTECT THE WORKING GIRL
A. Baldwin Sloane (w: Edgar Smith)
Chas. K. Harris—New York
1909
**Show:** *Tillie's Nightmare*
A satire on tearjerkers, it was sung in the show by Marie Dressler and published by the master of tearjerkers, proving Harris had a sense of humor. Interpolated in Rogers and Hart's show *Peggy Ann* (1926), it was revived for the musical *Sing Out, Sweet Land* (1944). Max Morath had fun with it on his 1963 LP, *A Program of Waltzes, Shouts, Novelties, Rags, Blues, Ballads and Stomps* (Epic LN-24066).

## HEIDELBERG (STEIN SONG)
Gustav Luders (w: Frank Pixley)
M. Witmark and Sons—New York
1902
**Show:** *The Prince of Pilsen*
Famous drinking song sung by the show's chorus. Harry MacDonough had the hit recording (Victor 1920). Barbershop singers have always found it a favorite.

## HELLO
Lionel Richie (w & m)
Brockman Music
1984
Number 1 hit for soft soulster Lionel Richie, holding that position for two out of seventeen weeks on the charts and selling over a million copies (Motown 1722).

Also an adult-contemporary and R&B number 1. A soft-rock ballad, it became something of a signature song for Richie.

## HELLO BLUEBIRD
Cliff Friend (w & m)
Jerome H. Remick—New York
1926
Introduced by Art Landry and His Orchestra (Victor 20285). It was revived in 1952 by Teresa Brewer (Coral 60873).

## HELLO CENTRAL, GIVE ME HEAVEN
Charles K. Harris (w & m)
Charles K. Harris—Milwaukee
1901
A classic tearjerker and a contrast to the earliest telephone song, "Hello Ma Baby." This is Charles K. Harris at his weepiest. Byron Harlan had the hit recording (Columbia 230). Went over well with children's acts.

## HELLO CENTRAL, GIVE ME NO MAN'S LAND
Jean Schwartz (w: Sam Lewis and Joe Young)
Waterson, Berlin and Snyder—New York
1918
Al Jolson introduced and sang this to success. His recording made it a World War I favorite (Columbia A-2542).

## HELLO, DOLLY!
Jerry Herman (w & m)
Edwin H. Morris—New York
1963
**Show:** *Hello Dolly!*
Carol Channing sang it in the show. Jazz trumpeter/vocalist Louis Armstrong knocked the Beatles off their number 1 positions with his number 1 hit, which charted for nineteen weeks (Kapp 573). A 1969 film was made starring Barbra Streisand (20th Century Fox), in which Armstrong reprised the song.

## HELLO! MA BABY
Joe E. Howard and Ida Emerson
T. B. Harms—New York
1899

This syncopated early telephone song became a million-seller and a standard beloved of glee clubs. Revived in Howard biopic *I Wonder Who's Kissing Her Now* (20th Century Fox 1947).

## HELLO YOUNG LOVERS
Richard Rodgers
(w: Oscar Hammerstein)
Williamson Music—New York
1951
**Show:** *The King and I*
Gertrude Lawrence sang it in the show and recorded it (Decca 40210). Perry Como had a number 27 hit (RCA Victor 20-4112), and Paul Anka revived it in 1960 with a number 23 hit (ABC-Paramount 10132).

## HELP!
John Lennon and Paul McCartney
Maclen Music—New York
1965
**Film:** *Help!* (United Artists)
The Beatles had the number 1 hit, which charted for twelve weeks and sold more than one million copies (Capitol 5476). It was the title song of their second movie, which had been provisionally titled "Eight Arms to Hold You."

## HELP ME, RHONDA
Brian Wilson (w & m)
Sea of Tunes—Hawthorne, California
1965
Number 1 hit for the Beach Boys, holding the top position for two out of eleven weeks on the charts (Capitol 5395). A classic by the group, it was originally recorded in a slightly different arrangement featuring a fading-in-and-out vocal and a flute solo (released first as an album track). Unhappy with the result, Brian Wilson rearranged it, and the result was a major success.

## HERE COMES MY BALL AND CHAIN
J. Fred Coots (w: Lou Davis)
Spier and Coslow—New York
1929
The Coon-Sanders Orchestra had the hit recording (Victor 21812).

## HERE COMES MY DADDY NOW
Lewis F. Muir (w: L. Wolfe Gilbert)
F. A. Mills—New York
1912
This raggy song was a vaudeville favorite by Brown and Small. Arthur Collins and Byron Harlan made a hit recording (Victor 17315). It was revived in 1953 by Joe "Fingers" Carr and vocalist Barbara Barr (Capitol F-2463).

## HERE COMES THE SHOW BOAT
Maceo Pinkard (w: Billy Rose)
Shapiro, Bernstein—New York
1927
**Show:** *Africana*
Originally interpolated into an all-black revue, Vaughn DeLeath introduced it on radio and as a result had a hit recording (Edison 52104). It was then interpolated into the first film version of *Show Boat* (Universal, 1929).

## HESITATING BLUES
W. C. Handy
Pace and Handy Music—Memphis
1915
Introduced in vaudeville by the Imperial Quartette. Prince's Orchestra made the hit recording (Columbia A-5772). Has remained popular among blues and folk musicians.

## HEY! BABY
Margaret Cobb and Bruce Channel
Le Bill Music—Fort Worth, Tex.
1961
Number 1 pop-rock hit in 1962 for Bruce Channel, holding the top spot for three out of twelve weeks on the charts (Smash 1731). Originally released on the small Le Com label in 1961. An early rock classic.

## HEY JUDE
John Lennon and Paul McCartney
Maclen Music—New York
1968
The Beatles' most popular song in their illustrious career, and the best-selling single of the 1960s. It held the number 1 position for nine of the nineteen weeks

charted (Apple 2276). At the time of its release, it was the longest pop single ever made, clocking in at over six minutes. The record sold over six million copies. Originally written by Paul McCartney addressed to John Lennon's son, Julian; McCartney felt that "Jude" was easier to sing and more melifluous than "Jules."

## HEY, MR. BANJO
Freddy Morgan and Norman Malkin
Mills Music—New York
1955
The Sunnysiders were a pop-vocal quartet, half of whom wrote this number 12 hit, which charted for ten weeks (Kapp 113).

## HEY, TAXI!
Ivon DeBie (w & m)
Zodiac Music—New York
1956
Introduced on television and on disc by Ernie Kovacs with Leroy Holmes and His Tugboat Eight (MGM 12408). A classic novelty song.

## HIAWATHA
Neil Moret (w: James O'Dea)
Whitney-Warner Publishing Co.—Detroit
1903
Started the trend of Indian songs, although it was first published (1901) as an instrumental, which John Philip Sousa featured in concert. Harry MacDonough had the hit recording (Victor 2351).

## HIGH FEVER
Joe Sanders (w: Charlie Harrison)
Ted Browne Music—Chicago
1926
Introduced by the Coon-Sanders Orchestra, which had the hit recording (Victor 20461). It was also done by Doc Cook and His Dreamland Orchestra featuring Freddie Keppard (Columbia 813-D).

## HIGH HOPES
James Van Heusen (w: Sammy Cahn)
Barton Music—New York
1959
**Film:** *A Hole in the Head* (United Artists)

Academy Award winner for Best Song. Frank Sinatra, starring in the film, had the number 30 hit (Capitol 4214).

## HIGH NOON
Dimitri Tiomkin (w: Ned Washington)
Leo Feist—New York
1952
**Film:** *High Noon* (United Artists)
Academy Award winner for Best Song. Frankie Laine had the number 5 hit, which charted for nineteen weeks (Columbia 39770).

## HIGH SOCIETY
Porter Steele
Brooks and Denton—New York
1901
Originally a march, now a Dixieland favorite. Prince's Band had the 1911 hit recording (Columbia A-1038). King Oliver's Jazz Band helped make it a jazz standard (Okeh 4933) in 1923. Abe Lyman and His Orchestra revived it in 1932 (Brunswick 6325), and Jelly Roll Morton's New Orleans Jazzmen revived it again in 1939 (Bluebird B-10434).

## HIGHER LOVE
Steve Winwood and Will Jennings
F. S. Music
1986
Steve Winwood had the number 1 hit, which charted for fourteen weeks (Island 28710). It was the singer's first number 1, and signaled his comeback after a long period of inactivity.

## HINDUSTAN
Oliver Wallace and Harold Weeks
Forster Music—Chicago
1918
Introduced by Jack LaFollette in vaudeville. A favorite with bands as a result of Joseph C. Smith and His Orchestra's recording (Victor 18507). Revived by Ted Weems and His Orchestra, with whistling by Elmo Tanner, in the 1948 number 24 hit (Mercury 5139).

## HIT THE ROAD JACK
Percy Mayfield (w & m)

Tangerine Music—New York

1961

Number 1 hit for Ray Charles, holding that position for two out of eleven weeks on the charts (ABC-Paramount 10244). Also a number 1 R&B hit. Charles has performed the song for over four decades, and it remains one of his most popular numbers.

## HIT THE ROAD TO DREAMLAND

Harold Arlen (w: Johnny Mercer)

Famous Music—New York

1942

**Film:** *Star Spangled Rhythm* (Warner Bros.)

Mary Martin, Dick Powell, and the Golden Gate Quartet sang it in the film. Freddie Slack and His Orchestra, with vocal by the Mellowaires, had the number 16 hit (Capitol 126).

## HITCHY KOO

Lewis F. Muir and Maurice Abrahams

(w: L. Wolfe Gilbert)

F. A. Mills—New York

1912

Introduced in vaudeville by Al Jolson. The American Quartet had the hit recording (Victor 17196).

## HOLD ON

Carnie Wilson/Glen Ballard/Chynna Phillips

MCA Music

1990

Wilson Phillips, a pop-vocal trio composed of the off-spring of Brian Wilson of the Beach Boys and Michelle and John Phillips of the Mamas and The Papas, had this number 1 hit lasting eighteen weeks on the chart (SBK 07322). It sold over half a million copies.

## HOLD ON TO THE NIGHTS

Richard Marx (w & m)

Chi-Boy Music

1987

Pop-singer hunk Richard Marx had the number 1 hit in 1988, which charted for fourteen weeks (EMI-Manhattan 50106).

## HOLIDAY FOR STRINGS

David Rose (w: Sam Gallop)

Bregman, Vocco and Conn—New York

1943

Introduced on disc by the composer and His Orchestra (Victor 27853). It sold over a million copies. Spike Jones and His City Slickers followed it up in 1945 with a marvelous parody that sold nearly as many (RCA Victor 20-1733).

## HOME AGAIN BLUES

Irving Berlin and Harry Akst

Irving Berlin—New York

1921

Introduced by the Original Dixieland Jazz Band (Victor 18729). Aileen Stanley had the vocal hit (Victor 18760). It was the last song on which Irving Berlin collaborated.

## HONEST AND TRULY

Fred Rose (w & m)

Leo Feist—New York

1924

Introduced in vaudeville and on disc by the composer (Brunswick 3768). Popularized by Jean Goldkette and His Orchestra (Victor 19528) and Isham Jones and His Orchestra (Brunswick 2767).

## HONEY

Bobby Russell (w & m)

Russell-Cason Music—Nashville

1968

Bobby Goldsboro had the number 1 hit with this soft-rock tearjerker, which held its top position for five of the thirteen weeks charted (United Artists 50283). It sold over one million copies.

## HONEY BOY

Albert Von Tilzer (w: Jack Norworth)

York Music Co.—New York

1907

Lyricist Norworth introduced it in vaudeville, where it became famous. Sophie Tucker, then an up-and-comer, used it to good effect in her act. Billy Murray had the hit recording (Victor 16818).

## HONEY MAN

Al Piantadosi (w: Joe McCarthy)

Leo Feist—New York

1911

Introduced in vaudeville by Stella Tracey. Fine syncopated tune popularized on disc by Dolly Connolly (Columbia A-1102).

## HONEYSUCKLE ROSE

Thomas Waller (w: Andy Razaf)

Santly Bros.—New York

1929

**Show:** *Load of Coal*

Fats Waller didn't get to record his standard until 1935 (Victor 24826). Lena Horne sang it in the film *Thousands Cheer* (MGM, 1943). Ken Page and Nell Carter revived it in the 1978 Fats Waller Broadway revue *Ain't Misbehavin'*. It remains a favorite of jazz vocalists and instrumentalists.

## HONKY TONK WOMEN

Mick Jagger and Keith Richards

Gidwon Music—New York

1969

The Rolling Stones had this number 1 hit, which held its top position for four out of fourteen weeks charted and sold over one million copies (Rolling Stone 19100). The band reprised it in an acoustic version as "Country Honk" on their *Sticky Fingers* album (Rolling Stones 59100).

## HOOKED ON A FEELING

Mark James (w & m)

Press Music—Nashville

1968

B. J. Thomas had the number 5 hit, which charted for twelve weeks and sold over one million copies (Scepter 12230). The Swedish septet Blue Swede revived it in 1974 making it a number 1 hit, which charted for fourteen weeks (EMI 3627). Their version also sold over one million copies.

## HOORAY FOR HOLLYWOOD

Richard Whiting (w: Johnny Mercer)

Harms—New York

1938

**Film:** *Hollywood Hotel* (Warner Bros.)

Frances Langford, Johnny "Scat" Davis, and Benny Goodman and His Orchestra sang and played it in the film. It became Jack Benny's closing theme on his radio

and television shows. It has become a standard song about the entertainment industry.

## HORSE WITH NO NAME, A

Dewey Bunnell (w & m)

Kinney Music—London

1972

Pop-rock vocal group America had this number 1 hit, which charted for twelve weeks (Warner 7555). It sold over one million copies. Many felt that the group's lead vocalist was imitating Neil Young in his delivery, creating some confusion among listeners and fans.

## HORSES

Richard Whiting and Byron Gay

Leo Feist—New York

1926

Introduced in vaudeville by the Oriole Orchestra. George Olsen and His Music had the hit recording (Victor 19977) and the Six Jumping Jacks had the hit novelty version (Brunswick 3109).

## HOT LIPS

Henry Lange/Henry Busse/Lou Davis

Leo Feist—New York

1922

Originally came from Henry Lange's *Puss 'n Boots*. Paul Whiteman made it a gigantic hit, featuring Henry Busse on trumpet (Victor 18920). When Busse formed his own orchestra, it became his theme song in 1934 (Columbia 2937-D).

## HOT STUFF

Pete Bellotte/Harold Faltermeyer/Keith Forsey

Rick's Music

1979

Donna Summer had the number 1 hit, which charted for seventeen weeks (Casablanca 978). It sold over two million copies. A classic of the disco era.

## HOTEL CALIFORNIA

Don Felder/Don Henley/Glenn Frey

Long Run Music

1976, 1977

The Eagles had this number 1 hit, which charted for fifteen weeks (Asylum 45386). The song was among the last hits for the group, which disbanded shortly there-after. It is a classic song depicting 1970s-era Southern California ennui. It sold over one million copies.

## HOUND DOG
Mike Stoller (w: Jerry Leiber)
Elvis Presley Music—New York
1956
Originally recorded by "Big" Mama Thornton for an R&B hit. Elvis Presley had the number 1 pop hit, which stayed in that position for eleven of the twenty-three weeks charted and sold over six million copies (RCA Victor 47-6604). In a famous clip, he sang it to a sad-eyed beagle on Steve Allen's variety TV program. The song inspired numerous imitations, including "Bear Cat" by Rufus Thomas (Sun 181).

## HOUSE I LIVE IN, THE
Earl Robinson
(w: Lewis Allan)
Chappell and Co.—New York
1942
**Film:** *The House I Live In* (RKO)
The film was an Academy Award winner for Best Short. Frank Sinatra sang this song in the short and also had the number 22 hit in 1946 (Columbia 36886). Earl Robinson, one of the song's writers, would be famous for his "Ballad for Americans," a folk-inspired radio work that enjoyed great popularity in the late 1940s. Lewis Allan, another left-leaning writer, was responsible for Billie Holiday's hit "Strange Fruit."

## HOUSE OF THE RISING SUN, THE
Alan Price (w & m)
Al Gallico Music—New York
1964
The Animals had the number 1 hit, which charted for ten weeks (MGM 13264). It was revived in 1970 by Frijid Pink, who had a number 7 hit that charted for eleven weeks and sold over one million copies (Parrot 341). The song is a version of a traditional American blues of the same name, collected by John and Alan Lomax. Animals's keyboardist Alan Price took writer's credit, although he probably based their version on an earlier recording by Bob Dylan.

## HOW ABOUT YOU?
Burton Lane (w: Ralph Freed)
Leo Feist—New York
1941
**Film:** *Babes on Broadway* (MGM)
Judy Garland and Mickey Rooney sang it in the film. Tommy Dorsey and His Orchestra with vocal by Frank Sinatra, had the number 8 hit in 1942 (Victor 27749).

## HOW ARE THINGS IN GLOCCA MORRA?
Burton Lane (w: E.Y. Harburg)
Crawford Music—New York
1946
**Show:** *Finian's Rainbow*
Ella Logan sang it in the show. Buddy Clark had the number 6 hit, which charted for eight weeks (Columbia 37223).

## HOW ARE YOU GOING TO WET YOUR WHISTLE WHEN THE WHOLE DARN WORLD GOES DRY?
Percy Wenrich/Francis Byrne/Frank McIntyre
Leo Feist—New York
1919
Hit recording by Billy Murray (Victor 18537). A novelty hit written in reaction to prohibition.

## HOW COME YOU DO ME LIKE YOU DO?
Gene Austin and Roy Bergere
Stark and Cowan—New York
1924
Marion Harris, accompanied by Phil Ohman, had the hit vocal (Brunswick 2610). Rosa Henderson, accompanied by Fletcher Henderson, also had a fine version (Vocalion 14795). The Original Memphis Five had a hit instrumental (Perfect 14322). It was revived in 1954 by Bill Krenz (Coral 9-61248). It remains a standard among Dixieland and jug band revivalists.

## HOW COULD I BE BLUE?
Dan Wilson and Andy Razaf
Clarence Williams Music—New York
1926
Introduced in vaudeville by Roger Wolfe Kahn. James P. Johnson and publisher Clarence Williams made a

splendid duet recording (Columbia 14502-D), and the Savoy Bearcats had a great orchestral arrangement (Victor 20307).

## HOW COULD RED RIDING HOOD?
A. P. Randolph (w & m)
Jack Mills—New York
1925
Introduced by Rube Wolf in vaudeville. This fabulous novelty was recorded by the Six Jumping Jacks (Brunswick 3254), the Seven Little Polar Bears (Cameo 1058), and by the Yacht Club Boys (Brunswick 3270).

## HOW DEEP IS THE OCEAN?
Irving Berlin (w & m)
Irving Berlin—New York
1932
Guy Lombardo and His Royal Canadians had the number 4 hit (Brunswick 6399). Bing Crosby sang it in the film *Blue Skies* (Paramount, 1946), and Frank Sinatra sang it in the film *Meet Danny Wilson* (Universal, 1952).

## HOW DEEP IS YOUR LOVE?
Barry, Robin and Maurice Gibb
Stigwood Music
1977
**Film:** *Saturday Night Fever* (Paramount)
The Bee Gees had this number 1 hit, which charted for an incredible twenty-six weeks (RSO 882). It sold over one million copies.

## HOW HIGH THE MOON
Morgan Lewis (w: Nancy Hamilton)
Chappell—New York
1940
**Show:** *Two for the Show*
Alfred Drake and Frances Comstock sang it in the show. Benny Goodman and His Orchestra, with vocal by Helen Forrest, had a number 6 hit (Columbia 35391). Les Paul and Mary Ford revived it in 1951 and had the number 1 hit that charted for twenty-five weeks and sold over one million copies (Capitol 1451). It has become a jazz and nightclub favorite.

## HOW LONG HAS THIS BEEN GOING ON?
George and Ira Gershwin

New World Music—New York
1927
**Show:** *Funny Face*
It was composed for *Funny Face* but dropped. It was then put into *Rosalie* (1928), where it was introduced by Bobbie Arnst. It did make the film version *Funny Face* (Paramount, 1957), where it was sung by Audrey Hepburn.

## HOW MUCH IS THAT DOGGIE IN THE WINDOW?
Bob Merrill (w & m)
Santly-Joy—New York
1952
Patti Page had the number 1 hit in 1953, which charted for twenty weeks and sold over one million copies (Mercury 70070). Still a popular song, particularly among the kiddie set.

## HOW WILL I KNOW?
George Merrill/Shannon Rubicam/
Narada Walden
Irving Music
1985
Whitney Houston had seven number 1 hits during the 1980s. This was her second, and it stayed on the charts for sixteen weeks, the longest of all (Arista 9434). It sold over one million copies. Her mother, Cissy, a one-time backup singer for Aretha Franklin and many others as a member of the Soul Inspirations, provided vocal harmonies on this track.

## HOW YA GONNA KEEP 'EM DOWN ON THE FARM?
Walter Donaldson (w: Sam Lewis and Joe Young)
Waterson, Berlin and Snyder—New York
1919
Tremendous hit in vaudeville by Eddie Cantor, Sophie Tucker, and Nora Bayes, the latter also having a hit record (Columbia A-2687). Arthur Fields also helped popularize it on disc (Victor 18537). It was revived when Judy Garland sang it in the film *For Me and My Gal* (MGM, 1942). Eddie Cantor sang it in his biopic *The Eddie Cantor Story* (Warner Bros., 1953). Pee Wee Hunt and Joe "Fingers" Carr revived it yet again in 1956 in their *Pee Wee and Fingers* LP (Capitol T-783).

## HOW'D YOU LIKE TO SPOON WITH ME?

Jerome Kern (w: Edward Laska)

T. B. Harms—New York

1905

**Show:** *The Earl and the Girl*

The composer's first song hit, interpolated into the show and sung by Georgia Caine and Victor Morley. It stopped the show nightly, as six girls on swings accompanied the duet. Revived in the biopic *Till the Clouds Roll By* (MGM, 1946) by Angela Lansbury.

## HUSTLE, THE

Van McCoy

Warner-Tamerlane Music—New York

1975

Van McCoy had the number 1 hit, which charted for twelve weeks and sold more than one million copies (Avco 4653). This instrumental, with the vocal interjection of "Do the Hustle," was a landmark in the disco movement, and remains one of the records most closely associated with the 1970s dance craze.

## I AIN'T GONNA GIVE NOBODY NONE O' THIS JELLY ROLL

Clarence Williams (w: Spencer Williams)

Williams and Piron—New Orleans

1919

It wasn't until 1934 that the composer recorded this with His Orchestra (Vocalion 2805). It has been a favorite of jazz bands and is a fun tune to sing.

## I AIN'T GOT NOBODY

Spencer Williams (w: Dave Peyton)

Frank K. Root—Chicago

1916

Introduced in vaudeville by Bert Williams and also used by Sophie Tucker with great success. She revived it on disc in 1927 with Miff Mole's Molers (Okeh 40837). Marion Harris had the hit recordings, the first in 1917 (Victor 18133), then a remake in 1921 (Columbia A-3371). Bessie Smith made a heart rending recording in 1925 (Columbia 14095). The Coon-Sanders Original Nighthawks made a superb disc, with the leaders dueting the vocal in 1927 (Victor 20785). It was revived in the film *Paris Honeymoon* (Paramount, 1939). Louis Prima revived it as part of his duet "Just A Gigolo/I Ain't Got Nobody" (first issued on V-Disc in 1944); hard-rocking vocalist David Lee Roth copied the arrangement for a 1985 number 12 pop hit (Warner Bros. 29040).

## I AIN'T NEVER HAD NOBODY CRAZY OVER ME

Jimmie Durante/Johnny Stein/Jack Roth

Fred Fisher—New York

1923

A jazzy blues number successfully recorded by the Broadway Syncopators (Vocalion 14598).

## I AM WOMAN

Helen Reddy and Ray Burton

Buggerlugs Music—Los Angeles

1971, 1972

Helen Reddy got this number 1 hit from the film *Stand Up and Be Counted* (Columbia, 1971) which charted for fourteen weeks (Capitol 3350). It sold over one million copies. It became a theme song for the 1970s feminist movement.

## I CAN DREAM, CAN'T I?

Sammy Fain (w: Irving Kahal)

Marlo Music—New York

1937

**Show:** *Right This Way*

Tamara sang it in the show. Tommy Dorsey and His Orchestra had the number 5 hit in 1938, which charted for eleven weeks (Victor 25741). The Andrews Sisters revived it in 1950 with a number 1 hit that charted for twenty-five weeks and sold over one million copies (Decca 24705).

## I CAN SEE CLEARLY NOW

Johnny Nash (w & m)

Cayman Music Ltd.—New York

1972

Number 1 reggae hit for Johnny Nash, holding that spot for four out of fourteen weeks on the charts; also a number 1 adult-contemporary hit (Epic 10902). Nash was accompanied on the original recording by Bob Marley's Wailers. Covered in 1994 by Jimmy Cliff (Chaos/Columbia 77207) for a number 18 hit that charted for fourteen weeks.

## I CAN'T BELIEVE THAT YOU'RE IN LOVE WITH ME

Jimmy McHugh (w: Clarence Gaskill)

Mills Music—New York

1926

Introduced in vaudeville by the composer. Roger Wolfe Kahn and His Orchestra had the hit recording (Victor 20573). The Ames Brothers had the number 22 hit in 1953 (RCA Victor 20-5530). It was revived again as background music in the film *Thoroughly Modern Millie* (Universal, 1967).

## I CAN'T DO THE SUM

Victor Herbert (w: Glen MacDonough)

M. Witmark and Sons—New York

1903

**Show:** *Babes in Toyland*

Mabel Barrison and a children's chorus sang it in the show; Charlotte Henry and children's chorus sang it in the film (MGM, 1934).

## I CAN'T GET NEXT TO YOU

Barrett Strong and Norman Whitfield

Jobete Music—Detroit

1969

The Temptations had the number 1 hit, which charted for fifteen weeks and sold over two million copies (Gordy 7093).

## (I CAN'T GET NO) SATISFACTION

Mick Jagger

(w: Keith Richard)

Saturday Music—New York

1965

The Rolling Stones had the number 1 hit, which charted for twelve weeks and sold over one million copies (London 9766). The famous riff played by Keith Richard has become a defining sound in rock and roll; the slightly risqué lyrics (for the time) also made this song a sensation upon its introduction.

## I CAN'T GET STARTED WITH YOU

Vernon Duke (w: Ira Gershwin)

Chappell—New York

1936

**Show:** *Ziegfeld Follies of 1936*

Bob Hope and Eve Arden sang it in the show. Bunny Berigan and His Orchestra, with Bunny as vocalist and trumpet soloist, had the number 10 hit in 1938 (Victor 25728), and used it as his theme song.

## I CAN'T GET THE ONE I WANT

Lou Handman (w: Herman Ruby and Billy Rose)

Irving Berlin—New York

1924

A favorite with dance bands: Paul Whiteman (Victor 19381), Varsity Eight (Cameo 567), Vincent Lopez (Okeh 40152), Paul Specht (Columbia 160-D), Lanin's Arcadians (Perfect 14283), and Ray Miller (Brunswick 2643) all made fine arrangements.

## I CAN'T GIVE YOU ANYTHING BUT LOVE

Jimmy McHugh (w: Dorothy Fields)

Jack Mills—New York

1928

**Show:** *Lew Leslie's Blackbirds of 1928*

Introduced in the flop 1927 revue *Delmar's Revels* by Patsy Kelly, it was interpolated into *Lew Leslie's Blackbirds of 1928*, where Aida Ward made it a hit. Later during the run of the show, it was sung by Adelaide Hall. Cliff Edwards had the hit recording (Columbia 1471-D) at first, followed by several hundred recordings, including the Teddy Wilson hit with vocalist Billie Holiday (Brunswick 7781) in 1936 and Rose Murphy's version in 1948 (Majestic 1204). Jazzmen through the years have featured and recorded it, notably Louis Armstrong (Okeh 8669, 1929), Benny Goodman (Victor 25678, 1937), and Fats Waller (Bluebird 10573, 1939). It was also featured in the romantic comedy *Bringing Up Baby*, sung by Katharine Hepburn (MGM, 1938). Late in his life, Andy Razaf claimed that he and Fats Waller were the actual writers of the song.

## I CAN'T GO FOR THAT

Daryl Hall (w: Hall/Oates/Sara Allen)

Hot-Cha Music

1981

Daryl Hall and John Oates had the number 1 hit in 1982, which charted for seventeen weeks (RCA 12357). It sold over one million copies.

## I CAN'T HELP MYSELF
Brian and Eddie Holland and Lamont Dozier
Jobete Music—Detroit
1965
The Four Tops had this number 1 hit, which charted for thirteen weeks (Motown 1076). Also known as "Sugar Pie, Honey Bunch."

## I CAN'T STOP LOVING YOU
Don Gibson (w & m)
Acuff-Rose—Nashville
1958
Ray Charles had the number 1 hit in 1962, and it held that position for five of the fourteen weeks on the chart (ABC-Paramount 10330). It sold over one million copies and was his biggest hit. Charles was one of the first R&B stars to cover country songs, which have proven to be a durable part of his repertory.

## I COULD BE HAPPY WITH YOU
Sandy Wilson (w & m)
Chappell—New York
1954
**Show:** *The Boy Friend*
Julie Andrews and John Hewer sang it in the show.

## I COULD HAVE DANCED ALL NIGHT
Frederick Loewe
(w: Alan Jay Lerner)
Chappell—New York
1956
**Show:** *My Fair Lady*
Julie Andrews sang it in the show. Sylvia Syms had the number 20 hit (Decca 29903). Audrey Hepburn "sang" it in the movie (Warner Bros., 1964); but the actual vocals were by Marnie Nixon).

## I COVER THE WATERFRONT
John W. Green (w: Edward Heyman)
Harms—New York
1933
Eddie Duchin and His Orchestra had the number 3 hit, which charted for six weeks (Victor 24325).

## I CRIED FOR YOU
Gus Arnheim and Abe Lyman (w: Arthur Freed)

Sherman, Clay—San Francisco
1923
Abe Lyman and His Orchestra introduced it in vaudeville. The Collegians had a hit (Victor 19093), but it wasn't until 1939 that Glen Gray's Casa Loma Orchestra, with vocal by Kenny Sargent had a major number 6 hit, which charted for thirteen weeks (Decca 1684). Judy Garland sang it in the film *Babes In Arms* (MGM, 1939). It was also featured in the Billy Holiday biopic *Lady Sings the Blues* (Paramount, 1972).

## I DIDN'T KNOW WHAT TIME IT WAS
Richard Rodgers (w: Lorenz Hart)
Chappell—New York
1939
**Show:** *Too Many Girls*
Marcy Westcott and Richard Kollmar sang it in the show. Benny Goodman and His Orchestra had the number 6 hit, which charted for thirteen weeks (Columbia 35230). Trudi Erwin sang it in the film version of the show (RKO, 1940), and Frank Sinatra sang it in the film *Pal Joey* (Columbia, 1957)

## I DIDN'T RAISE MY BOY TO BE A SOLDIER
Al Piantadosi (w: Alfred Bryan)
Leo Feist—New York
1915
An early antiwar song introduced in vaudeville by Ed Morton. The Peerless Quartet had the hit (Columbia A-1697). Two years later, the United States entered World War I.

## I DON'T CARE
Harry O. Sutton (w: Jean Lenox)
Shapiro, Remick—New York
1905
**Show:** *The Sambo Girl*
Eva Tanguay made this song her own, and it remained identified with her throughout her life. Judy Garland sang it in the film *In the Good Old Summertime* (MGM, 1949), and Mitzi Gaynor sang it in biopic *The I Don't Care Girl* (20th Century Fox, 1953).

## I DON'T CARE IF THE SUN DON'T SHINE
Mack David (w & m)

Famous Music—New York

1949

Patti Page had the number 8 hit in 1950, that charted for nine weeks (Mercury 5396). Elvis Presley revived it in 1954 (Sun 210).

## I DON'T KNOW WHY (I JUST DO)

Fred E. Ahlert (w: Roy Turk)

Leo Feist—New York

1931

Introduced in vaudeville by Kate Smith, who also had a popular disc (Columbia 2539-D). Walter Brown and His Orchestra had a popular instrumental (Victor 23314). Revived in 1946 by the Andrews Sisters (Decca 18899), and instrumentally by Tommy Dorsey and His Orchestra (RCA Victor 20-1901), after it appeared in the film *Faithful in My Fashion* (MGM, 1946).

## I DON'T WANNA CRY

Mariah Carey and Narada Walden

Vision of Love Songs

1990, 1991

Mariah Carey had this number 1 hit, which charted for fourteen weeks (Columbia 73743).

## I DON'T WANT TO MISS A THING

Diane Warren (w & m)

Realsongs

1998

**Film:** *Armageddon* (Touchstone)

Hard rockers Aerosmith had the number 1 hit, which charted for fourteen weeks (Columbia 78952). It sold over half a million copies.

## I DON'T WANT TO SET THE WORLD ON FIRE

Eddie Seiler/Sol Marcus/Bennie Benjamin/ Eddie Durham

Cherio Music—New York

1941

Horace Heidt and His Orchestra, with vocalists Larry Cotton, Donna Wood, and the Don Juans, had the number 1 hit, which charted for thirteen weeks (Columbia 36295). The Ink Spots had the number 4 hit, which charted for ten weeks (Decca 3987).

## I FOUND A MILLION DOLLAR BABY

Harry Warren (w: Billy Rose and Mort Dixon)

Remick Music—New York

1931

**Show:** *Billy Rose's Crazy Quilt*

Ted Healy, Fanny Brice, Phil Baker, and Lew Brice sang it in the show. Fred Waring's Pennsylvanians had a number 1 hit, which charted for six weeks (Victor 22707). Barbra Streisand sang it in the Fanny Brice biopic *Funny Lady* (Columbia, 1975). This song has become closely associated with the Depression era.

## I FOUND A ROSE IN THE DEVIL'S GARDEN

Fred Fisher and Willie Raskin

Fred Fisher—New York

1921

Introduced by Harry Raderman's Jazz Orchestra on both Okeh 4276 and Gennett 4716. Pete Wendling made a fine piano roll arrangement (QRS 1411).

## I GAVE YOU UP JUST BEFORE YOU THREW ME DOWN

Fred Ahlert/Harry Ruby/ Bert Kalmar

Waterson, Berlin and Snyder—New York

1922

Paul Whiteman and His Orchestra (Victor 19003), Arthur Fields (Banner 1158), and a piano-banjo duet by Harry Reser and Phil Ohman (Columbia A-3785) were the hit recordings.

## I GET A KICK OUT OF YOU

Cole Porter (w & m)

Harms—New York

1934

**Show:** *Anything Goes*

Ethel Merman and William Gaxton sang it in the show. Merman had a number 12 hit in 1935 with the song, which charted for five weeks (Brunswick 7342). She sang it in the film (Paramount, 1936). Ginny Simms sang it in the Cole Porter biopic *Night and Day* (Warner Bros., 1946). Jeanmaire sang it and danced to it in the film *Anything Goes* (Paramount, 1956). It remains one of Cole Porter's best-loved songs, often revived by nightclub chanteuses.

## I GET AROUND

Brian Wilson (w & m)

Sea of Tunes—Hawthorne, California

1964

Number 1 hit for surf-harmony singers the Beach Boys, holding that spot for two out of thirteen weeks on the charts, and selling over a million copies (Capitol 5118). An ode to innocent teen pastimes.

## I GOT PLENTY O' NUTTIN'

George Gershwin (w: Ira Gershwin and DuBose Heyward)

Gershwin Publishing—New York

1935

**Show:** *Porgy and Bess*

Todd Duncan sang it in the show. Leo Reisman and His Orchestra had the number 5 hit (Brunswick 7562). In the film *Porgy and Bess* (Columbia, 1959) it was sung by Robert McFerrin (opera singer and father of jazz-pop vocalist Bobby McFerrin).

## I GOT RHYTHM

George and Ira Gershwin

New World Music—New York

1930

**Show:** *Girl Crazy*

Ethel Merman and the Foursome sang it in the show. Red Nichols and His Five Pennies had the number 5 hit (Brunswick 4957). The Happenings revived it with a number 3 hit in 1967, which charted for nine weeks (B.T. Puppy 527). This remains one of the Gerhswins' most often performed songs. The tricky rhythm of the piece itself makes it a standout for jazz performers.

## I GOT YOU BABE

Sonny Bono (w & m)

Cotillion Music—New York

1965

Sonny and Cher had the number 1 hit, which charted for ten weeks and sold over one million copies (Atco 6359). It was their first and only number 1, and remains the song most closely associated with the duo.

## I GOTTA RIGHT TO SING THE BLUES

Harold Arlen (w: Ted Koehler)

Harms—New York

1932

**Show:** *Earl Carroll's Vanities*: 10th edition

Lillian Shade sang it in the show. Cab Calloway had the number 17 hit in 1933 (Brunswick 6460). Jack Teagarden recorded it in 1941 (Okeh 6272), after which he used it as his band's theme song.

## I GUESS I'LL HAVE TO CHANGE MY PLAN

Arthur Schwartz (w: Howard Dietz)

Harms—New York

1929

**Show:** *The Little Show*

Introduced in the show by Clifton Webb. Its hit recording came in 1932 with Rudy Vallee and His Orchestra (Columbia 2700D). It was revived in the film *The Band Wagon* (MGM, 1953).

## I HADN'T ANYONE TILL YOU

Ray Noble (w & m)

ABC Music—New York

1938

Ray Noble and His Orchestra, with vocal by Tony Martin, had the number 4 hit, which charted for twelve weeks (Brunswick 8079).

## I HEARD IT THROUGH THE GRAPEVINE

Norman Whitfield and Barrett Strong

Jobete Music—Detroit

1966, 1967

Marvin Gaye had the number 1 hit in 1968, and it held that position for seven of the fifteen weeks it charted (Tamla 54176). It had been recorded a year earlier by Gladys Knight and the Pips, who achieved a number 2 hit (Soul 35039), but it is Gaye's version that is best remembered. The song is a Motown classic and was prominently featured in the soundtrack to the film *The Big Chill* (Orion, 1983).

## I HONESTLY LOVE YOU

Peter Allen and Jeff Barry

Irving Music

1973

Olivia Newton-John had a number 1 hit with this syrupy pop ballad in 1974, and it charted for ten weeks (MCA 40280). It sold over one million copies.

## I JUST CALLED TO SAY I LOVE YOU
Stevie Wonder (w & m)
Jobete Music
1984
**Film:** *The Woman in Red* (Orion)
Academy Award winner for Best Song. Stevie Wonder had this number 1 hit, which stayed on the Top 40 chart for fifteen weeks (Motown 1745). It sold over one million copies.

## I JUST WANT TO BE YOUR EVERYTHING
Barry Gibb (w & m)
Brothers Gibb
1977
Andy Gibb's first number 1 hit, which charted for twenty-three weeks (RSO 872). It sold over one million copies.

## I KNOW THAT YOU KNOW
Vincent Youmans (w: Anne Caldwell)
Harms—New York
1926
**Show:** *Oh, Please!*
Beatrice Lillie and Charles Purcell sang it in the show. Among the hit recordings were those by Arden-Ohman Orchestra (Brunswick 3410), the Ipana Troubadours (Columbia 829-D), and Nat Shilkret and His Orchestra (Victor 20437). Benny Goodman and His Orchestra revived it in 1936 with a number 14 hit (Victor 25290), as did the Rod Cless Quartet in 1944, featuring James P. Johnson at the piano (Black and White 30). Doris Day and Gordon MacRae sang it in the film *Tea For Two* (Warner Bros., 1950).

## I LEFT MY HEART IN SAN FRANCISCO
George Cory and Douglass Cross
General Music—New York
1954
Tony Bennett had the number 19 hit in 1962, which charted for ten weeks and became a standard (Columbia 42332). Bennett continues to perform it nearly every time he appears on stage.

## I LOVE A PIANO
Irving Berlin (w & m)
Irving Berlin—New York
1915
**Show:** *Stop! Look! Listen!*
Harry Fox sang it in the show. Billy Murray had the hit (Victor 17945). It was revived in the film *Easter Parade* by Fred Astaire and Judy Garland (MGM, 1948).

## I LOVE A RAINY NIGHT
Eddie Rabbitt/Even Stevens/David Malloy
DebDave Music—Nashville
1980
Eddie Rabbitt had the number 1 hit in 1981, which charted for eighteen weeks (Elektra 47066). It sold over one million copies.

## I LOVE, I LOVE, I LOVE MY WIFE, BUT OH, YOU KID
Harry Von Tilzer (w: Jimmy Lucas)
Harry Von Tilzer—New York
1909
Trying to capitalize on the Armstrong-Clark hit earlier in the year ("I Love My Wife, But Oh, You Kid"), it became a favorite in vaudeville. Arthur Collins had the hit recording (Columbia A-707).

## I LOVE IT
Harry Von Tilzer (w: E. Ray Goetz)
Harry Von Tilzer Music—New York
1910
Arthur Collins had the hit (Columbia A-940).

## I LOVE ME (I'M WILD ABOUT MYSELF)
Edwin J. Weber (w: Jack Hoins and Will Mahoney)
Broadway Music—New York
1923
**Show:** *Passing Show of 1922*
Introduced in the show by Willie Howard. Popularized by the International Novelty Orchestra (Victor 19121) and the Broadway Dance Orchestra (Edison 51222).

## I LOVE MY BABY
Harry Warren (w: Bud Green)
Shapiro, Bernstein—New York
1925

Introduced by Dolly Kramer in vaudeville, Jimmy Gallagher on radio, and by Waring's Pennsylvanians on record (Victor 19905).

## I LOVE MY WIFE, BUT, OH, YOU KID!
Harry Armstrong and Billy Clark
Victor Kremer—Chicago
1909
Introduced in vaudeville by the writers. Not only did the song become a hit, but the title a catch phrase for years to follow. Ada Jones and Billy Murray had the hit recording (Columbia A-1000). Inspired the follow-up song "I Love, I Love, I Love My Wife, But Oh, You Kid."

## I LOVE PARIS
Cole Porter (w & m)
Buxton Hill—New York
1953
**Show:** *Can-Can*
Lilo sang it in the show. Les Baxter and His Orchestra had the number 13 hit, which charted for ten weeks (Capitol 2479). A nightclub standard.

## I LOVE ROCK 'N ROLL
Alan Merrill and Jake Hooker
Rak Publishing
1975, 1982
Joan Jett and the Blackhearts made their recording debut with their only number 1 hit, and it held that position for seven out of sixteen weeks on the Top 40 chart (Boardwalk 135). It sold over two million copies.

## I LOVE TO GO SWIMMIN' WITH WIMMEN
Sigmund Romberg (w: Ballard MacDonald)
M. Witmark and Sons—New York
1921
**Show:** *Love Birds*
Pat Rooney sang it in the show. It's a cheerful song that flopped, and it took fifty years for it to be revived by Al Stricker and the St. Louis Ragtimers (Paseo 102).

## I LOVE YOU
Harry Archer (w: Harlan Thompson)
Leo Feist—New York
1923

**Show:** *Little Jessie James*
John Boles and Margaret Wilson sang it in the show. Paul Whiteman, who led the band in the show, had the hit recording (Victor 19151). Carl Fenton's Orchestra, with duo pianists Victor Arden and Phil Ohman, also made a fine recording (Brunswick 2487).

## I LOVE YOU SUNDAY
Charley Straight (w: Charles F. Byrne)
Forster Music—Chicago
1920
Introduced by Isham Jones and His Orchestra in vaudeville and recorded by them (Brunswick 5031). The Benson Orchestra closely followed with their version (Victor 18701).

## I LOVE YOU TRULY
Carrie Jacobs-Bond (w & m)
Carrie Jacobs-Bond and Son—Chicago
1906
Sung by various performers in vaudeville, inspiring enormous sheet music sales. Elsie Baker (who sang under the name Edna Brown) made a great-selling disc (Victor 17121) in 1912. It has remained a favorite, and can be heard in the classic *It's A Wonderful Life* (RKO, 1946) when the young, newly wed Donna Reed and Jimmy Stewart are serenaded with it on their wedding night.

## I MAY BE CRAZY, BUT I AIN'T NO FOOL
Alex Rogers (w & m)
Attucks Music—New York
1904
**Show:** *In Dahomey*
Introduced successfully by Bert Williams in the show, he later took it to vaudeville.

## I MEET HER IN THE MOONLIGHT BUT SHE KEEPS ME IN THE DARK
Pete Wendling (w: Alfred Bryan and Willie Raskin)
Henry Waterson—New York
1926
A charming song introduced by its composer (Cameo 1064) with vocalist Frances Sper.

## I MIGHT BE YOUR ONCE-IN-A-WHILE

Victor Herbert (w: Robert B. Smith)

T. B. Harms—New York

1919

**Show:** *Angel Face*

John E. Young and Ada Meade sang it in the show. Olive Kline had the hit vocal disc (Victor 45173), and Joseph C. Smith and His Orchestra had the hit instrumental (Victor 18629). Mary Martin sang it in the biopic *The Great Victor Herbert* (Paramount, 1939).

## I NEED SOME PETTIN'

Ted Fiorito and Robert King (w: Gus Kahn)

Shapiro, Bernstein—New York

1924

Introduced in vaudeville by Sam Heiman's Orchestra. The best recording is by the Wolverine Orchestra featuring Bix Beiderbecke (Gennett 20062).

## I NEED YOU NOW

Jimmie Crane and Al Jacobs

Miller Music—New York

1953

Eddie Fisher had the number 1 hit in 1954, which charted for twenty-four weeks and sold over one million copies (RCA Victor 20-5830).

## I NEVER KNEW

Irving Berlin (w: Elsie Janis)

Irving Berlin—New York

1919

Popularized on disc by Arthur Fields (Emerson 10130).

## I NEVER KNEW

Tom Pitts/Ray Egan/Roy Marsh

Leo Feist—New York

1920

Paul Whiteman and His Orchestra had the instrumental hit (Victor 18734). Henry Burr and John Meyer had the vocal hit (Okeh 4043).

## I NEVER KNEW

Ted Fiorito (w: Gus Kahn)

Irving Berlin—New York

1925

A favorite in vaudeville, introduced by Elinor Gail. The hit recordings were by Gene Austin (Victor 19864) and Roger Wolfe Kahn and His Orchestra (Victor 19845). Sam Donohue and His Orchestra revived it in 1947 with a number 2 hit recording (Capitol 405). It was revived again in 1955 by the Glenn Brown Trio (Coronet 500).

## I NEVER SEE MAGGIE ALONE

Everett Lynton (w: Harry Tilsley)

Irving Berlin—New York

1926

Popularized by Irving Aaronson and his Commanders (Victor 20473). It was revived in 1949 by Art Mooney and His Orchestra, with vocal by Tex Fletcher (MGM 10548).

## I ONLY HAVE EYES FOR YOU

Harry Warren (w: Al Dubin)

Remick Music—New York

1934

**Film:** *Dames* (Warner Bros.)

Dick Powell and Ruby Keeler sang it in the film. Ben Selvin and His Orchestra had the number 2 hit, which charted for eight weeks (Columbia 2966-D). The Flamingos turned it into a doo-wop standard in 1959 with a number 11 hit that charted for eleven weeks (End 1046). Art Garfunkel revived it again in 1975 with a number 18 hit, which charted for twelve weeks (Columbia 10190).

## I SAW MOMMY KISSING SANTA CLAUS

Tommie Connor (w & m)

Harman Music—New York

1952

Jimmy Boyd had the number 1 hit, which only charted for five weeks but sold over one million copies (Columbia 39871). Spike Jones and His City Slickers had the number 4 hit the same year, with vocal by George Rock (RCA Victor 20-5067). It remains a novelty Christmas favorite.

## I SCREAM—YOU SCREAM—WE ALL SCREAM FOR ICE CREAM

Robert King/Howard Johnson/Billy Moll

Shapiro, Bernstein—New York

1927

Hit recording by Fred Waring's Pennsylvanians (Victor 21099). The Six Jumping Jacks also helped popularize it (Brunswick 3782). It remains a popular song on the playground.

## I SECOND THAT EMOTION
William Robinson and Alfred Cleveland
Jobete Music—Detroit
1967
Smokey Robinson and the Miracles had the number 4 hit, which charted for twelve weeks (Tamla 54159).

## I SHOT THE SHERIFF
Bob Marley (w & m)
Cayman Music—New York
1974
Eric Clapton had this number 1 hit, which charted for ten weeks (RSO 409). It sold over one million copies. Clapton's version helped popularize reggae in Europe and the U.S.

## I SURRENDER, DEAR
Harry Barris (w: Gordon Clifford)
Freed and Powers—Hollywood
1931
Gus Arnheim and His Orchestra, with vocal by Bing Crosby, had the number 3 hit that charted for ten weeks (Victor 22618). It success led CBS to offer Crosby his first radio program.

## I SWEAR
Gary Baker and Frank Myers
Rick Hall Music
1993, 1994
Soul vocal group All-4-One had three hits in the Top Ten during the 1990s. This one charted at number 1, holding that position for eleven out of the twenty-six chart weeks (Blitzz/Atlantic 87243). It sold over one million copies.

## I THINK I LOVE YOU
Tony Romeo (w & m)
Screen Gems-Columbia Music—New York
1970
The Partridge Family was a "family" pop-rock group created for the TV show of the same name; it starred Shirley Jones and featured her real-life son, teen heart-throb David Cassidy. This song was their only number 1 hit, but it charted for sixteen weeks (Bell 910). It sold over one million copies.

## I WANNA BE LOVED
Johnny Green (w: Billy Rose and Edward Heyman)
Famous Music—New York
1933
Although it was used in a Billy Rose nightclub revue, nothing happened until the Andrews Sisters made it a number 1 hit in 1950 that charted for twenty-one weeks (Decca 27007). Ricky Nelson revived it in 1959 with a number 20 hit that charted for eight weeks (Imperial 5614).

## I WANNA BE LOVED BY YOU
Harry Ruby and Herbert Stothart (w: Bert Kalmar)
Harms—New York
1928
**Show:** *Good Boy*
Introduced in the show by Helen Kane, who also had a hit recording (Victor 21684). It became her trade-mark. She added the phrase "boop-boop-a-doop," which led to the creation of the animated movie char-acter, Betty Boop. Kane dubbed the singing for Debbie Reynolds in the film *Three Little Words* (MGM, 1950). In a completely different, sultry interpretation, Mari-lyn Monroe sang it in the film *Some Like It Hot* (United Artists, 1959). The song is closely associated with the Jazz Age and all its glories and excesses.

## I WANNA DANCE WITH SOMEBODY
George Merrill and Shannon Rubicam
Irving Music
1986
Pop and adult-contemporary hit in 1987 for singer Whitney Houston, holding the number 1 position for two out of fourteen weeks on the pop charts and sell-ing over a million copies (Arista 9598).

## I WANNA GO WHERE YOU GO, DO WHAT YOU DO, THEN I'LL BE HAPPY
Cliff Friend (w: Sidney Clare and Lew Brown)
Irving Berlin—New York
1925

Introduced in vaudeville by Harry Rappi. Whispering Jack Smith had the hit vocal recording (Victor 19856). Russo and Fiorito's Oriole Orchestra (Victor 19917) and the University Six (Harmony 71-H) also had nice versions.

## I WANNA SAY HELLO
Jimmy MacDonald (w: Jack Hoffman)
Johnstone-Montei—New York
1951
Ellen Sutton, with Sir Hubert Pimm, had the number 21 hit in 1952 (Kem 2710).

## I WANT A GIRL (JUST LIKE THE GIRL THAT MARRIED DEAR OLD DAD)
Harry Von Tilzer (w: Will Dixon)
Harry Von Tilzer Music—New York
1911
Walter Van Brunt and the American Quartet had the first hit recording of this perennial barbershop favorite (Victor 16962). Revived by Eddie Cantor, Joan Davis, George Murphy, and Constance Moore in the film *Show Business* (RKO, 1944).

## I WANT A LITTLE GIRL
Murray Mencher (w: Billy Moll)
Shapiro, Bernstein—New York
1930
Introduced in vaudeville by Lester Allen. McKinney's Cotton Pickers, with vocal by George Thomas, was the popular recording (Victor 23000).

## I WANT TO BE HAPPY
Vincent Youmans (w: Irving Caesar)
Harms—New York
1924
**Show:** *No, No, Nanette*
Charles Winninger and Louise Groody sang it in the show. Jan Garber and His Orchestra had the hit recording (Victor 19404). It was featured in both film versions (First National, 1930 and RKO, 1940). Susan Watson, Jack Gilford, and Ruby Keeler sang it in the show's 1971 Broadway revival.

## I WANT TO HOLD YOUR HAND
John Lennon and Paul McCartney

Duchess Music—New York
1963
The Beatles' first hit in the U.S. It held the number 1 position in 1964 for seven of the fourteen weeks charted, and sold over one million copies (Capitol 5112).

## I WANT TO KNOW WHAT LOVE IS
Mick Jones (w & m)
Somerset Songs
1984
Number 1 power-rock ballad for Foreigner in 1985, holding the top spot for two out of sixteen weeks on the charts and selling over one million copies (Atlantic 89596). Has become a standard often heard at weddings.

## I WANT TO LINGER
Henry I. Marshall (w: Stanley Murphy)
Jerome H. Remick and Co.—New York
1914
Introduced in vaudeville by Ed Miller and Helen Vincent. Prince's Orchestra had the hit recording (Columbia A-5662). Revived in 1947 by Pete Daily's Chicagoans (Capitol 15095).

## I WHISTLE A HAPPY TUNE
Richard Rodgers (w: Oscar Hammerstein)
Williamson Music—New York
1951
**Show:** *The King and I*
Gertrude Lawrence and Sandy Kennedy sang it in the show.

## I WILL ALWAYS LOVE YOU
Dolly Parton (w & m)
Velvet Apple Music
1973
Originally recorded by songwriter Parton, the song was a minor country hit on its first release in 1974 (RCA 0234). However, it became a monster pop hit when Whitney Houston sang it in the film *The Bodyguard* (Warner Bros., 1992). Houston's version maintained the number 1 position for fourteen out of the twenty-four weeks on the chart (Arista 12490). It sold over five million copies.

## I WILL FOLLOW HIM
J. W. Stole and Del Roma (w: Norman Gimbel and Arthur Altman)
Leeds Music—New York
1962, 1963
Little Peggy March had the number 1 hit, which charted for eleven weeks (RCA Victor 8139).

## I WILL SURVIVE
Dino Fegaris and Freddie Perren
Perren Vibes Music
1978
Gloria Gaynor had this number 1 hit, which charted for seventeen weeks (Polydor 14508). It sold over two million copies. The song remains a classic of the disco era, and has been revived by Chantay Savage in a number 24 hit in 1996 (RCA 64492). Gaynor continues to perform it in her stage act over two decades later.

## I WISH I COULD SHIMMY LIKE MY SISTER KATE
A.J. Piron (w & m)
Clarence Williams Music—New York
1922
Originally composed by Louis Armstrong, although he did not receive credit. This now standard jazz song helped the dance called the shimmy, as popularized by Gilda Gray and Bee Palmer. The Virginians had the hit recording (Victor 18965), but fine versions were also done by the Cotton Pickers (Brunswick 2338), Jazzbo's Carolina Serenaders (Cameo 269), and the Original Memphis Five (Perfect 14051). It is in traditional jazz and jug band repertoires.

## I WISH'T I WAS IN PEORIA
Harry Woods (w: Billy Rose and Mort Dixon)
Irving Berlin—New York
1925
A favorite in vaudeville. The song's hit recordings were by the Russo and Fiorito Orchestra (Victor 19924) and the Orchestra Chez Fysher (Brunswick 3030). It is a standard with Dixieland jazz bands.

## I WONDER WHAT'S BECOME OF JOE?
Maceo Pinkard (w: Roy Turk)

Shapiro, Bernstein—New York
1926
Introduced in vaudeville by the Five Locust Sisters. Great comedy disc by the Seven Little Polar Bears (Lincoln 2536). Francis J. Carter made a fine piano solo (Okeh 40693). Revived in 1947 by Rosy McHargue and His Band (Jump 28).

## I WONDER WHERE MY BABY IS TONIGHT
Walter Donaldson
(w: Gus Kahn)
Irving Berlin—New York
1925
A dance-band favorite, with Isham Jones (Brunswick 3022), Paul Whiteman (Victor 19902), and the Knickerbockers (Columbia 494-D) all recording it. Frank Banta also cut a marvelous piano solo (Victor 19839). Spike Jones and His City Slickers revived it in a 1950 release (Victor 20-3677).

## I WONDER WHERE MY SWEET SWEET DADDY'S GONE
Ray Stark (w: T.A. Hammed)
Irving Berlin—New York
1921
Introduced in vaudeville by Aileen Stanley. A marvelous piano roll version was done by Doris Goodwin (Arto 1420). Bennie Krueger and His Orchestra had the hit recording (Brunswick 2105).

## I WONDER WHERE MY SWEETIE CAN BE
Eubie Blake (w: Noble Sissle)
Jack Mills—New York
1925
One of the few songs not written for a show by this team. They made a fabulous disc in London, England (Edison Bell Winner 4371).

## I WONDER WHO'S KISSING HER NOW
Joseph E. Howard (w: Will M. Hough and Frank R. Adams)
Chas. K. Harris—New York
1909
**Show:** *The Prince of Tonight*

It was established in 1947 that Harold Orlob composed the tune as a work for hire. It was a flop in the show, but when Howard sang it in the show *Miss Nobody from Starland* (1910), it started its success leading to a sale of over three million copies of sheet music. Henry Burr had the hit recording (Columbia A-707). It was revived in the biopic *I Wonder Who's Kissing Her Now* (20th Century Fox, 1947) sung by Buddy Clark. Perry Como's 1939 recording with the Ted Weems Orchestra made it a number 2 hit in 1947, when it charted for seventeen weeks (Decca 25078). The song remains an evergreen standard.

## I WRITE THE SONGS

Bruce Johnston (w & m)

Sunbury Music—New York

1975

Barry Manilow had this number 1 hit, which charted for sixteen weeks (Arista 0157). It sold over one million copies. Johnston, a long-time member of the Beach Boys, wrote the song in honor of the band's legendary and reclusive leader Brian Wilson.

## ICE ICE BABY

David Bowie/Queen/Earthquake/Vanilla Ice

Queen Music

1990

Vanilla Ice, a white rapper really named Robert Van Winkle and born in Florida, scored with this number 1 hit, which charted for fifteen weeks (SBK 07335). It sold over one million copies, but was his sole number 1, and the Vanilla Ice fad faded by mid-1991.

## I'D DO ANYTHING FOR LOVE

Jim Steinman (w & m)

Edward B. Marks Music—New York

1993

Big-throated rock singer Meat Loaf, whose real name is Marvin Lee Aday, had his only number 1 hit with this romantic pop ballad, which stayed on the chart for eighteen weeks (MCA 54626). It sold over one million copies.

## I'D LEAVE MA HAPPY HOME FOR YOU

Harry Von Tilzer (w: Will A. Heelan)

Shapiro, Bernstein and Von Tilzer—New York

1899

Blanche Ring achieved her first success with this "coon song" at Tony Pastor's Music Hall. The chorus was the first to use "oo-oo," which became a rage, encouraging other writers to include it.

## I'D RATHER BE BLUE OVER YOU

Fred Fisher (w: Billy Rose)

Irving Berlin—New York

1928

**Film:** *My Man* (Warner Bros.)

Introduced in the film by Fanny Brice, who also had a hit recording (Victor 21815). The Yankee Ten Orchestra had a nice version (Oriole 1457). It was revived in the Brice biopic *Funny Girl* by Barbra Streisand (Columbia, 1968).

## IDA! SWEET AS APPLE CIDER

Eddie Munson (w: Eddie Leonard)

Jos. W. Stern—New York

1903

Minstrel Eddie Leonard introduced it as a member of the Primrose and West show. Eddie Cantor took it up and performed it throughout his career on Broadway, in the movies, on radio, and television. He sang it in his biopic *The Eddie Cantor Story* (Warner Bros., 1953). Red Nichols and His Five Pennies had a million-selling disc in 1927 (Brunswick 3626). Max Kortlander made an outstanding piano roll version (QRS 100770) in 1919.

## IDOLIZING

Sam Messenheimer/Irving Abrahamson/Ray West

West Coast Music—Los Angeles

1926

Introduced in vaudeville by Abe Lyman and His Famous California Orchestra. Hit recording by Jean Goldkette and His Orchestra featuring Bix Beiderbecke (Victor 20270).

## IF EVER I WOULD LEAVE YOU

Frederick Loewe (w: Alan Jay Lerner)

Chappell—New York

1960

**Show:** *Camelot*

Robert Goulet sang it in the show. Franco Nero sang it in the film version (Warner Bros., 1967).

## IF I COULD BE WITH YOU ONE HOUR TONIGHT

James P. Johnson (w: Henry Creamer)

Jerome H. Remick—New York

1926

Introduced in vaudeville by Ruth Etting. McKinney's Cotton Pickers had a number 1 hit (Victor 38118). The composer made a lovely piano solo in 1944 (Decca 24883). Danny Thomas revived it in the film *The Jazz Singer* (Warner Bros., 1953).

## IF I DIDN'T CARE

Jack Lawrence (w & m)

Chappell—New York

1939

The Ink Spots had the number 2 hit that charted for nine weeks and became their theme song and most famous recording (Decca 2286). It was revived by the Hilltoppers in 1954 with a number 17 hit (Dot 15220). The Platters revived it in 1961 with a number 30 hit (Mercury 71749). It is a classic vocal-harmony piece.

## IF I GIVE MY HEART TO YOU

Jimmie Crane/Al Jacobs/Jimmy Brewster (aka Milt Gabler)

Miller Music—New York

1954

Doris Day had the number 3 hit, which charted for seventeen weeks (Columbia 40300). Denise Lor, who was featured on television's *The Garry Moore Show* (CBS-TV), had a number 8 hit, which charted for twelve weeks (Major 27).

## IF I HAD A TALKING PICTURE OF YOU

Ray Henderson (w: B. G. DeSylva and Lew Brown)

DeSylva, Brown and Henderson—New York

1929

**Film:** *Sunny Side Up* (Fox)

Introduced in the film by Charles Farrell and Janet Gaynor. It was revived in the team's biopic *The Best Things in Life Are Free* (20th Century Fox, 1956).

## IF I HAD MY WAY

James Kendis (w: Lou Klein)

Maurice Richmond Music—New York

1914

Ethel Green sang it in vaudeville. The Peerless Quartet showed other barbershop singers how to do it (Victor 17534). It was revived by Gale Storm and Phil Regan in the film *Sunbonnet Sue* (Monogram, 1945).

## IF I KNEW YOU WERE COMIN' I'D 'AVE BAKED A CAKE

Al Hoffman/Bob Merrill/Clem Watts

Robert Music—New York

1950

Eileen Barton had the number 1 hit, which remained in that position for ten of the sixteen weeks charted and sold over one million copies (National 9103).

## IF I LOVED YOU

Richard Rodgers (w: Oscar Hammerstein)

Williamson Music—New York

1945

**Show:** *Carousel*

John Raitt and Jan Clayton sang it in the show. Perry Como had the number 3 hit, which charted for thirteen weeks (Victor 20-1676). Roy Hamilton revived it in 1954 with a number 26 hit (Epic 9047). Chad and Jeremy revived it in 1965, gaining a number 23 hit (World Artist 1041).

## IF I WERE A BELL

Frank Loesser (w & m)

Susan—New York

1950

**Show:** *Guys and Dolls*

Isabel Bigley sang it in the show. Frankie Laine had a number 30 hit (Mercury 5500).

## IF MONEY TALKS, IT AIN'T ON SPEAKING TERMS WITH ME

J. Fred Helf (w & m)

Sol Bloom—Chicago

1902

Great comic song introduced in vaudeville by the Doherty Sisters. Dialect comedian/singer Arthur Collins made an important disc (Victor 1631).

## IF MY FRIENDS COULD SEE ME NOW
Cy Coleman (w: Dorothy Fields)
Notable Music—New York
1965
**Show:** *Sweet Charity*
Gwen Verdon sang it in the show. Shirley MacLaine sang it in the film version (Universal, 1969). She continued to perform it in revues and nightclub acts through the 1990s.

## IF THIS ISN'T LOVE
Burton Lane (w: E. Y. Harburg)
Crawford Music—New York
1946
**Show:** *Finian's Rainbow*
Ella Logan and Donald Richards sang it in the show.

## IF YOU DON'T KNOW ME BY NOW
Kenny Gamble and Leon Huff
Assorted Music—Philadelphia
1972
Harold Melvin and the Bluenotes had the number 3 hit, which charted for eleven weeks and sold more than one million copies (Philadelphia I. 3520). It was revived by Simply Red, who had a number 1 hit in 1989 that charted for fifteen weeks (Elektra 69297). It sold more than half a million copies. A wonderful, soulful ballad.

## IF YOU HAD MY LOVE
Rodney and Fred Jerkins/LaShawn Daniels/
Cory Rooney
EMI Blackwood Music
1999
Sultry actress/singer Jennifer Lopez had the number 1 hit, which held that position for five out of twenty weeks on the chart (Epic/Work 79163). It sold over one million copies.

## IF YOU KNEW SUSIE
Bud DeSylva (w & m)
Shapiro, Bernstein—New York
1925
**Show:** *Big Boy*
Introduced in the show by Al Jolson, who didn't like it and turned it over to Eddie Cantor. Cantor's recording

was a hit (Columbia 364-D), and he featured it in his act throughout his life. He sang it in his biopic *The Eddie Cantor Story* (Warner Bros., 1953).

## IF YOU LEAVE ME NOW
Peter Cetera (w & m)
Polish Prince Music
1976
Chicago had this number 1 hit on the chart for seventeen weeks (Columbia 10390). It sold over one million copies.

## IF YOU SHEIK ON YOUR MAMA, YOUR MAMMA'S GONNA SHEBA ON YOU
Chris Smith (w & m)
Dixon Lane Music—Chicago
1924
Comic novelty song, a favorite in vaudeville, revived in 1977 by the New Leviathan Oriental Foxtrot Orchestra on their LP *Old King Tut* (Camel Race Records).

## IF YOU TALK IN YOUR SLEEP, DON'T MENTION MY NAME
Nat D. Ayler (w: A. Seymour Brown)
Jerome H. Remick—New York
1911
Introduced in vaudeville by Alma Youlin. Billy Murray made a hit of this comic song (Victor 17025).

## I'LL BE A FRIEND WITH PLEASURE
Maceo Pinkard (w & m)
Mills Music—New York
1930
Introduced in vaudeville by Bernie Cummins and his Hotel New Yorker Orchestra. The hit recording was by Bix Beiderbecke and His Orchestra (Victor 23008).

## I'LL BE MISSING YOU
Sting (w & m)
Reggatta Music
1997
Puff Daddy and Faith Evans teamed up for this tribute to the Notorious B.I.G. It remained number 1 for eleven out of twenty-nine weeks on the charts (Bad Boy 79097) and sold over four million copies.

## I'LL BE SEEING YOU

Sammy Fain (w: Irving Kahal)

Williamson Music—New York

1938

**Show:** *Right This Way*

Tamara sang it in the show. Bing Crosby had the number 1 hit in 1944 that charted for twenty-four weeks (Decca 18595).

## I'LL BE THERE

Bob West/Hal Davis/Willie Hutch/Berry Gordy

Jobete Music—Detroit

1970

The Jackson five had the original number 1 hit, which held this position for five of the sixteen weeks it charted (Motown 1171). Mariah Carey revived it in 1992, and her version reached the number 1 position for two of its fourteen weeks on the chart (Columbia 74330).

## I'LL BE WITH YOU IN APPLE BLOSSOM TIME

Albert Von Tilzer (w: Neville Fleeson)

Broadway Music—New York

1920

Introduced in vaudeville by Nora Bayes, it has been a perennial standard, with Charles Harrison first making a hit recording (Victor 18693), followed by the Andrews Sisters number 5 1941 disc (Decca 3622), and Tab Hunter's 1959 version (Warner Bros. 5032).

## I'LL BUILD A STAIRWAY TO PARADISE

George Gershwin (w: Bud DeSylva and

Arthur Francis)

Harms—New York

1922

**Show:** *George White's Scandals*: 4th Edition

Introduced in the show by Winnie Lightner. Selvin's Dance Orchestra had a hit recording (Vocalion 14434). It was revived by Georges Guetary in the film *An American in Paris* (MGM, 1951).

## I'LL GET BY

Fred Ahlert (w: Roy Turk)

Irving Berlin—New York

1928

A standard that in its day sold over one million copies of sheet music. Ruth Etting had the first hit recording (Columbia 1733-D). Irene Dunne sang it in the film *A Guy Named Joe* (MGM, 1943). It became a hit all over again when Harry James and His Orchestra, with vocal by Dick Haymes, released their version in 1944, reaching number 1 (Columbia 36698). It was revived again by June Haver in the film of the same name (20th Century Fox, 1950). Judy Garland sang it in the film *A Star Is Born* (Warner Bros., 1954).

## I'LL KNOW

Frank Loesser (w & m)

Susan—New York

1950

**Show:** *Guys and Dolls*

Isabel Bigley and Robert Alda sang it in the show.

## I'LL MAKE LOVE TO YOU

Babyface (w & m)

Sony Songs I

1994

The popular soul vocal group Boyz II Men had this phenomenal hit, which charted number 1 for fourteen of the thirty-one weeks listed on the Top 40 (Motown 2257). It sold over one million copies.

## I'LL NEVER BE THE SAME

Matt Malneck and Frank Signorelli (w: Gus Kahn)

Robbins Music—New York

1932

Introduced in vaudeville by Isham Jones and His Orchestra. Guy Lombardo and His Orchestra had the number 8 hit instrumental disc (Brunswick 6350).

## I'LL NEVER FALL IN LOVE AGAIN

Burt Bacharach (w: Hal David)

Blue Seas Music

1968, 1969

A number 6 pop/number 1 adult-contemporary song for Dionne Warwick in 1970 (Scepter 12273), charting for ten weeks. Noteworthy for its somewhat cynical lyrics.

## I'LL NEVER SMILE AGAIN

Ruth Lowe (w & m)

Sun Music—New York

1939

Tommy Dorsey and His Orchestra, with vocals by Frank Sinatra and the Pied Pipers, had a number 1 hit in 1940, holding this position for twelve of the twenty weeks charted and selling over one million copies (Victor 26628). The Platters revived it in doo-wop style in 1961 with the number 25 hit (Mercury 71847).

## I'LL REMEMBER (IN THE STILL OF THE NITE)

Fredericke Parris (w & m)

Angel Music

1956

Number 3 R&B hit and number 24 pop hit for the Five Satins that helped define the doo-wop sound (Standard 200/Ember 1005). Parris wrote the song and recorded it in a church basement with the group while he was on leave from the Army. The song "hit" while he was still in service, so the group enlisted a new lead singer, Bill Baker, to tour and record a follow-up. The spelling of "Night" was changed to "Nite" to avoid confusion with the Cole Porter song; the song's original title was "I'll Remember." The Satins' original recording reentered the pop charts in 1961, and helped launch a mini doo-wop revival. Boyz II Men revived it for a number 3 pop hit in 1992, charting for seventeen weeks and selling over a million copies (Motown 2193). Their version featured in the TV biopic *The Jacksons: An American Dream*.

## I'LL SAY SHE DOES

Bud DeSylva/Gus Kahn/Al Jolson

Jerome H. Remick—New York

1918

**Show:** *Sinbad*

Al Jolson sang it in the show, and he also had a hit recording (Columbia A-2746).

## I'LL SEE YOU AGAIN

Noel Coward (w & m)

Harms—New York

1929

**Show:** *Bitter Sweet*

Evelyn Laye and Gerald Nodin sang it in the show. Leo Reisman and His Orchestra had the hit recording (Vic-

tor 22246). Jeanette MacDonald and Nelson Eddy sang it in the film version (MGM, 1940).

## I'LL SEE YOU IN C-U-B-A

Irving Berlin (w & m)

Irving Berlin—New York

1920

**Show:** *Greenwich Village Follies of 1919*

Ted Lewis and His Band sang and played it in the show and also had a hit recording (Columbia A-2927). Vocalist Billy Murray covered it that same year for a hit (Victor 18652). Bing Crosby and Olga San Juan sang it in the film *Blue Skies* (Paramount, 1946).

## I'LL SEE YOU IN MY DREAMS

Isham Jones (w: Gus Kahn)

Leo Feist—New York

1924

One of the great standards from bandleader Isham Jones, who made a hit recording conducting the Ray Miller Orchestra (Brunswick 2788). Doris Day revived it in the film of the same name (Warner Bros., 1951).

## I'LL WALK ALONE

Jule Styne (w: Sammy Cahn)

Mayfair Music—New York

1944

**Film:** *Follow the Boys* (Universal)

Dinah Shore sang it in the film and also had the number 1 hit, which charted for twenty-five weeks (Victor 20-1586). Don Cornell revived it in 1952 with a number 5 hit, which charted for nineteen weeks (Coral 60659).

## I'M A BELIEVER

Neil Diamond (w & m)

Screen Gems-Columbia Music—New York

1966

The Monkees were formed for a television show that aired from 1966 to 1968 to cash in on the success of the Beatles and their films. This was their second number 1 hit, holding that position for seven of the thirteen weeks that it charted and selling over one million copies (Colgems 1002).

## I'M A JONAH MAN

Alex Rogers (w & m)

M. Witmark and Sons—New York

1903

**Show:** *In Dahomey*

Bert Williams had a hit when he introduced it in the show. It helped create his hard-luck stage persona.

## I'M A LITTLE BLACKBIRD LOOKING FOR A BLUEBIRD

George Meyer and Arthur Johnston

(w: Grant Clark and Roy Turk)

Irving Berlin—New York

1924

**Show:** *Dixie to Broadway*

Introduced in the show by Florence Mills. The hit recording was by Eva Taylor with Clarence Williams' Blue Five (Okeh 40260).

## I'M ALABAMA BOUND

Robert Hoffman (w: John J. Puderer)

Jerome H. Remick—New York

1910

Introduced in vaudeville by the Rag Trio. Popularized on disc by Prince's Orchestra (Columbia A-901).

## I'M ALL BOUND ROUND WITH THE MASON DIXON LINE

Jean Schwartz (w: Sam Lewis and Joe Young)

Waterson, Berlin and Snyder—New York

1917

Hit recording by Al Jolson (Columbia A-2478). Revived in 1936 by Jimmy McPartland's Squirrels (Decca 18441).

## I'M ALL BROKEN UP OVER YOU

Joe Murphy and Carl Hoeffle (w: Joe Burke and Lou Herscher)

Leo Feist—New York

1924

One of the great syncopated fox-trots, Ted Weems and His Orchestra had the hit recording (Victor 19286).

## I'M ALWAYS CHASING RAINBOWS

Harry Carroll (w: Joseph McCarthy)

McCarthy and Fisher—New York

1918

**Show:** *Oh, Look!*

Harry Fox sang it in the show. It would be more proper to credit Harry Carroll with adapting this melody from Chopin's Fantasy Impromptu in C-sharp minor. It sold over one million copies of sheet music. Charles Harrison had the hit on disc (Victor 18496). It was revived in the biopic *The Dolly Sisters*, where it was sung by John Payne (20th Century Fox, 1945). Perry Como had the number 5 hit in 1946, which charted for eight weeks and sold over one million copies (Victor 20-1788).

## I'M CERTAINLY LIVING A RAGTIME LIFE

Robert S. Roberts (w: Gene Jefferson)

Sol Bloom—Chicago

1900

Gene Jefferson was the pseudonym of lyricist Raymond A. Browne. This became a vaudeville favorite because of Fannie Midgley, who performed it often to great acclaim. Max Morath revived it in his stage show and record album, *A Program of Waltzes, Shouts, Novelties, Rags, Blues, Ballads and Stomps* (Epic LN-24066) in 1963.

## I'M COMING VIRGINIA

Donald Heywood (w: Will Marion Cook)

Robbins-Engel—New York

1927

**Show:** *Miss Calico*

Introduced in the show (later to be titled *Africana*) by Ethel Waters, who also had the hit vocal recording (Columbia 14170). Paul Whiteman with the Rhythm Boys also had a hit (Victor 20751). The jazz favorite was by Frankie Trumbauer and His Orchestra, featuring cornetist Bix Beiderbecke (Okeh 40843). The Original Indiana Five (Harmony 501-H) also had a fine version. Revived in 1937 by Teddy Wilson and His Orchestra (Brunswick 7893). It remains a Dixieland jazz standard.

## I'M CRAZY 'BOUT MY BABY

Thomas Waller (w: Alexander Hill)

Joe Davis—New York

1931

Fats Waller made this piano solo with his vocal (Columbia 14593-D). He joined the Ted Lewis Band for another hit recording (Columbia 2428-D).

## I'M CROONIN' A TUNE ABOUT JUNE

J. Fred Coots (w: Lou Davis)

Walter Donaldson—New York

1929

A neat spoof about love; Noble Sissle and His Orchestra had a hit in England (HMV B-5731). It was revived in 1976 by Gary Lawrence and his Sizzling Syncopators (Blue Goose 2020).

## I'M EASY

Keith Carradine (w & m)

ABC Music—Los Angeles

1975

**Film:** *Nashville* (Paramount)

Academy Award winner for Best Song. Keith Carradine starred in the film as well as had the number 17 hit, which charted for twelve weeks (ABC 12117). Carradine portrayed a country-singing lothario, and wrote this song about his character at the request of the film's director, Robert Altman.

## I'M FALLING IN LOVE WITH SOMEONE

Victor Herbert (w: Rida Johnson Young)

M. Witmark and Sons—New York

1910

**Show:** *Naughty Marietta*

Orville Harrold sang it in the show. Nelson Eddy sang it in the film version (MGM, 1935) as well as scoring a number 4 hit with his recording (Victor 4280). Allan Jones sang it in the biopic *The Great Victor Herbert* (Paramount, 1939).

## I'M FOREVER BLOWING BUBBLES

Jaan Kenbrovin and John William Kellette

Jerome H. Remick—New York

1919

The joint composer/lyric credits were derived by combining the names of the song's composers, James Kendis, James Brockman, and Nat Vincent. June Caprice sang it in the *Passing Show of 1918*. It sold over two-and-a-half million copies of sheet music. Ben Selvin and His Orchestra had the hit recording, selling over half a million copies (Victor 18603). Jack Smith revived it in the film *On Moonlight Bay* (Warner Bros., 1951).

## I'M GETTING SENTIMENTAL OVER YOU

George Bassman (w: Ned Washington)

Mills Music—New York

1932

Tommy Dorsey and His Orchestra had the number 8 hit in 1936, and it became his band's theme song (Victor 25236).

## I'M GOIN' AWAY JUST TO WEAR YOU OFF MY MIND

Lloyd Smith/Clarence Johnson/Warren Smith

Original Home of Jazz—Chicago

1922

Introduced on record by King Oliver and His Creole Jazz Band (Gennett 5134). It was also given a great arrangement by the Original Memphis Five (Paramount 20142). Clarence Johnson made a splendid version on piano roll (QRS 2243).

## I'M GOIN' TO LIVE ANYHOW, TILL I DIE

Shepard N. Edmonds (w & m)

Jos. W. Stern—New York

1901

Introduced by Eddie Leonard, star of the Primrose and West Minstrels. It is one of the very few songs that tells of the hypocrisy of do-gooders. A wonderfully syncopated number, which the composer claimed sold over a million copies in sheet music. Covered as "I'm Goin' to Live It High, Till I Die" by Charlie Poole and His North Carolina Ramblers.

## I'M GOIN' TO SETTLE DOWN OUTSIDE OF LONDON TOWN

James V. Monaco (w: Joe McCarthy)

McCarthy and Fisher—New York

1919

Popularized on disc by Billy Murray and the Peerless Quartet (Columbia A-2702).

## I'M GOING TO DO WHAT I PLEASE

Ted Snyder (w: Alfred Bryan)

Ted Snyder—New York

1909

Introduced in vaudeville by Sophie Tucker. Popularized on disc by Stella Tobin (Columbia A-737).

## I'M GONNA CHARLESTON BACK TO CHARLESTON
Lou Handman (w: Roy Turk)
Jerome H. Remick—New York
1925
A great tune for a Charleston as recorded by the Missouri Jazz Band (Banner 1644) and Lou Gold and His Orchestra (Perfect 14476).

## I'M GONNA MAKE YOU LOVE ME
Jerry Ross/Ken Gamble/Jerry Williams
Act Three Music—New York
1966
Diana Ross and the Supremes combined with the Temptations to have this number 2 hit in 1969, which charted for twelve weeks and sold over two million copies (Motown 1137).

## I'M GONNA MEET MY SWEETIE NOW
Jesse Greer (w: Benny Davis)
Jerome H. Remick—New York
1927
One of the great songs of the 1920s. Jane Green had a hit recording (Victor 20509) as did Jean Goldkette and His Orchestra (Victor 20675).

## I'M GONNA SIT RIGHT DOWN AND WRITE MYSELF A LETTER
Fred Ahlert (w: Joe Young)
Crawford Music—New York
1935
Fats Waller and His Rhythm, with Fats as vocalist, made the most famous recording, which charted at number 5 (Victor 25044). Billy Williams revived it in 1957 when he had a number 3 hit, which charted for eighteen weeks and sold over one million copies (Coral 61830).

## I'M IN LOVE AGAIN
Cole Porter (w & m)
DeSylva, Brown and Henderson—New York
1925
**Show:** *Greenwich Village Follies*: 6th edition
Introduced in the show by the Dolly Sisters. Plugged in vaudeville by Ben Bernie and His Orchestra. Featured in the Porter biopic *Night and Day* (Warner Bros.,

1946). Revived again in 1951 by April Stevens with a number 6 hit recording (RCA Victor 20-4148).

## I'M IN LOVE AGAIN
Antoine Domino and Dave Bartholomew
Reeve Music—Hollywood
1956
Fats Domino had the number 3 hit, which charted for eighteen weeks and sold over one million copies (Imperial 5386).

## I'M IN THE MOOD FOR LOVE
Jimmy McHugh (w: Ted Koehler)
Robbins Music—New York
1935
**Film:** *Every Night at Eight* (Paramount)
Frances Langford sang it in the film and had a number 15 hit (Brunswick 7513). Little Jack Little and His Orchestra had the number 1 hit, which charted for fourteen weeks (Columbia 3069). Billy Eckstine revived it in 1946 with a number 12 hit (National 9016). The Chimes revived it again in 1961 with a number 38 hit (Tag 445). Spike Jones did a hilarious satire, "I'm in the Nude for Love," in 1954 (RCA Victor 20-5742).

## I'M JUST WILD ABOUT ANIMAL CRACKERS
Harry Link/Sam Coslow/Fred Rich
Henry Waterson—New York
1926
Introduced on records by Irving Aaronson and His Orchestra (Victor 20094). The Six Jumping Jacks also had a comic hit (Brunswick 3216). Duke Ellington and His Washingtonians made a fine version (Gennett 3342).

## I'M JUST WILD ABOUT HARRY
Eubie Blake (w: Noble Sissle)
M. Witmark and Sons—New York
1921
**Show:** *Shuffle Along*
Lottie Gee sang it in the show. It was originally composed as a waltz, according to Eubie Blake, but changed into a more upbeat lovesong. Paul Whiteman and His Orchestra had a hit recording (Victor 18938), as did Bennie Krueger and His Orchestra (Brunswick

2272). Eubie Blake conducted his theater orchestra as well as played piano in his splendid arrangement (Victor 18797). Alice Faye and Louis Prima's Band sang it in the film *Rose of Washington Square* (20th Century Fox, 1939), and Al Jolson sang it in the film *Jolson Sings Again* (Columbia, 1949). In 1948, candidate Harry S. Truman revived it as his campaign song, and it remained closely associated with him for the rest of his life.

## I'M LOOKING OVER A FOUR LEAF CLOVER
Harry Woods (w: Mort Dixon)
Jerome H. Remick—New York
1927
A phenomenal hit when recorded by Jean Goldkette and His Orchestra (Victor 20466) in 1927, it became another million-seller when Detroit bandleader Art Mooney made it a number 1 hit twenty-one years later in 1948 (MGM, 10119). Mooney's recording featured the banjo of Paul Whiteman's original banjoist, Mike Pingatore. His heavy-strumming style became a model for all Dixieland banjoists. The song remains popular among scout troups and campers everywhere.

## I'M MORE THAN SATISFIED
Thomas Waller (w: Ray Klages)
Robbins Music—New York
1927
Introduced in vaudeville by Eddie Peabody. Popularized on disc by Guy Lombardo and His Orchestra (Columbia 1451-D).

## I'M NOBODY'S BABY
Milton Ager/Benny Davis/Lester Santly
Leo Feist—New York
1921
A million-seller in sheet music and a favorite with female singers in vaudeville. Hit recordings were by Marion Harris (Columbia A-3433) and Aileen Stanley (Vocalion 14172). Judy Garland revived it in the film *Andy Hardy Meets Debutante* (MGM, 1940), and had a number 3 hit recording (Decca 3174).

## I'M SITTING ON TOP OF THE WORLD
Ray Henderson (w: Sam Lewis and Joe Young)

Shapiro, Bernstein—New York
1925
Al Jolson had a hit recording (Brunswick 3014). The orchestras of Isham Jones (Brunswick 3022), Roger Wolfe Kahn (Victor 19845), and Sam Lanin (Banner 1644) had great arrangements. It has become a standard.

## I'M SORRY I MADE YOU CRY
N. J. Clesi (w & m)
Leo Feist—New York
1918
June Elvidge and John Bowers sang it in vaudeville. Henry Burr had the hit (Victor 18462). Alice Faye sang it in the film *Rose of Washington Square* (20th Century Fox, 1939). Betty Hutton revived it in the film *Somebody Loves Me* (Paramount, 1952).

## I'M TELLING YOU NOW
Freddie Garrity and Mitch Murray
Miller Music—New York
1963
British invasion band Freddie and the Dreamers had the number 1 hit in 1965, and it charted for eight weeks (Tower 125).

## I'M THROUGH (SHEDDING TEARS OVER YOU)
Edwin J. Weber (w: Karyl Norman)
Jerome H. Remick—New York
1922
Introduced in vaudeville by female impersonator Karyl Norman. Guyon's Paradise Orchestra (Okeh 4737) and the Benson Orchestra (Victor 18994) had fine versions.

## I'M TOO SEXY
Fred Fairbrass/Richard Fairbrass/Rob Manzoli
Hit and Run Music
1991
Number 1 hit in 1992 for British trio R*S*F (Right Said Fred), which held the top spot for three out of seventeen chart weeks, and sold over a million copies (Charisma 98671). Used as an advertising theme on Revlon commercials in the mid-to-late 1990s.

## I'M WALKIN'
Antoine Domino and Dave Bartholomew

Reeve Music—Hollywood

1957

Fats Domino had the original number 4 hit, which charted for fourteen weeks and sold over one million copies (Imperial 5428). Ricky Nelson quickly released his cover version—his second single release—which also reached number 4 and charted for fifteen weeks (Verve 10047).

## I'M WALKING BEHIND YOU
Billy Reid (w & m)

Leeds Music—New York

1953

Eddie Fisher had the number 1 hit, which charted for twenty-five weeks and sold over one million copies (RCA Victor 20-5293).

## I'M YOUR ANGEL
R. Kelly (w & m)

Zomba Songs

1998

R. Kelly and Celine Dion combined to make this a number 1 hit for six out of its fifteen weeks on the Top 40 chart (Jive 42557). It sold over one million copies.

## IMAGINE
John Lennon & Yoko Ono

Lenono Music

1971

One of Lennon's best-loved solo recordings, although it only reached number 3 on the charts (Apple 1840). Lennon based the lyrics on Ono's poetry collected in the book *Grapefruit*, originally published in 1964. The piece was widely played at the time of Lennon's death and also on the anniversaries of his shooting.

## IMPOSSIBLE DREAM, THE
Joe Darion and Mitch Leigh

Sam Fox Publications—New York

1965

**Show:** *Man Of La Mancha*

Richard Kiley sang this showstopping ballad in the show. Jack Jones had the number 35 hit (Kapp 755).

## IN A LITTLE SPANISH TOWN
Mabel Wayne (w: Sam Lewis and Joe Young)

Leo Feist—New York

1926

Introduced in vaudeville by Vincent Lopez. Paul Whiteman and His Orchestra had the hit record (Victor 20266), with vocal by Jack Fulton.

## IN A MIST
Bix Beiderbecke

Robbins Music—New York

1928

Introduced on disc by the composer (Okeh 40916). It is one of the most complex ragtime piano solos ever devised. Beiderbecke's impressionistic solo draws on late-19th-century classical music as much as it does on jazz. Red Norvo revived it on xylophone in 1933 (Brunswick 6906), and Frankie Trumbauer and His Orchestra, with Roy Bargy at the piano, revived it in the following year (Brunswick 6997). Mel Henke created his piano solo in 1946 (Tempo 1232), and Harry James and His Orchestra recorded it in 1949 (Columbia 38902).

## IN A SHANTY IN OLD SHANTY TOWN
Little Jack Little and John Siras (w: Joe Young)

M. Witmark and Sons—New York

1932

Ted Lewis and His Band had the number 1 hit, which maintained that position for ten of the twenty-two weeks charted (Columbia 2652-D). It was revived by Johnny Long and His Orchestra in 1946 with a number 13 hit (Decca 23622), and again in 1956 by Somethin' Smith and the Redheads with their number 27 hit (Epic 9168).

## IN HONEYSUCKLE TIME
Eubie Blake (w: Noble Sissle)

M. Witmark and Sons—New York

1921

**Show:** *Shuffle Along*

Introduced in the show by Noble Sissle, who made a hit record with his Sizzling Syncopators (Emerson 10385).

## IN MY MERRY OLDSMOBILE
Gus Edwards (w: Vincent Bryan)

M. Witmark and Sons—New York

1905

All-time standard. It celebrated the first transcontinental trip made by two Oldsmobiles in forty-four days. Billy Murray had the vocal hit (Victor 4467). It was revived in 1927 by Jean Goldkette and His Orchestra featuring Bix Beiderbecke on cornet (Victor Special). Although the song has been used on radio and television to advertise Oldsmobiles, the composer never could get the company to give him one of their automobiles. It was revived again in the film *The Merry Monahans* (Universal, 1944).

## IN OLD NEW YORK
Victor Herbert (w: Henry Blossom)
M. Witmark and Sons—New York
1906
**Show:** *The Red Mill*
A successful song about New York that is still sung. Introduced in the show by its stars, Fred Stone and Dave Montgomery. When revived on Broadway in 1945, it starred Dorothy Stone (Fred's daughter) and Eddie Foy Jr.

## IN SOUDAN
Nat Osborne (w: Ballard MacDonald)
Shapiro, Bernstein—New York
1919
Zez Confrey made an outstanding piano roll (QRS 786).

## IN THE COOL, COOL, COOL OF THE EVENING
Hoagy Carmichael (w: Johnny Mercer)
Burke-Van Heusen—New York
1951
**Film:** *Here Comes the Groom* (Paramount)
Academy Award winner for Best Song. Bing Crosby and Jane Wyman starred in the film and had the number 11 hit that charted for six weeks (Decca 27678).

## IN THE GOOD OLD SUMMER TIME
George Evans (w: Ren Shields)
Howley, Haviland and Dresser—New York
1902
Show: *The Defender*
Minstrel George "Honey Boy" Evans wrote this for Blanche Ring in *The Defender*. It sold over three million copies. Sousa's Band had a hit the following year (Victor 1833). A film of the same name revived it (MGM, 1949). Les Paul and Mary Ford had a number 15 hit in 1952, which charted for seven weeks (Capitol 2123). It remains a perennial seasonal favorite.

## IN THE LAND O' YAMO YAMO
Fred Fisher (w: Joe McCarthy)
McCarthy and Fisher—New York
1917
Sung in vaudeville and on disc by Van and Schenck (Victor 18443).

## IN THE MOOD
Joe Garland (w: Andy Razaf)
Shapiro Bernstein—New York
1939
Glenn Miller and His Orchestra had the number 1 hit, which maintained that position for ten of the thirty weeks charted and sold over one million copies (Bluebird 10416). The piece was closely associated with Miller. It was revived by Johnny Maddox and the Rhythmasters in 1953 with a number 16 hit (Dot 15045). The Ernie Fields Orchestra revived it again in 1959, with a number 4 hit that charted for fourteen weeks (Rendezvous 110). A novelty recording made it a number 40 hit in 1977 by the Henhouse Five Plus Two (Warner 8301).

## IN THE SHADE OF THE OLD APPLE TREE
Egbert Van Alstyne (w: Harry Williams)
Shapiro, Remick—New York
1905
The Team's biggest hit, sung and played in vaudeville. Henry Burr had a hit recording (Victor 4338).

## IN THE STILL OF THE NIGHT
Cole Porter (w & m)
Chappell—New York
1937
**Film:** *Rosalie* (MGM)
Nelson Eddy sang it in the film. Tommy Dorsey and His Orchestra had the number 3 hit, which charted for five weeks (Victor 25663). It was revived in 1960 by Dion and the Belmonts with a number 38 hit (Laurie

3059). Not to be confused with the the Five Satins'
1956 hit, "In the Still of the Nite."

## IN THE STILL OF THE NITE
*See* I'LL REMEMBER (IN THE STILL OF THE NITE)

## IN THE YEAR 2525
Rick Evans (w & m)
Zerlad Music—New York
1968
Zager and Evans had the number 1 hit in 1969, which
charted for twelve weeks and sold over one million copies
(RCA Victor 0174). It was their sole hit but did help
launch a brief fad for science-fiction/space-themed rock
(brought to fruition by David Bowie in the early 1970s).

## INDIAN LOVE CALL
Rudolf Friml (w: Otto Harbach and
Oscar Hammerstein)
Harms Inc.—New York
1924
**Show:** *Rose Marie*
Introduced in the show by Dennis King and Mary Ellis.
Paul Whiteman and His Orchestra had the hit record-
ing (Victor 19517). Jeanette MacDonald and Nelson
Eddy sang it in the film version (MGM, 1936), and a
year later their recording also made the charts. Slim
Whitman revived it in 1952 and had a million-seller
(Imperial 8156).

## INDIAN SUMMER
Victor Herbert (w: Al Dubin)
M. Witmark and Sons—New York
1939
Melody originally composed twenty years earlier, the
publisher asked Al Dubin to add lyrics. Barry Winton
introduced it on radio and Tommy Dorsey and His
Orchestra had the number 1 hit, which charted for sixteen weeks (Victor 26390).

## INDIANA
James F. Hanley (w: Ballard MacDonald)
Shapiro, Bernstein—New York
1917
One of the great "place" songs. The Original Dixieland
Jazz Band was the first to record it (Columbia A-2297)

and it became a favorite of succeeding jazz bands. Red
Nichols and his Five Pennies had a hit in 1929
(Brunswick 4373), and it was revived in his biopic *The
Five Pennies* (Paramount, 1959).

## INVISIBLE TOUCH
Anthony Banks/Phil Collins/Michael Rutherford
Hit and Run Music
1986
Genesis had the number 1 hit, which charted for twelve
weeks (Atlantic 89407). Originally purveyors of progressive rock songs, the group established itself as pop
hit makers in the mid-1980s, beginning with this song.
However, it remains their only number 1 pop hit.

## IS IT TRUE WHAT THEY SAY ABOUT DIXIE?
Gerald Marks/Irving Caesar/Sammy Lerner
Irving Caesar—New York
1936
Al Jolson, for whom the composers wrote the song,
introduced it on radio. Jimmy Dorsey and His Orchestra, with vocal by Bob Eberly, had the number 1 hit,
which charted for ten weeks (Decca 768).

## IS SHE MY GIRL FRIEND?
Milton Ager (w: Jack Yellen)
Ager, Yellen and Bornstein—New York
1927
Introduced in vaudeville by Edwards and Lilyan. The
Coon-Sanders Orchestra had a hit recording (Victor
21148).

## ISLANDS IN THE STREAM
The Gibb Brothers (w & m)
Chappell Music
1983
Kenny Rogers and Dolly Parton teamed up for this
number 1 hit, which stayed on the chart for eighteen
weeks (RCA 13615). It sold over two million copies.

## ISN'T IT ROMANTIC
Richard Rodgers (w: Lorenz Hart)
Famous Music—New York
1932
**Film:** *Love Me Tonight* (Paramount)

Maurice Chevalier and Jeanette MacDonald sang it in the film. Harold Stern and His Orchestra had the number 13 hit (Columbia 2718). It remains a cabaret favorite.

## IT AIN'T GONNA RAIN NO MO'
Wendell W. Hall (w & m)
Forster Music—Chicago
1923
Introduced in vaudeville, radio, and on disc by the ukulele-playing singer and composer. His recording sold over two million copies (Victor 19171), and sheet music sales totalled over a million. Instrumental hits include those of Carl Fenton and His Orchestra (Brunswick 2568), the Bar Harbor Society Orchestra (Vocalion 14816), and Jack Linx and His Orchestra (Okeh 40188). It was revived in the film *Has Anybody Seen My Gal?* (Universal, 1952). The song was also popular among early country artists.

## IT AIN'T NECESSARILY SO
George and Ira Gershwin
Gershwin Publishing—New York
1935
**Show:** *Porgy and Bess*
John Bubbles sang it in the show. Leo Reisman and His Orchestra had the number 16 hit (Brunswick 7562). Sammy Davis Jr. sang it in the film version (Columbia, 1959).

## IT ALL DEPENDS ON YOU
Ray Henderson (w: Bud DeSylva and Lew Brown)
DeSylva, Brown and Henderson—New York
1926
**Show:** *Big Boy*
Introduced in the show by Al Jolson. Paul Whiteman (Victor 20513) and Ruth Etting (Columbia 908-D) had the hit recordings. Doris Day revived it in the Etting biopic *Love Me Or Leave Me* (MGM, 1955).

## IT GOES LIKE IT GOES
David Shire (w: Norman Gimbel)
Fox Fanfare Music—Los Angeles
1979
**Film:** *Norma Rae* (20th Century Fox)
Academy Award winner for Best Song. Jennifer Warnes sang it in the film.

## IT HAD TO BE YOU
Isham Jones (w: Gus Kahn)
Jerome H. Remick—New York
1924
Introduced by the composer (Brunswick 2614) and also by Marion Harris, accompanied by pianist Phil Ohman (Brunswick 2610). It was revived in 1944 with hit recordings by Helen Forrest and Dick Haymes (Decca 23349), Betty Hutton (Capitol 155), and Artie Shaw (RCA Victor 20-1593). This standard was featured in the Gus Kahn biopic *I'll See You in My Dreams* (Warner Bros., 1951). Diane Keaton sang it in the film *Annie Hall* (United Artists, 1977). It remains a perennial nightclub favorite.

## IT ISN'T FAIR
Richard Himber/Frank Warshauer/
Sylvester Sprigato
Keit-Engel—New York
1933
Bandleader Richard Himber used this as his theme song on radio, where he had a long career in the 1930s (Vocalion 25008). Isham Jones and His Orchestra had the number 8 hit (Victor 24367). It was revived in 1950 by Sammy Kaye and His Orchestra, with vocal by Don Cornell. Their version reached number 2, charted for twenty-four weeks, and sold over one million copies (RCA Victor 20-3609).

## IT LOOKS LIKE RAIN IN CHERRY BLOSSOM LANE
Joe Burke (w: Edgar Leslie)
Joe Morris—New York
1937
Guy Lombardo and his Royal Canadians had the number 1 hit, which charted for sixteen weeks (Victor 25572).

## IT MIGHT AS WELL BE SPRING
Richard Rodgers (w: Oscar Hammerstein)
Williamson Music—New York
1945
Film: *State Fair* (20th Century Fox)
Academy Award winner for Best Song. Dick Haymes starred in the film and had the number 5 hit that charted for twelve weeks (Decca 18706).

## IT TAKES A LONG TALL BROWN SKIN GAL

Will E. Skidmore (w: Marshall Walker)

Skidmore Music—Kansas City, Mo.

1917

Introduced in vaudeville by Rae Samuels. It was a favorite with other vaudevillians like Emma Carus. Popularized on disc by Howard Kopp and Frank Banta (Columbia A-2376).

## ITALIAN STREET SONG

Victor Herbert (w: Rida Johnson Young)

M. Witmark and Sons—New York

1910

**Show:** *Naughty Marietta*

Emma Trentini sang it in the show. Jeanette MacDonald sang it in the film version (MGM, 1935). Jane Powell sang it in the film *Holiday in Mexico* (MGM, 1946).

## IT'S A GRAND NIGHT FOR SINGING

Richard Rodgers (w: Oscar Hammerstein)

Williamson Music—New York

1945

**Film:** *State Fair* (20th Century Fox)

Dick Haymes and William Marshall sang this in the film. Haymes also had a number 21 hit in 1946 (Decca 18740).

## IT'S A LONG, LONG WAY TO TIPPERARY

Jack Judge (w: Harry Williams)

Chappell—New York

1912

Written in England two years before the beginning of World War I. Montgomery and Stone sang it in the Broadway show *Chin Chin* and Al Jolson sang it in *Dancing Around*. Irish tenor John McCormack made his treasured version at the end of 1914 (Victor 64476). It remains a classic military song, and has often been parodied through the decades.

## IT'S A LOVELY DAY TODAY

Irving Berlin (w & m)

Irving Berlin—New York

1950

**Show:** *Call Me Madam*

Russell Nype and Galina Talva sang it in the show. Doris Day had a number 30 hit in 1951 (Columbia 39055).

## IT'S A LOVELY DAY TOMORROW

Irving Berlin (w & m)

Irving Berlin—New York

1940

**Show:** *Louisiana Purchase*

Irene Bordoni sang it in the show. Television's *The Garry Moore Show* used it as its closing theme during the 1950s.

## IT'S A MOST UNUSUAL DAY

Jimmy McHugh (w: Harold Adamson)

Robbins Music—New York

1948

**Film:** *A Date With Judy* (MGM)

Jane Powell sang it in the film. Ray Noble and His Orchestra, with vocal by Anita Gordon, had the number 21 hit (Columbia 38206).

## IT'S A SIN TO TELL A LIE

Billy Mayhew (w & m)

Donaldson, Douglas and Gumble—New York

1936

Fats Waller had the number 1 hit, which charted for twelve weeks, and was forever associated with him (Victor 25342). Somethin' Smith and the Redheads revived it in 1955, scoring a number 7 hit, which charted for twenty-three weeks (Epic 9093).

## IT'S ALL IN THE GAME

General Charles G. Dawes (w: Carl Sigman)

Remick Music—New York

1912, 1951

General Dawes composed the tune and called it "Melody" in 1912, but it was nearly forty years later, in 1951, that Carl Sigman changed the title and wrote lyrics for it. Tommy Edwards first recorded the vocal version, and had a number 18 hit, which charted for nine weeks (MGM 11035). In 1958, Edwards rerecorded it and it became a number 1 hit, which charted for nineteen weeks and sold over one million copies (MGM 12688). Cliff Richard revived it in 1964 with a number 25 hit, which charted for seven weeks (Epic

9633). The Four Aces revived it yet again in 1970 with a number 24 hit that charted for eight weeks (Motown 1164).

## IT'S BEEN A LONG, LONG TIME
Jule Styne (w: Sammy Cah)
Edwin H. Morris—New York
1945
Bing Crosby with the Les Paul Trio had a number 1 hit, which charted for sixteen weeks (Decca 18708). That same year, Harry James and His Orchestra also had a number 1 hit, charting for seventeen weeks (Columbia 36838).

## IT'S MAGIC
Jule Styne (w: Sammy Cahn)
M. Witmark & Sons—New York
1948
Film: *Romance on the High Seas* (Warner Bros.)
Doris Day sang it in the film and also had a number 2, million-selling hit that charted for twenty-one weeks (Columbia 38188).

## IT'S MY PARTY
Herb Wiesner/Wally Gold/John Gluck Jr.
Arch Music
1963
Leslie Gore had the number 1 hit, which charted for eleven weeks (Mercury 72119). A classic teen-angst song of the early 1960s.

## IT'S NOT FOR ME TO SAY
Robert Allen (w: Al Stillman)
Kerwin Music—New York
1956
Johnny Mathis had the number 5 hit in 1957, which charted for twenty-three weeks and sold over one million copies (Columbia 40851).

## IT'S NOW OR NEVER
Aaron Schroeder and Wally Gold
Gladys Music—New York
1960
The songwriters took the 1899 Italian song "O Sole Mio" as the basis for this pop ballad. Elvis Presley turned into a number 1 hit, which charted for sixteen weeks and sold over two million copies (RCA Victor 47-7777).

## IT'S ONLY A PAPER MOON
Harold Arlen (w: Billy Rose and E. Y. Harburg)
Harms—New York
1933
**Show:** *Crazy Quilt of 1933*
**Film:** *Take a Chance* (Paramount)
June Knight and Charles "Buddy" Rogers sang it in the film. Paul Whiteman and His Orchestra had the number 9 hit that charted for eight weeks (Victor 24400). Ella Fitzgerald revived it in 1945 with a number 9 hit, which charted for three weeks (Decca 23425). The song has been strongly associated with the Depression. Peter Bogdonovich borrowed part of the song's title for his black-and-white comedy about a Depression-era grifter (Paramount, 1973).

## IT'S RIGHT HERE FOR YOU
Alex Belledna (w: Marion Dickerson)
Perry Bradford Music—New York
1920
Introduced in vaudeville by Sophie Tucker. Mamie Smith had the hit recording (Okeh 4169). Eubie Blake made a fabulous version on piano roll (Melodee S-2948).

## IT'S STILL ROCK AND ROLL TO ME
Billy Joel (w & m)
Impulsive Music
1980
Billy Joel had the number 1 hit (Columbia 11276) which stayed on the chart for nineteen weeks. It sold over one million copies. Joel was commenting on the so-called new wave of rock in this song.

## IT'S THE TALK OF THE TOWN
Jerry Livingston (w: Marty Symes and Al Neiburg)
Santly Bros.—New York
1933
Glen Gray and the Casa Loma Orchestra had the number 6 hit, which charted for eleven weeks (Brunswick 6626).

## IT'S TIGHT LIKE THAT
Thomas Dorsey and Hudson Whittaker

Melrose Bros.—Chicago

1928

Introduced on disc by the composers under the name Tampa Red's Hokum Jug Band (Vocalion 1228) with a vocal by Frankie "Half-Pint" Jaxon. McKinney's Cotton Pickers had the hit recording with vocalists George Thomas and Dave Wilborn (Victor V-38013). Thomas Dorsey, who also recorded as Georgia Tom, would later abandon the blues and become one of the pioneer composers of gospel music.

## IT'S TOO LATE

Carole King (w: Toni Stern)

Colgems Music—New York

1971

Carole King's sole number 1 hit, which appeared on the chart for fifteen weeks (Ode 66015). It sold over one million copies. Earlier in the 1960s, she had been half of the phenomenally successful songwriting duo of Goffin and King. Her album *Tapestry* (Ode 77009, 1971), from which this single was drawn, was the best-selling album of its day, selling over ten million copies.

## IT'S TULIP TIME IN HOLLAND

Richard Whiting (w: Dave Radford)

Jerome H. Remick—New York

1915

Hit recording by Henry Burr (Victor 17874). Its most unusual recording came from hurdy-gurdy player Signor Grinderino (Victor 17884).

## ITSY BITSY TEENIE WEENIE YELLOW POLKADOT BIKINI

Paul J. Vance and Lee Pockriss

George Pincus & Sons—New York

1960

Number 1 teen-pop novelty ode to the popular swimwear, recorded by Brian Hyland. It was originally issued on the tiny Leader label, and then licensed to Kapp (342). It sold over a million copies for the teenage chanter.

## I'VE BEEN FLOATING DOWN THE OLD GREEN RIVER

Joe Cooper (w: Bert Kalmar)

Waterson, Berlin and Snyder—New York

1915

**Show:** *Maid in America*

Introduced in the show by Florence Moore. It was revived by the Firehouse Five Plus Two in 1952 (Good Time Jazz L-12012).

## I'VE FOUND A NEW BABY

Jack Palmer and Spencer Williams

Clarence Williams Music—New York

1926

Introduced on radio by Billy Jones and Ernest Hare. Ted Lewis and His Band had a hit recording (Columbia 600-D). The publisher, with James P. Johnson, recorded it as a piano duet (Columbia 14502-D). The Dixie Stompers (Harmony 121-H) and the Bostonians (Vocalion 15298) also had fine arrangements. It is a great Dixieland jazz standard today.

## I'VE GOT A CRUSH ON YOU

George Gershwin (w: Ira Gershwin)

New World Music—New York

1930

**Show:** *Strike Up the Band*

Introduced in the show by Doris Carson and Gordon Smith. Lee Wiley revived it in 1939 (Liberty Music Shop L-282) and Frank Sinatra in 1948 (Columbia 38151).

## I'VE GOT A FEELING I'M FALLING

Thomas Waller and Harry Link (w: Billy Rose)

Santly Bros.—New York

1929

Gene Austin had a hit recording (Victor 22033), and Fats Waller made a beautiful piano solo recording (Victor 22092). It was revived by Nell Carter in the 1978 revue *Ain't Misbehavin'*.

## I'VE GOT MY HABITS ON

Jimmie Durante (w: Chris Smith and Bob Schafer)

Goodman and Rose—New York

1921

Introduced in vaudeville by Donald Kerr. Hit recording by Bennie Krueger and His Orchestra (Brunswick 2181). Miss Patricola had the hit vocal (Victor 18838).

## I'VE GOT MY LOVE TO KEEP ME WARM

Irving Berlin (w & m)

Irving Berlin—New York

1937

**Film:** *On the Avenue* (20th Century Fox)

E.E. Clive, Dick Powell, and Alice Faye sang it in the film. Ray Noble and His Orchestra had the number 3 hit, which charted for nine weeks (Victor 25507). Les Brown and His Orchestra recorded their version in 1946, but it went unreleased until three years later, when it became a number 1, million-selling hit, remaining on the charts for seventeen weeks (Columbia 38324).

## I'VE GOT RINGS ON MY FINGERS

Maurice Scott (w: Weston and Barnes)

T. B. Harms—New York

1909

**Show:** *The Midnight Sons*

Blanche Ring sang it in the show and became solely identified with it. She made a hit recording the following year (Victor 5737)

## I'VE GOT THE WORLD ON A STRING

Harold Arlen (w: Ted Koehler)

Mills Music—New York

1932

**Show:** *Cotton Club Parade of 1932*

Aida Ward sang it in the show. Cab Calloway and His Orchestra, who accompanied her in the show, had the number 18 hit (Brunswick 6424). Frank Sinatra revived it in 1953 with a number 14 hit (Capitol 2505).

## I'VE GOT YOU UNDER MY SKIN

Cole Porter (w & m)

Chappell—New York

1936

**Film:** *Born to Dance* (MGM)

Virginia Bruce sang it in the film. Ray Noble and His Orchestra, with vocal by Al Bowlly, had the number 3 hit that charted for nine weeks. Ginny Simms sang it in the Cole Porter biopic *Night and Day* (Warner Bros., 1946). Stan Freberg had a funny parody when he revived it in 1951 with a number 11 hit, which charted for five weeks (Capitol 1711). The four Seasons revived it—à la the original version—in 1966, scoring a number 9 hit that charted for eight weeks (Philips 40393).

## I'VE GOT YOUR NUMBER

Cy Coleman (w: Carolyn Leigh)

Edwin H. Morris—New York

1962

**Show:** *Little Me*

Swen Swenson sang it in the show.

## I'VE GROWN ACCUSTOMED TO HER FACE

Frederick Loewe (w: Alan Jay Lerner)

Chappell—New York

1956

**Show:** *My Fair Lady*

Rex Harrison sang it in the show and in the subsequent film (Warner Bros., 1964).

## (I'VE HAD) THE TIME OF MY LIFE

Franke Previte/Donald Markowitz/John DeNicol

Knockout Music

1987

**Film:** *Dirty Dancing* (Vestron)

Academy Award winner for Best Song. Bill Medley (half of the Righteous Brothers) and Jennifer Warnes had the number 1 hit, which charted for fifteen weeks (RCA 5224). It sold over one million copies.

## I'VE HEARD THAT SONG BEFORE

Jule Styne (w: Sammy Cahn)

Edwin H. Morris—New York

1943

**Film:** *Youth on Parade* (Republic)

Bob Crosby and His Orchestra sang and played it in the film. Harry James and His Orchestra, with vocalist Helen Forrest, had the million-selling number 1 hit, which charted for twenty-two weeks (Columbia 36668).

## I'VE NEVER SEEN A STRAIGHT BANANA

Ted Waite (w & m)

Irving Berlin—New York

1926

Popularized on disc by Fred Waring's Pennsylvanians (Victor 20562) and the Columbians (Columbia 916-D).

## I'VE TOLD EV'RY LITTLE STAR

Jerome Kern (w: Oscar Hammerstein)

T. B. Harms—New York

1932

**Show:** *Music in the Air*

Walter Slezak sang it in the show. Jack Denny and His Orchestra had the number 10 hit, which charted for five weeks (Victor 24183). Gloria Swanson sang it in the film version (Fox, 1934). Linda Scott revived it in 1961 with a number 3 hit, which charted for ten weeks (Canadian American 123).

## IVY (CLING TO ME)

Isham Jones and Jimmy Johnson (w: Alex Rogers)

Irving Berlin—New York

1922

Introduced in vaudeville by Isham Jones and His Orchestra, who also had the hit recording (Brunswick 2365). The Original Memphis Five (Pathe 020900) and Sam Lanin's Orchestra (Banner 1152) also had fine versions.

## JA-DA

Bob Carlton (w & m )

Leo Feist—New York

1918

Nonsense song with great appeal in vaudeville. Popular recording artist Arthur Fields made a hit recording (Victor 18522). It was revived by Alice Faye in the film *Rose of Washington Square* (20th Century Fox, 1939).

## JACK AND DIANE

John Cougar Mellencamp (w & m)

Riva Music

1982

Under the performing name of John Cougar, the composer had this number 1 hit, which stayed on the charts for seventeen weeks (Riva 210). It sold over one million copies. This ballad of a mid-American couple, taking them from courtship through rocky marriage, is Mellencamp's only number 1 pop hit.

## JAIL HOUSE BLUES

Bessie Smith and Clarence Williams

Clarence Williams Music—New York

1924

Of all the songs both written and recorded by Bessie Smith, this is the only one published. She is accompa-

nied by her publisher on piano on the original recording (Columbia A-4001). It has become a classic.

## JAILHOUSE ROCK

Mike Stoller (w: Jerry Leiber)

Elvis Presley Music—New York

1957

**Film:** *Jailhouse Rock* (MGM)

Elvis Presley had the number 1 hit, which charted for nineteen weeks and sold over four million copies (RCA Victor 47-7035). The choreographed number in the film is often cited as an early inspiration for music video.

## JAPANESE SANDMAN

Richard A. Whiting (w: Ray Egan)

Jerome H. Remick—New York

1920

Nora Bayes sang it in vaudeville. It sold over one million copies of sheet music. Paul Whiteman and His Orchestra made their debut with this recording and sold over two million copies (Victor 18690). Zez Confrey made an outstanding piano roll (QRS 1160). Benny Goodman and His Orchestra revived it in 1935 with a number 10 hit (Victor 25024). It was revived again in the film *Thoroughly Modern Millie* (Universal, 1967).

## JAVA JIVE

Ben Oakland (w: Milton Drake)

Advanced Music—New York

1940

The Ink Spots had the number 15 hit (Decca 3432).

## JAZZ ME BLUES

Tom Delaney (w & m)

Palmetto Music—New York

1921

A jazz standard ever since the Original Dixieland Jazz Band made their hit recording (Victor 18772). Bix Beiderbecke and His Gang made another hit in 1927 (Okeh 40923). Les Paul revived it as a guitar instrumental in 1951 (Capitol 1825).

## JEAN

Shelton Brooks (w & m)

Waterson, Berlin and Snyder—New York

1919

Popularized by Isham Jones and His Orchestra (Brunswick 5012) and the All Star Trio (Emerson 10194).

## JEEPERS CREEPERS
Harry Warren (w: Johnny Mercer)
M. Witmark and Sons—New York
1938
**Film:** *Going Places* (Warner Bros.)
Louis Armstrong with Maxine Sullivan sang it in the film. Armstrong had a number 12 hit in 1939 that charted for five weeks (Decca 2267), while Al Donohue and His Orchestra, with vocal by Paula Kelly, had the number 1 hit that year, charting for thirteen weeks (Vocalion 4513). It remains a perennial favorite.

## "JELLY ROLL" BLUES, THE
Ferd "Jelly Roll" Morton
Will Rossiter—Chicago
1915
The first published tune of the outstanding jazzman Jelly Roll Morton. His piano solo was made on June 9, 1924 (Gennett 5552) when he cut an incredible eleven tunes during a single session. His superb group, the Red Hot Peppers, recorded it on December 16, 1926 (Victor 20405). It is a favorite of Dixieland jazz bands, and part of the standard repertory.

## JERSEY BOUNCE
Bobby Plater/Tiny Bradshaw/Ed Johnson
(w: Robert Wright)
Lewis Music—New York
1941
Benny Goodman and His Orchestra had the number 1 instrumental hit in 1942, which charted for twenty-one weeks (Okeh 6590). It was revived in his biopic *The Benny Goodman Story* (Universal, 1956).

## JESSIE'S GIRL
Rick Springfield (w & m)
Robie Porter Music
1980, 1981
Rick Springfield had the number 1 hit on the chart for twenty-two weeks (RCA 122021). It sold over one million copies.

## JIMMY VALENTINE
Gus Edwards (w: Edward Madden)
Gus Edwards Music—New York
1911
Introduced in vaudeville by the Gus Edwards company of youngsters. The Peerless Quartet made the hit recording after the song was transferred in 1912 to the Jerome H. Remick Publishing Company (Victor 17036). Bing Crosby revived it in the Gus Edwards biopic *Star Maker* (Paramount, 1939).

## JIMTOWN BLUES
Charlie Davis (w: Fred Rose)
Melrose Bros.—Chicago
1925
Introduced in vaudeville by Jimmie Wade's Moulin Rouge Syncopaters. It has become a Dixieland jazz standard thanks to The Cotton Pickers (Brunswick 2766) and Tennessee Tooters (Vocalion 15022). It was revived in 1951 by Pee Wee Hunt and His Orchestra (Capitol 1879).

## JOE TURNER BLUES
W. C. Handy (w & m)
Pace and Handy Music Co.—Memphis
1915
Introduced in vaudeville by Ruby Darby. Prince's Orchestra made the first recording (Columbia A-5854). It was revived in 1941 by Henry "Hot Lips" Levine leading the Dixieland Group of NBC's Chamber Music Society of Lower Basin Street (Victor 27543).

## JOHNNY ANGEL
Lee Pockriss (w: Lyn Duddy)
Post Music—Hollywood
1962
Shelley Fabares had the number 1 hit, which charted for thirteen weeks (Colpix 621); a classic of girl pop.

## JOHNNY B. GOODE
Chuck Berry (w & m)
ARC Music—New York
1958
Chuck Berry had the number 8 hit, which charted for eleven weeks (Chess 1691). Berry's importance to the history of rock and roll isn't reflected by his ratings,

but rather, his influence on later composer/performers. His compositions are cornerstones in the genre.

## JOY TO THE WORLD

Hoyt Axton (w & m)

Lady Jane Music—Los Angeles

1970

Three Dog Night had this number 1 hit, which charted for fifteen weeks (Dunhill/ABC 4272). It sold over one million copies.

## JUMP

Jermaine Dupri (w & m)

EMI April Music

1992

Kris Kross was a one-hit wonder whose only number 1 hit held that position for eight of eighteen weeks on the charts (Ruffhouse 74197). It sold over three million copies.

## JUMP STEADY BLUES

Millard E. Coffin and Percy Terry

Joe Morris Music—New York

1922

Introduced in vaudeville by the Paramount Four. Popularized on disc by the Original Six (Okeh 4655).

## JUMPIN' JACK FLASH

Mick Jagger and Keith Richards (w & m)

Gideon Music—New York

1968

Number 3 hit for the British rockers, charting for eleven weeks (London 908). It remains in their repertory of "classics" over three decades later. Aretha Franklin revived it in the film of the same name (20th Century Fox, 1986), for a number 24 hit that charted for six weeks (Arista 9528).

## JUMPING JACK

Rube Bloom/Bernie Seaman/Marvin Smolev

Standard Music—New York

1928

Popularized by Zez Confrey and His Orchestra (Victor 21845), Sam Lanin and His Orchestra, with Rube Bloom at the piano (Okeh 41121), and the Varsity Four (Brunswick 4075).

## JUNE IS BUSTIN' OUT ALL OVER

Richard Rodgers (w: Oscar Hammerstein)

Williamson Music—New York

1945

**Show:** *Carousel*

Christine Johnson and Jan Clayton sang it in the show. Hildegarde, accompanied by Guy Lombardo and His Orchestra, had the number 11 hit (Decca 23428).

## JUNK MAN RAG

C. Luckeyth Roberts

Jos. W. Stern—New York

1913

Introduced in vaudeville by Maurice and Florence Walton. Popularized on disc by banjoist Fred Van Eps (Columbia A-1417) and the Victor Military Band (Victor 17489).

## JUST A-WEARYIN' FOR YOU

Carrie Jacobs-Bond (w: Frank Stanton)

Carrie Jacobs-Bond and Son—Chicago

1901

The first of the composer's art songs that was heard on the vaudeville stage, later in recital halls. Concert soprano Lucy Isabelle Marsh had a hit in 1916 (Victor 45090).

## JUST ANOTHER DAY WASTED AWAY

Charles Tobias (w: Roy Turk)

Shapiro, Bernstein—New York

1927

Introduced in vaudeville by Barney Barnum and Bill Bailey. Abe Lyman and His Orchestra had the popular recording (Brunswick 3615).

## JUST CROSS THE RIVER FROM QUEENS

Albert Von Tilzer (w: Neville Fleeson)

Harms—New York

1927

**Show:** *Bye Bye Bonnie*

A lovely song recorded by Edwin J. McEnelly's Orchestra (Victor 20601).

## JUST FRIENDS

John Klenner (w: Sam Lewis)

Robbins Music—New York

1931

Russ Columbo had the number 14 hit, which charted for three weeks (Victor 22909).

## JUST IN TIME

Jule Styne (w: Comden and Green)

Stratford Music—New York

1956

**Show:** *Bells Are Ringing*

Sydney Chaplin and Judy Holliday sang it in the show.

## JUST LIKE A WOMAN

Bob Dylan (w & m)

Bob Dylan Words and Music—New York

1966

Dylan had a number 33 hit with this tune, which stayed on the charts three weeks. It has remained one of his most popular songs (Columbia 43792).

## (JUST LIKE) STARTING OVER

John Lennon (w & m)

Lenono Music

1980

John Lennon's last number 1 hit, which stayed in that position for five out of nineteen weeks (Geffen 49604). It sold over one million copies. The song signaled Lennon's return to recording after a five-year self-imposed retirement to be a "house husband."

## JUST MY IMAGINATION

Barrett Strong and Norman Whitfield

Jobete Music—Detroit

1970, 1971

The Temptations had the number 1 hit, which charted for thirteen weeks (Gordy 7105). It sold over two million copies.

## JUST ONE OF THOSE THINGS

Cole Porter (w & m)

Harms—New York

1935

**Show:** *Jubilee*

June Knight and Charles Walters sang it in the show. Richard Himber and His Orchestra had the number 10 hit, which charted for five weeks (Victor 25161). It was a great favorite in a string of films, and sung by the most popular singers of their time: Lena Horne in

*Panama Hattie* (MGM, 1942); Ginny Simms in the Porter biopic *Night and Day* (Warner Bros., 1946); Doris Day in *Lullaby of Broadway* (Warner Bros., 1951); Peggy Lee, as a number 14 hit in 1952 (Decca 28313) and in *The Jazz Singer* (Warner Bros., 1953); Frank Sinatra in *Young at Heart* (Warner Bros., 1954); Maurice Chevalier in *Can-Can* (20th Century Fox, 1960); and Madeline Kahn in *At Long Last Love* (20th Century Fox, 1975).

## JUST THE WAY YOU ARE

Billy Joel (w & m)

Impulsive Music

1977

Major pop-rock ballad by Billy Joel, who scored a number 3 hit on the pop charts in 1978 and number 1 for four weeks on the adult-contemporary charts with the song, which also sold over a million copies (Columbia 10646). It has become a cabaret and wedding favorite. Ironically, the song was written for Joel's first wife, who at the time was also his manager; the couple subsequently divorced.

## JUST WAIT TILL YOU SEE MY BABY DO THE CHARLESTON

Clarence Williams/Clarence Todd/ Rousseau Simmons

Clarence Williams Music—New York

1925

Introduced on records by Clarence Williams's Blue Five (Okeh 8272). It has become a favorite of Dixieland bands since the 1980s.

## JUST WALKING IN THE RAIN

Johnny Bragg and Robert S. Riley

Golden West Melodies—Hollywood

1953

Johnnie Ray had the number 2 hit in 1956 that charted for twenty-three weeks and sold over one million copies (Columbia 40729).

## JUSTIFY MY LOVE

Lenny Kravitz (w & m)

Miss Bessie Music

1990

A number 1 hit for Maddona in 1991, holding that spot for two out of thirteen weeks on the charts (Sire 19485). It sold over a million copies.

## K-K-K-KATY

Geoffrey O'Hara (w & m)

Leo Feist—New York

1918

Written during the First World War, it was sung as "K-K-K-KP" by soldiers. Billy Murray had the hit record (Victor 18455). It was revived by Jack Oakie in the movie *Tin Pan Alley* (20th Century Fox, 1940).

## KA-LU-A

Jerome Kern (w: Anne Caldwell)

T. B. Harms—New York

1921

**Show:** *Good Morning, Dearie*

Oscar Shaw sang it in the show. This song depends upon a repeated one-measure bass line, identical to the bass line in "Dardanella," whose publisher, Fred Fisher, sued Kern and won. It is the only time a bass line was considered more important than the melody. Paul Whiteman and His Orchestra had the hit recording (Victor 18826). Other favorites include Selvin's Dance Orchestra (Vocalion 14261), Carl Fenton's Orchestra (Brunswick 2170), and the Knickerbockers Orchestra (Columbia A-3516).

## KANSAS CITY

Mike Stoller (w: Jerry Leiber)

Armo Music—Cincinnati

1952

Wilbert Harrison had the number 1 hit in 1959, which charted for twelve weeks and sold over one million copies (Fury 1023). It has become a standard in the modern blues repertoire.

## KANSAS CITY KITTY

Walter Donaldson (w: Edgar Leslie)

Donaldson, Douglas and Gumble—New York

1929

The Cotton Pickers had a classic recording (Brunswick 4325). Fred Seibert made an outstanding piano roll (Atlas 3734).

## KANSAS CITY STOMP

Ferd "Jelly Roll" Morton

Melrose Bros.—Chicago

1925

Introduced by the composer in a 1923 piano solo (Gennett 5218). It has become a standard for jazz bands ever since Jelly Roll Morton's Red Hot Peppers recorded it in 1928 (Victor 38010). The Tennessee Tooters recorded it as soon as the orchestration came out in 1925 (Vocalion 15022).

## KARMA CHAMELEON

Culture Club (w & m)

Pendulum Music

1983

This was the biggest success for the new-wave rock group Culture Club, featuring the colorful lead singer Boy George. It held its number 1 position for three out of sixteen weeks (Virgin/Epic 04221). It sold over one million copies.

## KATY-DID

Jerome Kern (w: Harry B. Smith)

T. B. Harms—New York

1913

**Show:** *Oh I Say*

A fresh and lively syncopated song introduced in the show by Lois Josephine and Wellington Cross.

## KEEP ON LOVING YOU

Kevin Cronin (w & m)

Fate Music

1980, 1981

Number 1 power-rock ballad by REO Speedwagon, charting for twenty weeks and selling over a million copies (Epic 50953). It was their first number 1 hit, after twelve years as a band.

## KEEPIN' OUT OF MISCHIEF NOW

Thomas Waller (w: Andy Razaf)

Con Conrad—New York

1932

Louis Armstrong had the number 17 hit (Okeh 41560). The Coon-Sanders Orchestra had a number 20 hit (Victor 22969).

## KIDS!

Charles Strouse (w: Lee Adams)

Edwin H. Morris—New York

1960

**Show:** *Bye Bye Birdie*
Paul Lynde and Marijane Maricle sang it in the show. Lynde, Dick Van Dyke, Maureen Stapleton, and Bryan Russell sang it in the film version (Columbia, 1963).

## KILLING ME SOFTLY WITH HIS SONG
Charles Fox (w: Norman Gimbel)
Fox-Gimbel Productions—Beverly Hills
1972
Roberta Flack won a Grammy award for this number 1 hit, which charted for thirteen weeks and sold over one million copies (Atlantic 2940). The Fugees, with lead singer Lauryn Hill, revived it in 1996, and scored a number 2 hit that charted for thirty weeks. The song was supposedly inspired by singer/songwriter Don McLean.

## KING CHANTICLEER
Nat D. Ayer (w: A. Seymour Brown)
Jerome H. Remick—New York
1910
A vaudeville favorite, it was recorded by both Prince's Band (Columbia A-1150) and Arthur Pryor's Band (Victor 17079). Doris Day revived it in 1953 (Columbia 39971).

## KING OF THE ROAD
Roger Miller (w & m)
Tree—Nashville
1964, 1965
A number 4 pop and number 1 country and adult-contemporary hit for Roger Miller, selling over a million copies (Smash 1965). It remains one of the classic truck driver songs.

## KING PORTER STOMP
Ferd "Jelly Roll" Morton
Melrose Bros.—Chicago
1924
A major work in jazz literature. Introduced by Jelly Roll Morton as a piano solo in 1923 (Gennett 5289) and again in 1926 (Vocalion 1020). Fletcher Henderson made an arrangement for His Orchestra in 1928 (Columbia 1543-D) that developed into such a sensation that he made a new orchestration in 1933 (Vocalion 2527). When Benny Goodman created his big band, his version, also arranged by Fletcher Hen-

derson and featuring trumpeter Bunny Berigan became a smashing success (Victor 25090). Morton made a new recording as a piano solo in 1939 (General 4005). It was featured in the film *The Benny Goodman Story* (Universal, 1955). It remains a classic.

## KINKAJOU, THE
Harry Tierney (w: Joseph McCarthy)
Leo Feist—New York
1926
**Show:** *Rio Rita*
Ada May sang it in the show. The hit recording was by Nat Shilkret and His Orchestra (Victor 20474). An unusual piano duet was by Constance Mering and Muriel Pollock (Columbia 952-D).

## KISS
Prince (w & m)
Controversy Music
1986
Number 1 hit for pop-funkster Prince, holding the top spot for two out of fourteen weeks on the charts and selling over half a million copies (Paisley Park 28751); also a number 1 R&B hit.

## KISS IN THE DARK, A
Victor Herbert (w: Bud DeSylva)
Harms—New York
1922
**Show:** *Orange Blossom*
Edith Day sang it in the show. Metropolitan Opera soprano Amelita Galli-Curci had the hit recording (Victor 959). Mary Martin sang it in the film *The Great Victor Herbert* (Paramount, 1939), and Gordon MacRae revived it in the Marilyn Miller biopic *Look For the Silver Lining* (Warner Bros., 1949).

## KISS ME AGAIN
Victor Herbert
(w: Henry Blossom)
M. Witmark and Sons—New York
1905
**Show:** *Mlle. Modiste*
This haunting waltz was composed for Fritzi Scheff, the show's star. She had to sing it ever after. While she never recorded it, Victor Herbert and His Orchestra

did in 1919 (Victor 45165). Susanna Foster sang it in the biopic *The Great Victor Herbert* (Paramount, 1939).

## KISS OF FIRE
Lester Allen and Robert Hill
Duchess Music—New York
1952
Georgia Gibbs had the number 1 hit, which charted for twenty weeks and sold over one million copies (Mercury 5823).

## KISS ON MY LIST
Daryl Hall and Janna Allen
Hot-Cha Music
1980, 1981
Daryl Hall and John Oates were the most successful pop-rock duo of the 1980s. This number 1 hit stayed on the chart for seventeen weeks (RCA 12142), and it sold over one million copies.

## KISS YOU ALL OVER
Mike Chapman and Nicky Chinn
Chinnichap Publishing
1978
Exile, a soft-rock group from Lexington, Kentucky, had this number 1 hit, which charted for seventeen weeks (Warner/Curb 8589). It sold over one million copies. In the 1980s, the band forged a new career in country music.

## KITTEN ON THE KEYS
Zez Confrey
Jack Mills Music—New York
1921
Two-million-selling novelty rag in sheet music, sparked by the composer's piano recording (Brunswick 2082) in 1921, followed by his huge recording success the following year with his orchestra (Victor 18900). Over the years, it has been recorded over two hundred times and is used as a test piece for pianists. It has remained in print since its original publication. Freddie Slack made a hit recording as a boogie-woogie solo with orchestra in 1945 (Capitol 20032), and Rafael Mendez and Orchestra turned it into a rhumba hit in the same year (Pan American 112). Its popularity continues as a virtuosic show piece.

## KNOCK THREE TIMES
Irwin Levine and I. Russell Brown
Pocket Full of Tunes—New York
1970
Dawn had this number 1 hit, which charted for sixteen weeks (Bell 938). It sold over one million copies.

## KOKOMO
Mike Love/Terry Melcher/John Phillips/
Scott McKenzie
Walt Disney Music
1988
**Film:** *Cocktail* (Touchstone)
The Beach Boys had the number 1 hit, which charted for fifteen weeks (Elektra 69385). It sold over two million copies.

## LA BAMBA
Ritchie Valens
Picture Our Music
1958
**Film:** *La Bamba* (Columbia)
Valens, the tragically short-lived rock star from Pomona, California, originally recorded this in 1959 for a number 22 hit, remaining on the charts for eight weeks (Del-Fi 410). Los Lobos, an innovative California-based band who play a wide range of music from Tex-Mex to their own original songs, revived it for the 1987 biopic film of the same name, scoring their only number 1 hit, which charted for fourteen weeks (Slash 28336).

## LADY
Lionel Richie (w & m)
Brockman Music—Beverly Hills, CA
1980
Kenny Rogers had his biggest song when this reached number 1 for six out of nineteen weeks on the charts (Liberty 1380). It sold over one million copies.

## LADY IS A TRAMP, THE
Richard Rodgers (w: Lorenz Hart)
Chappell—New York
1937
**Show:** *Babes in Arms*
Mitzi Green sang it in the show. Tommy Dorsey and His Orchestra, with vocal by Jack Leonard, had the

number 15 hit (Victor 25673). June Preisser sang it in the film version (MGM, 1939). Lena Horne sang it in the Rodgers and Hart biopic *Words and Music* (MGM, 1948). Frank Sinatra sang it in the film *Pal Joey* (Columbia, 1957), and the song thereafter was a staple of his nightclub and Vegas acts.

## LADY MADONNA
John Lennon and Paul McCartney
Maclen Music—New York
1968
The Beatles had the number 4 hit, which charted for ten weeks and sold over two million copies (Capitol 2138).

## LAND WHERE THE GOOD SONGS GO, THE
Jerome Kern
(w: P. G. Wodehouse)
T. B. Harms—New York
1917
**Show:** *Miss 1917*
Introduced in the show by the singers Elizabeth Brice and Charles King in order to revive older favorite songs. The song itself was revived in the Kern biopic *Till the Clouds Roll By* (MGM, 1946).

## LAST DANCE
Paul Jabara (w & m)
Primus Artists Music—New York
1977, 1978
**Film:** *Thank God It's Friday* (Columbia)
Academy Award winner for Best Song. Donna Summer had the number 3 hit that charted for fourteen weeks (Casablanca 926). It sold over one million copies; a disco classic.

## LAST TIME I SAW PARIS, THE
Jerome Kern (w: Oscar Hammerstein)
Chappell—New York
1940
**Film:** *Lady Be Good* (MGM)
Academy Award winner for Best Song in 1941. Kate Smith had the number 8 hit for the song that Hammerstein wrote in response to the Nazi takeover of Paris (Columbia 35802).

## LAST TRAIN TO CLARKSVILLE
Tommy Boyce and Bobby Hart
Screen Gems-Columbia Music—New York
1966
The Monkees had the number 1 hit, which charted for twelve weeks and sold over one million copies (Colgems 1001). It was their first single and gained heavily from the hoopla over the debut of their TV series.

## LAUGHIN' CRYIN' BLUES
Porter Grainger and Bob Ricketts
Zipf Music—New York
1923
Fabulous piano roll version by Thomas Waller (QRS 2213).

## LAUGHTER IN THE RAIN
Neil Sedaka and Phil Cody
Don Kirshner Music—New York
1974
Number 1 hit in 1975 for pop singer/songwriter Neil Sedaka, charting for fifteen weeks; also a number 1 adult-contemporary hit (Rocket 40313). Sedaka's first hit of his revived 1970s career, and his first charting song in eleven years.

## LAURA
David Raksin (w: Johnny Mercer)
Robbins Music—New York
1945
**Film:** *Laura* (20th Century Fox)
Also popularly known as "Laura's Theme," the instrumental version was played numerous times during the melodramatic film. Woody Herman and His Orchestra had the number 4 hit, which charted for twelve weeks (Columbia 36785).

## LAY, LADY, LAY
Bob Dylan (w & m)
Big Sky Music
1969
A number 7 hit for Dylan, charting for eleven weeks (Columbia 44926). The single was from his album, *Nashville Skyline* (Columbia 9825), in which Dylan adopted a new countrified personality, complete with a smoother singing voice.

## LAZY

Irving Berlin (w & m)

Irving Berlin—New York

1924

Hit vocal recording by Al Jolson, accompanied by Gene Rodemich and His Orchestra (Brunswick 2595). Paul Whiteman and His Orchestra had the hit instrumental (Victor 19299). It was revived in the films *Alexander's Ragtime Band* (20th Century Fox, 1938), *Holiday Inn* (Paramount, 1942), and *There's No Business like Show Business* (20th Century Fox, 1954).

## LAZY MOON

J. Rosamond Johnson (w: Bob Cole)

Jos. W. Stern—New York

1903

A beautiful ballad introduced in vaudeville by the writers.

## LAZYBONES

Hoagy Carmichael (w: Johnny Mercer)

Southern Music—New York

1933

Ted Lewis and His Band had the number 1 hit, which charted for eleven weeks (Columbia 2786-D). Mildred Bailey was associated with this song, and her disc, accompanied by The Dorsey Brothers Orchestra, was a number 9 hit (Brunswick 6587). Often revived by cabaret singers to this day.

## LE FREAK

Nile Rodgers and Bernard Edwards

Cotillion Music

1978

Chic was a New York group formed by the composers/producers. This number 1 hit lasted for nineteen weeks on the charts, and sold over two million copies (Atlantic 3519). It was a great favorite of the disco era.

## LEADER OF THE PACK

George Morton/Jeff Barry/Ellie Greenwich

Robert Mellin—London

1964

The Shangri-Las had the number 1 hit, which charted for ten weeks (Red Bird 10-014). Their recording featured motorcycle sound effects, a nice realistic touch.

## LEAN ON ME

Bill Withers (w & m)

Interior Music—Hollywood

1972

Bill Withers had this number 1 hit, which charted for fourteen weeks and sold over one million copies (Sussex 235). It was revived in 1987 by Club Nouveau, whose number 1 hit stayed on the charts for twelve weeks and also sold over one million copies (King Jay/Warner 28430).

## LEARNIN' THE BLUES

Dolores Vicki Silvers (w & m)

Barton Music—New York

1955

Number 1 hit for Frank Sinatra, holding that spot for two out of twenty-one weeks on the charts (Capitol 3102).

## LEAVE IT TO JANE

Jerome Kern (w: P. G. Wodehouse)

T. B. Harms—New York

1917

**Show:** *Leave It To Jane*

This rousing number was sung in the show by Edith Hallor, Oscar Shaw, Ann Orr, and the Girls. It was revived in the Kern biopic *Till the Clouds Roll By* (MGM, 1946), sung by June Allyson. It was revived again when the show opened Off-Broadway in 1959 for a staggering 928-performance run. In this revival, it was sung by Kathleen Murray, Angelo Mango, Jeanne Allen, and the Girls (CD - DRG 15017).

## LEAVING ON A JET PLANE

John Denver (w & m)

Cherry Lane Music—New York

1967, 1969

Peter, Paul and Mary had the number 1 hit in 1969, and it charted for fifteen weeks and sold over one million copies (Warner 7340).

## LEFT ALL ALONE AGAIN BLUES

Jerome Kern (w: Anne Caldwell)

T. B. Harms—New York

1920

**Show:** *The Night Boat*

Introduced in the show by Stella Hoban. Marion Harris had a hit recording (Columbia A-2939), as did the Joseph C. Smith Orchestra (Victor 18661). It was also popular among early country performers.

## LET A SMILE BE YOUR UMBRELLA
Sammy Fain (w: Irving Kahal and Francis Wheeler)
Waterson, Berlin and Snyder——New York
1927
Paul Ash introduced it in vaudeville. Roger Wolfe Kahn and His Orchestra had the hit recording (Victor 21233). Dan Dailey and Charles Winninger sang it in the film *Give My Regards to Broadway* (20th Century Fox, 1948).

## LET IT BE
John Lennon and Paul McCartney
Maclen Music——New York
1970
**Film:** *Let It Be* (United Artists)
The Beatles had this number 1 hit, which charted for thirteen weeks (Apple 2764). It sold over four million copies.

## LET IT SNOW! LET IT SNOW! LET IT SNOW!
Jule Styne (w: Sammy Cahn)
Edwin H. Morris——New York
1945
Vaughn Monroe had the number 1 hit, which charted for fourteen weeks (Victor 20-1759). A Christmas favorite.

## (LET ME BE YOUR) TEDDY BEAR
Bernie Lowe and Kal Mann
Gladys Music——New York
1957
**Film:** *Loving You* (Paramount)
Elvis Presley had the number 1 hit, which charted for eighteen weeks and sold over four million copies (RCA Victor 47-7000).

## LET ME CALL YOU SWEETHEART
Leo Friedman (w: Beth Slater Whitson)
Leo Friedman——Chicago
1910
This sold over six million copies of sheet music when it was transferred to Harold Rossiter Music. A tremendous hit in vaudeville. The Peerless Quartet had the original hit recording (Columbia A-1057). Nat Shilkret and the Victor Orchestra had a fine version in 1926 (Victor 20194). It was revived by Betty Grable in the film *Coney Island* (20th Century Fox, 1943) and again by Bette Midler in the film *The Rose* (20th Century Fox, 1979).

## LET ME GO, LOVER!
Jenny Lou Carson (w: Al Hill)
Hill and Range Songs——New York
1953, 54
**TV Show:** *Studio One* (CBS-TV)
Joan Weber sang this song on *Studio One*, and subsequently had the number 1 hit, which charted for sixteen weeks and sold over one million copies (Columbia 40366).

## LET THE REST OF THE WORLD GO BY
Ernest R. Ball (w: J. Keirn Brennan)
M. Witmark and Sons——New York
1919
Elizabeth Spencer and Charles Hart had the hit recording (Victor 18638). Dick Haymes sang it in the Ball biopic *Irish Eyes Are Smiling* (20th Century Fox, 1944).

## LET THE RIVER RUN
Carly Simon (w & m)
Warner Bros. Publications
1988, 1989
**Film:** *Working Girl* (20th Century Fox)
Academy Award winner for Best Song of 1988. Carly Simon sang it on the soundtrack of the film.

## LET'S CALL THE WHOLE THING OFF
George Gershwin (w: Ira Gershwin)
Chappell——New York
1937
**Film:** *Shall We Dance?* (RKO)
Fred Astaire and Ginger Rogers sang it in the film. Astaire had the number 5 hit, which charted for nine weeks (Brunswick 7857). The "tom-AY-to/tom-AH-to" lyric has become a part of America's cultural vocabulary.

## LET'S DO IT
Cole Porter (w & m)

Harms—New York

1928

**Show:** *Paris*

Irene Bordoni and Arthur Margetson sang it in the show. It was Porter's first real hit, one of his own personal favorites, and established him as a favorite of the sophisticates. Irving Aaronson and His Commanders had the hit recording, with vocals by Phil Saxe and Jack Armstrong (Victor 21745). Ginny Simms sang it in the Porter biopic *Night and Day* (Warner Bros., 1948) and it was revived by Frank Sinatra and Shirley MacLaine in *Can-Can* (20th Century Fox, 1960).

## LET'S DO IT AGAIN

Desmond O'Connor and Ray Hartley

Robbins Music—New York

1950

Happy song recorded by Margaret Whiting, accompanied by the happy sounds of Joe "Fingers" Carr (Capitol 1132).

## LET'S FALL IN LOVE

Harold Arlen (w: Ted Koehler)

Irving Berlin—New York

1933

**Film:** *Let's Fall in Love* (Columbia)

Art Jarrett sang it in the film. Eddie Duchin and His Orchestra had the number 1 hit in 1934, which charted for eleven weeks (Victor 24510). Peaches and Herb had a number 21 hit when they revived it in 1967 (Date 1523). It has become a cabaret standard.

## LET'S GET AWAY FROM IT ALL

Matt Dennis (w: Tom Adair)

Embassy Music—New York

1941

Tommy Dorsey and His Orchestra had the number 7 hit, with vocals by the Pied Pipers (Victor 27377).

## LET'S HANG ON

Bob Crewe/Sandy Linzer/Denny Randell

Saturday Music—New York

1965

The Four Seasons had the number 3 hit, which charted for twelve weeks (Philips 40317). A classic pop-rock, vocal-harmony song.

## LET'S HAVE ANOTHER CUP OF COFFEE

Irving Berlin (w & m)

Irving Berlin—New York

1932

**Show:** *Face the Music*

J. Harold Murray and Katherine Carrington sang it in the show. Fred Waring's Pennsylvanians had the number 5 hit, which charted for seven weeks (Victor 22936).

## LET'S HEAR IT FOR THE BOY

Tom Snow (w: Dean Pitchford)

Ensign Music—New York

1984

**Film:** *Footloose* (Paramount)

Deniece Williams had the number 1 hit, which charted for fourteen weeks (Columbia 04417). It sold more than two million copies.

## LET'S STAY TOGETHER

Willie Mitchell/Al Green/Al Jackson

JEC Music—Memphis, Tennessee

1971

Al Green's first number 1 hit, charting for fifteen weeks in 1972; also a number 1 R&B hit (Hi 2202), selling over one million copies. It began Green's successful string of 1970s hits, which lasted through 1974.

## LET'S TAKE AN OLD-FASHIONED WALK

Irving Berlin (w & m)

Irving Berlin—New York

1949

**Show:** *Miss Liberty*

Eddie Albert and Allyn McLerie sang it in the show. Perry Como had the number 15 hit (Victor 20-3469).

## LETTER, THE

Wayne Carson Thompson

Earl Barton Music—Springfield, Missouri

1967

Classic rock song of the 1960s, a number 1 hit for the Memphis-based group the Box Tops, featuring lead singer Alex Chilton. It held the top position for four out of thirteen weeks on the charts, and sold over a million copies (Mala 565). The song was also covered by the Arbors in 1969 (Date 1638) and Joe Cocker with Leon Russell a year later, achieving a number 7 hit (A&M 1174). Chilton has achieved cult status, thanks to his involvement in 1970 with the group Big Star and his subsequent solo performances and recordings.

## LIFE IS JUST A BOWL OF CHERRIES
Ray Henderson (w: Lew Brown)
DeSylva, Brown and Henderson—New York
1931
**Show:** *George White's Scandals*: 11th edition
Ethel Merman sang it in the show. Rudy Vallee made it famous on radio and had a number 3 hit that charted for five weeks (Victor 22783).

## LIGHT MY FIRE
The Doors (w & m)
Nipper Music
1967
The Doors had the number 1 hit, which charted for fourteen weeks and sold over one million copies (Elektra 45615). The long, midsong improvisatory solo by guitar and organ was cut from the original single release. The piece was also a tour-de-force for lead singer Jim Morrison, who gave it an appropriately orgiastic treatment.

## LIKE A PRAYER
Madonna Ciccone and Pat Leonard
WB Music
1989
Madonna had the number 1 hit, which charted for twelve weeks (Sire 27539). It sold over one million copies. The video for the song was controversial because it depicted Madonna kissing a black Jesus.

## LIKE A ROLLING STONE
Bob Dylan (w & m)
M. Witmark and Sons—New York
1965
Dylan's biggest hit, holding the number 2 spot for two out of its nine chart weeks in his original recording (Columbia 43346). A mighty, stream-of-consciousness, rock ballad, one of Dylan's signature songs. Revived by the Rolling Stones themselves for their 1994 European tour, documented on the 1995 album *Stripped* (Rolling Stones 41040).

## LIKE A VIRGIN
Billy Steinberg and Tom Kelly
Billy Steinberg Music
1984
Madonna's first number 1 disc. This stayed on the chart for fourteen weeks (Sire 29210), and sold over one million copies. Her performance of the song in a wedding dress on the first MTV Video Awards was a show stopper.

## LILA
Maceo Pinkard/Archie Gottler/Chas. Tobias
DeSylva, Brown and Henderson—New York
1928
Introduced by Watts and Marshall in vaudeville. Fred Waring's Pennsylvanians had the hit recording (Victor 21333).

## LIMEHOUSE BLUES
Philip Braham (w: Douglas Furber)
Harms—New York
1922
**Show:** *Andre Charlot's Revue of 1924*
Introduced in the show by Gertrude Lawrence, who made her U.S. debut. It was revived by Julie Andrews and Garrett Lewis in the Lawrence biopic *Star* (20th Century Fox, 1968). Paul Whiteman and His Orchestra had the original hit recording (Victor 19264). Cliff Jackson made a superb stride piano solo in 1944 (Black and White 26).

## LINDA
Jack Lawrence (w & m)
Edwin H. Morris—New York
1946
Ray Noble and His Orchestra, with vocal by Buddy Clark, had the number 1 hit, which charted for twenty-three weeks (Columbia 37215).

## LINGER AWHILE
Vincent Rose (w: Harry Owens)
Leo Feist—New York
1923
Introduced in vaudeville by Paul Whiteman, whose recording then sold two million copies (Victor 19211). It was featured in the film *Belles On Their Toes* (20th Century Fox, 1952).

## LION SLEEPS TONIGHT, THE (WIMOWEH)

Hugo Peretti/Luigi Creatore/
George David Weiss/Albert Stanton
Fokways Music—New York
1951, 1962

The Tokens had the number 1 hit in 1961, which charted for thirteen weeks and sold over one million copies (RCA Victor 7954). It was revived in 1972 with Robert John having the number 3 hit, which charted for thirteen weeks and also sold over one million copies (Atlantic 2846). The song was featured in the Disney animated film *The Lion King* (1994), and subsequently in the hit Broadway show based on it. It was originally a South African pop recording of the late 1940s that folk-lorist Alan Lomax introduced to the folk group the Weavers, and was performed and recorded by them as "Wimoweh," a number 14 hit in 1952 (Decca 27928).

## LITTLE BIT OF HEAVEN, A

Ernest R. Ball (w: J. Keirn Brennan)
M. Witmark and Sons—New York
1914
**Show:** *The Heart of Paddy Whack*
Chauncey Olcott sang it in the show. The famous Irish tenor John McCormack had a hit (Victor 64543). It was revived in the Ball biopic *Irish Eyes Are Smiling* (20th Century Fox, 1944), and by Dennis Morgan in the Olcott biopic *My Wild Irish Rose* (Warner Bros., 1947).

## LITTLE DRUMMER BOY, THE

Katherine Davis/Henry Onorati/Harry Simeone
Mills Music—New York
1960
Christmastime perennial, first recorded by the Harry Simeon Chorale in 1958, though not published until two years later. It charted thereafter in the Top twenty-five every year through 1962 (20th Century Fox 121).

## LITTLE FORD RAMBLED RIGHT ALONG, THE

Byron Gay (w: B. G. and C. R. Foster)
C. R. Foster—Los Angeles
1914
Billy Murray had the hit recording (Victor 17755).

## LITTLE GIRL

Francis Henry (w: Madeline Hyde)
Olman Music—New York
1931
Harold Arlen, accompanied by Joe Venuti's Blue Four, made a number 4 hit recording (Columbia 2488-D). Eubie Blake and His Orchestra had the instrumental hit (Victor 22735). It became the radio theme song for the popular Baby Snooks program, starring Fanny Brice. It was revived in the film *The Sting* (Universal, 1974).

## LITTLE THINGS MEAN A LOT

Edith Lindeman and Carl Stutz
Leo Feist—New York
1954
Kitty Kallen had the number 1 hit, which charted for twenty-six weeks and sold over one million copies (Decca 28904).

## LIVERY STABLE BLUES

Ray Lopez and Alcide Nuñez
Roger Graham Music Co.—Chicago
1917
Introduced in vaudeville and on record by the Original Dixieland Jazz Band (Victor 18255), and takes the credit as the first jazz recording. It has become a staple with Dixieland jazz bands, with hundreds of recordings made since.

## LIVIN' LA VIDA LOCA

Robi Rosa and Desmond Child
A Phantom Vox
1999
Ricky Martin's number 1 hit, which stayed on the charts for seventeen weeks, and sold over one million copies (C2/Columbia 79124). It helped introduce the Latino star to the U.S. pop market, thanks to his hip-swiveling performance on the 1999 Grammy Awards program.

## LIVIN' ON A PRAYER

Jon Bon Jovi/Richie Sambora/Desmond Child
Bon Jovi Publishing
1986
Bon Jovi had this number 1 hit, which stayed on the chart for thirteen weeks (Mercury 888184).

## LIZA
Maceo Pinkard and Nat Vincent
Harms—New York
1922
**Show:** *Liza*
Popularized on disc by Zez Confrey and His Orchestra (Victor 19055), Albert E. Short and his Tivoli Syncopators (Vocalion 14554), and the New Synco Jazz Band (Perfect 14104).

## LIZA
George Gershwin (w: Gus Kahn and
Ira Gershwin)
New World Music—New York
1929
**Show:** *Show Girl*
Introduced in the show by Ruby Keeler, accompanied by the Duke Ellington Orchestra, which was the pit band. Al Jolson, who had recently married Keeler, had the hit recording (Brunswick 4402). It quickly became a favorite of jazz musicians, and Teddy Wilson made a great piano solo (Brunswick 7563) in 1935. It was revived when Jolson sang it in his biopic *The Jolson Story* (Columbia, 1946). Liberace played it in the film *Sincerely Yours* (Warner Bros., 1955).

## LOCO-MOTION, THE
Gerry Goffin and Carole King
Aldon Music—New York
1962
Little Eva (Eva Narcissus Boyd) had the number 1 hit, which charted for twelve weeks and sold over one million copies (Dimension 1000). Eva was Goffin and King's babysitter, and was enlisted to do the vocal. It was her biggest hit, one she was never able to equal. Heavy rockers Grand Funk Railroad revived it in 1974 with their number 1 hit, which charted for fourteen weeks and also sold over one million copies (Capitol 3840). Australian popster Kylie Minogue revived it yet again in 1988, scoring a number 3 hit, which also sold over one million copies (Geffen 27752).

## LOLLIPOP
Beverly Ross and Julius Dixon
Edward B. Marks Music—New York
1958

Number 2 hit for the female vocal group the Chordettes, holding that position for two out of twelve weeks on the charts (Cadence 1349). The group hailed from Sheboygan, Wisconsin, and had been regulars on the Arthur Godfrey radio show from 1949 to 1953. They scored most of their hits in the mid-1950s.

## LONELY BOY
Paul Anka (w & m)
Spanka Music—New York
1958
**Film:** *Girls Town* (MGM)
Number 1 hit in 1959 for Paul Anka, holding that position four out of fourteen weeks on the charts and selling over a million copies (ABC-Paramount 10022); a classic of teen angst.

## LONESOME AND SORRY
Con Conrad (w: Benny Davis)
Henry Waterson—New York
1926
Introduced by Milton Berle in vaudeville. Ruth Etting had a hit recording (Columbia 644-D), as did Jean Goldkette and His Orchestra (Victor 20031).

## LONESOME, LOVESICK GOT-TO-HAVE-MY-DADDY BLUES
Ernie Erdman/Clarence Jones /Chester Cohn
Leo Feist—New York
1921
Introduced in vaudeville by Moody and Duncan. Warner's Seven Aces (Okeh 4924) and Lanin's Southern Serenaders (Regal 9164) helped make it a jazz standard.

## LONESOME MAMA BLUES
Billie Brown/A. W. Brown/E. Nickel
J. W. Jenkins Sons Music—Kansas City, Mo.
1922
Introduced in vaudeville by Eddie Jackson and Dot Taylor. It became a great favorite of jazz bands, particularly the Original Memphis Five (Banner 1068), the Virginians (Victor 18895), Ladd's Black Aces (Gennett 4886), and Jazzbo's Carolina Serenaders (Cameo 232).

## LONG AGO AND FAR AWAY
Jerome Kern (w: Ira Gershwin)

Crawford Music—New York

1944

**Film:** *Cover Girl* (Columbia)

Gene Kelly and Nan Wynn sang it in the film. Helen Forrest and Dick Haymes had the number 2 hit, which charted for eighteen weeks (Decca 23317).

## LONG AND WINDING ROAD, THE

John Lennon and Paul McCartney

Northern Songs—London

1970

The Beatles last number 1 hit, which charted for ten weeks (Apple 2832). McCartney's original solo piano version was a highlight of the film *Let It Be* (United Artists). Unfortunately, producer Phil Spector added strings and a swelling choir to the single, angering McCartney and further estranging him from his fellow group members. It sold over two million copies.

## LONG TALL SALLY

Enotris Johnson (w & m)

Venice Music—New York

1956

Little Richard had the original number 6 hit, which charted for twelve weeks and sold over one million copies (Specialty 572). Cover artist Pat Boone had a number 8 hit, which lasted nine weeks (Dot 15457). Little Richard's original was a favorite of Paul McCartney, who wrapped his tonsils around the song on the Beatles' second album (Capitol S 2080, 1964).

## LOOK FOR THE SILVER LINING

Jerome Kern (w: B. G. DeSylva)

T. B. Harms—New York

1920

**Show:** *Sally*

Introduced by Marilyn Miller and Irving Fisher. Miller also sang it in the 1929 version of the film (First National). Marion Harris had the hit recording (Columbia A-3367). It was sung in the Kern biopic *Till the Clouds Roll By* (MGM, 1946) and in the Miller biopic *Look For the Silver Lining* (Warner Bros., 1949).

## LOOKING AT THE WORLD THRU ROSE COLORED GLASSES

Tommie Malie and Jimmy Steiger

Milton Weil Music—Chicago

1926

Introduced in vaudeville by Jack Osterman. Popularized on disc by vocalist Jane Gray (Harmony 236-H) and as a piano solo by Jimmy Andrews (Banner 1831).

## LOOKING FOR A BOY

George and Ira Gershwin

Harms—New York

1925

**Show:** *Tip-Toes*

Introduced in the show by Queenie Smith. Hit recordings were by the Knickerbockers (Columbia 549-D) and Roger Wolfe Kahn and His Orchestra (Victor 19939).

## LOOKS LIKE WE MADE IT

Richard Kerr (w: Will Jennings)

Irving Music

1976, 1977

Barry Manilow had this number 1 hit that charted for thirteen weeks (Arista 0244). It sold over one million copies.

## LOT OF LIVIN' TO DO, A

Charles Strouse (w: Lee Adams)

Edwin H. Morris—New York

1960

**Show:** *Bye Bye Birdie*

Dick Gautier, Susan Watson, and the Teenagers sang it in the show. Jesse Pearson, Ann-Margaret, and Bobby Rydell sang it in the film version (Columbia, 1963).

## LOUIE LOUIE

Richard Berry (w & m)

Limax Music—New York

1957, 1963

The composer had the original recording in 1957; revived in 1963 by the Kingsmen, who had the number 2 hit, which charted for thirteen weeks (Wand 143). The song became a favorite of teenage boys and garage-rock bands everywhere; its indecipherable lyrics, on the Kingsmen's recording, made it the subject of endless speculation, and its simple and repetitive chord progression made it easy to master even for beginning guitarists. According to author Dave Marsh, the FBI investigated the song, trying to understand exactly what the Kingsmen were saying, but were unable to decipher it!

## LOUISE
Richard Whiting (w: Leo Robin)
Famous Music—New York
1929
**Film:** *Innocents of Paris* (Paramount)
Maurice Chevalier sang it in the film and also had the hit recording (Victor 21918); he revived it in the film *A New Kind of Love* (Paramount, 1963). Chevalier remained identified with it through his long career.

## LOVE AND MARRIAGE
James Van Heusen
(w: Sammy Cahn)
Barton Music—New York
1955
**TV Show:** *Our Town* (NBC-TV)
Frank Sinatra sang it in the show and had a number 5 hit that charted for fifteen weeks (Capitol 3260). His version was used as the theme song for the 1990s television series *Married With Children* (Fox-TV).

## LOVE CHILD
Pam Sawyer/R. Dean Taylor/Frank Wilson/
Deke Richards
Jobete Music—Detroit
1968
Diana Ross and the Supremes had the number 1 hit, which charted for fifteen weeks (Motown 1135). It was revived in 1990 by the female vocal trio Sweet Sensation, reaching number 13 (Atco 98983).

## LOVE IN BLOOM
Ralph Rainger (w: Leo Robin)
Famous Music—New York
1934
**Film:** *She Loves Me Not* (Paramount)
Bing Crosby and Kitty Carlisle sang it in the film. Crosby had the number 1 hit, which charted for fifteen weeks (Brunswick 6936). After Jack Benny performed it in the film *College Holiday* (Paramount, 1936), it became his radio—and then television—theme song for the rest of his life.

## LOVE IS A MANY-SPLENDORED THING
Sammy Fain (w: Paul Webster)
Miller Music—New York
1955
**Film:** *Love Is a Many-Splendored Thing* (20th Century Fox)
Academy Award winner for Best Song. The Four Aces had the number 1 hit, which charted for twenty-one weeks (Decca 29625). It sold over one million copies.

## LOVE IS BLUE
Andre Popp (w: Blackburn)
Crema Music—New York
1968
Paul Mauriat and His Orchestra had the number 1 hit as an instrumental that sold over one million copies. It retained its top chart position for five of the fifteen weeks charted (Philips 40495).

## LOVE IS HERE TO STAY
George and Ira Gershwin
Chappell—New York
1938
**Film:** *The Goldwyn Follies* (United Artists)
In this film, Kenny Baker sang the last song that George Gershwin wrote. Larry Clinton and His Orchestra had the number 15 hit (Victor 25761). It has become a cabaret favorite.

## LOVE IS JUST AROUND THE CORNER
Lewis Gensler (w: Leo Robin)
Famous Music—New York
1934
**Film:** *Here Is My Heart* (Paramount)
Bing Crosby sang it in the film. He also had the number 8 hit that charted for nine weeks (Decca 310).

## LOVE LETTERS IN THE SAND
J. Fred Coots (w: Nick and Charles Kenny)
Irving Berlin—New York
1931
Ted Black and His Orchestra had the number 6 hit, which charted for seven weeks (Victor 22799). It was revived by Pat Boone, who had a number 1 hit in 1957 that charted for twenty-four weeks and sold over one million copies (Dot 15570).

## LOVE ME DO
John Lennon and Paul McCartney

Ardmore and Beechwood Ltd.—London

1962

The Beatles's first hit in England and a number 1 hit in 1964 in the United States, where it charted for eleven weeks (Tollie 9008).

## LOVE ME OR LEAVE ME
Walter Donaldson (w: Gus Kahn)

Donaldson, Douglas and Gumble—New York

1928

**Show:** *Whoopee*

Ruth Etting sang it in the show and had the hit recording (Columbia 1680-D). Dinah Shore revived it in 1941, accompanied by Henry Levine and His Dixie Octet (Bluebird 11278). Etting's biopic (MGM, 1955) was named after the song. Sammy Davis Jr. revived the song for a number 12 hit in 1955 (Decca 29484).

## LOVE ME TENDER
Elvis Presley and Vera Matson

Elvis Presley Music—New York

1956

**Film:** *Love Me Tender* (20th Century Fox)

Elvis Presley had the number 1 hit from his first film, which charted for nineteen weeks and sold over five million copies (RCA Victor 47-6643). It was a change of pace for Presley—a languid love ballad that made teenage girls swoon. The song's melody is based on the 1861 minstrel song, "Aura Lee." Richard Chamberlain revived it in 1962 and had a number 21 hit (MGM 13075), and Percy Sledge revived it again in 1967 for a number 40 hit (Atlantic 2414).

## LOVE NEST, THE
Louis A. Hirsch (w: Otto Harbach)

Victoria—New York

1920

**Show:** *Mary*

Introduced in the show by Jack McGowan and Janet Velie. Joseph C. Smith and His Orchestra had a hit recording (Victor 18678). As the theme song for the Burns and Allen hit radio and television shows, it never left the public's consciousness.

## LOVE WILL FIND A WAY
Eubie Blake (w: Noble Sissle)

M. Witmark and Sons—New York

1921

**Show:** *Shuffle Along*

Introduced in the show by Roger Matthews and Lottie Gee. Sissle and Blake had the hit recording (Emerson 10396). The song had two instrumental hits, one by Selvin's Orchestra (Brunswick 2144), the other by Leroy Smith's Dance Orchestra (Vocalion 14218).

## LOVE WILL KEEP US TOGETHER
Neil Sedaka and Howard Greenfield

Don Kirshner Music—New York

1973, 1975

The Captain and Tennille had the number 1 hit, holding the top spot for four out of sixteen weeks on the charts (A&M 1672). It sold over one million copies.

## LOVE WILL LEAD YOU BACK
Diane Warren (w & m)

Realsongs

1989, 1990

Taylor Dayne, whose real name is Leslie Wundermann, had this number 1 hit, which lasted on the Top 40 chart for fifteen weeks (Arista 9938). It sold over half a million copies.

## LOVELY TO LOOK AT
Jerome Kern (w: Dorothy Fields and Jimmy McHugh)

T. B. Harms—New York

1935

**Film:** *Roberta* (RKO)

Irene Dunn sang it in the film. Eddy Duchin had the number 1 hit that charted for fourteen weeks (Victor 24871). Howard Keel sang it in the remake of the film, which took the song's name (MGM, 1952).

## LOVER
Richard Rodgers (w: Lorenz Hart)

Famous Music—New York

1933

**Film:** *Love Me Tonight* (Paramount)

Jeanette MacDonald sang it in the film. Paul Whiteman and His Orchestra, with vocal by Jack Fulton, had a number 3 hit that charted for seven weeks (Victor 24283). Peggy Lee revived it in 1952 with a number 3 hit, which charted for thirteen weeks and sold over one million copies (Decca 28215).

## LOVER, COME BACK TO ME
Sigmund Romberg (w: Oscar Hammerstein)
Harms—New York
1928
**Show:** *The New Moon*
Evelyn Herbert sang it in the show. The theme was taken from Tschaikovsky's "June Barcarolle." Rudy Vallee featured it on radio and had a hit recording (Victor 21868). Paul Whiteman and His Orchestra had the instrumental hit (Columbia 1731-D). Lawrence Tibbett sang it in the film version, which was called *New Moon* (MGM, 1930). The second time it was filmed, Jeanette MacDonald and Nelson Eddy sang it as a duet (MGM, 1940). It was revived as a number 16 hit in 1953 by Nat "King" Cole (Capitol 2610). Tony Martin and Joan Weldon sang it in the Romberg biopic *Deep in My Heart* (MGM, 1954).

## LOVIE JOE
Joe Jordan (w: Will Marion Cook)
Harry Von Tilzer—New York
1910
**Show:** *Ziegfeld Follies of 1910*
Fanny Brice sang it in the show, and it turned her into a star.

## LUCKY DAY
Ray Henderson (w: Bud DeSylva and Lew Brown)
Harms—New York
1926
**Show:** *George White's Scandals*
Introduced by Harry Richman in the show. George Olsen's Orchestra had the hit recording (Victor 20101), but Ohman and Arden with their Orchestra (Brunswick 3242) and Howard Lanin's Orchestra (Columbia 689-D) helped it along. As the radio theme song for *Your Hit Parade*, it was heard every week for almost twenty years. It was included in the writers' biopic *The Best Things in Life Are Free* (20th Century Fox, 1956).

## LUCKY IN LOVE
Ray Henderson (w: Lew Brown and B. G. DeSylva)
DeSylva, Brown and Henderson—New York
1927
**Show:** *Good News!*
Introduced in the show by Mary Lawlor and John Price Jones. George Olsen and His Music was the pit band in the show and recorded this number (Victor 20872), as did Fred Rich and His Orchestra (Columbia 1108-D). It was sung in the DeSylva, Brown, and Henderson biopic *The Best Things In Life Are Free* (20th Century Fox, 1956).

## LUCKY LINDY
Abel Baer (w: L. Wolfe Gilbert)
Leo Feist—New York
1927
The most popular of the Lindbergh songs; Vernon Dalhart's version was the hit (Columbia 1000-D).

## LUCY IN THE SKY WITH DIAMONDS
John Lennon and Paul McCartney
Maclen Music
1967
Recorded by the Beatles as part of their *Sergeant Pepper's Lonely Hearts Club Band* album (Capitol S 2653, 1967). The title was supposed to be based on a children's drawing made by Lennon's son Julian, although others read into it a drug reference (L-S-D). Elton John achieved the number 1 hit in 1975, when it was on the chart for ten weeks, and John Lennon played guitars on this recording (MCA 40344). He also promised to perform with John at Madison Square Garden if the song reached number 1; their performance together was one of Lennon's few live appearances in the 1970s. The record sold over one million copies.

## LULLABY OF BIRDLAND
George Shearing (w: B. Y. Forster)
Patricia Music—New York
1954
Jazz pianist George Shearing named this song for the famous New York City nightclub where he was performing. A French group, Blue Stars, had the number 16 hit in 1956 (Mercury 70742). It has remained a bebop standard.

## LULLABY OF BROADWAY
Harry Warren (w: Al Dubin)
M. Witmark and Sons—New York
1935
**Film:** *Gold Diggers of 1935* (Warner Bros.)
Academy Award winner for Best Song. Wini Shaw and Dick Powell sang it in the film. The Dorsey Brothers Orchestra had the number 1 hit, which charted for eleven weeks (Decca 370). Doris Day sang it in the film of the same name (Warner Bros., 1951).

## LYIN' EYES
Don Henley and Glenn Frey
Benchmark Music
1975
Number 2 hit for the country-rocking Eagles, holding that spot for two out of eleven weeks on the charts (Aslyum 45279). The song became a standard for the group.

## MA
Con Conrad (w: Sidney Clare)
Fred Fisher—New York
1921
**Show:** *The Midnight Rounders*
Eddie Cantor sang it in the show and for the rest of his life in show business. The Benson (Victor 18819) and Isham Jones Orchestras (Brunswick 5065) had hit recordings. Eubie Blake recorded a flashy piano solo that was the envy of his competitors (Emerson 10450). It was revived by Eddie Cantor in his biopic *The Eddie Cantor Story* (Warner Bros., 1953).

## MA BLUSHIN' ROSIE
John Stromberg (w: Edgar Smith)
M. Witmark and Sons—New York
1900
**Show:** *Fiddle-Dee-Dee*
Introduced by Fay Templeton in the Weber and Fields show, it became her greatest hit. Al Jolson sang it on the soundtracks to both *The Jolson Story* (Columbia, 1946) and *Jolson Sings Again* (Columbia, 1949). It also appeared in the film biopic, *Lillian Russel* (20th Century Fox, 1940), and in *The Daughter of Rosie O'Grady* (Warner Bros., 1950).

## MACARENA
Antonio Romero and Rafael Ruiz
Rightsong Music
1994
Los Del Rio (a fictional group, actually consisting of studio musicians led by the composers) charted with this peppy dance number for 37 weeks, fourteen of them in the number 1 position (RCA 64407). It sold more than five million copies. A short-lived dance craze, involving simple, repeated arm movements, was designed around the instrumental.

## MACARTHUR PARK
Jimmy Webb (w & m)
Canopy Music
1968, 1973
Richard Harris had the original recording of this melodramatic pop ballad, which reached number 2, remaining on the charts for ten weeks (Dunhill 4134). Donna Summer revived it for a number 1 hit in 1978, when it charted for fifteen weeks (Casablanca 939). Summer's version sold over one million copies. A kitsch classic, the song is one that you either love or hate (or both).

## MACK THE KNIFE ("MORITAT")
Kurt Weill (w: Marc Blitzstein)
Harms—New York
1928, 1955
**Show:** *The Three Penny Opera*
Taken from the German show of 1928, whose phenomenally long run at the Theatre De Lys in Greenwich Village, New York City, in English featured Scott Merrill singing this song. The Dick Hyman Trio had a number 8 hit in 1956, which charted for fifteen weeks and sold over one million copies under the title "Moritat" (MGM 12149). That same year, jazz great Louis Armstrong had a number 20 hit under the present title (Columbia 40587); Armstrong continued to feature the song in his concerts until his death in 1971. Teen popster Bobby Darin had a number 1 hit with it in 1959 that charted for twenty-two weeks and sold over one million copies (Atco 6147).

## MADELON
Camille Robert (w: Alfred Bryan)

Jerome H. Remick—New York
1918
Introduced by the Victor Military Band (Victor 18534) with a vocal by opera star Marcel Journet. It was revived by Willie the Lion Smith in 1972 (Jazz Odyssey 009).

## MAGGIE MAY
Rod Stewart and Martin Quittenton
Unichappell
1971
Rod Stewart started his solo career with this number 1 hit, which held this position for five of the fifteen weeks charted (Mercury 73224). It sold over one million copies. He was at the time lead singer for the Small Faces, but the group would soon splinter because of his solo success.

## MAGIC
John Farrar (w & m)
JF Music
1980
**Film:** *Xanadu* (Universal)
Olivia Newton-John starred in the film and had the number 1 hit, which charted for sixteen weeks (MCA 41247). It sold over one million copies. The film itself, an embarrassing musical featuring an aging Gene Kelly, was a box office bomb despite the success of this song.

## MAKE BELIEVE
Jerome Kern (w: Oscar Hammerstein)
T. B. Harms—New York
1927
**Show:** *Show Boat*
Howard Marsh and Norma Terris sang it in the show. Irene Dunne and Allan Jones sang it in the first film version (MGM, 1936), and Kathryn Grayson and Howard Keel sang it in the second (MGM, 1951). Grayson and Tony Martin sang it in the Kern biopic *Till the Clouds Roll By* (MGM, 1946). Paul Whiteman and His Orchestra had the original hit recording (Victor 21218).

## MAKE BELIEVE BALLROOM
Paul Denniker (w: Andy Razaf)
Joe Davis—New York
1936

Radio theme song for pioneer deejay Martin Block's show on WNEW in New York.

## MAKE IT WITH YOU
David Gates (w & m)
Screen Gems-Columbia Music—New York
1970
Number 1 hit for soft rockers Bread—their first single—which charted for thirteen weeks (Elektra 45686). It established them as pop hit makers through the early 1970s.

## MAKIN' WHOOPEE!
Walter Donaldson (w & m)
Donaldson, Douglas and Gumble—New York
1928
**Show:** *Whoopee!*
Eddie Cantor sang it in the show and had the hit recording (Victor 21831). He then sang it in the film version (United Artists, 1930); in another film, *Show Business* (RKO, 1944); and in his biopic *The Eddie Cantor Story* (Warner Bros., 1953).

## MAMA TOLD ME (NOT TO COME)
Randy Newman (w & m)
January Music—New York
1970
A hit for the pop-rock group Three Dog Night, holding the number 1 position for two out of thirteen weeks on the charts and selling over a million copies (Dunhill 4239).

## MAMA'S GONE, GOODBYE
Peter Bocage and Armand J. Piron
Clarence Williams Music—New York
1924
Introduced on disc by Piron's New Orleans Orchestra (Victor 19233), featuring Bocage on trumpet. The pianist in this Orchestra, Steve Lewis, made a fine piano roll (QRS 2699). It has since become a standard for Dixieland jazz bands.

## MAMMY BLOSSOM'S POSSUM PARTY
Theodore Morse (w: Arthur Fields)
Leo Feist—New York
1917

Introduced on disc by Collins and Harlan (Victor 18354).

## MAMMY JINNY'S JUBILEE
Lewis F. Muir (w: L. Wolfe Gilbert)
F. A. Mills—New York
1913
Introduced in vaudeville by Louise Bauer. Popularized on disc by Collins and Harlan (Victor 17411).

## MAMMY O' MINE
Maceo Pinkard (w: William Tracey)
Shapiro, Bernstein—New York
1919
A million-seller in sheet music, it was recorded by the Original Dixieland Jazz Band in England (Columbia 804). Joseph C. Smith and His Orchestra had the hit instrumental here (Victor 18615).

## MAMMY'S LITTLE COAL BLACK ROSE
Richard A. Whiting (w: Raymond Egan)
Jerome H. Remick—New York
1916
Introduced in vaudeville by Blossom Seeley. Popularized on disc by the Orpheus Quartet (Victor 18183).

## MAN I LOVE, THE
George Gershwin (w: Ira Gershwin)
Harms—New York
1924
**Show:** *Lady, Be Good!*
After it was dropped from the show during out-of-town tryouts, it became a favorite on the radio and with dance bands. Marion Harris had a hit recording (Victor 21116), as did the Troubadours (Victor 21233). Hazel Scott revived it at the piano for the Gershwin biopic *Rhapsody in Blue* (Warner Bros., 1945). Diana Ross sang it in the Billie Holiday biopic *Lady Sings the Blues* (Paramount, 1972). It remains a cabaret standard.

## MAN IN THE MIRROR
Glen Ballard and Siedah Garrett
Yellowbrick Road Music
1987

Number 1 hit in 1988 for Michael Jackson, holding that spot for two out of thirteen weeks on the charts (Epic 07668).

## MAN THAT GOT AWAY, THE
Harold Arlen (w: Ira Gershwin)
Harwin Music—New York
1954
**Film:** *A Star Is Born* (Warner Bros. )
Judy Garland sang it in the film and became identified with it because she used it as her theme song on radio, television, in nightclubs, and stage shows.

## MAÑANA
Peggy Lee and Dave Barbour
Barbour-Lee Music—New York
1948
Peggy Lee had the number 1 hit, which charted for twenty-one weeks and sold over one million copies (Capitol 15022).

## MANDY
Irving Berlin (w & m)
Irving Berlin—New York
1918
**Show:** *Yip-Yip-Yaphank*
Written for a minstrel group setting, it was then interpolated into the *Ziegfeld Follies of 1919*, where Van and Schenck sang it with Marilyn Miller and Ray Dooley. Eddie Cantor revived it in the movie *Kid Millions* (United Artists, 1934), and Trudy Stevens sang it in the film *White Christmas* (Paramount, 1954).

## MANDY
Richard Kerr and Scott English
Screen Gems-Columbia Music
1971, 1974
Originally written as "Brandy," the song was revived as the first single (and first number 1 hit) of popular 1970s-era singer Barry Manilow (Barry Alkan Pincus) under the name "Mandy." The song hit in 1975, charting for twelve weeks, and selling over one million copies.

## MANDY, MAKE UP YOUR MIND
George W. Meyer and Arthur Johnstone
(w: Roy Turk and Grant Clarke)

Irving Berlin—New York

1924

**Show:** *Dixie to Broadway*

Florence Mills sang it in the show. Paul Whiteman and His Orchestra had the hit recording (Victor 19492). It has since become a favorite with traditional jazz bands.

## MANEATER

Daryl Hall and John Oates (w: Sara Allen, Hall and Oates)

Unichappell Music

1982

Hall and Oates had this number 1 hit, which held that position for four out of seventeen weeks (RCA 13354). It sold over one million copies.

## MANHATTAN

Richard Rodgers (w: Lorenz Hart)

Edward B. Marks Music—New York

1925

**Show:** *Garrick Gaieties*

June Cochrane and Sterling Holloway sang it in the show. Paul Whiteman and His Orchestra had a hit recording (Victor 19769). Tom Drake, Mickey Rooney, and Marshall Thompson sang it in the Rodgers and Hart biopic *Words and Music* (MGM, 1948). Its urbane lyrics long have made it a favorite song about New York.

## MANHATTAN SERENADE

Louis Alter

Robbins Music—New York

1928

Theme song for the radio show *The Easy Aces*, starring Jane and Goodman Ace. Tommy Dorsey and His Orchestra had a hit recording in 1943 (Victor 27962).

## MANSION OF ACHING HEARTS

Harry Von Tilzer (w: Arthur J. Lamb)

Harry Von Tilzer—New York

1902

One of the few sequel songs to make a hit, this was a follow-up to "A Bird in a Gilded Cage." This tearjerker was successfully featured in vaudeville by Florence Gill and Charles Ennis. Harry MacDonough had the hit recording (Victor 1415).

## MAORI

William H. Tyers (w: Henry S. Creamer)

Gotham-Attucks Music—New York

1909

Popularized on disc by the Rishell Band (Rishell 5092) and in a piano solo by Mike Bernard in 1913 (Columbia A-1427).

## MAPLE LEAF RAG

Scott Joplin

John Stark and Son—Sedalia, Mo.

1899

The greatest rag ever written, it established the rag genre as a popular music. It was the first rag to sell a million copies of sheet music. It became a famous test piece for budding pianists, and was recorded innumerable times. African-American composer Joplin (1868–1917) won a Pulitzer Prize for composition in 1975. *They All Played the Maple Leaf Rag* CD contains twenty-seven performances throughout eighty-five years (Archive Productions CD-1600).

## MARGIE

Con Conrad and J. Russel Robinson (w: Benny Davis)

Waterson, Berlin and Snyder—New York

1920

Five-year-old Marjorie Cantor, daughter of the famous comedian Eddie, inspired this song, which was added to his Broadway revue *The Midnight Rounders*. Gene Rodemich and His Orchestra had the first instrumental hit (Brunswick 2060), followed by Eddie Cantor's vocal hit (Emerson 10301). But it was the Original Dixieland Jazz Band's recording that holds the record (if you'll pardon the pun) for staying in print continuously for sixty years (Victor 18717).

## MARIE

Irving Berlin (w & m)

Irving Berlin—New York

1928

**Film:** *The Awakening* (United Artists)

Rudy Vallee popularized it on radio and in his hit recording (Harmony 834-H). Tommy Dorsey revived it in his 1937 recording (Victor 25523), which sold over a million copies. The vocal is by Jack Leonard and the boys in the band. He played it in his biopic *The Fabulous Dorseys* (United Artists, 1947). It was revived in a number 15 hit recording by the Bachelors in 1965 (London 9762).

## MARSHMALLOW WORLD, A
Peter DeRose (w: Carl Sigman)
Shapiro, Bernstein—New York
1950
Bing Crosby had the number 24 hit in 1951 (Decca 27230).

## MARY LOU
Abe Lyman/George Waggner/J. Russel Robinson
Henry Waterson—New York
1926
Introduced with a hit recording by Abe Lyman and His Orchestra (Brunswick 3135). The Ipana Troubadours also enjoyed a hit (Columbia 738-D). The seldom-recorded Pete Wendling, who made over seven hundred piano rolls, made a gem of a piano recording (Cameo 1064) with vocalist Frances Sper. Joe "Fingers" Carr revived it on his 1959 *Swingin' Strings* LP (Capitol T-1217).

## MARY'S A GRAND OLD NAME
George M. Cohan (w & m)
F. A. Mills—New York
1905
**Show:** *Forty Five Minutes From Broadway*
Introduced in the show by Donald Brian. James Cagney sang it in biopic *Yankee Doodle Dandy* (Warner Bros., 1942), and he and Bob Hope danced to it in *The Seven Little Foys* (Paramount, 1955).

## MASCULINE WOMEN! FEMININE MEN!
James V. Monaco (w: Edgar Leslie)
Clarke and Leslie Songs—New York
1925
Introduced in vaudeville by Maureen Englin. There is a great recording of this comic number by the Six Jumping Jacks (Brunswick 3095).

## MATERIAL GIRL
Peter Brown and Robert Rans
Minong Publishing
1985

Number 2 hit for Madonna, which held that position for two out of twelve weeks on the charts (Sire 29083). It was a signature song for Madonna during the early part of her career; many, failing to see the song's humor, faulted her for her proud espousal of "materialism." It was promoted through a video homage to Marilyn Monroe's production number for "Diamonds Are a Girl's Best Friend," from *How to Marry a Millionaire.*

## MAYBE
George Gershwin (w: Ira Gershwin)
Harms—New York
1926
**Show:** *Oh, Kay!*
Introduced in the show by Gertrude Lawrence and Oscar Shaw. George Gershwin recorded a piano solo (Columbia 812-D), and Nat Shilkret and the Victor Orchestra had a fine version (Victor 20392).

## MAYBE BABY
Norman Petty and Charles Hardin
Nor Va Jak Music—New York
1957
Buddy Holly and the Crickets had the number 17 hit in 1958 that charted for eight weeks (Brunswick 55053).

## MAYBELLENE
Chuck Berry/Russ Fratto/Alan Freed
ARC Music—New York
1955
Chuck Berry's first success and number 5 hit, which charted for eleven weeks (Chess 1604). A rock and roll classic, it is based on the traditional country song, "Ida Red."

## MAZIE
Lew Gold/Sid Caine/Eli Dawson
Jack Mills—New York
1921
Marvelous song popularized on disc by the All Star Trio (Victor 18738), Banjo Wallace and His Orchestra (Okeh 4280), and the Yerkes Jazarimba Orchestra (Columbia A-3393).

## ME AND BOBBY MCGEE
Kris Kristofferson and Fred Foster

Combine Music—Nashville

1969

Country singer Kris Kristofferson's best-known song, thanks to Janis Joplin's number 1 recording, which charted for twelve weeks in 1971 following her tragic death (Columbia 45314). The opening line of the chorus, "Freedom is just another name for nothing left to lose," became a catchphrase of the era.

## ME AND MY SHADOW

Dave Dreyer and Al Jolson (w: Billy Rose)

Irving Berlin—New York

1927

Hit recordings were by Whispering Jack Smith (Victor 20626) and Nat Shilkret and the Victor Orchestra (Victor 20675). Revived in the film *Funny Lady* (Columbia, 1975). A perennial favorite.

## ME AND THE BOY FRIEND

Jimmie Monaco (w: Sidney Clare)

Jerome H. Remick—New York

1924

Introduced in vaudeville and on records by Jane Green (Victor 19502). Popularized on disc by Ray Miller and His Orchestra (Brunswick 2753) and Isabelle Patricola with the Ambassadors (Vocalion 14906).

## MEAN TO ME

Fred E. Ahlert (w: Roy Turk)

DeSylva, Brown and Henderson—New York

1929

Popular torch song, with the original hit recording by Ruth Etting (Columbia 1762-D). There is a fine instrumental version by the Yankee Ten Orchestra (Oriole 1536). Revived in 1937 by Teddy Wilson and His Orchestra, with a vocal by Billie Holiday (Brunswick 7903). Doris Day sang it in the Etting biopic *Love Me Or Leave Me* (MGM, 1955), and Diana Ross sang it in the Holiday biopic *Lady Sings the Blues* (Paramount, 1972). Nell Carter revived it in the 1978 show *Ain't Misbehavin'*.

## MEET ME IN ST. LOUIS, LOUIS

Kerry Mills (w: Andrew B. Sterling)

F. A. Mills—New York

1904

Occasioned by the St. Louis World's Fair, it became an enormous hit. Like most pop standards from the first decade of the twentieth century, it was a waltz. Billy Murray had the hit (Victor 2850). It became the name of a film starring Judy Garland (MGM, 1944) who then had a number 22 hit (Decca 23360), and was sung in the musical film *By the Light of the Silvery Moon* (Warner Bros., 1953).

## MEET ME TONIGHT IN DREAMLAND

Leo Friedman

(w: Beth Slater Whitson)

Leo Friedman—Chicago

1909

The biggest selling song of 1909, eventually selling around five million copies in sheet music. Henry Burr made the hit recording (Columbia A-905). Judy Garland revived it in the movie *In The Good Old Summertime* (MGM, 1949). It was also featured in *The Eddie Cantor Story* (Warner Bros., 1953).

## MELANCHOLY LOU

Ray Hibbeler (w & m)

Garrick Music—Chicago

1925

A popular song in vaudeville. Howard Lanin and His Orchestra had a hit recording (Victor 19797) as did the Little Ramblers (Columbia 423-D).

## MELLOW YELLOW

Donovan Leitch (w & m)

Peer International—New York

1966

Donovan had the number 2 hit, which charted for ten weeks and sold over one million copies (Epic 10098). Some believed that the title referred to a popular tranquilizer.

## MEMORIES

Egbert Van Alstyne (w: Gus Kahn)

Jerome H. Remick—New York

1915

A million-seller in sheet music, Henry Burr had a hit recording (Columbia A-1923). It was revived in the Kahn biopic *I'll See You In My Dreams* (Warner Bros., 1951).

## MEMORIES ARE MADE OF THIS
Terry Gilkyson/Richard Dehr/Frank Miller
Blackwood Music—New York
1955
Dean Martin had the number 1 hit, which charted for nineteen weeks and sold over one million copies (Capitol 3295).

## MEMORIES OF YOU
Eubie Blake (w: Andy Razaf)
Shapiro, Bernstein—New York
1930
**Show:** *Lew Leslie's Blackbirds of 1930*
Blake's best-loved song. Minto Cato sang it in the show. That same year, Ethel Waters had the first recording (Columbia 2288-D), and Louis Armstrong and His Orchestra scored a number 18 hit (Okeh 41463). Garland Wilson made an outstanding piano solo in 1932 (Okeh 41556). Glen Gray and his Casa Loma Orchestra revived it in a 1937 disc that became a classic (Decca 1672), and the Ink Spots revived it in 1940 as a harmony vocal piece, getting a number 29 hit (Decca 2966). It was featured by the Benny Goodman Trio in the film *The Benny Goodman Story* (Universal, 1956); that year the trio, with vocalist Rosemary Clooney, had a number 20 hit (Columbia 40616) with the song. Eubie Blake recorded a splendid piano solo version on his 1969 double LP *The Eighty-Six Years of Eubie Blake* (Columbia C2S-847).

## MEMORY
Andrew Lloyd Webber (w: Trevor Nunn)
The Really Useful Group
1981
Show: *Cats*
Betty Buckley sang it in the show on Broadway. Barry Manilow had the hit recording in 1983 (Arista 1025). It has since been covered endlessly by cabaret artists and pop concert singers.

## MEMPHIS BLUES
W. C. Handy
Theron C. Bennett
1912
Introduced in vaudeville by Honey Boy Evans's Minstrel Band, it was given a splendid recording by the Victor Military Band (Victor 17619). Ted Lewis and His Band revived it as a number 9 hit in 1927 (Columbia 1050-D). It has become a standard and was featured in the Handy biopic *St. Louis Blues* (Paramount, 1958). The song was originally titled "Mr. Crump," and was written as a campaign song for the Memphis mayorial candidate.

## MERRY WIDOW WALTZ, THE
Franz Lehar
Anglo-American Music—New York
1907
**Show:** *The Merry Widow*
Danced by Ethel Jackson and Donald Brian in the wildly successful Broadway musical import from Vienna. When the operetta was made into the film, Jeanette MacDonald and Maurice Chevalier danced it (MGM, 1934). The remake featured Lana Turner and Fernando Lamas (MGM, 1952). The tune was also the dark theme song for the murderous Uncle Charlie, "The Merry Widow Murderer," in the Hitchcock film *Shadow of a Doubt* (Universal, 1943).

## MERRY WIDOW'S GOT A SWEETIE NOW, THE
Lew Porter and Sam A. Perry
Handy Bros.—New York
1928
Lew Weimer's Black and Gold Aces had the best recording of this great Charleston number (Gennett 6540).

## MERRY-GO-ROUND BROKE DOWN, THE
Cliff Friend and Dave Franklin
Harms—New York
1937
Russ Morgan and His Orchestra had the number 1 hit that charted ten weeks (Brunswick 7888).

## MESSIN' AROUND
Charles L. Cooke (w: John A. St. Cyr)
Will Rossiter—Chicago
1926
A jazz standard with the initial recording made by the composer and lyricist in Cookie's Gingersnaps (Okeh 8390). Joe Candullo and His Orchestra also made a fine version (Domino 3772).

## MIDNIGHT TRAIN TO GEORGIA

Jim Weatherly (w & m)

Keca Music—Hollywood

1971, 1973

Gladys Knight and the Pips had their lone 1970s number 1 hit with this song, which charted for sixteen weeks (Buddah 383). It sold over one million copies.

## MIGHTY LAK' A ROSE

Ethelbert Nevin (w: Frank L. Stanton)

John Church—Cincinnati

1901

This coon song is referred to as "an art song in dialect." It gained popularity in vaudeville and subsequently sold a million copies in sheet music. Opera star Geraldine Farrar, accompanied by violinist Fritz Kreisler, made an outstanding record (Victor 88537) in 1916. Deanna Durbin revived it in the film *The Amazing Mrs. Holiday* (Universal, 1943).

## MILENBERG JOYS

Ferd "Jelly Roll" Morton/Leon Roppolo/
Paul Mares (w: Walter Melrose)

Melrose Bros. Music—Chicago

1925

Introduced in vaudeville by Ted Lewis and His Orchestra, who also recorded it (Columbia 439-D). Introduced on disc by the New Orleans Rhythm Kings in 1923 (Gennett 3076, tk. 1, and Gennett 5217, tk. 4). and also popularized on disc by Busse's Buzzards (Victor 19782), Jimmy Joy and His Orchestra (Okeh 40251), the Cotton Pickers (Brunswick 2937), and Perry's Hot Dogs (Banner 1618). It has become a standard and a favorite with traditional jazz bands.

## MINE

James F. Hanley (w: B. G. DeSylva)

Shapiro, Bernstein—New York

1927

Lovely song popularized by Horace Heidt's (Victor 20608) and the Arden-Ohman orchestra (Brunswick 3457). Fred Elizalde made a fabulous syncopated piano solo (English Brunswick 102).

## MINNIE THE MERMAID

Bud DeSylva (w & m)

Leo Feist—New York

1923

Introduced in vaudeville by Rudy Vallee and revived in 1949 by Pete Daily and his Chicagoans (Capitol 1055). A favorite of Dixieland bands.

## MISS ANNABELLE LEE

Lew Pollack (w: Sidney Clare)

Irving Berlin—New York

1927

Introduced in vaudeville by Harry Richman. Hit recording by the Knickerbockers (Columbia 1088-D), and Jane Gray had a nice vocal (Diva 2464-G). Revived in the film *Gentlemen Marry Brunettes* (United Artists, 1955). A standard and favorite of jazz bands.

## MISS YOU

Mick Jagger and Keith Richards

Colgems-EMI Music

1978

Number 1 hit for the Rolling Stones, a position it held for one out of the sixteen weeks it charted (Rolling Stones 19307). It is (to date) the band's last number 1 hit, and it was also their last single to sell over a million copies. It was notable at the time because the band adopted a disco beat for the song, a major heresy to their hard-rock fans.

## MISS YOU MUCH

James Harris III and Terry Lewis

Flyte Tyme Tunes

1989

Janet Jackson had this number 1 hit on the chart for thirteen weeks (A&M 1445). It sold over one million copies.

## M-I-S-S-I-S-S-I-P-P-I

Harry Tierney (w: Bert Hanlon and Benny Ryan)

William Jerome Music—New York

1916

One of the most popular of the spelling songs, it was introduced in vaudeville by Frances White (who dressed up as a little girl). Anna Wheaton had the hit recording in 1917 (Columbia A-2224).

## MISSISSIPPI MUD

Harry Barris (w & m)

Shapiro, Bernstein—New York

1927

Paul Whiteman and His Orchestra had the hit recording with the composer and Bing Crosby on vocals (Victor 21274). Also popularized by the Dixie Jazz Band (Oriole 1275) and the Seven Little Polar Bears (Cameo 8188).

## MISSOURI WALTZ

Frederic Knight Logan (w: J. R. Shannon)

Forster Music—Chicago

1915

Composer Logan actually stole the song from ragtime composer Edgar Settle, who called it "The Graveyard Waltz." Nonetheless, Logan's version sold over three million copies of sheet music. The Victor Military Band had a hit recording (Victor 18026). It received a tremendous amount of airplay when Harry Truman became president, as he constantly played it on the piano at the White House and on television. It became the official state song of Missouri.

## MISTER SANDMAN

Pat Ballard (w & m)

Edwin H. Morris—New York

1954

The Chordettes had the number 1 hit, which charted for twenty weeks and sold over one million copies (Cadence 1247). It was revived in 1981 by Emmylou Harris, who had a number 37 hit (Warner 49684). It is a vocal-group favorite.

## MOBILE BLUES

Albert E. Short and Fred Rose

Melrose Bros. Music—Chicago

1924

Introduced on disc by Jimmy Wade's Moulin Rouge Orchestra (Paramount 20295). Other fine versions include Gene Rodemich and His Orchestra (Brunswick 2599) and the Bucktown Five (Gennett 5405).

## MO' LASSES

C. Luckeyth Roberts (w: Alex Rogers)

Shapiro, Bernstein—New York

1923

**Show:** *Go-Go*

Outstanding piano roll made by the composer (QRS 2306).

## MOLASSES, MOLASSES

Larry Clinton (w & m)

Warwick Music—New York

1950

Teresa Brewer had the hit vocal version (London 794).

## MOMENTS TO REMEMBER

Robert Allen (w: Al Stillman)

Beaver Music—New York

1955

The Four Lads had the number 2 hit, which charted for twenty-five weeks and sold over one million copies (Columbia 40539).

## MONA LISA

Jay Livingston and Ray Evans

Famous Music

1949

**Film:** *Captain Carey, U.S.A.* (Paramount)

Academy Award winner for Best Song of 1950. Nat "King" Cole had the number 1 hit in 1950, and it held that position for eight of the twenty-seven chart weeks, selling three million discs (Capitol 1010). The song remains strongly associated with Cole.

## MONDAY, MONDAY

John and Michelle Phillips

Trousdale Music—Beverly Hills, CA.

1966

The Mamas and the Papas had their first (and only) number 1 hit with this song, which charted for ten weeks and sold over one million copies (Dunhill 4026). The Bangles's "Manic Monday" (Columbia 05757, 1986, number 2 pop hit), written by Prince, owes an obvious debt to this song.

## MONEY FOR NOTHING

Mark Knopfler (w & m)

Almo Music

1985

Number 1 hit for Scottish rock group Dire Straits, holding that spot for three out of thirteen chart weeks (Warner 28950). The song satirized pop consumerism, and featured harmony vocals by pop singer Sting.

## MONSTER MASH
Bobby Pickett and Leonard Capizzi
Acoustic Music—Nashville, Tennessee
1962
Number 1 teen novelty hit for Bobby "Boris" Pickett, holding that spot for two out of twelve chart weeks (Garpax 44167). It sold over a million copies. The original recording featured the backup band "The Cryptkickers" made up of L.A. session musicians, including pianist Leon Russell. A follow-up, "Monsters' Holiday," saw little action and Pickett disappeared from the charts. However, eleven years later, the original "Monster Mash" charted once again, this time reaching number 10.

## MOOD INDIGO
Duke Ellington/Albany Bigard/Irving Mills
Gotham Music Service—New York
1931
Duke Ellington and His Cotton Club Orchestra had the number 3 hit, which charted for ten weeks and became one of the most beloved recordings of all time, featuring a solo by the clarinetist/composer Barney Bigard (Victor 22587). The Norman Petty Trio revived it in 1954 with a number 14 hit that charted for nine weeks ("X" 0040). It remains a jazz standard.

## MOON IS BLUE, THE
Herschel Burke Gilbert (w: Sylvia Fine)
Santly-Joy—New York
1953
**Film:** *The Moon Is Blue* (United Artists)
The Sauter-Finegan Orchestra had the number 20 hit with vocalist Sally Sweetland, and it charted for three weeks (RCA Victor 20-5359).

## MOON OVER MIAMI
Joe Burke (w: Edgar Leslie)
Irving Berlin—New York
1935
Eddy Duchin and His Orchestra had the number 1 hit in 1936 that charted for eleven weeks (Victor 25212).

## MOON RIVER
Henry Mancini (w: Johnny Mercer)
Famous Music—New York
1961
**Film:** *Breakfast at Tiffany's* (Paramount)
Academy Award winner for Best Song. Jerry Butler had the number 11 hit, which charted for eleven weeks (Vee-Jay 405). Henry Mancini and His Orchestra also had an instrumental hit at number 11 that charted for sixteen weeks (RCA Victor 7916). This is one of Mancini's best-loved songs, and is often revived.

## MOONGLOW
Will Hudson/Eddie DeLange/Irving Mills
Exclusive—New York
1934
Benny Goodman and His Orchestra had the number 1 hit, which charted for fifteen weeks (Columbia 2927-D). It was revived in the film *Picnic* (Columbia, 1956), and the soundtrack recording reached number 1, with Morris Stoloff conducting the Columbia Pictures Orchestra (Decca 29888).

## MOONLIGHT
Con Conrad (w & m)
Waterson, Berlin and Snyder—New York
1921
Hit recording by Paul Whiteman and His Orchestra (Victor 18756).

## MOONLIGHT AND ROSES
Neil Moret (w: Edwin H. Lemare and
Ben Black )
Villa Moret—San Francisco
1925
Introduced in vaudeville by Art Kahn. Hit recording by Ray Miller and His Orchestra (Brunswick 2866). Lanny Ross used it as his radio theme song, and Betty Grable sang it in the film *Tin Pan Alley* (20th Century Fox, 1940). Revived in 1954 by the pop vocal group Three Suns (RCA Victor 20-5768).

## MOONLIGHT BAY
Percy Wenrich (w: Edward Madden)
Jerome H. Remick—New York
1912

Huge barbershop-quartet song as exemplified by the American Quartet's hit (Victor 17034). It was sung in vaudeville by the composer's wife, Dolly Connolly, who also had a hit recording (Columbia A-1128). It was revived by Alice Faye in the film *Tin Pan Alley* (20th Century Fox, 1943) and again by Doris Day in the film *On Moonlight Bay* (Warner Bros., 1951). Also in 1951, Bing and Gary Crosby had a number 14 hit with the song, which then charted for six weeks (Decca 27577).

## MOONLIGHT COCKTAIL

Luckey Roberts (w: Kim Gannon)

Jewel Music—New York

1941

Glenn Miller and His Orchestra had the number 1 hit in 1942, which charted for nineteen weeks and sold over one million copies (Bluebird 11401).

## MOONLIGHT IN VERMONT

Karl Suessedorf (w: John Blackburn)

Michael Goldsen—New York

1945

Billy Butterfield and His Orchestra, with Margaret Whiting on vocals, had the number 15 hit, which sold over one million copies (Capitol 182). Whiting revived it in 1954, accompanied by Lou Busch and His Orchestra (Capitol 2681).

## MOONLIGHT ON THE GANGES

Sherman Myers (w: Chester Wallace)

Harms—New York

1926

Paul Whiteman and His Orchestra had the hit recording (Victor 20139), but Fred Rich also had a fine version (Columbia 734-D). It was revived during the swing band era when Tommy Dorsey's Orchestra had a hit (Victor 27876) in 1942.

## MOONLIGHT SERENADE

Glenn Miller (w: Mitchell Parish)

Robbins Music—New York

1939

Glenn Miller's best-known theme song. His recording was a number 3 hit and charted for fifteen weeks. It sold over one million copies (Bluebird 10214).

## MORE THAN YOU KNOW

Vincent Youmans (w: William Rose and Edward Eliscu)

Miller Music—New York

1929

**Show:** *Great Day!*

Mayo Methot sang it in the show. Ruth Etting had the hit recording (Columbia 2038-D). Tony Martin sang it in the film *Hit the Deck* (MGM, 1955), and Barbra Streisand sang it in *Funny Lady* (Columbia, 1975). Martika revived it with a number 18 hit in 1989 (Columbia 08103).

## MORNING AFTER, THE

Al Kasha and Joel Hirschhorn

Twentieth Century Music—Los Angeles

1972

**Film:** *The Poseidon Adventure* (20th Century Fox)

Academy Award winner for Best Song. Maureen McGovern had the number 1 hit, which charted for eleven weeks (20th Century 2010). It sold over one million copies.

## MORNING TRAIN

Florrie Palmer (w & m)

Chappell Music

1981

This was Sheena Easton's first (and only) number 1 hit, and it charted for fifteen weeks (EMI America 8071). It sold over one million copies, and launched the singer's 1980s-era career.

## MOROCCO BLUES

Joe Jordan (w: Clarence Williams)

Clarence Williams Music—New York

1926

Introduced in vaudeville by Rita Gould. Recorded by Joe Jordan's Ten Sharps and Flats (Columbia 14144-D, Banner 1821). It has since become a staple of Dixieland jazz bands.

## MOST BEAUTIFUL GIRL, THE

Norris Wilson/Billy Sherrill/Rory Bourke

Al Gallico Music—New York

1973

Charlie Rich had his only number 1 pop hit with this upbeat love song, which charted for a spectacular seventeen weeks and it sold over one million copies (Epic 11040). Rich's career spanned four decades, and ranged from rockabilly to countrypolitan and mainstream pop.

## M-O-T-H-E-R

Theodore Morse (w: Howard Johnson)

Leo Feist—New York

1915

Great spelling song. Introduced in vaudeville by Al Wohlman; its hit recording was by tenor Henry Burr (Victor 17913).

## MOTHER MACHREE

Chauncey Olcott and Ernest R. Ball

(w: Rida Johnson Young)

M. Witmark and Sons—New York

1910

**Show:** *Barry of Ballymore*

Chauncey Olcott sang it in the show and also had a hit recording (Columbia A-1337). It became a staple in John McCormack's repertory when his recording was a tremendous hit (Victor 64181). It was revived by Dick Haymes in the Ball biopic *Irish Eyes Are Smiling* (20th Century Fox, 1944) and by Dennis Morgan in the Olcott biopic *My Wild Irish Rose* (Warner Bros., 1947).

## MOTHER-IN-LAW

Allen Toussaint (w & m)

Minit Music—New York

1961

Number 1 hit for Cajun pop-rocker Ernie K-Doe, charting for twelve weeks; also a number 1 R&B hit (Minit 623). It is a classic of early 1960s swamp rock, written by the famous New Orleans producer Allen Toussaint.

## MOXIE (1 STEP)

Norman Leigh (w: Dennis J. Shea)

Moxie Co.—Boston

1921

A great song commissioned by the Moxie Company for their soda drink. They even issued a double-sided record to promote the song, one side featuring Arthur Fields singing and the other side Raderman's Orchestra

(Moxie). The Shannon Four recorded it for Vocalion, as did the Aeolian Dance Orchestra (Vocalion 14250).

## MR. JAZZ HIMSELF

Irving Berlin (w & m)

Irving Berlin—New York

1917

Introduced in vaudeville by the Watson Sisters.

## MR. MOON MAN TURN OFF YOUR LIGHT

Jack Norworth and Nora Bayes

Norworth Music—New York

1910

**Show:** *Little Miss Fix-It*

Nora Bayes and Jack Norworth sang it in the show. Their recording illustrates the lilting quality in Bayes's voice (Victor 70038).

## MR. TAMBOURINE MAN

Bob Dylan (w & m)

M. Witmark and Sons—New York

1965

The Byrds had the number 1 hit, which charted for ten weeks (Columbia 43271). The song was one of Dylan's earliest nonprotest numbers, inspired by a trip to New Orleans in 1963.

## MRS. ROBINSON

Paul Simon (w & m)

Charing Cross Music—New York

1967, 1968

**Film:** *The Graduate* (United Artists, 1967)

Simon and Garfunkel had the number 1 hit, which charted for twelve weeks and sold over one million copies (Columbia 44511); it was written for the soundtrack of the Mike Nichols comedy; Mrs. Robinson (portrayed by Anne Bancroft) was the older woman in the film who seduced young Dustin Hoffman.

## MUDDY WATER

Peter DeRose and Harry Richman (w: Jo Trent)

Broadway Music—New York

1926

Introduced in vaudeville by Nora Bayes. Popularized on disc by Ben Bernie and His Orchestra (Brunswick

3414) and by Paul Whiteman and His Orchestra, with a vocal by Bing Crosby (Victor 20508).

## MUSCLE SHOALS BLUES
George W. Thomas
George W. Thomas—Chicago
1921
Popularized on disc by Harry Raderman's Orchestra (Okeh 4477). It was Thomas "Fats" Waller's first piano solo (Okeh 4757).

## MUSIC GOES 'ROUND AND AROUND, THE
Edward Farley and Michael Riley (w: Red Hodgson)
Select Music—New York
1935
The Riley-Farley Orchestra had a number 1 hit with their novelty song, which charted for eleven weeks (Decca 578). Its sheet music sales were more than two million copies. The band was featured performing the song in the film *The Music Goes Round* (Columbia 1936). In 1938, Tommy Dorsey and his Clambake Seven, with vocal by Edythe Wright, scored a number 1 hit with it, which charted for nine weeks (Victor 25201). This led to a reissue of the original Decca recording, which reached number 15 on the charts.

## MUSIC! MUSIC! MUSIC!
Stephen Weiss and Bernie Baum
Cromwell Music—New York
1950
Teresa Brewer had the number 1 hit, which charted for seventeen weeks and sold over one million copies (London 30023). The song's success helped spur the Dixieland revival (she was accompanied by the Dixieland All-Stars, including Max Kaminsky on trumpet and Cutty Cutshall on trombone). The song remained closely associated with Brewer throughout her career. Joe "Fingers" Carr revived it on his *Swinging Strings* LP in 1959 (Capitol T-1217). It was actually composed by Mel Glazer, who allowed Weiss and Baum to take credit for it.

## MY BABY JUST CARES FOR ME
Walter Donaldson (w: Gus Kahn)
Donaldson, Douglas and Gumble—New York
1930

**Film:** *Whoopee!* (United Artists)
Eddie Cantor sang it in the film. Ted Weems and His Orchestra had the number 4 hit, which charted for seven weeks (Victor 22499). The Hi-Los revived it in 1954 for a number 29 hit (Trend 74).

## MY BEAUTIFUL LADY
Ivan Caryll (w: CMS McLellan)
Chappell—New York
1911
**Show:** *The Pink Lady*
Introduced as a waltz in the show by Hazel Dawn. Lucy Isabelle Marsh made the hit record (Victor 60040).

## MY BLACKBIRDS ARE BLUEBIRDS NOW
Cliff Friend (w: Irving Caesar)
Leo Feist—New York
1928
**Show:** *Whoopee!*
Introduced in the show by Eddie Cantor. Introduced in vaudeville by Benny Meroff. Ruth Etting had the hit vocal record (Columbia 1595-D), and Jean Goldkette and His Orchestra had the hit instrumental (Victor 21805).

## MY BLUE DAYS BLEW OVER
Max Rich (w: Tot Seymour)
Arthur Behim Songs—New York
1931
Popularized on disc by Eubie Blake and His Orchestra (Victor 22735).

## MY BLUE HEAVEN
Walter Donaldson (w: George Whiting)
Leo Feist—New York
1927
Introduced in the *Ziegfeld Follies of 1927* by Eddie Cantor. It became a standard, selling over a million copies of sheet music; Gene Austin's recording (Victor 20964) sold over five million copies. Notable orchestral recordings include those of Fred Rich's Dance Orchestra (Regal 8417), and Paul Whiteman, featuring trumpeter Red Nichols (Victor 20828). Sammy Kaye and His Orchestra revived the song in 1939 (Vocalion 4199), as did Fats Domino in 1956 (Imperial 5386). The song was revived as a title theme song for a minor

musical drama starring Betty Grable and Dan Dailey in 1950 (MGM), and forty years later for a Steve Martin comedy about a small-time gangster who is relocated as part of a witness protection program (Orion, 1990).

## MY BOYFRIEND'S BACK
Robert Feldman/Gerald Goldstein/
Richard Gotteherer
Blackwood Music—New York
1963
The Angels had the number 1 hit, which charted for twelve weeks (Smash 1834). This is one of the greatest of all the girl group recordings of the early 1960s.

## MY BUDDY
Walter Donaldson (w: Gus Kahn)
Jerome H. Remick—New York
1922
First hit by Donaldson and Kahn, and a favorite in vaudeville. Henry Burr had the hit recording (Victor 18930). It was revived in the Gus Kahn biopic *I'll See You In My Dreams* (Warner Bros., 1951).

## MY CASTLE IN THE AIR
Jerome Kern (w: P. G. Wodehouse)
T. B. Harms—New York
1916
**Show:** *Miss Spingtime*
Geoge MacFarlane sang it in the show as well as on record (Victor 45110).

## MY CASTLE ON THE NILE
Rosamond Johnson (w: James Weldon Johnson and Bob Cole)
Jos. W. Stern—New York
1901
**Show:** *Sons of Ham*
Bert Williams introduced it in his show. It became such a showstopper that he recorded it (Victor 991).

## MY CHERIE AMOUR
Stevie Wonder (w & m)
Jobete Music—Detroit
1969
Number 2 pop hit for Stevie Wonder, holding that spot for two out of eleven weeks on the charts (Tamla

54174). A wonderful love ballad, it has often been covered.

## MY CUTIE'S DUE AT TWO-TO-TWO TODAY
Albert Von Tilzer /Irving Bibo/Leo Robin
Bibo, Bloedon and Lang—New York
1926
Introduced in vaudeville by Vaughn DeLeath. Popularized on disc by the Clevelanders (Brunswick 3279) and the Missouri Jazz Band (Banner 1799).

## MY DARLING, MY DARLING
Frank Loesser (w & m)
Edwin H. Morris—New York
1948
**Show:** *Where's Charley*
Byron Palmer and Doretta Morrow sang it in the show. Jo Stafford and Gordon MacRae had the number 1 hit, which charted for seventeen weeks (Capitol 15270).

## MY DING-A-LING
Chuck Berry (w & m)
Carlin Music—New York
1970
Oddly enough, the only number 1 hit the famous rock and roll singer/guitarist achieved on the pop charts (in 1972), long after his hit-making days of the 1950s. It held this spot for two out of twelve chart weeks, and sold over one million copies (Chess 2131).

## MY FAVORITE THINGS
Richard Rodgers (w: Oscar Hammerstein)
Williamson Music—New York
1959
**Show:** *The Sound of Music*
Patricia Neway and Mary Martin sang it in the show. John Coltrane made a famous instrumental recording of it in a modern jazz setting in 1960, and it was among his most popular numbers on lp (Atlantic 1361).

## MY FOOLISH HEART
Victor Young (w: Ned Washington)
Santly-Joy—New York
1949
**Film:** *My Foolish Heart* (RKO)

Susan Hayward sang it in the film. Gordon Jenkins and His Orchestra, with vocalist Eileen Wilson, had the number 3 hit, which charted for twenty-three weeks (Decca 24830). Billy Eckstine had a number 6 hit, which charted for nineteen weeks and sold over one million copies (MGM 10623).

## MY FUNNY VALENTINE
Richard Rodgers (w: Lorenz Hart)
Chappell—New York
1937
**Show:** *Babes in Arms*
Mitzi Green sang it in the show. Hal McIntyre and His Orchestra had the number 16 hit in 1945 (Bluebird 0837). It has become a cabaret standard.

## MY GAL SAL
Paul Dresser (w & m)
Paul Dresser Music—New York
1905
The composer's last song and greatest hit, but he died before Louise Dresser could make it into a success in vaudeville. Byron G. Harlan had the hit recording in 1907 (Victor 4918). Revived in 1924 by Ted Weems and His Orchestra (Victor 19287), and in 1934 by Claude Hopkins and His Orchestra (Brunswick 6864). Dresser's biopic was named after the song (20th Century Fox, 1942), which played throughout the film.

## MY GIRL
William "Smokey" Robinson and Ronald White
Jobete Music—Detroit
1964, 1965
The Temptations had the number 1 hit, which charted for eleven weeks and sold over 2 million copies (Gordy 7038). One of the classic Motown songs.

## MY GUY
William "Smokey" Robinson (w & m)
Jobete Music
1964
Mary Wells had the number 1 hit, which charted for thirteen weeks (Motown 1056). Wells's version is noteworthy for the clever vocal tag. It was covered in 1982 by soul vocalists Sister Sledge, whose version reached number 23 (Cotillion 47000).

## MY HAPPINESS
Barney Bergantine (w: Betty Peterson)
Blasco Music—Kansas City, Mo.
1933, 1948
Although written in 1933, the song went nowhere until Jon and Sandra Steele revived it for a number 2 hit in 1948. Their version charted for thirty weeks and sold over one million copies (Damon 11133). The Pied Pipers also had a million-seller that year with their number 3 hit, which charted for twenty-seven weeks (Capitol 15094). Connie Francis revived it in 1959 with a number 2 hit that charted for fourteen weeks and also sold over one million copies (MGM 12738).

## MY HEART BELONGS TO DADDY
Cole Porter (w & m)
Chappell—New York
1938
**Show:** *Leave It to Me*
Mary Martin made her Broadway debut and sang this song, which made her reputation in the show. She had the number 9 hit in 1939, accompanied by Eddy Duchin's Orchestra (Decca 8282). She was outdone, however, by Larry Clinton and His Orchestra, whose recording reached number 4 that same year (Victor 26100). Mary Martin sang it in the Porter biopic *Night and Day* (Warner Bros., 1946). Marilyn Monroe revived it in the film *Let's Make Love* (20th Century Fox, 1960).

## MY HEART CRIES FOR YOU
Percy Faith (w: Carl Sigman)
Massey Music—New York
1950
Guy Mitchell had the number 2 hit, which charted for twenty-one weeks and sold over one million copies (Columbia 39067).

## MY HEART STOOD STILL
Richard Rodgers (w: Lorenz Hart)
Harms—New York
1927
**Show:** *A Connecticut Yankee*
Introduced in the show by William Gaxton and Constance Carpenter. George Olsen and His Orchestra had a hit recording (Victor 21034). It was used in the

Rodgers and Hart biopic *Words and Music* (MGM, 1948). It has become a jazz and cabaret standard.

## MY HEART WILL GO ON
James Horner (w: Will Jennings)
Famous Music
1997
**Film:** *Titanic* (Paramount/20th Century Fox)
Academy Award winner for Best Song. Canadian chanteuse Celine Dion had the number 1 hit, which charted for sixteen weeks (500 Music/Epic 78825). It sold over half a million copies.

## MY HERO
Oscar Straus
(w: Stanislaus Stange)
Jerome Remick—New York
1909
**Show:** *The Chocolate Soldier*
Introduced by Ida Brooks Hunt in the show, it regained popularity in the film version (MGM, 1941). Ralph Flanagan's Orchestra made a number 27 hit of it in his 1949 recording (Bluebird 0006).

## MY HONEY'S LOVIN' ARMS
Joseph Meyer (w: Herman Ruby)
Fred Fisher—New York
1922
Zez Confrey made a fabulous piano roll version (QRS 1944). Isham Jones and His Orchestra (Brunswick 2301), the Virginians (Victor 18881), and Jazzbo's Carolina Serenaders (Cameo 218) had fine recordings. A favorite with traditional jazz bands, it was revived in a 1955 LP by the Firehouse Five Plus Two (Good Time Jazz L-12014).

## MY ISLE OF GOLDEN DREAMS
Walter Blaufuss (w: Gus Kahn)
Jerome H. Remick and Co.—New York
1919
Introduced in vaudeville by the Dolly Sisters. Hit recording by Ben Selvin's Orchestra (Victor 18633). Revived in 1939 by Glenn Miller and His Orchestra (Bluebird 10399). It became the theme song for Phil Spitalny and his All Girl Orchestra on his radio show *Hour of Charm.*

## MY LIFE
Billy Joel (w & m)
Impulsive Music
1978
Number 3 hit for Joel in 1979 that remained on the chart for sixteen weeks (Columbia 10853). This adolescent declaration-of-independence was among Joel's most popular early hits.

## MY LITTLE BIMBO DOWN ON THE BAMBOO ISLE
Walter Donaldson (w: Grant Clarke)
Irving Berlin—New York
1920
**Show:** *Silks and Satins*
Aileen Stanley sang it in the show. Roy Bargy made a fabulous piano roll arrangement (Imperial 91192). The Benson Orchestra (Victor 18698) and the Happy Six (Columbia A-3304) had fine versions. Clancy Hayes and the Salty Dogs revived it on their 1964 LP (Delmark DL-210).

## MY LOVE
Paul and Linda McCartney
MPL Communication
1973
Number 1 hit for McCartney and Wings, holding the top spot for four out of fifteen chart weeks (Apple 1861); also a number 1 adult-contemporary hit. A treacly love ballad, nonetheless somewhat of a pop standard.

## MY LOVIN' (YOU'RE NEVER GONNA GET IT)
Thomas McElroy and Denzil Foster
Irving Music
1992
Soulful and sexy female singers En Vogue had a number 2 hit with this song, which charted for twenty-two weeks and sold over a million copies (EastWest 98586). It was effectively promoted by a sultry video.

## MY MAMMY
Walter Donaldson (w: Sam Lewis and Joe Young)
Irving Berlin—New York
1921

Identified with Al Jolson who used it for the next 29 years. He sang it in the pioneer sound film *The Jazz Singer* (Warner Bros., 1927) and recorded it the next year (Brunswick 3912). Isham Jones and His Orchestra had a hit recording in 1921 (Brunswick 5046). Jolson sang it again in the films *The Singing Fool* (Warner Bros., 1929), *Rose of Washington Square* (20th Century Fox, 1939), and his two biopics *The Jolson Story* (Columbia, 1946) and *Jolson Sings Again* (Columbia, 1949). It was after the first biopic that Jolson rerecorded it and this new version sold over one million copies (Decca 23614). The Happenings revived it in 1967 with a number 13 hit (B.T. Puppy 530).

## MY MAN
Maurice Yvain (w: Channing Pollock)
Leo Feist—New York
1921
**Show:** *Ziegfeld Follies of 1921*
Introduced in the show by Fanny Brice who had the hit record (Victor 45263) and who became identified with it throughout her life. When she sang it in the film *My Man* (Warner Bros., 1929), her new recording made another hit (Victor 21168). After Alice Faye sang it in the Brice biopic *Rose of Washington Square* (20th Century Fox, 1939), Wayne King and His Orchestra had a hit recording (Victor 26231). Barbra Streisand revived it again in the film *Funny Girl* (Columbia, 1968).

## MY MELANCHOLY BABY
Ernie Burnett (w: George A. Norton)
Theron C. Bennett—New York
1912
Originally published as "Melancholy." It was introduced in vaudeville by Winsome June Le Vey. It has become a standard with many hit recordings, starting with Walter Van Brunt in 1915 (Edison 50923); followed by Gene Austin's number 3 hit of 1927 (Victor 21015); and Teddy Wilson's Orchestra's number 6 hit of 1936, with vocalist Ella Fitzgerald (Brunswick 7729). Tenor sax player Sam Donohue had a number 5 hit in 1947 (Capitol 357), while Tommy Edwards had the number 26 hit in 1959 (MGM 12794).

## MY NAME IS MORGAN BUT IT AIN'T J.P.
Halsey K. Mohr (w: Will A. Mahoney)

P. J. Howley—New York
1906
A great comic number originally recorded by Bob Roberts (Zonophone 369). Revived on a 1963 LP by Max Morath (Epic LN-24066).

## MY ONE AND ONLY
George Gershwin (w: Ira Gershwin)
New World Music—New York
1927
**Show:** *Funny Face*
Gertrude MacDonald sang it in the show, while Fred Astaire and Betty Compton danced to it. Tommy Tune and Honi Coles revived it in the 1983 Broadway show of the same name.

## MY PILLOW AND ME
Tim Brymn/Chris Smith/Clarence Williams
Clarence Williams Music—New York
1922
Introduced in vaudeville by Lada's Louisiana Orchestra. Popularized on disc by Lizzie Miles, accompanied by Clarence Johnson on piano (Brunswick 2462).

## MY PONY BOY
Charley O'Donnell (w: Bobby Heath)
Jerome H. Remick—New York
1909
**Show:** *Miss Innocence*
Introduced by Lillian Lorraine in the show. Ada Jones had the hit recording (Victor 16356).

## MY PRAYER
Georges Boulanger
(w: Jimmy Kennedy)
Skidmore Music—New York
1939
Glenn Miller and His Orchestra, with vocal by Ray Eberle, had the number 2 hit, which charted for fifteen weeks (Bluebird 10404). The Platters revived it in 1956 with a number 1 hit, which charted for twenty weeks and sold over one million copies (Mercury 70893), after which it became a doo-wop favorite.

## MY SHARONA
Doug Fieger and Berton Averre

Eighties Music

1979

The Knack had this sole number 1 hit, which kept that position for six of the sixteen weeks on the chart (Capitol 4731). It sold over one million copies. Much heralded when they first appeared on the scene, the Knack were a new-wave band who produced artful pop music. However, they were unable to replicate their initial success with "My Sharona," and quickly faded from the scene.

## MY SILENT LOVE

Dana Suesse (w: Edward Heyman)

Famous Music—New York

1932

Ruby Newman and His Orchestra had the number 3 hit, which charted for six weeks. The song was adapted from Suesse's instrumental "Jazz Nocturne" (Victor 24042).

## MY SUNDAY GIRL

Sam H. Stept (w: Herman Ruby and Bud Cooper)

Irving Berlin—New York

1927

A lovely song that was given a fine arrangement by Edwin J. McEnelly and His Orchestra, with a piano break by Frankie Carle (Victor 20589). Also popularized by Joe Candullo and His Orchestra (Harmony 361-H) and the Cliquot Club Eskimos (Columbia 921-D).

## MY SUNNY TENNESSEE

Bert Kalmar/Harry Ruby/Herman Ruby

Waterson Berlin and Snyder—New York

1921

**Show:** *Midnight Rounders of 1921*

Introduced in the show by Eddie Cantor. Popularized on disc by the Benson Orchestra (Victor 18819), Isham Jones and His Orchestra (Brunswick 5066), Lanin's Southern Serenaders (Emerson 10467), and Harry Raderman's Jazz Orchestra (Okeh 4441). Revived in the Kalmar-Ruby biopic *Three Little Words* (MGM, 1950).

## MY SWEET LORD

George Harrison (w & m)

Harrisongs Music—New York

1970, 1971

George Harrison had the number 1 hit, which held that position for four of thirteen weeks charted (Apple 2995). It sold over one million copies. However, the courts in 1976 said that it was "unconcious[ly] plagiarized" from the Ronald Mack hit of 1963, "He's So Fine." Harrison settled with the original song's publishers at that time.

## MY SWEETIE TURNED ME DOWN

Walter Donaldson (w: Gus Kahn)

Irving Berlin—New York

1925

The Dixie Stars had a hit recording featuring a piano chorus by J. Russel Robinson (Columbia 389-D).

## MY TIME IS YOUR TIME

Leo Dance (w: Eric Little)

Chappell-Harms—New York

1924

Rudy Vallee's theme song for his radio show *The Fleishmann Yeast Hour*. He had the hit recording (Victor 21924) in 1929. The song had been written in England by R. S. Hooper and H. M. Tennent, who used the pseudonyms of Dance and Little. Vallee secured the American rights five years later. He sang it in the biopic *The Helen Morgan Story* (Warner Bros., 1957).

## MY TRULY, TRULY FAIR

Bob Merrill (w & m)

Santly-Joy—New York

1951

Guy Mitchell had the number 2 hit, which charted for nineteen weeks and sold over one million copies (Columbia 39415).

## MY WILD IRISH ROSE

Chauncey Olcott (w & m)

M. Witmark and Sons—New York

1899

**Show:** *A Romance of Athlone*

One of the first Irish ballads to sell a million copies, it was also used as the title of the biopic starring Dennis Morgan, who also sang it (Warner Bros. 1947). It remains a perennial St. Patrick's Day favorite.

## NAGASAKI

Harry Warren (w: Mort Dixon)

Remick Music—New York

1928

Introduced on disc by Paul Mares's Friars Society Orchestra (Okeh 41574). The Ipana Troubadours had a hit (Columbia 1463-D). Willie "the Lion" Smith used it as a specialty throughout his life in nightclubs and first recorded it in 1949 (Royal Jazz 743).

## NAT'AN! NAT'AN! TELL ME FOR WHAT ARE YOU WAITIN', NAT'AN?

James Kendis (w & m)

Kendis Music—New York

1916

Introduced in vaudeville by Rhoda Bernard. A typical comic dialect song of the era.

## NAUGHTY LADY OF SHADY LANE, THE

Sid Tepper and Roy C. Bennett

George Paxton—New York

1954

The Ames Brothers had the number 3 hit, which charted for fifteen weeks and sold over one million copies (RCA Victor 47-5897).

## NAVAJO

Egbert Van Alstyne (w: Harry H. Williams)

Shapiro, Bernstein—New York

1903

**Show:** *Nancy Brown*

Marie Cahill introduced the song in the show. Billy Murray had the hit recording in 1904 (Columbia 1655).

## NEAR YOU

Francis Craig (w: Kermit Goell)

Supreme Music—New York

1947

Francis Craig and His Orchestra, with vocalist Bob Lamm, had the number 1 hit, which held that position for seventeen of the charted twenty-five weeks, and sold over one million copies (Bullet 1001). It became Milton Berle's television theme song. It was revived in 1958 by Roger Williams, who had a number 10 hit that charted for eleven weeks (Kapp 233).

## NEARNESS OF YOU, THE

Hoagy Carmichael (w: Ned Washington)

Famous Music—New York

1940

Glenn Miller and His Orchestra had the number 5 hit, which charted for eleven weeks (Bluebird 10745).

## 'NEATH THE SOUTHERN MOON

Victor Herbert (w: Rida Johnson Young)

M. Witmark and Sons—New York

1910

**Show:** *Naughty Marietta*

Marie Duchene sang it in the show. Jeanette MacDonald and Nelson Eddy sang it in the film version (MGM, 1935).

## NEVER AGAIN

Isham Jones (w: Gus Kahn)

Milton Weil Music—Chicago

1924

Introduced in vaudeville and nightclubs by the composer, who also had the hit recording (Brunswick 2577). Ruth Mack made an outstanding piano roll (Vocalstyle 12994).

## NEVER GONNA GIVE YOU UP

Stock/Aitken/Waterman

Terrace Music

1987

Pop singer Rick Astley had the number 1 hit in 1988 that charted for fourteen weeks (RCA 5347). It sold over one million copies.

## NEVER LET NO ONE MAN WORRY YOUR MIND

Will E. Skidmore and Jack Baxley

Skidmore Music—New York

1920

Introduced in vaudeville and on disc by Marion Harris (Columbia A-3328). J. Russel Robinson made an outstanding piano roll (QRS 1179).

## NEVER ON SUNDAY

Manes Hadjidakis (w: Billy Towne)

Esteem Music and Sidmore Music—New York

1960

**Film:** *Never On Sunday* (Lopert)

Academy Award winner for Best Song. Don Costa and His Orchestra had the number 19 hit (United Artists

234). One of the few pop instrumentals to feature the Greek bouzouki!

## NEVERTHELESS
Bert Kalmar and Harry Ruby
DeSylva, Brown and Henderson—New York
1931
Jack Denny and His Orchestra had the number 5 hit, which charted for five weeks (Brunswick 6114). Fred Astaire, Red Skelton, and Anita Ellis sang it in the Kalmar-Ruby biopic *Three Little Words* (MGM, 1950), which gave the song a second life. The best of the new recordings were by Paul Weston and His Orchestra, with vocal by the Norman Luboff Choir, which charted for eighteen weeks peaking at number 2 (Columbia 38982), and the Mills Brothers version, which reached number 4 with seventeen weeks on the charts (Decca 27253).

## NICE WORK IF YOU CAN GET IT
George Gershwin (w: Ira Gershwin)
Gershwin Publishing—New York
1937
**Film:** *A Damsel In Distress* (RKO)
Fred Astaire, Jan Duggan, Mary Dean, and Pearl Amatore sang and danced it in the film. Astaire also had a number 1 hit that charted for fifteen weeks (Brunswick 7983). The Andrews Sisters had a number 12 hit in 1938 (Decca 1562).

## NIGHT AND DAY
Cole Porter (w & m)
Harms—New York
1932
**Show:** *Gay Divorce*
Fred Astaire and Claire Luce sang it in the show. In the film, which changed the title to *The Gay Divorcee* (RKO, 1934), Fred Astaire and Ginger Rogers sang and danced to it. Fred Astaire with Leo Reisman's Orchestra had the number 1 hit in 1932, which maintained its position for ten of the eighteen weeks charted (Victor 24193). Cary Grant and Alexis Smith sang it in the Porter biopic *Night and Day* (Warner Bros., 1946). It remains one of Porter's best-known and best-loved songs.

## NIGHT FEVER
Barry, Robin, Maurice Gibb

Stigwood Music
1977
**Film:** *Saturday Night Fever* (Paramount)
The Bee Gees' biggest hit was number 1 for eight of the eighteen weeks charted (RSO 889). It sold over two million copies. The *Saturday Night Fever* soundtrack album was an enormous success, and it showed how a film could effectively promote pop songs and vice versa. It also revitalized the Bee Gees' career, which had been in a serious slump.

## NIGHT THEY INVENTED CHAMPAGNE, THE
Frederick Loewe (w: Alan Jay Lerner)
Lowal Corp.—New York
1958
**Film:** *Gigi* (MGM)
Betty Wand, Louis Jourdan, and Hermione Gingold sang it in the film.

## NIGHTS IN WHITE SATIN
Justin Haward (w & m)
TRO—New York
1967, 1968
A number 2 hit in 1972 for art-rockers the Moody Blues, holding that spot for two out of fourteen weeks on the charts (Deram 85023). The song originally appeared on their classic 1968 album *Days of the Future Passed* (Deram 18012), which was recorded with the London Festival Orchestra. It was an early example of progressive—or art—rock.

## 9 TO 5
Dolly Parton
Velvet Apple Music
1980
**Film:** *9 to 5* (20th Century Fox, 1980)
Dolly Parton, who was one of the stars of the film, had the number 1 hit in 1981 that charted for eighteen weeks (RCA 12133). Her recording sold over one million copies. This was at the height of Parton's crossover success; previously, most of her hits had been on the country charts.

## NO MORE
Leo DeJohn (w: Julie and Dux DeJohn)

Maple Leaf Music—New York

1954

The DeJohn Sisters had the number 6 hit in 1955, which charted for thirteen weeks (Epic 9085).

## NO, NO, NORA

Ted Fiorito and Ernie Erdman (w: Gus Kahn)

Leo Feist—New York

1923

Introduced by bandleader Ted Fiorito in vaudeville. Eddie Cantor had a hit recording (Columbia A-3964), as did the Benson Orchestra (Victor 19121). Phil Ohman and Victor Arden recorded a piano duet (Brunswick 2512) and Max Kortlander made an extraordinary piano roll (QRS 2398). It was revived in the Gus Kahn biopic *I'll See You in My Dreams* (Warner Bros., 1951).

## NO, NOT MUCH

Robert Allen (w: Al Stillman)

Beaver Music—New York

1956

Pop-vocal group the Four Lads had the number 2 hit, which charted for nineteen weeks and sold over one million copies (Columbia 40629). The Vogues revived it in 1969 for a number 34 hit (Reprise 0803).

## NO OTHER LOVE

Richard Rodgers (w: Oscar Hammerstein)

Williamson Music—New York

1953

**Show:** *Me and Juliet*

Isabel Bigley and Richard Hayes sang it in the show. The music was taken from the score of the television series *Victory At Sea* (NBC-TV, 1952), comprised of twenty-six patriotic documentary films scored by Rodgers. Perry Como had the number 1 hit, which charted for twenty-two weeks (RCA Victor 20-5317).

## NOBODY

Bert A. Williams (w: Alex Rogers)

The Attucks Publishing Co.—New York

1905

Introduced by the composer in vaudeville, this song was identified with him throughout his life. Williams's stage character—a small-time, somewhat pathetic but

also comic creation—was perfectly described by the song's lyric. His greatest recording was made in 1913 (Columbia A-1289). Revived in the Broadway revue *Bubbling Brown Sugar* by Avon Long (1976).

## NOBODY DOES IT BETTER

Marvin Hamlisch (w: Carole Bayer Sager)

Unart Music

1977

Film: *The Spy Who Loved Me* (United Artists)

Number 2 hit for singer/songwriter Carly Simon, holding that position for three out of fifteen weeks charted; also a number 1 adult-contemporary hit that sold over a million copies (Elektra 45880). Written as a theme song for a film in the long-lived James Bond franchise, the song has become something of a pop standard.

## NOBODY KNOWS AND NOBODY SEEMS TO CARE

Irving Berlin (w & m)

Irving Berlin—New York

1919

Irving and Jack Kaufman had the hit vocal recording (Columbia A-2795) and the Art Hickman Trio had the instrumental hit (Columbia A-2839).

## NOBODY KNOWS WHAT A RED HEAD MAMA CAN DO

Sammy Fain (w: Al Dubin and Irving Mills)

Jack Mills—New York

1924

Margaret Young had a hit vocal recording (Brunswick 2806), while the hit instrumentals belonged to Ray Miller and His Orchestra (Brunswick 2778) and George Olsen and His Music (Victor 19580).

## NOBODY LIED (WHEN THEY SAID THAT I CRIED OVER YOU)

Edwin Webber (w: Karyl Norman and Hyatt Berry)

Jerome H. Remick—New York

1922

Introduced in vaudeville by Karyl Norman, the fashion plate. Marion Harris had the hit vocal (Columbia A-3646), while Isham Jones and His Orchestra (Brunswick

2301), the Virginians (Victor 18913), and Markels Orchestra (Okeh 4648) had hit instrumentals.

## NOBODY'S LOOKIN' BUT DE OWL AND DE MOON
Rosamond Johnson (w: Bob Cole and
James Weldon Johnson)
Jos. W. Stern—New York
1901
**Show:** *The Sleeping Beauty and the Beast*
A lovely ballad written by African-American composers for an all-white show.

## NOBODY'S SWEETHEART
Elmer Schoebel and Ernie Erdman (w: Billy Meyers and Gus Kahn)
Jack Mills—New York
1924
Isham Jones and His Orchestra had the hit recording (Brunswick 2578). Paul Whiteman revived it in 1930 (Columbia 2098-D), and the Mills Brothers had a million-seller in 1934 (Brunswick 6197). It has remained a standard for jazz bands. It was featured in the Gus Kahn biopic *I'll See You in My Dreams* (Warner Bros., 1951).

## NOLA
Felix Arndt
Sam Fox—Cleveland
1916
Extremely popular piano solo made famous by Vincent Lopez, who used it as his theme song. In addition to his recording (Okeh 4579), it was heard at the beginning and end of his many radio programs. To this day, piano students play it.

## NOODLIN' RAG
Robert Allen (w: Allan Roberts)
Bregman, Vocco and Conn—New York
1952
Perry Como had the number 23 hit (RCA Victor 20-4542) and Joe "Fingers" Carr had the instrumental hit (Capitol 2009).

## NOTHING COMPARES 2 U
Prince (w & m)

Controversy Music
1985, 1986
Irish singer Sinead O'Connor had this number 1 hit in 1990. It held its number 1 position for four of the fifteen weeks it charted and sold over one million copies (Ensign/Chrysalis 23488).

## NOTHING'S GONNA STOP US NOW
Albert Hammond and Diane Warren
Albert Hammond Music
1986, 1987
Starship had the number 1 hit, which charted for fifteen weeks (Grunt 5109). It sold over one million copies.

## NOW HE'S GOT A BEAUTIFUL GIRL
Ted Snyder (w: Grant Clarke and Edgar Leslie)
Waterson, Berlin and Snyder—New York
1916
**Show:** *Robinson Crusoe, Jr.*
Al Jolson sang this extremely syncopated song in the show in addition to making the best recording (Columbia A-2080).

## NOW'S THE TIME TO FALL IN LOVE
Al Sherman and Al Lewis
DeSylva, Brown and Henderson—New York
1931
**Film:** *Palmy Days* (United Artists)
Eddie Cantor sang it in the film and on his radio show, and continued to use it for the rest of his career. He sang it in his biopic *The Eddie Cantor Story* (Warner Bros., 1953). Ben Selvin and His Orchestra had the number 17 hit in 1932 (Columbia 2575-D).

## NOWHERE TO RUN
Brian Holland/Lamont Dozier/
Eddie Holland
Jobete Music—Detroit
1965
Martha and the Vandellas had the number 8 hit, which charted for eight weeks (Gordy 7039).

## OBJECT OF MY AFFECTION, THE
Pinky Tomlin/Coy Poe/Jimmie Grier
Irving Berlin—New York
1934

Jimmie Grier and His Orchestra, with vocal by Pinky Tomlin, had the number 1 hit, which charted for thirteen weeks (Brunswick 7308). A year later, pop-jazz vocal trio The Boswell Sisters, backed by the Jimmie Grier Orchestra, also scored a number 1 hit that charted for ten weeks (Brunswick 7348).

## OCEANA ROLL, THE
Lucien Denni (w: Roger Lewis)
Jerome H. Remick—New York
1911
Introduced in vaudeville by Eddie Morton, who also made a hit recording (Victor 16908). Revived in 1952 by Teresa Brewer (London 1083).

## ODE TO BILLIE JOE
Bobbie Gentry (w & m)
Larry Shane Music—New York
1967
Bobbie Gentry had the number 1 hit, which charted for twelve weeks and sold over one million copies (Capitol 5950). The "mystery" of what Billie Joe threw off the Talahatchie bridge has never been solved. The sultry vocal and its pop accompaniment made this an unusual success for a singer promoted as a "country" artist.

## OH!
Arnold Johnson and Byron Gay
Leo Feist—New York
1919
A hit in vaudeville by the Paul Biese Orchestra, who also recorded it (Victor 18647). Ted Lewis's Jazz Band also had a hit (Columbia A-2844). It was revived in 1953 by Pee Wee Hunt and His Orchestra, who had a number 3 hit that charted for twenty-five weeks and sold over one million copies (Capitol 2442).

## OH BABY
Walter Donaldson (w: Bud DeSylva)
Irving Berlin—New York
1924
A dance band favorite in vaudeville. Fred Waring's Pennsylvanians had the hit recording (Victor 19254), followed by the Ambassadors (Vocalion 14808) and the Lanin Orchestra (Okeh 40111). Charles Stanfield did a

nice vocal, accompanied by Jesse Crump on piano (Starr 20057).

## OH, BABY
Owen Murphy (w & m)
Ager, Yellen and Bornstein—New York
1928
**Show:** *Rain or Shine*
Ted Lewis (Columbia 1391-D) and the Dixie Stompers (Harmony 636-H) both had hits with this tune. It subsequently became a Dixieland favorite.

## OH! BOY, WHAT A GIRL
Frank Wright and Frank Bessinger (w: Bud Green)
Shapiro, Bernstein—New York
1925
**Show:** *Gay Paree*
Introduced by Winnie Lightner in the show. Eddie Cantor had the hit vocal (Columbia 457-D) and Isham Jones had the hit instrumental (Brunswick 2963).

## OH, BY JINGO!
Albert Von Tilzer (w: Lew Brown)
Broadway Music—New York
1919
**Show:** *Linger Longer Letty*
Charlotte Greenwood sang it in the show. Frank Crumit had the hit in 1920 (Columbia A-2935). Spike Jones and His City Slickers revived it in 1943 with a number 20 hit (Bluebird 0812), and it has been a favorite of jazz bands since. Betty Hutton sang it in the film *Incendiary Blonde* (Paramount, 1945), and Vivian Blaine sang it in the film *Skirts Ahoy* (MGM, 1952).

## OH DADDY BLUES
Will Russell and Ed Herbert
Clarence Williams Music—New York
1923
Introduced in vaudeville by Worth and Willing. Bessie Smith had the hit recording, accompanied by the publisher on piano (Columbia A-3888), which made it a jazz classic.

## OH, DIDN'T HE RAMBLE
Will Handy (pseud. of Bob Cole and
J. Rosamond Johnson)

Jos. W. Stern—New York

1902

Introduced by minstrel George Primrose in his shows. Famous as a tune jazz bands play on the way home from a funeral. Jelly Roll Morton's New Orleans Jazzmen made a recording recreating the effect in 1939 (Bluebird 10249). It was also popular among early country performers, thanks to a recording by Charlie Poole and His North Carolina Ramblers.

## OH! GEE, OH! GOSH, OH! GOLLY, I'M IN LOVE

Ernest Breuer (w: Olsen and Johnson)

Waterson, Berlin and Snyder—New York

1923

**Show:** *Ziegfeld Follies of 1923*

Olsen and Johnson sang it in the show. Eddie Cantor had the vocal hit (Columbia A-3934), and the Garber-Davis Orchestra had the instrumental hit (Victor 19164).

## OH GEE, SAY GEE, YOU OUGHT TO SEE MY GEE GEE FROM THE FIJI ISLES

Albert Von Tilzer (w: Lew Brown)

Broadway Music—New York

1920

Billy Murray had the hit recording (Victor 18712). Chuck Thomas and His Dixieland Band revived it in 1949 (Capitol 746).

## OH! HOW I HATE TO GET UP IN THE MORNING

Irving Berlin (w & m)

Waterson, Berlin and Snyder—New York

1918

The composer wrote it for himself to perform in the show *Yip, Yip, Yaphank* when he was a soldier in the First World War. He reprieved it in his all-soldier World War II show *This Is the Army,* which was subsequently released in a film version (Warner Bros., 1943). It was also featured in the biggest musical film of the 1930s, *Alexander's Ragtime Band* (20th Century Fox, 1938).

## OH, JOHNNY, OH, JOHNNY, OH!

Abe Olman (w: Ed Rose)

Forster Music—Chicago

1917

Henry Jackson sang it in the show *Follow Me.* The American Quartet had the hit (Victor 18279). Orrin Tucker and His Orchestra, with vocal by Wee Bonnie Baker, had the number 2 hit in 1939, and it charted for fourteen weeks (Columbia 35228). The tune is also used to accompany Western square dances.

## OH, LADY BE GOOD

George Gershwin (w: Ira Gershwin)

Harms—New York

1924

**Show:** *Lady, Be Good!*

Walter Catlett sang it in the show. Paul Whiteman and His Orchestra had the hit recording (Victor 19551). Ann Southern, Robert Young, Red Skelton, and John Carroll sang it in the film version (MGM, 1941). Joan Leslie sang it in the Gershwin biopic *Rhapsody in Blue* (Warner Bros., 1945). It is a favorite of jazz singers and instrumentalists.

## OH ME! OH MY! (OH YOU!)

Vincent Youmans (w: Arthur Francis)

T. B. Harms—New York

1921

**Show:** *Two Little Girls in Blue*

Introduced in the show by Oscar Shaw and Marion Fairbanks. Paul Whiteman and His Orchestra had the hit recording (Victor 18778). It was revived in the film *Tea for Two* (Warner Bros., 1950).

## OH! MISTER GALLAGHER AND MISTER SHEAN

Ed Gallagher and Al Shean

Jack Mills—New York

1922

**Show:** *Ziegfeld Follies of 1922*

Introduced in the show by Gallagher and Shean, whose recording sold over a million copies (Victor 18941). Bennie Krueger and His Orchestra also made a fine disc (Brunswick 2327). It was revived in 1938 by Bing Crosby and Johnny Mercer (Decca 1960).

## OH, PRETTY WOMAN

Roy Orbison and Bill Dees

Acuff-Rose-Opryland Music—Nashville

1964

Roy Orbison had the number 1 hit, which charted for fourteen weeks and sold more than one million copies (Monument 851). Orbison's tiger-like growl and the repetitive guitar riff are but two of the joys of the original recording. A classic rock song by one of the most unusual rock singers.

## OH SISTER, AIN'T THAT HOT
Will Donaldson and Harry White
Stark and Cowan—New York
1923
Popularized on disc by Gene Rodemich and His Orchestra (Brunswick 2474), Frank Westphal and His Orchestra (Columbia 22-D), and Charles Dornberger and His Orchestra (Victor 19138).

## OH THAT NAVAJO RAG
Egbert Van Alstyne (w: Harry Williams)
Jerome H. Remick—New York
1911
A favorite in vaudeville, made famous on disc by the American Quartet, with soloist Billy Murray (Victor 17000).

## OH WHAT A BEAUTIFUL MORNIN'
Richard Rodgers (w: Oscar Hammerstein)
Marlo Music—New York
1943
**Show:** *Oklahoma!*
Alfred Drake sang it in the show. Bing Crosby had the number 4 hit (Decca 18564).

## OH! WHAT A PAL WAS MARY
Pete Wendling (w: Edgar Leslie and Bert Kalmar)
Waterson, Berlin and Snyder—New York
1919
Henry Burr's recording (Victor 18606) helped to sell one million copies of sheet music.

## OH, YOU BEAUTIFUL DOLL
Nat D. Ayer (w: A. Seymour Brown)
Jerome H. Remick—New York
1911
Mose Gumble, chief song plugger of Remick's, made this a million-seller in sheet music. The American Quartet, with Billy Murray, made the hit vocal disc

(Victor 16979), while Arthur Pryor's Band had the instrumental hit (Victor 17063). Judy Garland revived it in the film *For Me and My Gal* (MGM, 1942).

## O-HI-O (DOWN BY THE)
Abe Olman (w: Jack Yellen)
Forster Music—Chicago
1920
Introduced in vaudeville by Van and Schenck. Billy Murray and Victor Roberts had the hit recording (Victor 18723). It was revived in 1940 by the Andrew Sisters (Decca 3065).

## OKLAHOMA
Richard Rodgers (w: Oscar Hammerstein)
Marlo Music—New York
1943
**Show:** *Oklahoma!*
The entire cast, which included Alfred Drake and Joan Roberts, had a million-selling hit with the original cast album reaching number 9 in four charted weeks (Decca 359). This was the first cast album ever released, and it set the pattern for many more successful recordings.

## OL' MAN RIVER
Jerome Kern (w: Oscar Hammerstein)
T. B. Harms—New York
1927
**Show:** *Show Boat*
Introduced in the show by Jules Bledsoe. It has become a classic. Paul Whiteman and His Orchestra had the hit recording (Victor 21218), followed by Al Jolson (Brunswick 3867) and Paul Robeson accompanied by Paul Whiteman's Orchestra (Victor 35912). Bledsoe sang it in the first film version (Universal, 1929), Robeson sang it in the second version (MGM, 1936), and William Warfield sang it in the third version (MGM, 1951).

## OLD FASHIONED LOVE
James P. Johnson (w: Cecil Mack)
Harms—New York
1923
**Show:** *Runnin' Wild*
Introduced in the show by Adelaide Hall. Sissle and Blake made a hit recording (Victor 19253) and the

composer revived it in a 1944 piano solo (Decca 24882). It is a favorite of cabaret singers and jazz bands.

## OLD PIANO ROLL BLUES, THE
Cy Coben (w & m)

Leeds Music—New York

1949

Hoagy Carmichael and Cass Daley had the number 11 hit in 1950 that charted for ten weeks (Decca 24977).

## OLD-FASHIONED GARDEN
Cole Porter (w & m)

T. B. Harms—New York

1919

**Show:** *Hitchy-Koo of 1919*

Lillian Kemble Cooper sang it in the show. It was Cole Porter's first hit song. Revived by Cary Grant and Selena Royle in the Porter biopic *Night and Day* (Warner Bros., 1946).

## OLE BUTTERMILK SKY
Hoagy Carmichael and Jack Brooks

Burke and Van Heusen—New York

1946

**Film:** *Canyon Passage* (Universal)

Hoagy Carmichael sang it in the film, and also had a number 2 hit, which charted for nineteen weeks (ARA 155). However, Kay Kyser and His Orchestra, with vocalist Mike Douglas, bested him with their number 1 hit, which also charted for nineteen weeks (Columbia 37073).

## ON A SLOW BOAT TO CHINA
Frank Loesser (w & m)

Susan—New York

1948

Kay Kyser and His Orchestra had the number 2 hit, which charted for twenty weeks and sold over one million copies (Columbia 38301).

## ON A SUNDAY AFTERNOON
Harry Von Tilzer (w: Andrew B. Sterling)

Harry Von Tilzer—New York

1902

A two-million-selling sheet music success, it was introduced in vaudeville by Ira Kessner. J. W. Myers had the hit recording (Columbia 106). Constance Moore revived it in the film *Atlantic City* (Republic, 1944).

## ON BENDED KNEE
James Harris III and Terry Lewis

Flyte Tyme Tunes

1994

Vocal group Boyz II Men had this number 1 hit, which remained on the charts for twenty-five weeks (Motown 0244). It sold over one million copies.

## ON BROADWAY
Barry Mann/Cynthia Weil/Jerry Leiber/

Mike Stoller

Aldon Music

1963

Although only a number 9 hit for the Drifters, this is one of the classics of teen-pop (Atlantic 2182). It has been since covered by many others, most successfully by jazz guitarist/singer George Benson in 1978, whose version reached number 7 (Warner 8542).

## ON MY OWN
Burt Bacharach and Carole Bayer Sager

Carole Bayer Sager Music

1985, 1986

Patti LaBelle and Michael McDonald had the number 1 hit, which charted for fifteen weeks (MCA 52770. It sold over one million copies.

## ON THE ATCHISON, TOPEKA AND THE SANTE FE
Harry Warren (w: Johnny Mercer)

Leo Feist—New York

1945

**Film:** *The Harvey Girls* (MGM)

Academy Award winner for Best Song of 1946. Johnny Mercer had the number 1 hit, which charted for eighteen weeks (Capitol 195). Judy Garland, who starred in the film, had the number 10 hit (Decca 23436).

## ON THE LEVEL YOU'RE A LITTLE DEVIL
Jean Schwartz (w: Joe Young)

Waterson, Berlin and Snyder—New York

1918

**Show:** *Passing Show of 1918*

This one escaped everyone's notice when it first came out. It wasn't until Rick Benjamin unearthed the Arthur Pryor arrangement for his Paragon Ragtime Orchestra in 1987 that we could hear it (Newport Classic CD-60039). It seems to be a steal from Jerome Kern's "The Sun Shines Brighter" from his show *Leave It to Jane* (1917).

## ON THE MISSISSIPPI
Harry Carroll and Arthur Fields
(w: Ballard MacDonald)
Shapiro Music—New York
1912
Harry Cooper sang it in vaudeville, as did Al Jolson. The American Quartet had the hit vocal recording (Victor 17237) and the Victor Military Band had the hit instrumental (Victor 17277). Mitzi Gaynor revived it in the film *The I Don't Care Girl* (20th Century Fox, 1953).

## ON THE STREET WHERE YOU LIVE
Frederick Loewe (w: Alan Jay Lerner)
Chappell—New York
1956
**Show:** *My Fair Lady*
Michael King sang it in the show. Vic Damone had a number 4 hit, which charted for sixteen weeks (Columbia 40654). Jeremy Brett sang it in the film (Warner Bros., 1964).

## ON THE SUNNY SIDE OF THE STREET
Jimmy McHugh (w: Dorothy Fields)
Shapiro Bernstein—New York
1930
**Show:** *Lew Leslie's International Revue*
Harry Richman sang it in the show. Ted Lewis and His Band had the number 2 hit, which charted for seven weeks (Columbia 2144-D). Tommy Dorsey and His Orchestra, with vocal by the Sentimentalists, revived it in 1945 with a number 16 hit (Victor 20-1648). It has become a cabaret and jazz standard.

## ON TREASURE ISLAND
Joe Burke (w: Edgar Leslie)
Joe Morris—New York
1935
Tommy Dorsey and His Orchestra, with vocal by Edythe Wright, had the number 1 hit, which charted for fourteen weeks (Victor 25144).

## ONCE IN AWHILE
Michael Edwards (w: Bud Green)
Miller Music—New York
1937
Tommy Dorsey and His Orchestra had the number 1 hit, which maintained its position for seven of the fourteen weeks charted (Victor 25686). Patti Page revived it in 1952 with her number 9 hit, which charted for eleven weeks (Mercury 5867). The Chimes also revived it in 1961 for a number 11 hit (TAG 444).

## ONCE IN LOVE WITH AMY
Frank Loesser (w & m)
Edwin H. Morris—New York
1948
**Show:** *Where's Charley?*
Ray Bolger sang it in the show. He had the number 16 hit in 1949 when it charted for seven weeks (Decca 40065). He became forever identified with the song.

## ONE ALONE
Sigmund Romberg (w: Otto Harbach and
Oscar Hammerstein)
Harms—New York
1926
**Show:** *The Desert Song*
Robert Halliday sang it in the show. Arden-Ohman Orchestra had a hit recording (Brunswick 3410). John Boles sang it in the 1929 film version (Warner Bros.), Dennis Morgan sang it in the 1943 version (Warner Bros.), and Gordon MacRae and Kathryn Grayson sang it in the 1953 version (Warner Bros.). It was danced to in the Romberg biopic *Deep in My Heart* (MGM, 1954) by Cyd Charisse and James Mitchell.

## ONE BAD APPLE
George Jackson (w & m)
Fame—Muscle Shoals, Ala.
1970, 1971
This was teen vocal group the Osmonds only number 1 hit, charting for twelve weeks (MGM 14193). It sold over one million copies.

## ONE FOR MY BABY

Harold Arlen (w: Johnny Mercer)

Edwin H. Morris—New York

1943

**Film:** *The Sky's the Limit* (RKO)

Fred Astaire sang it in the film. Lena Horne had the number 21 hit in 1945 (Victor 20-1616).

## ONE HOUR WITH YOU

Richard Whiting (w: Leo Robin)

Famous Music—New York

1932

**Film:** *One Hour With You* (Paramount)

Jeanette MacDonald, Maurice Chevalier, Genevieve Tobin, Charles Ruggles, and Donald Novis sang it in the film. Jimmie Grier and His Orchestra, with vocal by Donald Novis, had the number 2 hit, which charted for eleven weeks (Victor 22971). Eddie Cantor used it as his closing theme on both his radio and television shows.

## ONE I LOVE BELONGS TO SOMEBODY ELSE, THE

Isham Jones (w: Gus Kahn)

Milton Weil—Chicago

1924

Al Jolson had the hit vocal (Brunswick 2567) and the composer had the hit instrumental (Brunswick 2555). It was revived in 1938 by Tommy Dorsey, with a vocal by Jack Leonard (Victor 25741). Doris Day sang it in the Gus Kahn biopic *I'll See You in My Dreams* (Warner Bros., 1951).

## ONE MORE NIGHT

Phil Collins (w & m)

Pun Music

1984, 1985

Phil Collins had the number 1 hit, which charted twelve weeks (Atlantic 89588). It sold over one million copies, and it helped Collins establish his success as a mid-1980s pop crooner, separate from his role as drummer/ vocalist for the popular group Genesis.

## ONE SWEET DAY

Mariah Carey and Boys II Men

Sony Music—Nashville

1995

Mariah Carey and Boyz II Men had the number 1 hit, which held that position for sixteen of the twenty-seven weeks charted and sold over three million copies (Columbia 78074). This song held the number 1 position the longest of any pop single issued since 1955. Mariah Carey was the leading artist of the 1990s, having nineteen songs in the Top 5. Typical of her work, this song emphasized her vocal gymnastics, artfully supported by the more restrained vocalizing of the popular group Boyz II Men.

## ONE THAT YOU LOVE, THE

Graham Russell (w & m)

Careers Music—Los Angeles

1980

The Australian pop-rock group Air Supply had this number 1 hit in 1981 that charted for fourteen weeks (Arista 0604). It sold over one million copies. It was their only chart-topper in a five-year career on the pop charts.

## ONLY A ROSE

Rudolf Friml (w: Brian Hooker)

Henry Waterson—New York

1925

**Show:** *The Vagabond King*

Dennis King and Carolyn Thompson sang it in the show and on a hit recording (Victor 19897). King and Jeanette MacDonald sang it in the first film version (Paramount, 1930). Oreste and Kathryn Grayson sang it in the second film version (Paramount, 1956).

## ONLY YOU

Buck Ram and Ande Rand

Wildwood Music—New York

1955

The Platters had the number 5 hit, which charted for twenty weeks and sold over one million copies (Mercury 70633). Ringo Starr revived it in 1975 with a number 6 hit that charted for ten weeks (Apple 1876). It is a doo-wop standard.

## OOGIE OOGIE WA WA

Archie Gottler (w: Grant Clarke and Edgar Leslie)

Stark and Cowan—New York

1922

Introduced in vaudeville by Margaret Young. Instrumental hit by the Benson Orchestra (Victor 18917). Revived in 1952 by Debbie Reynolds (MGM 30493).

## OPEN YOUR HEART
Madonna Ciccone/Gardner Cole/Peter Rafelson
WB Music
1986
Madonna had this number 1 hit on the Top 40 chart for fourteen weeks (Sire 28508).

## OPPOSITES ATTRACT
Oliver Leiber (w & m)
Virgin Music
1988
Paula Abdul had the number 1 hit in 1990 that charted for fourteen weeks and sold over half a million copies (Virgin 99158).

## ORIENTAL BLUES
Jack Newlon
Jack Newlon—Glenside, Penn.
1933
Introduced in vaudeville by the composer. Revived in 1950 by Ernie Kovacs as his television theme song, as played by the Tony De Simone Trio (Decca 29183).

## ORIGINAL DIXIELAND ONE-STEP
Dominic James LaRocca
Edward B. Marks Music—New York
1937
Introduced in vaudeville and on record in 1917 by the Original Dixieland Jazz Band (Victor 18255)—the first jazz record. Because it ran into copyright difficulties, it wasn't published until decades later, when the band reassembled to celebrate their twentieth anniversary. "Nick" LaRocca was the band's leader and cornetist. It is a jazz classic and has become part of the jazz band repertoire. It has never gone out of style.

## OUR DAY WILL COME
Mort Carson (w: Bob Hilliard)
Rosewood Music
1963
Ruby and the Romantics had the number 1 hit, which charted for ten weeks (Kapp 501). Twelve years later,

Frankie Valli, one-time lead singer of the four Seasons, covered it for a number 11 hit (Private St. 45.043).

## OUT OF NOWHERE
John Green (w: Edward Heyman)
Famous Music—New York
1931
Bing Crosby had the number 1 hit, which charted for eight weeks (Brunswick 6090). Helen Forest sang it in the film *You Came Along* (Paramount, 1945).

## OVER THE RAINBOW
Harold Arlen (w: E.Y. Harburg)
Leo Feist—New York
1939
**Film:** *The Wizard of Oz* (MGM)
Academy Award winner for Best Song. Judy Garland, who sang it in the film and used it as her theme song until 1954 had the number 5 hit, which charted for twelve weeks (Decca 2672). Glenn Miller and His Orchestra had the number 1 hit, holding the top spot for seven out of fifteen weeks charted (Bluebird 10366). It was revived in 1960 by the Demensions, who had the number 16 hit that charted for nine weeks (Mohawk 116). It has become a cabaret singer's favorite as well as a jazz standard.

## OVER THERE
George M. Cohan (w & m)
William Jerome—New York
1917
The most famous song of World War I. Nora Bayes introduced it at a Red Cross war-bond rally and had a hit recording (Victor 45130). Enrico Caruso also had a hit (Victor 87294). James Cagney and Frances Langford sang it in the Cohan biopic *Yankee Doodle Dandy* (Warner Bros., 1942). Joel Grey sang it in the 1968 musical *George M!*

## PACK UP YOUR TROUBLES IN YOUR OLD KIT BAG AND SMILE, SMILE, SMILE
Felix Powell (w: George Asaf)
Chappell—New York
1915
An English war song that became more famous in this country. James Harrison and the Knickerbocker Quartet

had a hit record (Columbia A-2181), as did the Victor Military Band, with a stirring arrangement (Victor 18218).

## PADDLIN' MADELIN HOME
Harry Woods (w & m)
Shapiro, Bernstein—New York
1925
Cliff Edwards had the vocal hit recording (Pathe 025149) and a year later the Ipana Troubadours had the instrumental hit (Columbia 503-D).

## PAGAN LOVE SONG
Nacio Herb Brown (w: Arthur Freed)
Robbins Music—New York
1929
**Film:** *The Pagan* (MGM)
Introduced in the film by Ramon Novarro. Bob Haring and his Copley Plaza Orchestra had the hit recording (Brunswick 4321). Howard Keel sang it in the film *The Pagan Love Song* (MGM, 1950).

## PAINT IT, BLACK
Mick Jagger and Keith Richards
Gideon Music—New York
1966
Nihilistic rock song that held the number 1 position for two out of ten weeks it charted for the Rolling Stones (London 901). The recording was notable because lead-guitarist Brian Jones played the Indian sitar on it, giving it an exotic flavor. It also is notable for the most unusual use of a comma in a rock song title.

## PAINTING THE CLOUDS WITH SUNSHINE
Joe Burke (w: Al Dubin)
M. Witmark and Sons—New York
1929
**Film:** *Gold Diggers of Broadway* (Warner Bros.)
Nick Lucas sang it in the film and had the hit recording (Brunswick 4418). Dennis Morgan sang it in the film *Painting the Clouds with Sunshine* (Warner Bros., 1951).

## PALESTEENA
Con Conrad and J. Russel Robinson
Shapiro Bernstein—New York
1920

Writtten for Eddie Cantor, who had the hit vocal recording (Emerson 10292), but it was the Original Dixieland Jazz Band who had the major hit (Victor 18717).

## PAPA BETTER WATCH YOUR STEP
Gilbert Wells and Bud Cooper
Goodman and Rose—New York
1923
Margaret Young had the hit vocal recording (Brunswick 2459). It was also popularized by the Gulf Coast Seven (Columbia A-3978), and the Emerson Dance Orchestra (Emerson 10623).

## PAPA DON'T PREACH
Brian Elliot (w: Madonna)
WB Music
1986
Madonna had the number 1 hit, which charted for thirteen weeks (Sire 28660). It sold over one million copies. The song was controversial because it depicted a young girl deciding to have a child out of wedlock.

## PAPER DOLL
Johnny S. Black (w & m)
Edward B. Marks—New York
1942
The Mills Brothers had the number 1 hit, which stayed in that position for twelve of the thirty-six weeks charted. It sold over six million copies (Decca 18318).

## PARTY DOLL
James Bowen and Buddy Knox
Patricia Music—New York
1957
Buddy Knox, with the Rhythm Orchids, had the number 1 hit which charted for fifteen weeks and sold over one million copies (Roulette 4002). It is a classic rockabilly song.

## PARTY'S OVER, THE
Jule Styne (w: Comden and Green)
Stratford—New York
1956
**Show:** *Bells Are Ringing*
Judy Holliday sang it in the show.

## PEANUT VENDOR, THE
Moises Simons (w: Marion Sunshine and
L. Wolfe Gilbert)
Edward B. Marks Music—New York
1930
Don Azpiazu and His Havana Casino Orchestra, with
vocal by Arturo Machin, had the number 1 hit, which
charted for twenty-eight weeks (Victor 22483). In
1931, Louis Armstrong and his Sebastian New Cotton
Club Orchestra covered it for a number 15 hit; the
same recording was reissued a decade later for a number 25 hit (Okeh 41478). The tune helped introduce
Latin rhythms into popular music and jazz. It remains a
standard among Latin-Jazz orchestras.

## PEG O' MY HEART
Fred Fisher (w: Alfred Bryan)
Leo Feist—New York
1913
**Show:** *Peg o' My Heart*
Inspired by actress Laurette Taylor, who had starred in a
straight play the year before, the song was sung by José
Collins in the *Ziegfeld Follies of 1913*. Charles Harrison had
a major hit (Victor 17412). It was revived in 1947 by the
Harmonicats, with a number 1 hit that charted for twenty-
six weeks and sold over one million copies (Vitacoustic 1).

## PEGGY SUE
Jerry Allison and Norman Petty
Nor Va Jak Music—New York
1957
Buddy Holly and the Crickets had the number 3 hit,
which charted for sixteen weeks and sold over one million copies (Coral 61885). It is one of Holly's most
famous numbers, inspiring the follow-up, "Peggy Sue
Got Married." Holly's stuttering vocal ("p-p-pretty, p-
p-pretty, p-p-pretty little Peggy Sue") and the rolling
drum rhythm make this a classic recording.

## PENNIES FROM HEAVEN
Arthur Johnston (w: Johnny Burke)
Select Music—New York
1936
**Film:** *Pennies From Heaven* (Columbia )
Bing Crosby sang it in the film and had the number 1
hit, which charted for fifteen weeks (Decca 947).

Revived in 1978 as the theme song for the BBC-TV
series of the same name, which took the conventions of
1930s musicals and satirized them by placing the songs
into a modern story. The series inspired a film,
directed by Herbert Ross and starring Steve Martin
(United Artists, 1981).

## PENNSYLVANIA 6-5000
Jerry Gray (w: Carl Sigman)
Robbins Music—New York
1940
Glenn Miller and His Orchestra had the number 5 hit,
which charted for twelve weeks and sold over one million copies (Bluebird 10754). This was the telephone
number of the Hotel Pennsylvania, across the street
from the Pennsylvania Railroad Station in New York
City. The hotel was a popular place for bandmembers
to stay while on the road.

## PENNY LANE
John Lennon and Paul McCartney
Maclen Music—New York
1967
The Beatles had the number 1 hit, which charted for
nine weeks and sold over one million copies (Capitol
5810). This nostalgic song was Paul McCartney's
"answer" to John Lennon's childhood-memory ballad,
"Strawberry Fields Forever." They were released as a single together. Prominently featured on the recording is a
baroque trumpet, an instrument McCartney had heard
in a recording of one of the Brandenberg Concerti and
specifically asked producer George Martin to use.

## PENTHOUSE SERENADE
Will Jason and Val Burton
Famous Music—New York
1931
The Arden-Ohman Orchestra had the number 3 hit in
1932 under the title "When We're Alone," and it
charted for seven weeks (Victor 22910). Ruth Etting
had the number 8 hit (Columbia 2630-D).

## PEOPLE
Jule Styne (w: Bob Merrill)
Chappell-Styne—New York
1963, 1964

**Show:** *Funny Girl*

Barbra Streisand, who starred in both the show and the film version (Columbia, 1968), had the number 5 hit, which charted for twelve weeks (Columbia 42965). The song became one of the trademark ballads of her nightclub and concert acts.

## PEOPLE GOT TO BE FREE

Felix Cavaliere and Edward Brigati

Slacsar Publishing—New York

1968

The Rascals had this number 1 hit, which held its top position for five of the thirteen weeks charted (Atlantic 2537). It sold over one million copies and remained their biggest hit. In fitting with the era, it was a song advocating personal, social, and sexual freedom.

## PEOPLE WILL SAY WE'RE IN LOVE

Richard Rodgers

(w: Oscar Hammerstein)

Marlo Music—New York

1943

**Show:** *Oklahoma!*

Alfred Drake and Joan Roberts sang this in the show. Bing Crosby had the number 2 hit, which charted for seventeen weeks (Decca 18564).

## PEPPERMINT TWIST

Joey Dee and Henry Glover

Pietro Deiro Publications—New York

1961

Joey Dee and the Starliters had the number 1 hit in 1962, which charted for fourteen weeks and sold over one million copies (Roulette 4401). It was named for the New York City nightclub, the Peppermint Lounge, where the Starliters were the house band.

## PERFECT DAY, A

Carrie Jacobs-Bond (w & m)

Carrie Jacobs-Bond—Chicago

1910

A five-million-selling success in sheet music, it is an art song that crossed to the pop market. Elsie Baker had the hit record (Victor 17387) in 1913. It has since been used at weddings and at funerals.

## PETER GINK

George L. Cobb

Walter Jacobs—Boston

1918

Clever take-off of Edvard Grieg's "Peer Gynt." Popularized on disc by the Six Brown Brothers (Emerson 1055) and the Okeh Dance Band (Okeh 4002).

## PHILADELPHIA FREEDOM

Elton John (w: Bernie Taupin)

Big Pig Music

1975

The Elton John Band recorded this tribute to tennis star Billie Jean King and had the number 1 hit, which charted for seventeen weeks (MCA 40364). It sold over two million copies.

## PHYSICAL

Steve Kipner and Terry Shaddick

April Music

1981

Olivia Newton-John's biggest hit of the 1980s, which charted for twenty-one weeks (MCA 51182). It sold over two million copies. The song was somewhat controversial, because it went against her good-girl image. The video, in which Newton-John works out using a mix of aerobic and disco moves, was considered particularly risqué, although by today's standards it is fairly tame.

## PIANOFLAGE

Roy Bargy

Sam Fox—Cleveland

1922

One of the outstanding novelty rags, introduced by the composer on piano rolls in August 1920 (Imperial 513130) and on disc two years later (Victor 18969). Fate Marable and His Orchestra made a fine arrangement in 1924 (Okeh 40113). Revived in 1952 by Ray Turner (Capitol 2094).

## PICCOLO PETE

Phil Baxter (w & m)

J. W. Jenkins Sons Music—Kansas City, Mo.

1929

Hit recordings by Ted Weems and His Orchestra (Victor 22037) and the Six Jumping Jacks (Brunswick 4457).

## PLAY THAT BARBERSHOP CHORD
Lewis F. Muir (w: William Tracey)

J. Fred Help—New York

1910

Introduced in vaudeville by Bert Williams, whose recording of it helped make it a big seller (Columbia A-929). It was revived in the film *In the Good Old Summertime* (MGM, 1949).

## PLAY THAT FUNKY MUSIC
R. Parissi (w & m)

Bema Music

1976

Number 1 hit for disco/funksters Wild Cherry, holding that spot for three out of eighteen weeks on the charts, and selling over a million copies; also a number 1 R&B hit (Epic 50225). White rapper Vanilla Ice covered it in 1991 for a number 4 hit that sold over half a million copies (SBK 07339).

## PLEASE
Ralph Rainger (w: Leo Robin)

Famous Music—New York

1932

**Film:** *The Big Broadcast* (Paramount)

Bing Crosby sang it in the film and had a number 1 hit that charted for sixteen weeks (Brunswick 6394). He revived it in 1941 with a new version that was a number 24 hit (Decca 3450). John Lennon admired the song for its clever wordplay ("Please, hear my pleas") and said it inspired the lyric to the Beatles's "Please Please Me."

## PLEASE DON'T GO
Harry Wayne Casey and Richard Finch

Sherlyn Publication

1979

KC and the Sunshine Band had the number 1 hit in 1980, which charted for eighteen weeks (T.K. 1035).

## PLEASE DON'T TALK ABOUT ME WHEN I'M GONE
Sam Stept (w: Sidney Clare)

Remick Music—New York

1930

Gene Austin had the number 3 hit in 1931, which charted for five weeks (Victor 22635). Johnny Ray revived it in 1953 with a number 29 hit (Columbia 40090).

## PLEASE LET ME SLEEP
James T. Brymn (w: R. C. McPherson)

Harry Von Tilzer—New York

1902

Very popular in vaudeville, where the publisher introduced it during minstrel Arthur Deming's performance. Other vaudevillians, such as Harry Short, helped to make it famous.

## PLEASE, MR. POSTMAN
Brianbert/Freddie Gorman/
Georgia Dobbins/William Garrett

Jobete Music—Detroit

1961

A number 1 pop and R&B hit for the Marvelettes, an early Motown vocal group; it charted for fifteen weeks and sold over a million copies (Tamla 54046). Covered by the Beatles, among many others, and revived in 1975 by the Carpenters, yielding another number 1, which charted for twelve weeks and sold over a million discs (A&M 1646).

## PLEASE PLEASE ME
John Lennon and Paul McCartney

Concertone Songs—New York

1962

The Beatles's second U.K. single, and a major hit there in 1962. However, it did little on the U.S. charts until Beatlemania kicked in with the group's appearance on the *Ed Sullivan Show* in early 1964. It then reached number 3, charting for ten weeks (Vee Jay 581). The driving drum beat, three-part harmonies, and exuberant "C'mon-c'mon" chorus made this an irresistible pop song.

## PLEASURE MAD
Sidney Bechet (w: Rousseau Simmons)

Fred Fisher—New York

1924

Introduced in vaudeville by Blossom Seeley. Bennie Krueger and His Orchestra had the hit recording (Brunswick 2667). The Ambassadors also had a fine version (Vocalion 14851). It was revived in 1928 by the State Street Ramblers (Gennett 6454).

## PLEDGING MY LOVE

Don Robey and Ferdinand Washington

Lion Publishing—New York

1955

Johnny Ace had the number 17 hit, which charted for nine weeks (Duke 136). Teresa Brewer recorded a cover version, which also reached number 17 (Coral 61362). Recognized as a classic of 1950s soul.

## PONY TIME

Don Covay and John Berry

Harvard Music—New York

1961

Chubby Checker had the number 1 hit, which charted for thirteen weeks (Parkway 818). After the success of the twist, Checker's handlers had him record a series of other dance numbers, including the hucklebuck, the mess around, the fly, and the limbo—but the twist remained the most popular.

## POOR BUTTERFLY

Raymond Hubbell

(w: John L. Golden)

T. B. Harms—New York

1916

**Show:** *The Big Show*

When introduced in the show, it flopped. But the recording by the Victor Military Band (Victor 35605) proved so successful that the sheet music sold a couple of million copies and became the biggest seller of the publisher up to that time. It was revived in 1954 by the Hilltoppers, who had the number 12 hit, which charted for five weeks (Dot 15156).

## POOR PEOPLE OF PARIS, THE

Marguerite Monnot

Reg Connelly Music—New York

1954

Les Baxter had the number 1 hit in 1956, which charted for twenty weeks and sold over one million copies (Capitol 3336).

## POPULARITY

George M. Cohan

F. A. Mills—New York

1906

Hit recording by banjoist Vess L. Ossman (Columbia 3529).

## PORTER'S LOVE SONG TO A CHAMBERMAID, A

James P. Johnson (w: Andy Razaf)

Joe Davis—New York

1930, 1932

Fats Waller had the number 20 hit in 1934 (Victor 24648). A decade later, in 1944, the composer James P. Johnson recorded his piano solo (Decca 24884).

## PORTUGUESE WASHERWOMAN, THE

Andre Popp and Roger Lucchesi

Remick Music—New York

1956

Joe "Fingers" Carr had the number 19 hit, which charted for ten weeks (Capitol 3418).

## POTOMAC RIVER BLUES

Maceo Pinkard (w & m)

Down South Music—New York

1923

**Show:** *Shuffle Along*

Introduced in the touring company of the show by lead Gertrude Saunders, who also recorded it with the composer at the piano (Victor 19159).

## POWDER YOUR FACE WITH SUNSHINE

Carmen Lombardo and Stanley Rochinski

Lombardo Music—New York

1948

Evelyn Knight, with the Starlighters, had the number 1 hit, which charted for twenty weeks (Decca 24530).

## POWER OF LOVE, THE

Mary Applegate and Jennifer Rush

EMI Songs

1986

Canadian pop vocalist Celine Dion had the number 1 hit in 1994, which charted for twenty-six weeks (550 Music/Epic 77230). It sold over one million copies. It had been previously recorded by Laura Branigan in 1988, but only reached number 26 (Atlantic 89191).

## POWER OF LOVE, THE
Johnny Colla/Chris Hayes/Huey Lewis
Hulex Music
1985
**Film:** *Back To the Future* (Universal)
Huey Lewis and the News wrote, performed musically, and acted in the film. This number 1 hit stayed on the chart for fifteen weeks (Chrysalis 42876). It sold over one million copies.

## PREACHER AND THE BEAR, THE
Joe Arzonia (w & m)
Capitol Music House—Columbus, Ohio
1904
Arzonia bought the song from George Fairman. Arthur Collins, a dialect comedy singer, made a two million selling recording (Victor 4431). Phil Harris revived it on radio and on Victor (20-2143) in 1947. As a comic novelty, it enjoyed several decades of popularity, and still remains a campfire favorite.

## PRETTY BABY
Tony Jackson and Egbert Van Alstyne
(w: Gus Kahn)
Jerome H. Remick—New York
1916
**Show:** *Passing Show of 1916*
Dolly Hackett sang it in the show. It also appeared in the show *A World of Pleasure*. Billy Murray had the hit recording (Victor 18102).

## PRETTY GIRL IS LIKE A MELODY, A
Irving Berlin (w & m )
Irving Berlin—New York
1919
**Show:** *Ziegfeld Follies of 1919*
Introduced by John Steel, whose recording was a hit (Victor 18588). After this show, it became the theme song for all of the Follies. It has been used by beauty pageants and fashion shows ever since. It was revived in the biopic *The Great Ziegfeld* (MGM, 1936) and used in several all-Berlin movies, especially *There's No Business like Show Business* (20th Century Fox, 1954).

## PRINCE OF WAILS
Elmer Schoebel (w & m)

Leo Feist—New York
1924
Introduced in vaudeville by L. Carlos Meier. The composer's version with his Friar Society Orchestra (Brunswick 4652) is the best. Other interesting versions include those of the Cotton Pickers (Brunswick 2766), the Varsity Eight (Lincoln 2289), and the Tennessee Tooters (Vocalion 14952).

## PRIVATE EYES
Daryl Hall/Warren Pash/Sara Allen/Janna Allen
Hot-Cha Music
1981
Daryl Hall and John Oates had the number 1 hit, which charted for seventeen weeks (RCA 12296). It sold over one million copies.

## PROUD MARY
John C. Fogerty (w & m)
Jondora Music—Oakland
1968
Creedence Clearwater Revival had the number 2 hit, which charted for twelve weeks and sold over two million copies (Fantasy 616). It was revived in 1971 by Ike and Tina Turner, who had a number 4 hit that sold over one million copies (Liberty 56216). Their energetic version, featuring Tina's incredible high-heeled strutting, became the duo's signature song. Even since their breakup, Tina Turner continues to include it in her stage shows.

## PROUD OF A BABY LIKE YOU
Paul R. Helmick (w: Chris Schonberg and Leonard Stevens)
Villa Moret—San Francisco
1926
Introduced in vaudeville by the Foursome. Hit recording by Jean Goldkette and His Orchestra, featuring Bix Beiderbecke (Victor 20469).

## PUFF (THE MAGIC DRAGON)
Peter Yarrow and Leonard Upton
Pepamar Music
1963
Peter, Paul and Mary had the number 2 hit, which charted for eleven weeks (Warner 5348). A favorite children's song to this day.

## PULLMAN PORTERS PARADE

Maurice Abrahams (w: Ren G. May)

Maurice Abrahams Music—New York

1913

Introduced in vaudeville by songwriters Harry Armstrong and Billy Clark. Al Jolson had a hit recording (Columbia A-1374). It is known that the lyricist was Irving Berlin (the pseudonym "Ren G. May" is an anagram for "Germany").

## PURPLE PEOPLE EATER, THE

Sheb Wooley (w & m)

Cordial Music—Hollywood

1958

Sheb Wooley had the number 1 hit, which charted for fourteen weeks and sold over one million copies (MGM 12651). This is a classic rock novelty song of the period.

## PURPLE ROSE OF CAIRO, THE

A. J. Piron and Steve Lewis (w: Jimmie Dupre)

A. J. Piron—New Orleans

1920

Zez Confrey made an outstanding piano roll of this jazz band standard (QRS 1163). The tune was used as the title theme for Woody Allen's film about a Depression-era woman whose life is transformed when she falls in love with a screen hero (Orion, 1985).

## PUT A LITTLE LOVE IN YOUR HEART

Jimmy Holiday/Randy Myers/Jackie DeShannon

Unart Music—New York

1969

A number 4 hit for Jackie DeShannon, which sold over a million records (Imperial 66385). Revived by Annie Lennox and Al Green (A&M 1255) for the film *Scrooged* (Paramount, 1988), it reached number 9 in 1989. A wonderful gospel-pop sounding number.

## PUT ON A HAPPY FACE

Charles Strouse (w: Lee Adams)

Edwin H. Morris—New York

1960

**Show:** *Bye Bye Birdie*

Dick Van Dyke sang it in the show. Van Dyke and Janet Leigh sang it in the film version (Columbia, 1963).

## PUT ON YOUR OLD GRAY BONNET

Percy Wenrich (w: Stanley Murphy)

Jerome H. Remick—New York

1909

Spurred by the Haydn Quartet's hit recording (Victor 16377), it has become a favorite of barbershop quartets and community sings.

## PUT YOUR ARMS AROUND ME, HONEY

Albert Von Tilzer (w: Junie McCree)

York Music—New York

1910

Introduced in vaudeville by Alta Virginia Houston. It was also popularized in vaudeville by Elizabeth Murray and Blossom Seeley. Collins and Harlan had the hit record (Victor 16708). It was revived in 1943 by Dick Kuhn and His Orchestra, who had a number 4 hit that charted for ten weeks (Decca 4337). Judy Garland sang it in the film *In the Good Old Summertime* (MGM, 1949).

## PUT YOUR HEAD ON MY SHOULDER

Paul Anka (w & m)

Spanka Muisc—New York

1958

Number 2 hit in 1959 for teen popster Anka, holding that spot for three out of fourteen weeks on the charts (ABC-Paramount 10040). A classic late-1950s teen love song.

## PUTTIN' ON THE RITZ

Irving Berlin (w & m)

Irving Berlin—New York

1929

**Film:** *Puttin' On The Ritz* (United Artists)

Harry Richman sang it in the film. He also had the hit recording (Brunswick 4677). Fred Astaire revived it in the film *Blue Skies* (Paramount, 1946). In homage to Astaire, Gene Wilder and Peter Boyle, portraying Frankenstein and his monster, sang and danced to it in the Mel Brooks film *Young Frankenstein* (20th Century Fox, 1974). Taco revived it again in 1983 as a number 4 hit that sold over one million copies (RCA 13574).

## RACING WITH THE MOON

Johnny Watson (w: Vaughn Monroe and Pauline Pope)

Robbins Music—New York

1941

Vaughn Monroe and His Orchestra's recording only reached number 25, but after it became Monroe's theme song it made a greater impact than indicated by its chart position (Bluebird 11070).

## RAG DOLL

Bob Crewe and Bob Gaudio

Saturday Music

1964

The Four Seasons had the number 1 hit, which charted for eleven weeks and sold over one million copies (Philips 40211). A pop vocal-harmony gem.

## RAGS TO RICHES

Richard Adler and Jerry Ross

Saunders—New York

1953

Tony Bennett had the number 1 hit, which charted for twenty-five weeks and sold over one million copies (Columbia 40048). Elvis Presley revived it in 1971, when it charted for four weeks (RCA Victor 47-9980), though it only reached number 33.

## RAGTIME COWBOY JOE

Lewis F. Muir and Maurice Abrahams

(w: Grant Clarke)

F. A. Mills—New York

1912

Introduced in vaudeville by Harry Prescott. Bob Roberts had the hit recording (Victor 17090). Revived in 1949 by Jo Stafford, with piano accompaniment by Lou Busch, it became a number 10 hit (Capitol 57-710). It remains a popular novelty song.

## RAILROAD MAN

Elmer Schoebel (w: Ernie Erdman and Billy Meyers)

Jack Mills—New York

1923

Outstanding recordings by Gene Rodemich and His Orchestra (Brunswick 2399), the Original Memphis Five (Pathe 020888), and Gene Fosdick's Hoosiers (Vocalion 14585).

## RAINBOW CONNECTION

Paul Williams and Kenny Ascher

Welbeck Music

1979

Film: *The Muppet Movie* (AFD)

Jim Henson was the voice of Kermit the Frog, and had the number 25 hit that charted for seven weeks (Atlantic 3610). The song has become a favorite of cabaret singers.

## RAINDROPS KEEP FALLIN' ON MY HEAD

Burt Bacharach (w: Hal David)

Blue Seas Music—New York

1969

**Film:** *Butch Cassidy and the Sundance Kid* (20th Century Fox)

Academy Award winner for Best Song. B. J. Thomas had the number 1 hit in 1970 that charted for nineteen weeks (Scepter 12265).

## RAINY DAY WOMEN #12 & #35

Bob Dylan (w & m)

Bob Dylan Words & Music—New York

1966

Number 2 hit for Bob Dylan, his highest-charting recording ever, charting for nine weeks (Columbia 43592). Famous for its chorus, "Everybody must get stoned!"

## RAMONA

Mabel Wayne (w: L. Wolfe Gilbert)

Leo Feist—New York

1927

**Film:** *Ramona* (United Artists)

Introduced on radio by the star of the silent film, Delores Del Rio. She also sang it in personal appearances. The sheet music sold over two million copies. Gene Austin's recording (Victor 21334) also sold over two million discs. Paul Whiteman's recording with vocalist Austin Young (Victor 21214) was also a bestseller. It was revived in 1953 by the Gaylords (Mercury 70112).

## RAPTURE

Chris Stein (w: Deborah Harry)

Rare Blue Music—Los Angeles

1980

Number 1 hit in 1981 for new-wave group Blondie, holding that position for two out of fourteen weeks on the charts, and selling over a million copies (Chrysalis 2485). One of the earliest pop songs to refer to the (then new) fad of rapping.

## REACH OUT I'LL BE THERE

Brian Holland/Lamont Dozier/
Eddie Holland

Jobete Music—Detroit

1966

The Four Tops had the number 1 hit, which charted for twelve weeks and sold over one million copies (Motown 1098). A very dramatic recording, with a driving beat, making it one of the best of all of the Motown productions.

## REACHING FOR THE MOON

Irving Berlin (w & m)

Irving Berlin—New York

1930

Ruth Etting had the number 6 hit in 1931 that charted for six weeks (Columbia 2377-D).

## RED HOT HENRY BROWN

Fred Rose (w & m)

Leo Feist—New York

1925

Introduced in vaudeville by Alice Morley. Margaret Young had the vocal hit (Brunswick 2939) and Busse's Buzzards had the instrumental (Victor 19782).

## RED HOT MAMA

Fred Rose/Gilbert Wells/Bud Cooper

Rainbow Music—New York

1924

A great syncopated favorite, with Ray Miller and His Orchestra (Brunswick 2681), Bob Haring and His Orchestra (Cameo 562), and the Original Memphis Five (Emerson 10782) having particularly fine arrangements. It was perfect for Sophie Tucker, whose successful recording gave her the title "the last of the red hot mamas" (Okeh 40129).

## RED LIPS KISS MY BLUES AWAY

Pete Wendling/James Monaco/Alfred Bryan

Henry Waterson—New York

1927

Jack Ward made the finest piano roll arrangement (Welte 75273). Mike Markel and His Orchestra had the hit recording (Okeh 40805).

## RED, RED WINE

Neil Diamond (w & m)

Tallyrand Music

1966, 1983

Diamond originally recorded the song in 1966, but his version never charted. UB40 revived it in 1988 for a number 1 hit, which charted for twelve weeks (A&M 1244). It sold over one million copies.

## RED ROSE RAG

Percy Wenrich (w: Edward Madden)

Jerome H. Remick—New York

1911

One of the raggiest songs ever written, it was introduced in vaudeville by Dolly Connolly, wife of the composer. She also had the hit recording (Columbia A-1028). Comedian George Burns kept singing it throughout his lengthy career in show business.

## RED ROSES FOR A BLUE LADY

Sid Tepper and Roy Brodsky

Mills Music—New York

1948

Vaughn Monroe had the number 3 hit in 1949, which charted for twenty-two weeks (RCA Victor 20-3319). It was revived in 1965 by Vic Dana, who had a number 10 hit (Dolton 304). It remains a lounge singer favorite.

## RED WING

Kerry Mills (w: Thurland Chattaway)

F. A. Mills—New York

1907

Huge success as an Indian song at first with a hit recording by Frank Stanley and Henry Burr (Columbia 3681), then became a dixieland standard from the 1920s on. It was Spike Jones's first recording in 1941 (Bluebird 11282). It also provided the melody for numerous folk songs, including Woody Guthrie's "Reuben James."

## REDHEAD
Burt Green (w: Irene Franklin)
Leo Feist—New York
1908
Introduced in the show *The Summer Widowers,* interpolated by author-singer Irene Franklin, who also recorded it with husband-composer-pianist Burt Green in 1913 (Columbia A-1873).

## REFLEX, THE
Duran Duran (w & m)
Tritec Music
1983, 1984
British synth-pop stars of the 1980s, Duran Duran had their first number 1 hit with this song, which stayed on the chart for fifteen weeks (Capitol 5345). It sold over one million copies.

## RELEASE ME
Carnie and Wendy Wilson and Chynna Phillips
EMI Music
1990
The second release—and second number 1 hit—for early 1990s pop trio Wilson Phillips; it charted for fifteen weeks, and sold over half a million copies (SBK 07327).

## REMEMBER
Irving Berlin (w & m)
Irving Berlin—New York
1925
A great hit for Ruth Etting, who introduced it in vaudeville. Isham Jones and His Orchestra had the hit recording (Brunswick 2963). It was sung by Alice Faye in the film *Alexander's Ragtime Band* (20th Century Fox, 1938).

## RESPECT
Otis Redding Jr. (w & m)
East Publishing—New York
1967
Aretha Franklin had the number 1 hit, which charted for eleven weeks and sold over one million copies (Atlantic 2403). The song became her signature piece, and the "Sock it to me" chorus introduced that phrase into the pop speech of the day. A great, modern spelling song.

## RHINESTONE COWBOY
Larry Weiss (w & m)
WB Music
1973
Glen Campbell had this number 1 hit in 1975 that charted for eighteen weeks (Capitol 4095). It sold over one million copies and became Campbell's theme song for about the next decade.

## RIO RITA
Harry Tierney (w: Joseph McCarthy)
Leo Feist—New York
1926
**Show:** *Rio Rita*
Ethelind Terry and J. Harold Murray sang it in the show. Nat Shilkret and His Orchestra had a hit recording (Victor 20474), as did Sam Lanin's Orchestra (Okeh 40781). John Boles sang it in the first film version (RKO, 1929) while John Carroll sang it in the second version (MGM, 1942).

## RISE 'N SHINE
Vincent Youmans (w: Bud DeSylva)
Harms—New York
1932
**Show:** *Take a Chance*
Ethel Merman sang it in the show. Lillian Roth sang it in the film version (Paramount 1933). After the film was released, Paul Whiteman and His Orchestra had the number 16 hit (Victor 24197).

## RIVERBOAT SHUFFLE
Dick Voynow/Hoagie Carmichael/
Irving Mills
Jack Mills—New York
1925
Introduced on records by Dick Voynow's Wolverines, featuring Bix Beiderbecke (Gennett 5454). Isham Jones and His Orchestra had the hit recording (Brunswick 2854). It is a Dixieland jazz classic and a staple in the repertoire.

## ROCK AND ROLL MUSIC

Chuck Berry (w & m)

ARC Music—New York

1957

Chuck Berry had the number 8 hit, which charted for thirteen weeks (Chess 1671). It became an early rock favorite, and was covered by the Beatles as an album track in 1964 (Capitol S 2080). The Beach Boys revived it in 1976 with a number 5 hit that charted for thirteen weeks (Brother/Reprise 1354).

## ROCK AND ROLL WALTZ

Shorty Allen (w: Dick Ware)

Sheldon Music—New York

1955

Kay Starr had the number 1 hit in 1956 that charted for twenty weeks and sold over one million copies (RCA Victor 47-6359).

## ROCK AROUND THE CLOCK

Max Freedman and Jimmy DeKnight

Myers Music—New York

1953

Bill Haley and His Comets recorded their number 1 hit on April 12, 1954. It wasn't until it was used in the film *Blackboard Jungle* (MGM, 1955) that it became a smash, charting for twenty-four weeks and selling over one million copies (Decca 29124). Haley and his Comets appeared the next year in the film *Rock around the Clock* (Columbia, 1956) and the following year in *Don't Knock the Rock* (Columbia, 1957) performing the song each time. The recording eventually sold over thirty million copies worldwide. It was revived in 1974, when the original recording was used as the opening theme for the TV series "Happy Days." Cowriter DeKnight's name was a pseudonym for publisher James Myers.

## R.O.C.K. IN THE U.S.A.

John Mellencamp (w & m)

Riva Music

1985

Number 2 hit for John Cougar Mellencamp, charting for eleven weeks in 1986 (Riva 88455). An homage to 1960s rock, the song is among Mellencamp's best-loved.

## ROCK-A-BYE YOUR BABY WITH A DIXIE MELODY

Jean Schwartz (w: Sam Lewis and Joe Young)

Waterson, Berlin and Snyder—New York

1918

**Show:** *Sinbad*

Al Jolson sang it in the show and throughout his career, single-handedly turning it into a standard. His first hit recording came that year of publication (Columbia A-2560). It was revived when he sang it in the film *Rose of Washington Square* (20th Century Fox, 1939). When he sang it in his biopic *The Jolson Story* (Columbia, 1946), it was also released as a disc (Brunswick 6502), which sold tremendously. It became so popular again that he included it in his second biopic, *Jolson Sings Again* (Columbia, 1949). Comedian Jerry Lewis revived it yet again in 1956 with a number 10 hit, which charted for fifteen weeks and sold over one million copies (Decca 30124).

## ROCKIN' CHAIR

Hoagy Carmichael (w & m)

Southern Music—New York

1930

The Mills Brothers had the number 4 hit in 1932, which charted for six weeks (Brunswick 6278). Mildred Bailey, despite being known as "The Rockin' Chair Lady," didn't get a hit until 1937, when her recording reached number 13 (Vocalion 3553).

## ROCKIN' ROBIN

Jimmie Thomas (w & m)

Recordo Music—New York

1958

Bobby Day had the number 2 hit, which charted for nineteen weeks and sold over one million copies (Class 229). Michael Jackson revived it in 1972 with a number 2 hit which charted for eleven weeks (Motown 1197). A classic 1950s pop confection, it is best remembered for the "Tweedle-dee" chorus.

## ROLL OVER, BEETHOVEN

Chuck Berry (w & m)

ARC Music—New York

1956

Chuck Berry had the number 29 hit (Chess 1626). Despite its low pop-chart position, it remains one of

Berry's best-loved classics. The Beatles covered it on their *Second Album* (Capitol S 2080)

## ROLL WITH IT
Steve Winwood and Will Jennings
F. S. Music
1988
Steve Winwood had this number 1 hit, which topped the charts for four of its fourteen-week run (Island 99326). However, it was the last major hit of his comeback career.

## ROSE AND A BABY RUTH, A
John Loudermilk (w & m)
Bentley Music—Chapel Hill, N.C.
1956
George Hamilton IV had the number 6 hit, which charted for fourteen weeks and sold over one million copies (ABC-Paramount 9765).

## ROSE GARDEN
Joe South (w & m)
Lowery Music—Atlanta, Georgia
1967, 1970
A number 3 hit for country-pop singer Lynn Anderson. It sold over a million copies during its fourteen-week chart run (Columbia 45252).

## ROSE OF THE RIO GRANDE
Harry Warren and Ross Gorman (w: Edgar Leslie)
Stark and Cowan—New York
1922
Marion Harris had the hit vocal recording (Brunswick 2370) and the Virginians had the hit instrumental (Victor 19001). It was revived in 1949 by Chuck Thomas and His Dixieland Band (Capitol 746).

## ROSE OF WASHINGTON SQUARE
James Hanley (w: Ballard MacDonald)
Shapiro, Bernstein—New York
1920
**Show:** *Ziegfeld Midnight Frolic*
Introduced in the show by Fanny Brice. Best-selling recordings were by the All Star Trio (Victor 18659) and the Kentucky Serenaders (Columbia A-2908). It was revived in the film of the same name and sung by Alice Faye (20th Century Fox, 1939). Benny Goodman

and His Orchestra had a number 10 hit recording in 1939 (Victor 26230). It was revived again by Ann Dee in the film *Thoroughly Modern Millie* (Universal, 1967).

## ROSE ROOM
Art Hickman (w: Harry Williams)
Sherman, Clay—San Francisco
1918
Introduced in vaudeville by the composer, who had a five-piece dance band. His recording, the first of many through the years, was a hit (Columbia A-2858). It was revived by Duke Ellington and His Famous Orchestra in 1932 with a number 15 hit (Brunswick 6265).

## ROSY CHEEKS
Richard A. Whiting (w: Seymour Simons)
Irving Berlin—New York
1927
A great song popularized by the Six Hottentots with a vocal by Irving Kaufman (Banner 1962). Henry Halstead and His Orchestra also had a hit (Victor 20691).

## ROUMANIA
Clarence Williams/Dave Peyton/Spencer Williams
Williams and Piron Music—Chicago
1920
Introduced on disc by Clarence Williams as Johnson's Jazz Boys (Okeh 8021). Eubie Blake (Melodee S-2988) and James P. Johnson (QRS 1479) made the important piano roll versions.

## ROW ROW ROW
Jimmy V. Monaco (w: William Jerome)
Harry Von Tilzer—New York
1912
**Show:** *Ziegfeld Follies of 1912*
Lillian Lorraine sang it in the show. Ada Jones had the hit recording (Victor 17205).

## ROYAL GARDEN BLUES
Clarence Williams (w: Spencer Williams)
Shapiro, Bernstein—New York
1919
Introduced in vaudeville by the Original Dixieland Jazz Band, whose recording helped make this a standard for jazz bands (Victor 18798).

## RUBY TUESDAY

Mick Jagger and Keith Richards

Gideon Music—New York

1967

Number 1 hit for the Rolling Stones, although it held this position only one out of nine weeks that it charted (London 903). Nonetheless, the single sold over a million copies. It was notable at the time for being a soft-rock ballad, featuring a prominent flute solo, marking the beginning of the Stones's brief psychedelic period.

## RUDOLPH THE RED-NOSED REINDEER

Johnny Marks (w & m)

St. Nicholas Music—New York

1949

Gene Autry, the singing cowboy, had the number 1 hit which became the perennial Christmas favorite, selling over ten million copies (Columbia 38610). David Seville's Chipmunks revived it in 1960 with a number 21 hit (Liberty 55289).

## RUNAWAY

Del Shannon and Max Crook

Mole Hole Music

1961

**TV Show:** *Crime Story*

Del Shannon had the number 1 hit, which charted for twelve weeks (Big Top 3067) and sold more than one million copies. The song is a classic of early rock.

## RUNNIN' WILD

A. Harrington Gibbs (w: Joe Grey and Leo Wood)

Leo Feist—New York

1922

A great favorite in vaudeville. Ted Lewis and His Orchestra had a hit recording (Columbia A-3790), as did the Great White Way Orchestra (Victor 19063). The Cotton Pickers had a fine arrangement (Brunswick 2382). It was revived in 1937 by the Emilio Cacares Trio (Victor 26109). It was revived again in the film *The Five Pennies* (Paramount, 1959).

## RUNNING BEAR

J. P. Richardson (w & m)

Big Bopper Music

1959

Johnny Preston had the number 1 hit in 1960, which charted for fourteen weeks and sold over one million copies (Mercury 71474).

## RUNNING SCARED

Roy Orbison and Joe Melson

Acuff-Rose Publications—London

1961

Operatic-voiced Roy Orbison had the number 1 hit, which charted for fifteen weeks (Monument 438).

## RUSH RUSH

Peter Lord (w & m)

EMI April Music

1991

Paula Abdul had this number 1 hit, which held this position for five out of the fifteen weeks on the charts (Virgin 98828). It sold over half a million copies. The song was promoted with a video recreating the famous street race scene from *Rebel without a Cause* (Warner Bros., 1955).

## 'S WONDERFUL

George and Ira Gershwin

New World Music—New York

1927

**Show:** *Funny Face*

Introduced in the show by Allen Kearns and Adele Astaire. It was the hit song of the show and is now a standard. Frank Crumit had the hit recording (Victor 21029). It was featured in the Gershwin biopic *Rhapsody in Blue* (Warner Bros., 1945), the film *An American in Paris* (MGM, 1951), and the film version of the original show (Paramount, 1957). It was revived in the 1983 Broadway show *My One and Only* by Tommy Tune and Twiggy.

## SAILING

Christopher Cross (w & m)

BMG Songs

1979

Christopher Cross had the number 1 hit in 1980, which charted for thirteen weeks (Warner 49507). It was the first of only two number 1 hits that he would achieve (the second was for "Arthur's Theme").

## SAILING DOWN THE CHESAPEAKE BAY

George Botsford (w: Jean Havez)

Jerome H. Remick—New York

1913

This happy, syncopated song was given a hit recording by Henry Burr and Albert Campbell (Columbia A-1378). It was revived in 1949 by Pete Daily and His Chicagoans (Capitol 57-728).

### SAM, THE OLD ACCORDION MAN

Walter Donaldson (w & m)

Leo Feist—New York

1927

Ruth Etting had the hit recording (Columbia 908-D). Doris Day sang it in the Etting biopic *Love Me or Leave Me* (MGM, 1955).

### SAM'S SONG

Lew Quadling (w: Jack Elliott)

Sam Weiss Music—New York

1950

There were two versions released in 1950 that charted: those of Bing and Gary Crosby, who had a number 3 hit that charted for nineteen weeks (Decca 27112), and Joe "Fingers" Carr, whose recording reached number 7, charting for thirteen weeks (Capitol 962).

### SAN

Lindsay McPhail and Walter Hirsch

L. B. Curtis—New York

1920

A very popular song in vaudeville. The hit recording was by the Benson Orchestra (Victor 18779). Also with fine arrangements were Abe Lyman's Sharps and Flats (Brunswick 3964), Markel's Orchestra (Okeh 40098), and Ben Selvin's Orchestra (Vocalion 14851). It was revived in 1953 in a million-selling disc by Pee Wee Hunt (Capitol 2442).

### SAN FRANCISCO

Bronislaw Kaper and Walter Jurmann

(w: Gus Kahn)

Robbins Music—New York

1936

**Film:** *San Francisco* (MGM)

Jeanette MacDonald sang it in the film. Tommy Dorsey and His Orchestra had the number 10 hit, which charted for five weeks (Victor 25352).

### SAN FRANCISCO (BE SURE TO WEAR FLOWERS IN YOUR HAIR)

John Phillips (w & m)

Trousdale Music—New York

1967

Number 4 hit for Bay Area singer/songwriter Scott McKenzie, the song inspired a rush of hippies to settle in the Haight-Ashbury neighborhood of San Francisco (Ode 103). Unofficial anthem of the "Summer of Love."

### SAN FRANCISCO BOUND

Irving Berlin (w & m)

Waterson, Berlin and Snyder—New York

1913

Amy Butler introduced this highly syncopated song in vaudeville. The Peerless Quartet had the hit recording (Victor 17367).

### SANTA CLAUS IS COMIN' TO TOWN

J. Fred Coots (w: Haven Gillespie)

Leo Feist—New York

1934

George Hall and His Orchestra, with vocal by Sonny Schuyler, had the number 12 hit (Bluebird 5711). Bing Crosby and the Andrews Sisters had the number 22 hit in 1947 (Decca 23281). The Four Seasons revived it in 1962 with a number 23 hit (Vee-Jay 478). It has become a Christmas favorite.

### SAVE IT FOR ME

Bob Cole (w: James Weldon Johnson)

Jos. W. Stern—New York

1903

Marie Cahill introduced it in vaudeville. Max Morath revived it in his 1964 album, *Oh, Play That Thing!* (Epic BN-26106).

### SAVE THE BEST FOR LAST

Wendy Waldman/Jon Lind/Phil Galdston

Windswept Pacific Entertainment

1989

Vanessa Williams had this number 1 hit in 1992, which topped the charts for five of its twenty-three-week run (Wing 865136). It was her first chart-topping release, helped launch her career as a pop singer, and sold over a million copies.

## SAVING ALL MY LOVE FOR YOU

Michael Masser

(w: Gerry Goffin)

Warner Bros. Publishing

1978, 1985

Whitney Houston's first number 1 hit—her second released single—charted for fifteen weeks (Arista 9381). It sold over one million copies.

## SAY IT ISN'T SO

Irving Berlin (w & m)

Irving Berlin—New York

1932

George Olsen and His Orchestra had the number 1 hit, which charted for nine weeks (Victor 24124).

## SAY IT WITH MUSIC

Irving Berlin (w & m)

Irving Berlin—New York

1921

**Show:** *Music Box Review*

Introduced in the show by Wilda Bennett and Joseph Santley. Paul Whiteman and His Orchestra had the hit recording (Victor 18803). Rudy Wiedoeft and His Orchestra also had a fine arrangement (Brunswick 2139). Ethel Merman sang it in the film *Alexander's Ragtime Band* (20th Century Fox, 1938).

## SAY IT WITH YOUR HEART

Steve Nelson and Norman Kaye

Leo Feist—New York

1952

Bob Carroll had the number 14 hit, which charted for four weeks (Derby 814).

## SAY, SAY, SAY

Paul McCartney and Michael Jackson

MPL Communications

1983

Two of pop music's icons collaborated on both song and recording to produce a number 1 hit that charted for eighteen weeks (Columbia 04168). It sold over two million copies.

## SAY YOU, SAY ME

Lionel Richie (w & m)

Brockman Music

1985

**Film:** *White Knights* (Columbia)

Academy Award winner for Best Song. Lionel Richie had the number 1 hit, which charted for sixteen weeks (Motown 1819). It sold over one million copies.

## SCHOOL DAY

Chuck Berry (w & m)

ARC Music—New York

1957

Chuck Berry had the number 3 hit, which charted for fifteen weeks (Chess 1653).

## SCHOOL DAYS

Gus Edwards (w: Will D. Cobb)

Gus Edwards Music—New York

1907

A three-million selling sheet music hit, introduced by the composer in vaudeville. Byron G. Harlan had this hit recording (Victor 5086). Bing Crosby sang it in the biopic *The Star Maker* (Paramount, 1939). It remains a singalong favorite.

## SEARCHIN'

Mike Stoller (w: Jerry Leiber)

Tiger Music—New York

1957

The Coasters had the number 3 hit, which charted for twenty-two weeks and sold over one million copies (Atco 6087).

## SECOND HAND ROSE

James F. Hanley (w: Grant Clarke)

Shapiro, Bernstein—New York

1921

**Show:** *Ziegfeld Follies of 1921*

Fanny Brice sang it in the show and also had a hit recording (Victor 45263). She also sang it in the film *My Man* (Warner Bros., 1929). Ted Lewis and his Band had the instrumental hit (Columbia A-3453). Barbra Streisand had the number 32 hit in 1966 (Columbia 43469); she also sang it in the Fanny Brice biopic *Funny Girl* (Columbia, 1968).

## SECRET LOVE

Sammy Fain (w: Paul Webster)

Remick Music—New York

1953

**Film:** *Calamity Jane* (Warner Bros.)

Academy Award winner for Best Song. Doris Day, who starred in the film, had the number 1 hit that charted for twenty-two weeks and sold over a million copies (Columbia 40108).

## SEE YOU LATER, ALLIGATOR

Robert Guidry (w & m)

ARC Music—New York

1956

**Film:** *Rock Around the Clock* (Columbia)

Bill Haley and His Comets played and sang it in the film. Their single was a number 6 hit, which charted for fifteen weeks and sold over one million copies (Decca 29791). The expression entered the slang of the day.

## SEEMS LIKE OLD TIMES

Carmen Lombardo and John Jacob Loeb

Leo Feist—New York

1946

Arthur Godfrey's radio and TV theme song. Guy Lombardo and His Orchestra had a number 7 hit that charted for seven weeks (Decca 18737). Vaughn Monroe with the Norton Sisters also had a number 7 hit (Victor 20-1811).

## SEND IN THE CLOWNS

Stephen Sondheim (w & m)

Revelation Music—New York

1973

**Show:** *A Little Night Music*

Glynis Johns sang it in the show. Judy Collins released her version in 1975, for a minor hit, but it reached number 19 when it was reissued two years later (Elektra 45253). The song has become a standard among cabaret stars and remains in Collins's performance repertory.

## SENTIMENTAL JOURNEY

Bud Green/Les Brown/Ben Homer

Edwin H. Morris—New York

1944

Les Brown and His Orchestra, with vocalist Doris Day, had the number 1 hit, which maintained its position for nine of the twenty-eight weeks on the chart and sold over one million copies (Columbia 36769). Ringo Starr used it as the title cut for his first solo album, a collection of standards issued in 1970 (Apple 3365).

## SEPTEMBER SONG

Kurt Weill (w: Maxwell Anderson)

Crawford Music—New York

1938

**Show:** *Knickerbocker Holiday*

Walter Huston sang it in the show, and his recording reached number 12, charting for five weeks in 1939 (Brunswick 8272). Frank Sinatra revived it in 1946 with a number 8 hit (Columbia 37161).

## SERENADE IN BLUE

Harry Warren (w: Mack Gordon)

Bregman, Vocco and Conn—New York

1942

**Film:** *Orchestra Wives* (20th Century Fox)

Glenn Miller and His Orchestra had the number 2 hit, which charted for eighteen weeks and became one of his theme songs (Victor 27935).

## SEVENTY SIX TROMBONES

Meredith Willson (w & m)

Frank Music—New York

1957

**Show:** *The Music Man*

Robert Preston sang it in the show and the film version (Warner Bros., 1962). It was one of the most popular numbers in the show.

## SHADOW DANCING

The Brothers Gibb

Stigwood Music

1978

Andy Gibb, the youngest brother of Barry, Robin, and Maurice, had a big solo career in the late 1970s. This hit stayed in the number 1 position for seven of the nineteen weeks it charted on the Top 40 (RSO 904). It sold over two million copies.

## SHADOW OF YOUR SMILE, THE

Johnny Mandel (w: Paul F. Webster)

United Artists Music—Los Angeles

1965

**Film:** *The Sandpiper* (MGM)
Academy Award winner for Best Song. Has become a lounge favorite.

## SHAKE IT AND BREAK IT
Lou Chiha (w: H. Qualli Clark)
Handy Bros. Music—New York
1920
A jazz standard, it has been featured by Dixieland bands since the revival in the 1940s. Sherry Magee and his Dixielanders were the first to record it (Vocalion 5281) in 1940 followed by Pete Daily's Chicagoans in 1946 (Jump 24). Pee Wee Hunt and his Dixieland Band made an outstanding version in the mid-1950s (Capitol T-312).

## SHAKE, RATTLE AND ROLL
Charles Calhoun (w & m) (pseudonym of Jesse Stone)
Progressive Music—New York
1954
Joe Turner introduced this first rock and roll hit in August when it charted at number 22 (Atlantic 1026). Bill Haley and His Comets quickly covered it for a number 7 hit, which charted for twenty-seven weeks and sold over one million copies (Decca 29204). Arthur Conley revived it in 1967 when he had the number 31 hit (Atco 6494).

## SHAKE YOUR BOOTY
Harry Wayne Casey and Richard Finch
Sherlyn Music—Hialeah, Fl.
1976
Number 1 disco hit for KC and the Sunshine Band, charting for sixteen weeks; also a number 1 R&B hit (T.K. 1019). A classic of the disco era, noted for its "Shake shake shake" chorus.

## SHAKING THE BLUES AWAY
Irving Berlin (w & m)
Irving Berlin—New York
1927
**Show:** *Ziegfeld Follies of 1927*
Introduced in the show by Ruth Etting, who also had the hit recording (Columbia 1113-D). Doris Day sang it in the Etting biopic *Love Me or Leave Me* (MGM, 1955).

## SHAKY EYES
Harry Armstrong and Billy Clark
M. Witmark and Sons—New York
1909
Introduced by the composers in vaudeville. Arthur Collins had the hit recording (Columbia A-811).

## SH-BOOM
James Keyes/Claude Feaster/Carl Feaster/
Floyd McRae/James Edwards
Hill and Range Songs—New York
1954
The black doo-wop group the Chords introduced it in July 1954, when it was a number 5 hit that charted for sixteen weeks (Cat 104). White cover artists the Crew-Cuts had the first rock and roll number 1 hit with their version, which held that position for nine of the twenty weeks that it charted and sold over one million copies (Mercury 70404). Stan Freberg did his devastating parody with The Toads and had a number 14 hit (Capitol 2929). Nonetheless, it remains a doo-wop classic.

## SHE CAME IN THROUGH THE BATHROOM WINDOW
John Lennon and Paul McCartney
Maclen Music—New York
1969
The Beatles recorded this on their *Abbey Road* album (Apple 383) as part of the long medley of songs on the album's second side. Joe Cocker covered it in a particularly memorable version, achieving a number 30 hit in 1970 (A&M 1147).

## SHE DIDN'T SAY "YES"
Jerome Kern (w: Otto Harbach)
T. B. Harms—New York
1931
**Show:** *The Cat and the Fiddle*
Bettina Hall sang it in the show. Leo Reisman and His Orchestra had the number 13 hit in 1932 (Victor 22839). Jeanette MacDonald sang it in the film version (MGM, 1934). The Wilde Twins sang it in the Kern biopic *Till the Clouds Roll By* (MGM, 1946).

## SHE LOVES YOU
John Lennon and Paul McCartney

Gil Music—New York

1963

The Beatles had the number 1 hit in 1964 that charted for fourteen weeks (Swan 4152). It was their second U.S. number 1, after "I Want to Hold Your Hand." The "yeah-yeah-yeah" chorus is the song's trademark.

## SHEIK OF ARABY, THE

Ted Snyder (w: Harry B. Smith and
Francis Wheeler)
Waterson, Berlin and Snyder—New York
1921

A favorite in vaudeville. The Club Royale Orchestra had the hit recording (Victor 18831). Alice Faye, Betty Grable, Billy Gilbert, and the Nicholas Brothers sang and danced to it in the film *Tin Pan Alley* (20th Century Fox, 1940). Spike Jones and His City Slickers made a memorable version in 1943 (Bluebird 0812). The Super-Sonics had a number 22 hit in 1953 (Rainbow 214).

## SHEPHERD SERENADE

Fred Spielman (w: Kermit Goell)
Sheppard Music—New York
1941

Horace Heidt and His Orchestra had the number 7 hit, with vocalists Gordon MacRae, Larry Cotton, and Fred Lowery (Columbia 36370).

## SHERRY

Bob Gaudio (w & m)
Bo Bob Music—New York
1962

The Four Seasons had this number 1 hit, which held its top position for five of the twelve weeks charted (Vee-Jay 456). It sold over one million copies. The soaring high falsetto vocals of Frankie Valli made their recording a classic.

## SHINE

Ford Dabney (w: Cecil Mack and Lew Brown)
Shapiro, Bernstein—New York
1924

Introduced in vaudeville by Art Landry and His Band. The original hit recordings of this standard were made by Herb Wiedoeft and His Orchestra (Brunswick 2542), the Virginians (Victor 19334), and the Original Mem-

phis Five (Perfect 14275). It was revived in 1932 by Bing Crosby and the Mills Brothers in a number 7 hit recording (Brunswick 6276). It was revived again in 1942 by Henry "Hot Lips" Levine and his Strictly from Dixie Jazz Band (Victor 27831). Frankie Laine had a number 9 hit recording in 1948 (Mercury 5091). It was featured in the biopic *The Benny Goodman Story* (Universal, 1956).

## SHINE ON, HARVEST MOON

Nora Bayes and Jack Norworth (w: Jack Norworth)
Jerome H. Remick—New York
1908
**Show:** *The Follies of 1908*

Introduced by Nora Bayes in the show, the song remained in her repertoire for life. Her lyricist-singer husband also used it in his vaudeville act. Ada Jones and Billy Murray had a hit recording in 1909 (Edison 10134). Ruth Etting revived it in the show *Ziegfeld Follies of 1931*. It appeared in the movie of the same name (Warner Bros., 1944). It remains a perennial among amateur singers everywhere.

## SHINE ON YOUR SHOES, A

Arthur Schwartz (w: Howard Dietz)
Harms—New York
1932
**Show:** *Flying Colors*

Dancers Vilma and Buddy Ebsen, singer Monette Moore, and harmonica whiz Larry Adler sang, played, and danced to it in the show. Fred Astaire sang and danced to it in the film *Band Wagon* (MGM, 1953). Roger Wolfe Kahn and His Orchestra had the number 12 hit in 1932 (Columbia 2722-D).

## SHINING STAR

Maurice White/Philip Bailey/Larry Dunn
Saggiflame Music—Los Angeles
1975

Earth Wind and Fire had this number 1 hit, which charted for fourteen weeks (Columbia 10090). It sold over one million copies.

## SHOE SHINE BOY

Saul Chaplin (w: Sammy Cahn)
Mills Music—New York
1936

**Show:** *Connie's Hot Chocolates of 1936*
Louis Armstrong and His Orchestra sang and played it in the show. The Mills Brothers had a memorable disc (Decca 961).

## SHOP AROUND
Berry Gordy Jr. and Bill Smokey Robinson
Jobete Music—Detroit
1961
Number 2 hit for the Miracles, their first single release; also a number 1 R&B song (Tamla 54034). A classic Motown song and arrangement. Covered in 1974 by the Captain and Tenille for a number 4 hit (A&M 1817).

## SHORT PEOPLE
Randy Newman (w & m)
Six Pictures Music
1977
Number 2 novelty hit for wry singer-songwriter Randy Newman; it held that position for three of thirteen chart weeks in 1978 (Warner 8492). Although a universally revered composer, Newman has had no other chart hits.

## SHOUT!
Isley Brothers
Wemar Music
1962
**Film:** *Hey Let's Twist* (Paramount)
Number 6 hit for teen popsters Joey Dee and the Starlighters (Roulette 4416). Revived as part of the soundtrack of the classic comedy *National Lampoon's Animal House* (Universal, 1978). Also used as a jingle to sell the detergent of the same name.

## SHOW ME THE WAY TO GO HOME
Irving King (w & m)
Harms—New York
1925
A standard of the drinking set, it was made famous in the recording by Perry's Hot Dogs (Banner 1615) and Vincent Lopez and His Orchestra (Okeh 40516).

## SIDE BY SIDE
Harry Woods (w & m)
Shapiro, Bernstein—New York
1927

Introduced in vaudeville by Cliff Edwards, who also had a hit record (Perfect 11640). Paul Whiteman with the Rhythm Boys had another hit (Victor 20627). It was revived in 1953 by Kay Starr in a number 3 hit (Capitol 2334).

## SIDEWALK BLUES
Ferd "Jelly Roll" Morton (w: Walter Melrose)
Melrose Bros. Music—Chicago
1926
Introduced on record by Jelly Roll Morton's Red Hot Peppers (Victor 20252). Doc Cook and His Dreamland Orchestra (Columbia 862-D) and Ross Gorman's Virginians (Harmony 322-H) also had fine arrangements.

## SIGN, THE
Buddha/Joker/Jenny and Linn
Megasong Pub.
1993
Ace of Base, a Swedish pop vocal group, had this enormous number 1 hit, which charted for thirty-three weeks (Arista 12653). It sold over one million copies. It featured a disco-esque beat and harmonies reminiscent of the earlier Swedish pop sensation, ABBA.

## SILLY LOVE SONGS
Paul McCartney (w & m)
McCartney Music
1976
Wings had this number 1 hit as their biggest of the 1970s. It was in this position for five of the fifteen weeks charted (Capitol 4256). It sold over one million copies. McCartney wrote the song in answer to critics who found some of his 1970s hits to be lightweight.

## SILVER BELL
Percy Wenrich (w: Edward Madden)
Jerome H. Remick—New York
1910
A big hit in vaudeville, the Peerless Quartet had the successful recording (Victor 16646).

## SIMPLE MELODY (AKA PLAY A SIMPLE MELODY)
Irving Berlin (w & m)

Irving Berlin—New York

1914

**Show:** *Watch Your Step*

This is the first of Berlin's double songs (a song for two vocalists, featuring two different melodies sung simultaneously). It was sung in the show by Sallie Fisher and Charles King. Billy Murray and Edna Brown made the hit recording (Victor 18051). It was revived in 1950 by Bing and Gary Crosby, whose number 2 hit charted nineteen weeks and sold over one million copies (Decca 27112). It was revived again by Ethel Merman and Dan Dailey in the film *There's No Business like Show Business* (20th Century Fox, 1954).

## SINCE MY BEST GAL TURNED ME DOWN

Ray Lodwig and Howdy Quicksell

Denton and Haskins Music—New York

1927

The hit recording was by Bix Beiderbecke and His Gang (Okeh 41001).

## SINCERELY

Harvey Fuqua and Allen Freed

Regent Music—New York

1954

The McGuire Sisters had the number 1 hit, which held that position for ten of the twenty-one weeks charted and sold over one million copies (Coral 61323). Freed was a popular disc jockey who was undoubtedly given a piece of the composer credit for the song in exchange for air play.

## SINGIN' IN THE RAIN

Nacio Herb Brown (w: Arthur Freed)

Robbins Music—New York

1929

**Film:** *Hollywood Revue of 1929* (MGM)

Cliff Edwards sang it in the film and had a hit recording (Columbia 1869-D). It was revived in the film *Singin' In the Rain* in a now famous sequence sung and danced to by Gene Kelly (MGM, 1952). The film has become a classic, ensuring the continued popularity of the song.

## SINGIN' THE BLUES

Con Conrad and J. Russel Robinson

(w: Sam Lewis and Joe Young)

Waterson, Berlin and Snyder—New York

1920

Aileen Stanley had a hit vocal recording (Victor 18703). It was also part of the Original Dixieland Jazz Band's version of "Margie," which sold over one million copies (Victor 18717). Frankie Trumbauer and His Orchestra revived it in 1927, featuring the cornet artistry of Bix Beiderbecke (Okeh 40072). Connee Boswell, backed by the Lawson-Haggart Jazz Band, revived it again in 1953 (Decca 28498).

## SINGING THE BLUES

Melvin Endsley (w & m)

Acuff-Rose Publications—Nashville

1954

Guy Mitchell had the number 1 hit in 1956 that stayed in that position for ten of the twenty-two weeks charted and sold over one million copies (Columbia 40769). It is considered a classic of early rockabilly, and was the best-selling single of 1956.

## SIREN'S SONG, THE

Jerome Kern (w: P. G. Wodehouse)

T. B. Harms—New York

1917

**Show:** *Leave It to Jane*

Edith Hallor sang it in the show. When it was revived in the Off-Broadway show (1959) which ran for a record-breaking 928 performances, it was sung by Kathleen Murray, whose performance can be found on the DRG CD (15017).

## SISTER SUSIE'S SEWING SHIRTS FOR SOLDIERS

Hermann E. Darewski (w: R. P. Weston)

T. B. Harms—New York

1914

Introduced in vaudeville by Al Jolson, whose recording was a hit (Columbia A-1671). A neat tongue-twister novelty. Follow-up the following year by Lerch and Cox, with "Betty's Basting Belly Bands for Belgians."

## SITTIN' IN A CORNER

George W. Meyer (w: Gus Kahn)

Irving Berlin—New York

1923

One of the most popular songs of the year, it was recorded by the Broadway Syncopators (Vocalion 14675), Paul Whiteman (Victor 19161), Isham Jones (Brunswick 2508), and the Broadway Music Masters (Grey Gull 1186), among many others.

## (SITTIN' ON) THE DOCK OF THE BAY
Steve Cropper and Otis Redding
East/Memphis Music
1968
Otis Redding had the number 1 hit, which held its top position for four of the fourteen weeks charted (Volt 157). It sold over one million copies and was recorded three days before his death in a plane crash.

## SIXTEEN TONS
Merle Travis (w & m)
American Music—Hollywood
1947
"Tennessee" Ernie Ford had the number 1 hit in 1955, which charted for nineteen weeks and sold over one million copies (Capitol 3262). Travis had originally recorded it as part of an album of "folk songs" that he composed. Ford's finger-snappin' version remained in his repertory. It inspired the parody by Mickey Katz, "Sixteen Tons (of Kosher Salami)."

## SLEEPY HEAD
Walter Donaldson (w: Gus Kahn)
Robbins Music—New York
1934
**Film:** *Operator 13* (MGM)
The Mills Brothers had the number 2 hit, which charted for nine weeks (Brunswick 6913).

## SLEEPY TIME GAL
Richard Whiting and Ange Lorenzo
(w: Joseph Alden and Ray Egan)
Leo Feist—New York
1925
A standard brought to prominence by Ben Bernie and His Orchestra, with vocal by Arthur Fields (Brunswick 2992). Art Landry also had a hit (Victor 19843). It was featured in the film of the same name (Republic, 1942). Harry James's 1939 recording was rereleased in 1944 and became a number 21 hit (Columbia 36713).

## SLOW HAND
Michael Clark & John Bettis
Warner-Tamerlane
1981
Number 2 hit for the pop vocal trio the Pointer Sisters, holding that spot for three out of sixteen chart weeks, and selling over a million records (Planet 47929). Famed for its rather explicit lyrics, hidden behind a soft-pop arrangement.

## SLOW POKE
Pee Wee King/Redd Stewart/Chilton Price
Ridgeway Music—New York
1951
Pee Wee King and His Golden West Cowboys had the number 1 hit, which charted for twenty-four weeks and sold over one million copies (RCA Victor 20-0489).

## SMILES
Lee S. Roberts (w: Will J. Callahan)
LSR—Chicago
1917
This standard started out as a flop. It wasn't until Jerome H. Remick bought it from the composer that it became a hit. It then sold over three million copies in sheet music. Joseph C. Smith's Orchestra had the hit recording in 1918 (Victor 18473) with a vocal by Harry MacDonough. It was used in the 1920s as the theme song for the Ipana Troubadours' radio program. Judy Garland sang it in the film *For Me and My Gal* (MGM 1942). It was also used as a recurring theme in the film *Ice Palace* (Warner Bros., 1960).

## SMILIN' THROUGH
Arthur A. Penn (w & m)
M. Witmark and Sons—New York
1919
Baritone Reinald Werrenrath had the hit recording (Victor 45166). It was used as background in the 1932 MGM film of the same name as well as the 1941 MGM Jeanette MacDonald version.

## SMOKE GETS IN YOUR EYES
Jerome Kern (w: Otto Harbach)
T. B. Harms—New York
1933

**Show:** *Roberta*

Tamara sang it in the show. Paul Whiteman and His Orchestra had the number 1 hit in 1934 that charted for fifteen weeks (Victor 24455). It was revived by the doo-wop group the Platters in 1958 with a number 1 hit that charted for sixteen weeks and sold over one million copies (Mercury 71383). It remains a nightclub favorite.

## SMOKE RINGS

Eugene Gifford (w: Ned Washington)

American Academy of Music—New York

1933, 1934

Clyde McCoy had the number 8 hit in 1933 (Columbia 2794-D). Glen Gray and the Casa Loma Orchestra used it as their theme song because the composer was their arranger, and had a number 15 hit in 1937 (Decca 1473). Les Paul and Mary Ford revived it in 1952 with a number 14 hit (Capitol 2123).

## SMOKY MOKES

Abe Holzmann

Feist and Frankenthaler—New York

1899

Outstanding cakewalk with five-string banjo virtuoso Vess L. Ossman making the first of his several versions in May 1900 (Berliner 6311) and the Columbia Orchestra reviving it in February 1902 (Columbia 627).

## SMOOTH

Rob Thomas and Itaal Shur

EMI Blackwood Music

1999

Rob Thomas, lead singer for the pop-rock group Matchbox 20 joined with legendary rock guitarist Carlos Santana for this monster hit, which was number 1 for twelve out of the fifty weeks it held the charts (Arista 13718). It sold over one million copies.

## SNOOKY OOKUMS

Irving Berlin (w & m)

Waterson, Berlin and Snyder—New York

1913

Introduced in vaudeville by Clark and Bergman. This comic number was recorded successfully by Billy Murray (Victor 17313). It was revived in 1950 by Joe "Fingers" Carr and the Carr Hops (Capitol 1074).

## SO IN LOVE

Cole Porter (w & m)

Buxton Hill—New York

1948

**Show:** *Kiss Me Kate*

Sung by Patricia Morrison in the show. Patti Page had the number 13 hit in 1949, which led the field of several charted versions (Mercury 5230).

## SO LONG! OO-LONG

Harry Ruby (w: Bert Kalmar)

Waterson, Berlin and Snyder—New York

1920

Introduced in vaudeville by the composers. Frank Crumit had the hit recording (Columbia A-2935). Fred Astaire and Red Skelton sang it in the Kalmar-Ruby biopic *Three Little Words* (MGM, 1950).

## SOBBIN' BLUES

Arthur Kassell and Victor Burton

Melrose Bros. Music—Chicago

1923

Introduced on records by King Oliver's Creole Jazz Band (Okeh 4906) and then by the New Orleans Rhythm Kings (Gennett 5219). The Benson Orchestra had a hit recording (Victor 19130), as did Art Kahn and His Orchestra (Columbia 16-D), and Albert E. Short and His Tivoli Syncopators (Vocalion 14600). It remains a Dixieland jazz favorite. Its name is derived from the crying effect played by the lead clarinet.

## SOLDIER BOY

Florence Green and Luther Dixon

Ludix Music—London

1962

The Shirelles had the number 1 hit, which charted for thirteen weeks and sold over one million copies (Scepter 1228).

## SOME ENCHANTED EVENING

Richard Rodgers (w: Oscar Hammerstein)

Williamson Music—New York

1949

**Show:** *South Pacific*

Ezio Pinza sang it in the show and had a number 7 hit that sold over one million copies (Columbia 4559). But

Perry Como bested him with his number 1 hit, which charted for twenty-six weeks and also sold over one million copies (RCA Victor 20-3402). It was revived in 1965 by Jay and the Americans for a number 13 hit (United Artists 919). It is so well known that it even inspired its own knock-knock joke.

## SOME LITTLE BUG IS GOING TO FIND YOU

Silvio Hein (w: Benjamin H. Burt and Roy Atwell)
T. B. Harms—New York
1915
**Show:** *Alone At Last*
Roy Atwell sang it in the show. He also performed it in the 1917 musical *All Over Town*.

## SOME OF THESE DAYS

Shelton Brooks (w & m)
Wm. Foster Co.—Chicago
1910
Introduced in vaudeville by Sophie Tucker, who thenceforth used it as her theme song. Her 1927 number 1 hit recording with Ted Lewis's Band was her biggest seller (Columbia 826-D). The song had languished until publisher Will Rossiter acquired it, and Tucker popularized it, leading to sheet music sales of over two million copies.

## SOMEBODY LOVES ME

George Gershwin (w: Ballard MacDonald and Bud DeSylva)
Harms—New York
1924
**Show:** *George White's Scandals*
Introduced in the show by Winnie Lightner. Hit recordings were made by Marion Harris (Brunswick 2735) and Paul Whiteman (Victor 19414). It has become one of Gershwin's most famous standards. Benny Goodman revived it in 1936 (Victor 25497) and Henry Levine and his Strictly from Dixie Jazz Band revived it, with vocalist Linda Keene, in 1942 (Victor 27831).

## SOMEBODY STOLE MY GAL

Leo Wood (w & m)
Meyer Cohen Music Co.—New York
1918

A flop when originally issued (it was taken from a Maceo Pinkard tune called "If I Can't Have You All of the Time" of 1917), it became a hit when it was reissued by Denton and Haskins Publishers, with a 1922 recording by the Original Memphis Five (Perfect 14322). Ted Weems' Orchestra had a million-selling recording in 1924 (Victor 19212) thanks to pianist Dewey Bergman's arrangement. Famous jazz cornetist Bix Beiderbecke made an outstanding recording with His Gang (Okeh 41030) in 1928. It was revived by Joe "Fingers" Carr in 1952 in his LP *Rough House Piano* (Capitol T-345). Johnnie Ray had a number 8 hit in 1953 (Columbia 39961).

## SOMEDAY SWEETHEART

John C. Spikes (w & m)
Spikes Bros. and Carter—Los Angeles
1919
Later copyrighted by Melrose Bros. of Chicago in 1924, adding Benjamin Spikes to the credits. However, the music was composed by Jelly Roll Morton, who never received credit but made a splendid recording with his Red Hot Peppers (Victor 20405). Gene Austin had a best-selling disc (Victor 20561). Traditional jazz bands have always featured it, especially the Bucktown Five (Gennett 5405) and the Original Indiana Five (Harmony 501-H).

## SOMEDAY WE'LL BE TOGETHER

Jackey Beavers/Johnny Bristol/Harvey Fuqua
Jobete Music—Detroit
1961, 1969
Diana Ross and the Supremes had the number 1 hit, which charted for fifteen weeks and sold over two million copies (Motown 1156). It was their swan-song single.

## SOMEONE IS LOSIN' SUSAN

George W. Meyer (w: Roy Turk)
Henry Waterson—New York
1926
Pete Wendling made a sensational piano recording (Cameo 1021) and Philip Spitalny and His Orchestra made the hit instrumental (Victor 20196).

## SOMEONE TO WATCH OVER ME

George Gershwin (w: Ira Gershwin)
Harms—New York
1926

**Show:** *Oh, Kay!*

Gertrude Lawrence sang it in the show and also had a hit recording (Victor 20331). George Gershwin recorded it as one of his few piano solos (Columbia 802-D). It was featured in the Gershwin biopic *Rhapsody in Blue* (Warner Bros., 1945). It has become a cabaret favorite and one of Gershwin's most often performed songs.

## SOMETHING

George Harrison (w & m)

Harrisongs Ltd.—New York

1969

Harrison's first major hit with the Beatles, reaching number 3 with sixteen weeks on the charts, selling over a million copies (Apple 2654). It became a standard, even covered by singers like Frank Sinatra. Harrison borrowed the first line of his song from James Taylor's 1968 composition, "Something in the Way She Moves."

## SOMETHING'S GOTTA GIVE

Johnny Mercer (w & m)

Robbins Music—New York

1955

**Film:** *Daddy Long Legs* (20th Century Fox)

Fred Astaire sang it in the film. The McGuire Sisters had the number 5 hit, which charted for fourteen weeks (Coral 61423).

## SOMETIMES I'M HAPPY

Vincent Youmans (w: Irving Caesar)

Harms—New York

1927

**Show:** *Hit the Deck*

It was originally used in the show *A Night Out*, which closed in Philadelphia in 1925 before it reached Broadway. Louise Groody and Charles King sang it in the 1927 show. Roger Wolfe Kahn and His Orchestra had its hit recording (Victor 20599). Benny Goodman and His Orchestra had its first hit using Fletcher Henderson's arrangement in 1935, which helped to solidify Goodman's position as "King of Swing" (Victor 25090). Polly Walker and Jack Oakie sang it in the first film version (RKO, 1930), and Jane Powell and Vic Damone sang it in the second (MGM, 1955).

## SONG OF INDIA

N. Rimsky-Korsakov (arrangement: Ferde Grofe)

Sherman, Clay—San Francisco

1921

Paul Whiteman took the "Chanson Indoue" from Rimsky-Korsakov's 1897 opera *Sadko* and made it a tremendous popular hit (Victor 18777). Tommy Dorsey and His Orchestra revived it in 1937 with a number 5 hit that sold over one million copies (Victor 25523).

## SONG SUNG BLUE

Neil Diamond (w & m)

Prophet Music—Los Angeles

1972

Neil Diamond had this number 1 hit, which charted for twelve weeks (Uni 55326). It sold over one million copies.

## SOONER OR LATER

Stephen Sondheim (w & m)

Hal Leonard Publications—Milwaukee

1990

**Film:** *Dick Tracy* (Warner Bros.)

Academy Award winner for Best Song.

## SOPHISTICATED LADY

Duke Ellington (w: Mitchell Parish and Irving Mills)

Mills Music Inc.—New York

1933

Duke Ellington and His Famous Orchestra had the number 3 hit, which charted for sixteen weeks (Brunswick 6600). Billy Eckstine revived it in 1948 with a number 24 hit (National 9049). It is among Ellington's most famous compositions, and served as the name of the Broadway revue of his songs staged in the 1980s.

## SOUL MAN

David Porter and Isaac Hayes

Birdees Music

1967

Number 2 hit for Memphis duo Sam and Dave, holding the number 2 spot for three out of eleven charted weeks and selling over half-a-million records; also a number 1 R&B hit (Stax 231). A classic of the Stax sound. It was lovingly revived by comedians Dan Ackroyd and John Belushi, as the Blues Brothers, in their film of the same name (Universal, 1980); their version reached number 14 in 1979 (Atlantic 3545).

## SOUND OF SILENCE, THE
Paul Simon (w & m)
Charing Cross Music—New York
1964, 1965
Simon and Garfunkel had the number 1 hit in 1966, which charted for twelve weeks and sold over one million copies (Columbia 43396). They had originally recorded the song in 1964 with just acoustic guitar accompaniment. Simon then went to England; while he was away, Columbia added electric guitar, bass, and drums to the song, and it became a big hit. It launched the duo's career as pop hit makers.

## SOUTH AMERICA, TAKE IT AWAY
Harold Rome (w & m)
M. Witmark and Sons—New York
1946
**Show:** *Call Me Mister*
Betty Garrett sang it in the show. Bing Crosby and the Andrews Sisters had the number 2 hit that charted for nineteen weeks (Decca 23569).

## SOUTH OF THE BORDER
Jimmy Kennedy and Michael Carr
Shapiro, Bernstein—New York
1939
**Film:** *South of the Border* (Republic)
Gene Autry sang it in the film and had a number 12 hit that charted for four weeks (Vocalion 5122), but he was outdone by Shep Fields and His Rippling Rhythm, who had the number 1 hit that charted for eighteen weeks (Bluebird 10376). Frank Sinatra revived it in 1953 with a number 18 hit, charting for four weeks (Capitol 2638).

## SPAIN
Isham Jones (w: Gus Kahn)
Milton Weil—Chicago
1924
Introduced by bandleader Isham Jones, who also had the hit recording (Brunswick 2600). Paul Whiteman's version also did well (Victor 19330).

## SPANISH SHAWL
Elmer Schoebel (w: Billy Meyers and Walter Melrose)
Melrose Bros. Music—Chicago
1925
Introduced in vaudeville by Blossom Seeley, who also had the hit vocal (Columbia 613-D). The hit instrumental belongs to Boston bandleader Edwin J. McEnelly's Orchestra, with pianist Frankie Carle (Victor 19851). Ray Miller and His Orchestra (Brunswick 2989) and the Missouri Jazz Band (Banner 1662) had nice versions as well.

## SPEEDOO
Esther Navarro (w & m)
Benell Music—New York
1955
The Cadillacs had the number 17 hit in 1956 that charted for five weeks (Josie 785). Lead vocalist Earl Carroll got his nickname from the song's title. A doo-wop classic.

## SPLISH SPLASH
Bobby Darin and Jean Murray
Portrait Music—New York
1958
Bobby Darin had the number 3 hit, which charted for thirteen weeks and sold over one million copies (Atco 6117). A teenybopper classic.

## SPREADIN' RHYTHM AROUND
Jimmy McHugh (w: Ted Koehler)
Robbins Music—New York
1935
Film: *King of Burlesque* (Fox)
Alice Faye sang it in the film and on a disc (Melotone 60308). Fats Waller and His Rhythm, with a Fats vocal, had the important version (Victor 25211).

## SQUEEZE ME
Clarence Williams and Thomas Waller
Clarence Williams—New York
1926
A Jazz standard first recorded by Clarence Williams's Blue Five (Okeh 8254) with vocal by Eva Taylor. Louis Armstrong (Okeh 8641), Bessie Smith (Columbia

14133-D), and Chick Webb (Decca 1716), among many others, made fine recordings. Fats Waller made a marvelous piano roll (QRS 3352).

## ST. LOUIS BLUES

W. C. Handy (w & m)

Pace and Handy Music Co.—Memphis

1914

This masterpiece is the most recorded blues of all time. The 1921 recording by the Original Dixieland Jazz Band sold more than any other (Victor 18772). Bessie Smith's 1925 hit recording is a classic (Columbia 14064-D). The Mills Brothers had a number 2 hit in 1932 (Brunswick 6330). It was featured in the biopic sung by Nat "King" Cole (Paramount, 1958).

## STAIRWAY TO THE STARS

Matt Malneck and Frank Signorelli

(w: Mitchell Parish)

Robbins Music—New York

1935

With lyrics added in 1939, Glenn Miller and His Orchestra, with vocal by Ray Eberle, had the number 1 hit, which charted for thirteen weeks (Bluebird 10276).

## STAND BY ME

Ben E. King/Mike Stoller/Jerry Leiber

Trio Music

1961

A classic R&B love song, originally recorded by Ben E. King, who had a number 4 pop hit and number 1 R&B hit with the song (Atco 6194). It has been covered dozens of times, including versions by John Lennon (Apple 1881) in 1975 and Mickey Gilley (Full Moon 46640) in 1980; King "covered" his original recording in 1986, reaching number 9 (Atlantic 89361).

## STANDING ON THE CORNER

Frank Loesser (w & m)

Frank Music—New York

1956

**Show:** *The Most Happy Fella*

Shorty Long, John Henson, Alan Gilbert, and Roy Lazarus sang it in the show. The Four Lads had the number 3 hit that charted for eighteen weeks (Columbia 40674).

## STAR DUST

Hoagy Carmichael (w: Mitchell Parish)

Mills Music—New York

1929

One of the most recorded standards in popular music. Isham Jones had the first great recorded hit (Brunswick 4586), which established the song. Bing Crosby had the vocal hit (Brunswick 6159). Tommy Dorsey seemed to have a stranglehold on the song as his 1936 version (Victor 25320) made a hit, as did his 1941 version with Frank Sinatra and the Pied Pipers (Victor 27233). This version became a hit again in 1943 when it was rereleased (Victor 27520). Benny Goodman also had a hit with his arrangement (Victor 25320). Artie Shaw's version (Victor 27230) in 1941 was voted the greatest record of all-time in the *Billboard* poll of disk jockeys. It was also featured in the film of the same name (20th Century Fox, 1940). Willie Nelson used it as the title for his 1978 album of standards, which reintroduced it to an entirely new audience (Columbia 35305).

## STARS FELL ON ALABAMA

Frank Perkins (w: Mitchell Parish)

Mills Music—New York

1934

Guy Lombardo and His Royal Canadians had the number 1 hit, which charted for nine weeks (Decca 104).

## STAY IN YOUR OWN BACKYARD

Lyn Udall (w: Karl Kennett)

M. Witmark and Sons—New York

1899

First pop song to deal with the realities of segregation. Louise Dresser made it a hit in vaudeville.

## STEP BY STEP

Maurice Starr (w & m)

EMI Music

1990

Boy band New Kids On The Block had this number 1 hit, which charted for eleven weeks and sold over one million copies (Columbia 73343).

## STEPPIN' IN SOCIETY

Harry Akst (w: Alex Gerber)

Shapiro, Bernstein—New York

1925

A great syncopated favorite in vaudeville, it had great recordings by Paul Whiteman (Victor 19692), Ben Selvin (Vocalion 15038), and the Knickerbockers (Columbia 391-D).

## STEPPIN' OUT

Con Conrad (w: John S. Howard)

Jerome H. Remick—New York

1923

Al Jolson had the vocal hit (Brunswick 2567) and Vincent Lopez had the instrumental (Okeh 40024). The Original Memphis Five had a fine arrangement (Banner 1296).

## STEPPIN' OUT WITH MY BABY

Irving Berlin (w & m)

Irving Berlin—New York

1947

**Film:** *Easter Parade* (MGM)

Fred Astaire sang it in the film.

## STOP! IN THE NAME OF LOVE

Brian Holland/Lamont Dozier/Eddie Holland

Jobete Music—Detroit

1965

The Supremes had the number 1 hit, which charted for ten weeks and sold over one million copies (Motown 1074). A Holland/Dozier/Holland classic.

## STORMY WEATHER

Harold Arlen (w: Ted Koehler)

Mills Music—New York

1933

**Show:** *Cotton Club Parade*

Ethel Waters sang it in the show and had a number 1 hit that charted for eleven weeks (Brunswick 6564). Composer Harold Arlen, with Leo Reisman's Orchestra also had a number 1 hit that charted for nineteen weeks (Victor 24262). Lena Horne sang it in the film of the same name (20th Century Fox, 1943) and her version reached number 21 (Victor 27819). It has become a cabaret standard.

## STORY BOOK BALL, THE

Billie Montgomery and George Perry

Will Rossiter—Chicago

1917

Introduced by Sophie Tucker in vaudeville. Since the 1970s, it has become a favorite with Dixieland jazz bands.

## STOUT HEARTED MEN

Sigmund Romberg (w: Oscar Hammerstein)

Harms—New York

1928

**Show:** *The New Moon*

Robert Halliday and a male chorus sang it in the show. Lawrence Tibbett sang it in the first film version (MGM, 1930) and Nelson Eddy sang it in the second (MGM, 1940). Opera star Helen Traubel sang it in the Romberg biopic *Deep in My Heart* (MGM, 1954).

## STRANGE FRUIT

Lewis Allan (w & m)

Edward B. Marks Music—New York

1940

Billie Holiday made this highly controversial recording about a lynching of a black man in the South that was banned on radio, and her record label (Decca) would not issue it. Instead, the small Commodore label, run as part of Milt Gabler's Commodore Record Shop, released it. Despite all of these obstacles, the record became a number 16 pop hit in 1939, a remarkable achievement (Commodore 526). It became her signature song at New York's Café Society, and has become a jazz classic. Diana Ross sang it in Holiday's biopic *Lady Sings the Blues* (Paramount, 1972). Allan was the pen name of schoolteacher/liberal activisit Abel Meropol (who later adopted the Rosenberg children).

## STRANGER IN PARADISE

Robert Wright and George Forrest

Frank Music—New York

1953

**Show:** *Kismet*

Richard Kiley and Doretta Morrow sang it in the show. Tony Bennett had the number 2 hit, which charted for nineteen weeks and sold over one million copies (Columbia 40121).

## STRANGERS IN THE NIGHT
Bert Kaempfert (w: Charles Singleton and
Eddie Snyder)
Champion Music and Roosevelt Music—New York
1966
**Film:** *A Man Could Get Killed* (Universal)
Frank Sinatra had the number 1 hit, which charted for
eleven weeks and sold over one million copies (Reprise
0470). It was a surprise hit for the crooner during the
rock era. The "Doobie-doobie-doo" chorus became a
favorite device for Sinatra imitators and parodists.

## STREETS OF PHILADELPHIA
Bruce Springsteen (w & m)
CPP Belwin
1993
**Film:** *Philadelphia* (TriStar)
Academy Award winner for Best Song. Bruce Springsteen
had the number 9 hit, which charted for fifteen weeks
(Columbia 77384). It sold over half a million copies.

## STRIKE UP THE BAND
George Gershwin (w: Ira Gershwin)
New World Music—New York
1927
**Show:** *Strike Up the Band*
Jerry Goff and Jim Townsend sang it in the 1930 ver-
sion of the show that opened on Broadway. It was used
in a dance sequence in the film version (MGM, 1940).
Red Nichols, who led the pit band in the 1930 show on
Broadway, had the hit recording (Brunswick 4695).
Tommy Tune revived it in the 1983 Broadway show *My
One and Only*.

## STRING OF PEARLS, A
Jerry Gray (w: Eddie DeLange)
Mutual Music—New York
1942
Glenn Miller and His Orchestra had the number 1
instrumental hit, which charted for twenty-one weeks
and sold over one million copies (Bluebird 11382).
Benny Goodman's version was a better arrangement,
but only reached number 15 (Okeh 6590).

## STROLL, THE
Clyde Otis and Nancy Lee

Meridian Music—New York
1957
The Diamonds, with Nancy Lee, had the number 4 hit
in 1958, which charted for fourteen weeks and sold
over one million copies (Mercury 71242).

## STUCK ON YOU
Aaron Schroeder and J. Leslie McFarland
Gladys Music—New York
1960
Elvis Presley had the number 1 hit, which charted for
thirteen weeks and sold over two million copies
(RCA Victor 47-7740).

## STUCK WITH YOU
Chris Hayes and Huey Lewis
Hulex Music—Universal City, CA
1986
Huey Lewis and the News had this number 1 hit,
which lasted thirteen weeks on the chart (Chrysalis
43019).

## STUMBLING
Zez Confrey (w & m)
Leo Feist—New York
1922
One of the great standards, a syncopated masterpiece.
Paul Whiteman had the hit instrumental (Victor
18899) and Billy Murray the hit vocal (Victor 18906).
But Ray Miller (Columbia A-3611), Bennie Krueger
(Brunswick 2272), and the Golden Gate Orchestra
(Cameo 227) also had fine versions. Revivals included
Bob Crosby's Bobcats 1937 disc (Decca 1593) and Joe
"Fingers" Carr 1952 recording (Capitol 2187).

## STUTTERING
Maceo Pinkard (w: Sidney Mitchell)
Broadway Music—New York
1922
Great takeoff on "Stumbling." Zez Confrey made an out-
standing piano roll (QRS 2079), which incorporated a
little of his piece to illustrate the parody. The Benson
Orchestra had the hit recording (Victor 18948).

## SUBTERRANEAN HOMESICK BLUES
Bob Dylan (w & m)

Blossom Music—London

1965

Bob Dylan had the number 39 hit, which charted for one week but had enormous influence on would-be folk rockers (Columbia 43242).

## SUDDENLY THERE'S A VALLEY

Chuck Meyer and Biff Jones

Warman Music—New York

1955

Gogi Grant had the number 9 hit, which charted for ten weeks and sold over one million copies (ERA 1003).

## SUGAR BLUES

Clarence Williams (w: Lucy Fletcher)

Williams and Piron Music—Chicago

1919

Made famous by bandleader Clyde McCoy as his theme song. He first recorded it in 1931, scoring a number 2 hit (Columbia 2389-D), and then he revived it when he moved to Decca in 1935 for a number 6 hit (Decca 381). Johnny Mercer brought it back once again in 1947 with a number 4 hit that charted for eight weeks (Capitol 448).

## SUGAR FOOT STOMP

Joe Oliver (w: Walter Melrose)

Melrose Bros.—Chicago

1926

Introduced on disc by King Oliver's Creole Jazz Band in 1923 as "Dippermouth Blues" (Gennett 3076). It has become a classic recording, with every clarinetist replicating Johnny Dodds's solo in the second strain. It is also a standard in the Dixieland repertoire, recorded by practically every jazz band. Under the "Sugar Foot" title, Fred Hamm and His Orchestra (Victor 20023) and Fletcher Henderson and His Orchestra (Columbia 395-D) recorded fine versions.

## SUGAR PLUM

Joseph Meyer (w: Bud DeSylva)

Harms—New York

1925

**Show:** *Gay Paree*

One of the great 1920s ballads. Beautiful arrangements by Markel and His Orchestra (Columbia 475-D) and

by Herb Wiedoeft (Brunswick 2976). George Olsen and His Music had a hit recording (Victor 19859).

## SUGAR SHACK

Keith McCormack and Faye Voss

Dundee Music—Clovis, New Mexico

1962, 1963

Jimmy Gilmer and the Fireballs had the number 1 hit, which held its position for five of the thirteen weeks (Dot 16487). It sold over one million copies.

## SUGAR, SUGAR

Jeff Barry and Andy Kim

Don Kirshner Music—New York

1969

The Archies were based on the television cartoon series, which was based on the comic book and radio show. Producer Don Kirshner—who had previously helped fabricate the Monkees—was responsible for putting together the music for the show. The "group" had a number 1 hit with this piece of bubblegum pop that held its top position for four of the eighteen weeks charted (Calendar 1008). It sold over one million copies.

## SUMMER IN THE CITY

John and Mark Sebastian and Steve Boone

Faithful Virtue Music—New York

1966

The Lovin' Spoonful had the number 1 hit, which charted for ten weeks and sold more than one million copies (Kama Sutra 211). One of the group's most hard-edged and evocative tracks, featuring an effective use of city sound effects, including the sound of jack hammers.

## SUMMERTIME

George Gershwin (w: DuBose Heyward)

Gershwin Publishing—New York

1935

**Show:** *Porgy and Bess*

Abbie Mitchell sang it in the show. Billie Holiday had the number 12 hit in 1936 (Vocalion 3288). Loulie Jean Norman sang it in the film version (Columbia, 1959). Billy Stewart revived it in 1966 with a number 10 hit (Chess 1966). An all-time jazz classic.

## SUN SHINES BRIGHTER, THE
Jerome Kern (w: P. G. Wodehouse)
T. B. Harms—New York
1917
**Show:** *Leave It to Jane*
Oscar Shaw and Ann Orr sang it in the show. Angelo Mango and Jeanne Allen sang it in the 1959 Off-Broadway revival (DRG CD 15017).

## SUNDAY
Ned Miller/Chester Cohn/Jules Stein/
Bennie Krueger
Leo Feist—New York
1926
Cliff Edwards had the hit recording (Perfect 11633) vocally, and Jean Goldkette had it instrumentally, featuring Bix Beiderbecke (Victor 20273). It was used as the theme song for the Phil Harris-Alice Fay radio show (1948–54).

## SUNNY
Jerome Kern (w: Otto Harbach and
Oscar Hammerstein)
Harms—New York
1925
**Show:** *Sunny*
Paul Frawley sang it in the show. George Olsen and His Music had the hit recording (Victor 19840). The song was featured in both film adaptations of the show (First National, 1930, and RKO, 1941). It was sung by Judy Garland in the Kern biopic *Till the Clouds Roll By* (MGM, 1946). June Haver sang it in the Marilyn Miller biopic *Look for the Silver Lining* (Warner Bros., 1949).

## SUNNY DISPOSISH
Philip Charig (w: Ira Gershwin)
Harms Inc.—New York
1926
**Show:** *Americana*
Introduced in the show by Arline and Edgar Gardiner. Jean Goldkette and His Orchestra had the hit recording (Victor 20493).

## SUNNY SIDE UP
Ray Henderson (w: Bud DeSylva and Lew Brown
DeSylva, Brown and Henderson—New York
1929

**Film:** *Sunny Side Up* (Fox)
Introduced in the film by Janet Gaynor and Charles Farrell. Fred Rich and His Orchestra had a hit recording (Velvet Tone 2020). It was used in the DeSylva-Brown-Henderson biopic *The Best Things In Life Are Free* (20th Century Fox, 1956).

## SUNRISE SERENADE
Frankie Carle (w: Jack Lawrence)
Jewel Music—New York
1939
Glen Gray and the Casa Loma Orchestra, with composer Frankie Carle at the piano, had the number 1 hit, which charted for sixteen weeks (Decca 2321). Glenn Miller and His Orchestra version only reached number 7, but it charted for eleven weeks and sold over one million copies (Bluebird 10214).

## SUNRISE, SUNSET
Jerry Bock (w: Sheldon Harnick)
Sunbeam Music—New York
1964
**Show:** *Fiddler on the Roof*
Zero Mostel and Maria Karnilova sang it in the show.

## SUNSHINE OF YOUR LOVE
Jack Bruce/Peter Brown/Eric Clapton
Casserole Music—New York
1968
Cream had the number 5 hit, which charted for twelve weeks and sold over one million copies (Atco 6544). A classic piece of psychedelia by the famous power trio.

## SUNSHINE ON MY SHOULDER
John Denver/Mike Taylor/Dick Kniss
Cherry Lane Music
1971
John Denver had this number 1 hit in 1974 that charted for thirteen weeks (RCA Victor 0213). It sold over one million copies.

## SUPERSTITION
Stevie Wonder (w & m)
Stein and Van Stock—Hollywood
1972

Number 1 hit in 1973 for singer/songwriter Stevie Wonder, charting for thirteen weeks; also a number 1 R&B hit (Tamla 54226). Noted for its early use of synthesized keyboards. An oft-sampled backing track.

## SURF CITY
Brian Wilson and Jan Berry
Screen Gems-Columbia Music—New York
1963
Jan and Dean had the number 1 hit, which charted for eleven weeks (Liberty 55580). Coauthor Wilson was the leader of the rival Beach Boys.

## SURFIN' U.S.A.
Chuck Berry (w: Brian Wilson)
Arc Music—New York
1963
Number 3 hit for the Beach Boys, introducing the craze for surf songs (Capitol 4777); it was reissued in 1974. The melody was borrowed from Chuck Berry, although he originally went uncredited; later, he was awarded a portion of the proceeds.

## SURRENDER
Mort Shuman (w: Doc Pomus)
Elvis Presley Music—New York
1960
Elvis Presley had the number 1 hit in 1961. The melody is based on the Italian song "Come Back To Sorrento." It stayed on the chart for eleven weeks and sold more than two million copies (RCA Victor 47-7850).

## SURREY WITH THE FRINGE ON TOP, THE
Richard Rodgers (w: Oscar Hammerstein)
Marlo Music—New York
1943
**Show:** *Oklahoma!*
Alfred Drake, Joan Roberts, and Betty Garde sang it in the show. Alfred Drake had the number 22 hit (Decca 23284).

## SUSIE
C. Naset (w: Gus Kahn)

Jerome H. Remick—New York
1924
Made famous by the Wolverine Orchestra, featuring Bix Beiderbecke (Gennett 5454).

## SUSPICIOUS MINDS
Mark James (w & m)
Press Music—Nashville
1968
Comeback number 1 hit for Elvis Presley, returning him to his Memphis roots sound. It charted for thirteen weeks in 1969 and sold over a million copies (RCA 47-9764). The song has been covered frequently since by both pop and country artists, including a 1992 recording by Dwight Yoakum (Epic Sound 74753).

## SUSSUDIO
Phil Collins (w & m)
Pun Music
1984
Collins's second number 1 hit in 1985, from his album *No Jacket Required* (Atlantic 89560).

## SWANEE
George Gershwin (w: Irving Caesar)
T. B. Harms—New York
1919
**Show:** *Sinbad* (orig. Capitol Theatre: *Demi Tasse*)
Although it became the composer's biggest commercial success, it was not well received when it was used for the opening of the Capitol Theatre in New York City. It took Al Jolson, who interpolated it into his show *Sinbad,* to turn the song into a million-selling hit (Columbia A-2884). He used it for the rest of his career and on the soundtracks of his biopics *The Jolson Story* (Columbia, 1946) and *Jolson Sings Again* (Columbia, 1949). Judy Garland made a memorable performance in the film *A Star Is Born* (Warner Bros., 1954).

## SWANEE BLUES
J. Milton Delcamp (w: Frank Goodman)
Al Piantadosi—New York
1920
Outstanding piano roll made by the composer (Republic 35218), followed by another fine roll made by Clarence Jones (Imperial 91069).

## SWEEPIN' THE CLOUDS AWAY

Sam Coslow (w & m)

Famous Music—New York

1930

**Film:** *Paramount on Parade* (Paramount)

Maurice Chevalier sang it in the film and also recorded it (Victor 22378).

## SWEET ADELINE

Henry W. Armstrong (w: Richard H. Gerard)

M. Witmark and Sons—New York

1903

The Quaker City Four introduced it in vaudeville where it became a stunning hit. The Haydn Quartet had the enormous hit recording in 1904 (Victor 2934). It was used in a successful mayoral campaign in 1906 by John F. "Honey" Fitzgerald in Boston. Revived in 1939 by the Mills Brothers, with a number 10 hit (Decca 2285). Barbershop singers have adopted it and it still brings down the house.

## SWEET DREAMS ARE MADE OF THIS

Annie Lennox and David A. Stewart

RCA Music

1983

Synth-pop duo the Eurythmics had the number 1 hit, which charted for seventeen weeks and sold over one million copies (RCA 13533).

## SWEET GEORGIA BROWN

Maceo Pinkard/Ken Casey/Ben Bernie

Jerome H. Remick—New York

1925

Introduced and popularized by bandleader Ben Bernie (Vocalion 15002). Isham Jones and His Orchestra had a fine recording (Brunswick 2913). Oliver Naylor and His Orchestra used the Charleston beat on his recording (Victor 19688). It was revived in 1949 by Brother Bones and His Shadows (Tempo 652); this recording was used as the theme song for the exhibition basketball team the Harlem Globetrotters for decades. The song was used in the film *Some Like It Hot* (United Artists, 1959), and sung by Vivian Reed in the 1976 show *Bubbling Brown Sugar*. It is a jazz and nightclub standard.

## SWEET LADY

Frank Crumit and Dave Zoob (w: Howard Johnson)

Leo Feist—New York

1921

**Show:** *Tangerine*

Introduced in the show by Julia Sanderson and Frank Crumit. Crumit made a hit recording (Columbia A-3475), as did Irving Kaufman, accompanied by Eubie Blake (Emerson 10450). Paul Whiteman (Victor 18803) and Carl Fenton (Brunswick 2143) had fine instrumental versions.

## SWEET LEILANI

Harry Owens (w & m)

Select Music—New York

1937

**Film:** *Waikiki Wedding* (Paramount)

Academy Award winner for Best Song. Bing Crosby, who sang it in the movie, had the number 1 hit, which held that position for ten of the twenty-five weeks on the chart (Decca 1175).

## SWEET LITTLE SIXTEEN

Chuck Berry (w & m)

ARC Music—New York

1958

Chuck Berry had the number 2 hit, which charted for eleven weeks (Chess 1683).

## SWEET LORRAINE

Cliff Burwell (w: Mitchell Parish)

Mills Music—New York

1928

Introduced on radio by Rudy Vallee and his Connecticut Yankees (the composer was Vallee's pianist). It is a standard that has been recorded by dance bands, jazz pianists, and jazz bands. The King Cole Trio's recording (Decca 8520) established Nat Cole as a singer. Teddy Wilson had a hit recording (Brunswick 7520) in 1935.

## SWEET MAN

Maceo Pinkard (w: Roy Turk)

Leo Feist—New York

1925

Isham Jones and His Orchestra had the hit recording (Brunswick 2970). Frank Banta made a fine piano solo

(Victor 19839). Zez Confrey turned out a piano roll with a Charleston beat (Ampico 206571).

## SWEET SAVANNAH SUE
Thomas Waller and Harry Brooks (w: Andy Razaf)
Mills Music—New York
1929
**Show:** *Hot Chocolates*
Margaret Simms, Paul Bass, and the Jubilee Singers sang it in the show. Fats Waller made a fabulous piano solo (Victor 22108). Louis Armstrong and His Orchestra made a fine recording, with a vocal by Armstrong (Okeh 8717).

## SWEET SUE—JUST YOU
Victor Young (w: Will J. Harris)
Shapiro, Bernstein—New York
1928
Introduced in vaudeville by Sue Carol, for whom the song was written. Ben Pollack and His Orchestra had the hit recording, with vocalist Franklin Bauer (Victor 21437). The Mills Brothers revived it in 1932 (Brunswick 6330), as did Tommy Dorsey in 1939 (Victor 26105). Johnny Long had a hit in 1949 (Signature 15243). It was played on the soundtrack to the *Eddy Duchin Story* (Columbia, 1956) by Carmen Cavallero. It has become a jazz standard.

## SWEETHEART OF SIGMA CHI, THE
F. Dudleigh Vernor
(w: Byron D. Stokes)
Richard E. Vernor—Albion, Mich.
1912
It started out as a college favorite, but by the 1920s became a favorite of all. Fred Waring's Pennsylvanians had the hit record in 1927 (Victor 20820) and shortly after, Rudy Vallee made it a radio and nightclub hit. It remains a standard.

## SWEETHEARTS
Victor Herbert (w: Robert B. Smith)
G. Schirmer—New York
1913
**Show:** *Sweethearts*
It was introduced in the show by Christie MacDonald. Another MacDonald, Jeanette, sang it in the film ver-

sion (MGM, 1938). Opera diva Dorothy Kirsten sang it in the film *The Great Caruso* (MGM, 1951).

## SWEETHEARTS ON PARADE
Carmen Lombardo (w: Charles Newman)
Milton Weil Music—Chicago
1928
Introduced with a hit recording by Guy Lombardo and His Orchestra (Columbia 1628-D). Louis Armstrong also had a hit when his 1930 recording was released in 1932 (Columbia 2688-D). Marvin Ash and His Band revived it in 1949 (Capitol 855).

## SWINGIN' DOWN THE LANE
Isham Jones (w: Gus Kahn)
Leo Feist—New York
1923
One of the great standards, it was introduced and popularized by the bandleader/composer (Brunswick 2438). The Columbians (Columbia A-3874), Vincent Lopez and His Orchestra (Okeh 4881), and the Great White Way Orchestra (Victor 19058) also had fine arrangements. Doris Day and Danny Thomas sang it in the Gus Kahn biopic *I'll See You in My Dreams* (Warner Bros., 1951).

## SWINGING ON A STAR
Jimmy Van Heusen (w: Johnny Burke)
Burke and Van Heusen—New York
1944
**Film:** *Going My Way* (Paramount)
Academy Award winner for Best Song. Bing Crosby had the hit, which kept its number 1 position for nine of the twenty-eight weeks charted (Decca 18597). Has become a favorite song, especially for young listeners.

## SYMPATHY
Rudolf Friml (w: Otto Hauerbach)
G. Schirmer—New York
1912
**Show:** *The Firefly*
Audrey Maple and Melville Stewart sang it in the show. Helen Clark and Walter Van Brunt had the hit recording (Victor 17270). Jeanette MacDonald and Allan Jones sang it in the film version (MGM, 1937).

## 'TAIN'T NOBODY'S BIZNESS IF I DO
Porter Grainger and Everett Robbins
Clarence Williams Music—New York
1922
**Show:** Seven O'Hearts
Hit vocal recording by Bessie Smith (Columbia A-3989). The Tennessee Ten had the instrumental hit (Victor 19109). Fats Waller made a splendid piano roll (QRS 2270).

## TAKE A BOW
Madonna Ciccone and Babyface
WB Music Corp.
1994, 1995
Madonna scored fifteen hits in the Top 10 in the 1990s. This was number 1 for seven of the twenty-seven weeks it charted (Maverick/Sire 18000). It sold over half a million copies.

## TAKE FIVE
Paul Desmond
Derry Music—San Francisco
1960, 1961
A modern jazz classic, this Dave Brubeck Quartet piece, written in 5/4 time, reached number 25 and remained on the charts for seven weeks (Columbia 41479). It was the group's only charting recording.

## TAKE GOOD CARE OF MY BABY
Gerry Goffin and Carole King
Aldon Music—New York
1961
Bobby Vee had the number 1 hit, which charted for eleven weeks and sold over one million copies (Liberty 55354).

## TAKE ME OUT TO THE BALL GAME
Albert Von Tilzer
(w: Jack Norworth)
York Music—New York
1908
The most recognized song about our national sport, it was composed twenty years before Albert Von Tilzer saw his first game. He introduced it in vaudeville. Nora Bayes also featured it in her act to great success. Billy Murray and the Haydn Quartet had the hit recording (Victor 5570). It was heard in the Bayes-Norworth biopic *Shine On Harvest Moon* (Warner Bros., 1944).

## TAKE ME TO THE MIDNIGHT CAKE WALK BALL
Maurice Abrahams/Eddie Cox/Arthur Jackson
Maurice Abrahams Music—New York
1915
Introduced by Daphne Pollard in the *Passing Show of 1915*. Revived in 1947 by Marvin Ash (available on the LP *The Jazz Piano of Marvin Ash* [Fairmont 104], released in 1973).

## TAKE MY BREATH AWAY
Giorgio Moroder and Tom Whitlock
Famous Music—New York
1986
**Film:** *Top Gun* (Paramount)
Academy Award winner for Best Song. European synth-pop band Berlin had the number 1 hit, which charted for thirteen weeks (Columbia 05903). It sold over one million copies.

## TAKE YOUR GIRLIE TO THE MOVIES
Pete Wendling (w: Edgar Leslie and Bert Kalmar)
Waterson, Berlin and Snyder—New York
1919
Introduced on records by Billy Murray (Victor 18592), who sang it to success. Revived in 1940 by Blue Barron and His Orchestra (Bluebird 10672).

## TAKING A CHANCE ON LOVE
Vernon Duke (w: John Latouche and Ted Fetter)
Leo Feist—New York
1940
**Show:** *Cabin in the Sky*
Ethel Waters sang it in the show. Benny Goodman and His Orchestra (with vocalist Helen Forrest) recorded the song in November 1940, but it went unreleased until 1943, when it became a number 1 hit, charting for fourteen weeks (Columbia 35869).

## TALK OF THE TOWN, THE
Chester Cohn (w: Gus Kahn)
Leo Feist—New York
1929

Ted Weems and His Orchestra had the hit recording (Victor 22304).

## TALK TO THE ANIMALS
Leslie Bricusse (w & m)
Hastings Music—New York
1967
**Film:** *Doctor Doolittle* (20th Century Fox)
Academy Award winner for Best Song. Rex Harrison sang it in the film.

## TAMMY
Jay Livingston and Ray Evans
Northern Cross Music—New York
1956, 1957
**Film:** *Tammy and the Bachelor* (Universal-International)
Debbie Reynolds had the number 1 hit, which charted for twenty-three weeks and sold over one million copies (Coral 61851).

## TEA FOR TWO
Vincent Youmans (w: Irving Caesar)
Harms—New York
1924
**Show:** *No, No, Nanette*
Louise Groody and John Barker sang it in the show. It is one of the most recorded standards of Tin Pan Alley. Marion Harris had the first vocal hit (Brunswick 2747) and the Benson Orchestra had the first instrumental hit (Victor 19438). Jazz performers Bob Crosby, with Bob Zurke on piano (Decca 1850), and Teddy Wilson and His Orchestra, featuring Ben Webster on tenor sax, revived it in 1937 (Brunswick 7816). Willie "the Lion" Smith made a piano solo in 1939 (Commodore 518). The two film versions featured the song (First National, 1930 and RKO, 1940). Doris Day, Gordon MacRae, and Gene Nelson sang it in the third remake, this time entitled *Tea for Two* (Warner Bros., 1950). "Tea for Two Cha Cha," by the Tommy Dorsey Orchestra led by Warren Covington, was a number 7 hit in 1958; it charted for fourteen weeks and sold over one million copies (Decca 30704).

## TEARS OF A CLOWN, THE
Henry Cosby/William Robinson/Stevie Wonder
Jobete Music
1967

Smokey Robinson and the Miracles had this number 1 hit in 1970, which charted for fourteen weeks (Tamla 54199). It was originally an album track of theirs from 1967.

## TEASING
Albert Von Tilzer (w: Cecil Mack)
York Music—New York
1904
The first song success of the composer and publisher, and the first Tin Pan Alley hit written by an interracial duo. Billy Murray made the hit recording (Columbia 1857).

## TEEN ANGEL
Jean and Red Surrey
Acuff-Rose Publications—Nashville
1959
Mark Dinning, whose sister Jean cowrote the song, had the number 1 hit in 1960, which charted fourteen weeks and sold over one million copies (MGM 12845). An oft-parodied teenybopper love song.

## TELL HER ABOUT IT
Billy Joel (w & m)
Joel Songs
1983
Billy Joel had the number 1 hit, which charted for fifteen weeks (Columbia 04012).

## TELL ME PRETTY MAIDEN
Leslie Stuart (w: Owen Hall)
T. B. Harms—New York
1900
**Show:** *Florodora*
Sung by a double sextet, several of the "Florodora girls" (as they became known) actually married millionaires. The show had a tremendous run in London and an equally successful run on Broadway. It toured with road companies for eight years and was revived with similar success in 1920. Harry MacDonough and Grace Spencer had the hit recording in 1901 (Victor 1362).

## TELL ME WHY
Marty Gold (w: Al Albert)
Signet Music—New York
1951

The Four Aces had the number 2 hit, which charted for twenty-four weeks and sold over one million copies (Decca 27860). Eddie Fisher also had a number 4 hit in 1952, which charted for nineteen weeks and sold over one million copies (RCA Victor 20-4444). Bobby Vinton revived it in 1964 with a number 13 hit (Epic 9687).

## TEMPTATION RAG
Henry Lodge
M. Witmark and Sons—New York
1909
An extremely popular piano rag, it was given its first recording by Prince's Band (Columbia A-854). Arthur Pryor's Band followed up in 1910 (Victor 16511). Wally Rose revived it in 1942 (Jazz Man 7) and Benny Goodman's Sextet in 1950 (Columbia 39121).

## TEN CENTS A DANCE
Richard Rodgers (w: Lorenz Hart)
Harms—New York
1930
**Show:** *Simple Simon*
Ruth Etting sang it in the show and also had the number 5 hit that charted for eleven weeks (Columbia 2146-D). Doris Day sang it in the Etting biopic *Love Me or Leave Me* (MGM, 1955).

## TENDER TRAP, THE
James Van Heusen (w: Sammy Cahn)
Barton Music—New York
1955
**Film:** *The Tender Trap* (MGM)
Frank Sinatra sang it in the film and had the number 7 hit that charted for nine weeks (Capitol 3290).

## TENDERLY
Walter Gross (w: Jack Lawrence)
Edwin H. Morris—New York
1947
Sarah Vaughan, primarily a jazz singer, had the number 27 hit of what is now a pop standard (Musicraft 504). Rosemary Clooney revived it in 1952 for a number 17 hit that sold more than one million copies (Columbia 39648). Bert Kaempfert and His Orchestra revived it again in 1961, when it charted number 31 (Decca 31236).

## TENNESSEE WALTZ
Redd Stewart and Pee Wee King
Acuff-Rose—Nashville
1948
Patti Page, who sold more records than any other female vocalist in the 1950s had this number 1 hit in 1950; it held the top position for thirteen of the twenty-six weeks charted, it sold over six million copies, and became the official state song of Tennessee (Mercury 5534). It was revived in 1964 by Sam Cooke, who had the number 35 hit (RCA Victor 8368). The song was originally recorded by Pee Wee King (RCA Victor 20-2680) for the country audience, charted for thirty-five weeks, and was among the first country songs to be successfully covered by a pop artist, inspiring a slew of other covers. It also inspired many other state waltzes, including Bill Monroe's "Kentucky Waltz."

## TEQUILA
Chuck Rio
Jat Music—Hollywood
1958
Number 1 hit for the instrumental group the Champs, holding that top position for five out of sixteen weeks on the chart; also a number 1 R&B hit (Challenge 1016). The group was made of a floating collection of studio musicians; they took their name from Gene Autry's horse. The piece has become a garage-rock standard.

## THANK GOD I'M A COUNTRY BOY
John Martin Sommers (w & m)
Cherry Lane Music
1974
John Denver had a nice career as an actor (*Oh, God*) and a better one as a singer. This number 1 hit charted for fifteen weeks (RCA Victor 10239). It sold over one million copies.

## THANK YOU (FALETTINME BE MICE ELF AGIN)
Sylvester Stewart (w & m)
Stone Flower Music—New York
1969
Number 1 hit in 1970 for funk-rock group Sly & the Family Stone, holding that spot for two out of twelve chart weeks; also a number 1 R&B hit (Epic 10555).

## THANKS FOR THE MEMORY

Ralph Rainger (w: Leo Robin)

Paramount Music—New York

1937

**Film:** *Big Broadcast of 1938* (Paramount)

Academy Award winner for Best Song. Bob Hope and Shirley Ross sang it in the film and recorded it (Decca 2219). Hope used it thereafter for the rest of his career as his theme song on radio, television, and personal appearances. Shep Fields and His Rippling Rhythm Orchestra had the number 1 hit, which charted for fourteen weeks (Bluebird 7318).

## THAT CERTAIN PARTY

Walter Donaldson (w: Gus Kahn)

Irving Berlin—New York

1925

This standard was given its first recorded hit by the Russo and Fiorito Oriole Orchestra (Victor 19917). Ernest Hare and Billy Jones had the first vocal hit (Victor 19865). Dave Gwin made a splendid piano roll (Capitol 1355). Dean Martin and Jerry Lewis revived it in 1948 (Capitol 15249).

## THAT INTERNATIONAL RAG

Irving Berlin (w & m)

Waterson, Berlin and Snyder—New York

1913

Introduced in vaudeville by Sophie Tucker. The Victor Military Band had a hit recording (Victor 17487).

## THAT LUCKY OLD SUN

Beasley Smith (w: Haven Gillespie)

Robbins Music—New York

1949

Frankie Laine had the number 1 hit, which charted for twenty-two weeks and sold over one million copies (Mercury 5316). It was revived in 1963 by Ray Charles, who had a number 20 hit (ABC-Paramount 10509).

## THAT OLD BLACK MAGIC

Harold Arlen (w: Johnny Mercer)

Famous Music—New York

1942

**Film:** *Star Spangled Rhythm* (Paramount)

Johnny Johnson sang it in the film. Glenn Miller and His Orchestra, with vocals by Skip Nelson and the Modernaires, had the number 1 hit in 1943 (Victor 20-1523). Spike Jones had a successful parody (Victor 20-1895). Sammy Davis Jr. revived it in 1955 with his number 13 hit (Decca 29541). Bobby Rydell revived it again in 1961 with his number 21 hit (Cameo 190). It remains a nightclub favorite.

## THAT OLD FEELING

Sammy Fain (w: Lew Brown)

Leo Feist—New York

1937

**Film:** *Vogues of 1938* (United Artists)

Virginia Verrill sang it in the film. Shep Fields and His Rippling Rhythm Orchestra had the number 1 hit that charted for fourteen weeks (Bluebird 7066).

## THAT THING CALLED LOVE

Perry Bradford (w & m)

Pace and Handy Music—New York

1920

Introduced in vaudeville by Sophie Tucker. The hit recording was by Mamie Smith and her Jazz Hounds (Okeh 4113). Zez Confrey made a splendid piano roll (QRS 918).

## THAT'LL BE THE DAY

Buddy Holly/Norman Petty/
Jerry Allison

Nor Va Jak Music—New York

1957

The first number 1 hit for Buddy Holly and the Crickets, it charted for sixteen weeks and sold over one million copies (Brunswick 55009). It became a signature tune for Holly, featuring his unusual hiccupy vocal mannerisms, fine guitar playing, and lean accompaniment, and "wop-wop" background vocals from the Crickets. Linda Ronstadt revived it in 1976 with a number 11 hit that charted for eleven weeks (Asylum 45340).

## THAT'S A PLENTY (RAG)

Lew Pollack

Joe Morris Music—New York

1914

A piano rag that got its start with Prince's Band (Columbia A-5582). During the 1950s it was comedian Jackie Gleason's "And away we go" music.

## THAT'S AMORE
Harry Warren (w: Jack Brooks)
Paramount Music—New York
1953
**Film:** *The Caddy* (Paramount)
Dean Martin sang it in the film and had the number 2 hit that charted for twenty-two weeks and sold more than one million copies (Capitol 2589). His recording was prominently featured in the 1987 film *Moonstruck* (MGM, 1987).

## THAT'S MY DESIRE
Helmy Kresa (w: Carroll Loveday)
Sterling Songs—New York
1931
Lanny Ross introduced it on radio. It only became a hit when Frankie Laine rediscovered it in 1947. Laine's disc was a number 4 hit that charted for twenty-six weeks and sold over one million copies (Mercury 5007).

## THAT'S MY WEAKNESS NOW
Sam Stept (w: Bud Green)
Green and Stept—New York
1928
Introduced in vaudeville by Helen Kane, who shoved in a few "boop-boop-a-doops" that made her famous. Her recording was a hit (Victor 21557). Paul Whiteman had the hit instrumental (Columbia 1444-D). It was revived in 1949 by Russ Morgan and His Orchestra (Decca 24692).

## THAT'S THE KIND OF BABY FOR ME
J. C. Egan (w: Alfred Harriman)
Broadway Music—New York
1917
**Show:** *Ziegfeld Follies of 1917*
Introduced in the show by Eddie Cantor, who made a name for himself with this song and also had the hit recording (Victor 18342).

## THAT'S THE WAY (I LIKE IT)
H. W. Casey and R. Finch

Sherlyn Music—Hialeah, Fla.
1975
Number 1 hit for KC and the Sunshine Band, holding that position for two out of thirteen chart weeks; also a number 1 R&B hit (T.K. 1015). A classic of the disco era.

## THAT'S THE WAY LOVE GOES
Janet Jackson/James Harris/Terry Lewis
Black Ice
1993
Janet Jackson's number 1 hit was on top for eight of the twenty weeks it charted (Virgin 12650). It sold over one million copies.

## THAT'S WHAT FRIENDS ARE FOR
Carole Bayer Sager and Burt Bacharach
Warner Bros.—Secaucus, NJ
1982, 1985
Dionne Warwick, Elton John, Gladys Knight, and Stevie Wonder created this number 1 hit that stayed on the chart for seventeen weeks and sold more than one million copies (Arista 9422). It was released as a benefit record for AIDS victims.

## THAT'S WHY THEY CALL ME "SHINE"
Ford Dabney (w: Cecil Mack)
Shapiro, Bernstein—New York
1910
**Show:** *His Honor the Barber*
Introduced in the show by Aida Overton Walker. With added words by Lew Brown in 1924, it became a standard. It was revived by Bing Crosby and the Mills Brothers in 1932 for a number 7 hit (Brunswick 6276) and by Frankie Lane in 1948 for a number 9 hit (Mercury 5091). Harry James played it in the biopic *The Benny Goodman Story* (Universal, 1956).

## THEM THERE EYES
Maceo Pinkard/William Tracey/
Doris Tauber
Irving Berlin—New York
1930
Gus Arnheim and His Orchestra, with vocal by Bing Crosby and the Rhythm Boys, had the number 7 hit in 1931 (Victor 22580). Billie Holiday was most closely

associated with the song (Vocalion 5021). Diana Ross sang it in the Holiday biopic *Lady Sings the Blues* (Paramount, 1972).

## THEME FROM "A SUMMER PLACE"
Max Steiner (w: Mack Discant)
M. Witmark and Sons—New York
1959, 1960
**Film:** *A Summer Place* (Warner Bros.)
Percy Faith and His Orchestra had the number 1 hit, holding that position for nine of the seventeen weeks on the chart (Columbia 41490). It sold more than one million copies.

## THEME FROM SHAFT
Isaac Hayes (w & m)
East/Memphis Music—Los Angeles
1971
**Film:** *Shaft* (MGM)
Academy Award winner for Best Song. Isaac Hayes, accompanied by the Bar-Kays, had the number 1 hit, which charted for twelve weeks (Enterprise 9038). It sold over one million copies.

## THEN CAME YOU
Phil Pugh and Sherman Marshall
Mighty Three Music
1974
Dionne Warwick combined with the Spinners to create this number 1 hit, which charted for fifteen weeks (Atlantic 3202). It sold over one million copies.

## THEN I'LL BE HAPPY
See "I Wanna Go Where You Go, Do What You Do, Then I'll Be Happy."

## THERE, I'VE SAID IT AGAIN
Redd Evans and Dave Mann
Valiant Music—New York
1941
Vaughn Monroe had the number 1 hit, which charted for twenty-nine weeks and sold more than two million copies (Victor 20-1637). Bobby Vinton revived it in 1964 with a number 1 hit that charted for twelve weeks (Epic 9638).

## THERE'LL BE SOME CHANGES MADE
W. Benton Overstreet (w: Billy Higgins)
Edward B. Marks Music—New York
1923
A jazz standard made famous by Ethel Waters (Black Swan 2021), Marion Harris (Brunswick 2651), and Ted Lewis (Columbia 170-D). It was revived in 1941 by Benny Goodman and His Orchestra with vocal by Louise Tobin (Columbia 35210). Ted Weems and His Orchestra had two hits with the same recording (Decca 3044 in 1939, reissued in 1947 as Decca 25288).

## THERE'S A KIND OF HUSH
Les Reed and Geoff Stephens
Leo Feist—New York
1966
Herman's Hermits had the number 4 hit in 1967 that charted for nine weeks and sold over one million copies (MGM 13681). It was revived by the Carpenters in 1976 with a number 12 hit which charted for eight weeks (A&M 1800).

## THERE'S A SMALL HOTEL
Richard Rodgers (w: Lorenz Hart)
Chappell—New York
1936
**Show:** *On Your Toes*
Ray Bolger and Doris Carson sang it in the show. Hal Kemp and His Orchestra had the number 1 hit that charted for fifteen weeks (Brunswick 7634). Betty Garrett sang it in the Rodgers and Hart biopic *Words and Music* (MGM, 1948). Frank Sinatra sang it in the film *Pal Joey* (Columbia, 1957).

## THERE'S NO BUSINESS LIKE SHOW BUSINESS
Irving Berlin (w & m)
Irving Berlin—New York
1946
**Show:** *Annie Get Your Gun*
William O'Neal, Ray Middleton, Marty May, and Ethel Merman sang it in the show. Bing Crosby, the Andrews Sisters, and Dick Haymes had the number 25 hit (Decca 40039). It has become a standard song about the business of entertainment.

## THESE BOOTS ARE MADE FOR WALKIN'

Lee Hazelwood (w & m)

Criterion Music—New York

1966

Nancy Sinatra, daughter of Frank, had her first number 1 hit with this song, which charted for twelve weeks and sold over one million copies (Reprise 0432). It helped establish her sexy-girl-with-an-attitude persona.

## THESE FOOLISH THINGS REMIND ME OF YOU

Jack Strachey and Harry Link (w: Holt Marvel)

Irving Berlin—New York

1935

**Show:** *Spread It Abroad* (London)

Benny Goodman and His Orchestra, with vocal by Helen Ward, had the number 1 hit, which charted for thirteen weeks (Victor 25351).

## THEY CAN'T TAKE THAT AWAY FROM ME

George and Ira Gershwin

Chappell—New York

1937

**Film:** *Shall We Dance?* (RKO)

Fred Astaire sang it in the film and had the number 1 hit that charted for eleven weeks (Brunswick 7855). He also sang it in the film *The Barkleys of Broadway* (MGM, 1949).

## THEY DIDN'T BELIEVE ME

Jerome Kern (w: Herbert Reynolds)

T. B. Harms—New York

1914

**Show:** *The Girl From Utah*

Introduced in the show by Julia Sanderson. With the recording by Harry MacDonough and Alice Green (Victor 35491), the sheet music sales topped two million. It was the first Kern song to become a standard. It was sung by Dinah Shore in the Kern biopic *Till the Clouds Roll By* (MGM, 1946).

## THEY GO WILD SIMPLY WILD OVER ME

Fred Fisher (w: Joe McCarthy)

McCarthy and Fisher—New York

1917

A fine comic number for vaudevillians. Marion Harris had the hit recording (Victor 18343).

## THEY GOTTA QUIT KICKIN' MY DAWG AROUND

Cy Perkins (w: Webb M. Oungst)

Stark Music—St. Louis

1912

Carrie B. Stark used the Perkins pseudonym. Publisher M. Witmark and Sons purchased the copyright from Stark and then sold it to Champ Clark to use in his campaign against Woodrow Wilson for the Democratic nomination. Unfortunately, he lost.

## (THEY LONG TO BE) CLOSE TO YOU

Burt Bacharach (w: Hal David)

Blue Seas Music—New York

1963

The Carpenters, who were the top-selling act in the 1970s, had this, their first number 1 hit, in 1970; it was on the chart for fifteen weeks and sold over one million copies (A&M 1183).

## THINK OF ME

Al Eldridge (w & m)

Jack Mills—New York

1923

Lovely song introduced by Isham Jones and His Orchestra (Brunswick 2374), as the composer was the pianist/arranger for Jones.

## THINKING OF YOU

Harry Ruby (w: Bert Kalmar)

Harms—New York

1927

**Show:** *The Five O'Clock Girl*

Oscar Shaw and Mary Eaton sang it in the show. Nat Shilkret and the Victor Orchestra had the hit recording (Victor 20996). Fred Astaire and Vera Ellen performed it in the Ruby-Kalmar biopic *Three Little Words* (MGM, 1950). That same year saw two hit recordings: Don Cherry's number 4 hit (Decca 27128) and Eddie Fisher's number 5 hit (RCA Victor 20-3901).

## THIRD MAN THEME, THE

Anton Karas

Chappell—New York

1949

**Film:** *The Third Man* (Selznick)

This instrumental was featured in the film by the composer, an Austrian zither player. His recording was the number 1 hit, holding that position for eleven of the twenty-seven weeks charted in 1950. It sold over two million copies (London 536). Guy Lombardo and His Royal Canadians also had a hit, featuring Don Rodney on guitar, that was number 1 in 1950 for eleven of the twenty-seven weeks charted, and sold over one million copies (Decca 24839).

## THIS CAN'T BE LOVE

Richard Rodgers

(w: Lorenz Hart)

Chappell—New York

1938

**Show:** *The Boys from Syracuse*

Eddie Albert and Marcy Westcott sang it in the show. Benny Goodman and His Orchestra had the number 2 hit in 1939 that charted for thirteen weeks (Victor 26099). Rosemary Harris sang it in the film version (Universal, 1940).

## THIS DIAMOND RING

Al Kooper/Irwin Levine/Bob Brass

Sea-Lark Enterprises—New York

1964, 1965

Gary Lewis and the Playboys had the number 1 hit, which charted for eleven weeks and sold more than one million copies (Liberty 55756). It was their first release and only number 1 hit.

## THIS GUY'S IN LOVE WITH YOU

Burt Bacharach (w: Hal David)

Blue Seas Music—New York

1968

Number 1 hit for Herb Alpert, his first vocal hit after years of leading the Tijuana Brass. It held the top spot for four out of twelve chart weeks, and sold over a million records; it also was a number 1 adult-contemporary hit (A&M 929). A year later, a regendered version ("This *Girl's* In Love with You") scored a number 7 hit for Dionne Warwick (Scepter 12241).

## THIS MAGIC MOMENT

Mort Shuman (w: Doc Pomus)

Rumbalero Music—New York

1960

Jay and the Americans had the number 6 hit in 1969 that charted for ten weeks and sold over one million copies (United Artists 50475). It had previously been recorded by the Drifters in 1960, but their version only charted number 15 pop (Atlantic 2050).

## THIS USED TO BE MY PLAYGROUND

Madonna Ciccone and Shep Pettibone

WB Music

1992

**Film:** *A League of Their Own*—Columbia

Madonna, who costarred in the film, had the number 1 hit, which charted for fourteen weeks (Sire 18822).

## THOSE PANAMA MAMAS

Irving Bibo (w: Howard Johnson)

Maurice Abrahams—New York

1924

A syncopated gem from the mid-1920s. Eddie Cantor had the hit vocal (Columbia 256-D), while the Cotton Pickers (Brunswick 2879) and the Varsity Eight (Lincoln 2289) had the hit instrumental versions.

## THOU SWELL

Richard Rodgers (w: Lorenz Hart)

Harms—New York

1927

**Show:** *A Connecticut Yankee*

Introduced in the show by William Gaxton and Constance Carpenter, it is a standard and favorite of jazz bands. Bix Beiderbecke and his Gang made the outstanding version (Okeh 41030).

## THREE COINS IN THE FOUNTAIN

Jule Styne (w: Sammy Cahn)

Robbins Music—New York

1954

**Film:** *Three Coins in the Fountain* (20th Century Fox)

Academy Award winner for Best Song. The Four Aces had the number 1 hit that charted for eighteen weeks (Decca 29123).

## THREE LITTLE WORDS

Harry Ruby (w: Bert Kalmar)

Harms—New York

1930

**Film:** *Check and Double Check* ( RKO)

Duke Ellington and His Famous Orchestra, with vocals
by Bing Crosby and the Rhythm Boys, had the number 1
hit, which charted for thirteen weeks (Victor 22528);
they were also featured in the film. Fred Astaire sang it in
the Ruby-Kalmar biopic *Three Little Words* (MGM, 1950).

## THREE TIMES A LADY

Lionel Richie (w & m)

Jobete Music—Hollywood

1978

The Commodores, with Lionel Richie on vocals and saxophone, had this number 1 hit, which charted for sixteen
weeks (Motown 1443). It is a classic soft-pop love ballad.

## TICKET TO RIDE

John Lennon and Paul McCartney

Maclen Music—New York

1965

**Film:** *Help* (United Artists)

The Beatles had the number 1 hit, which charted for
nine weeks (Capitol 5407).

## TICKLE TOE, THE

Louis A. Hirsch (w: Otto Harbach)

M. Witmark and Sons—New York

1917

**Show:** *Going Up*

Edith Day and Allen Fagan sang it in the show.

## TIDE IS HIGH, THE

John Holt (w & m)

Gemrod Music—New York

1968, 1972

Blondie had the number 1 hit in 1981, that charted for
seventeen weeks (Chrysalis 2465). It sold over one
million copies, and it was one of the first pop songs to
feature a reggae-like rhythm by a non-Jamaican group.

## TIE A YELLOW RIBBON ROUND THE OLE OAK TREE

Irwin Levine and L. Russell Brown

Tridem Music

1972, 1973

Tony Orlando and Dawn was a successful pop vocal
trio best remembered for this number 1 hit, which
charted for seventeen weeks (Bell 45.318), and it sold
over one million copies. At various times of crisis, such
as during the Gulf War, yellow ribbons have been tied
to trees as signs of support. This practice has continued
during other times of national emergency or stress.

## TIGER RAG

D. J. LaRocca

Leo Feist—New York

1917

The most famous dixieland jazz standard, introduced
in vaudeville and on records by the Original Dixieland
Jazz Band (Victor 18472). Jelly Roll Morton claims to
have originated the piece by taking an old French
quadrille and adapting it to a Dixieland style. It was
revived by the Mills Brothers in 1931; this, their first
recording, became a number 1 hit (Brunswick 6197).
It was revived again in 1952 by Les Paul and Mary
Ford, who had a number 2 hit (Capitol 1920).

## TILL I WALTZ AGAIN WITH YOU

Sidney Prosen (w & m)

Village Music—New York

1952

Teresa Brewer had the number 1 hit, which charted for
twenty-four weeks and sold over one million copies
(Coral 60873). However, it's not even a waltz!

## TILL THE CLOUDS ROLL BY

Jerome Kern (w: P. G. Wodehouse and
Jerome Kern)

T. B. Harms—New York

1917

**Show:** *Oh, Boy!*

Introduced in this enormously popular show by Anna
Wheaton and Tom Powers. Wheaton and James Harod
had the hit recording (Columbia A-2261). It was
Jerome Kern's favorite of all his songs, and was used in
his biopic of the same name (MGM, 1946).

## TILL THEN

Guy Wood/Sol Marcus/Eddie Seiler

Pickwick Music—New York

1944

The Mills Brothers had the number 8 hit, which charted for sixteen weeks (Decca 18599). It was revived in 1954 by the Hilltoppers, with a number 10 hit (Dot 15132), and in 1963 by the Classics, with a number 20 hit (Musicnote 1116).

## TILL THERE WAS YOU

Meredith Willson (w & m)

Frank Music—New York

1950, 1957

**Show:** *The Music Man*

Robert Preston and Barbara Cook sang it in the show. Anita Bryant had the number 30 hit in 1959 (Carlton 512).

## TILL WE MEET AGAIN

Richard Whiting (w: Raymond B. Egan)

Jerome H. Remick—New York

1918

A three-and-a-half million seller in sheet music. The most popular recording was by Henry Burr and Albert Campbell (Columbia A-2668). It was revived by Doris Day and Gordon MacRae in the film *On Moonlight Bay* (Warner Bros., 1951).

## TIME AFTER TIME

Cyndi Lauper and Rob Hyman

Rella Music

1983

Cyndi Lauper had the number 1 hit in 1984 that charted for fourteen weeks, selling over one million copies (Portrait 04432). It was revived in 1998 by Inoj, who had a number 6 hit that charted for fifteen weeks and sold over half a million copies (So So Def 79016).

## TIME IN A BOTTLE

Jim Croce (w & m)

Blendingwell Music—New York

1971, 1972

This was Jim Croce's last number 1 hit, which charted for twelve weeks (ABC 11405). It sold over one million copies.

## TIME ON MY HANDS

Vincent Youmans (w: Mack Gordon and

Harold Adamson)

Vincent Youmans—New York

1930

**Show:** *Smiles*

Paul Gregory sang it in the show. Both Smith Ballew and Leo Reisman and their orchestras had number 6 hits (Columbia 2544-D and Victor 22839, respectively). It became the theme song of the *Chase and Sanborn Hour*, an NBC radio series.

## TIN ROOF BLUES

New Orleans Rhythm Kings (w: Walter Melrose)

Melrose Bros.—Chicago

1923

A jazz standard composed, introduced, and recorded by the New Orleans Rhythm Kings (Gennett 5105) Ted Lewis and His Jazz Band made a hit recording (Columbia 439-D). New lyrics were created in 1954 and the song was retitled "Make Love To Me."

## TIP TOE THRU THE TULIPS

Joe Burke (w: Al Dubin)

M. Witmark and Sons—New York

1929

**Film:** *Gold Diggers of Broadway* (Warner Bros.)

Nick Lucas sang it in the film and had a hit recording (Brunswick 4418). It was also sung in the second film version, titled *Painting the Clouds with Sunshine* (Warner Bros., 1951). It was revived in 1968 with a number 17 hit record by novelty ukulele strummer Tiny Tim (Reprise 0679).

## TISHOMINGO BLUES

Spencer Williams (w & m)

Jos. W. Stern—New York

1917

A jazz favorite since its introduction in vaudeville; the 1928 recording by Duke Ellington and His Orchestra featured a solo by Bubber Miley (Brunswick 3987).

## TO KNOW HIM IS TO LOVE HIM

Phil Spector (w & m)

Warman Music—New York

1958

The Teddy Bears, Phil Spector's first pop group and the only one in which he actually performed, had the number 1 hit that charted for eighteen weeks and sold over one million copies (Dore 503). The title is taken from Spector's father's tombstone.

## TO SIR, WITH LOVE
Marc London (w: Don Black)
Screen Gems-Columbia—New York
1967
**Film:** *To Sir, with Love* (Columbia)
Lulu, who appeared in the film, had the number 1 hit, which maintained its top position for five of its fifteen weeks on the charts (Epic 10187). It sold over one million copies.

## TOGETHER FOREVER
Stock/Aitken/Waterman
All Boys USA Music
1987
Rick Astley had the number 1 hit in 1988 that charted for twelve weeks (RCA 8319).

## TOMORROW
Charles Strouse (w: Martin Charnin)
MPL—New York
1977
**Show:** *Annie*
Andrea McArdle sang it in the show. Aileen Quinn sang it in the film version (Columbia, 1982). Popular among big-lunged belters and would-be Broadway stars.

## TONIGHT YOU BELONG TO ME
Lee David (w: Billy Rose)
Henry Waterson—New York
1926
Gene Austin had the hit recording of this very popular song (Victor 20371). The Cavaliers also had a nice arrangement (Columbia 860-D). It was revived in 1956 by Patience and Prudence, who were eleven and fourteen years old (Liberty 55022); their record reached number 4 and charted for seventeen weeks, selling over one million copies. They were accompanied by their father Mack McIntyre's Orchestra.

## TOO CLOSE
Darren Lightly/Keir Gist/Robert Huggar

WB Music Corp.
1997, 1998
Next, a pop vocal trio, scored a number 1 hit that remained on the chart for an astonishing forty-nine weeks (Arista 13456). It sold over one million copies.

## TOO MARVELOUS FOR WORDS
Richard Whiting (w: Johnny Mercer)
Harms—New York
1937
**Film:** *Ready, Willing and Able* (Warner Bros.)
Wini Shaw and James Newill sang it in the film. Bing Crosby had the number 1 hit, which charted for ten weeks (Decca 1185).

## TOO YOUNG
Sid Lippman (w: Sylvia Dee)
Jefferson Music—New York
1951
Nat "King" Cole had the number 1 hit, which charted for twenty-nine weeks and sold over one million copies (Capitol 1449). It was revived in 1972 by Donny Osmond, who had a number 13 hit (MGM 14407).

## TOO-RA-LOO-RA-LOO-RAL
James Royce Shannon (w & m)
M. Witmark and Sons—New York
1913
**Show:** *Shameen Dhu*
Chauncey Olcott sang it in the show. Bing Crosby revived it in the film *Going My Way* (Paramount, 1944) and in a number 4 hit that charted for twelve weeks and sold over one million copies (Decca 18621). A St. Patrick's Day favorite.

## TOOT, TOOT, TOOTSIE!
Dan Russo/Ernie Erdman/Gus Kahn
Leo Feist—New York
1922
**Show:** *Bombo*
Al Jolson sang it in the show and had a hit recording (Columbia A-3705). It became a lifelong specialty. The Oriole Terrace Orchestra (Dan Russo, coleader); (Brunswick 2337) and the Benson Orchestra (Victor 18954) had the instrumental hits. Al Jolson sang it in the films *The Jazz Singer* (Warner Bros., 1927), *Rose of*

*Washington Square* (20th Century Fox, 1939), and his two biopics *The Jolson Story* (Columbia, 1946) and *Jolson Sings Again* (Columbia, 1949). It also appeared in the Gus Kahn biopic *I'll See You in My Dreams* (Warner Bros., 1951). Art Mooney and His Orchestra had a number 19 hit recording in 1949 (MGM 10548).

## TOP BANANA
Johnny Mercer (w & m)
Chappell-Mercer Music—New York
1951
**Show:** *Top Banana*
Phil Silvers sang it in the show; it became his theme song.

## TOP HAT, WHITE TIE AND TAILS
Irving Berlin (w & m)
Irving Berlin—New York
1935
**Film:** *Top Hat* (RKO)
Fred Astaire sang it in the film and had the number 2 hit that charted for thirteen weeks (Brunswick 7487).

## TOP OF THE WORLD
Richard Carpenter (W: John Bettis)
Almo Music
1972
The Carpenters had this number 1 hit, which charted for sixteen weeks (A&M 1468). It sold over one million copies.

## TOSSIN' AND TURNIN'
Malou Rene and Ritchie Adams
Havard Music
1961
Bobby Lewis had the number 1 hit, which charted for seventeen weeks (Beltone 1002).

## TOTAL ECLIPSE OF THE HEART
Jim Steinman (w & m)
Lost Boys Music
1982, 1983
Bonnie Tyler had the number 1 hit, which charted for eighteen weeks and sold over one million copies (Columbia 03906). It was revived in 1995 by Nicki French, who gained a number 2 hit that charted for twenty-one weeks and sold over half a million copies (Critique 15539).

## TOUCH OF YOUR HAND, THE
Jerome Kern (w: Otto Harbach)
T. B. Harms—New York
1933
**Show:** *Roberta*
Tamara and William Hain sang it in the show. Leo Reisman and His Orchestra had the number 10 hit that charted for five weeks (Brunswick 6715). Ginger Rogers sang it in the film version (RKO, 1935), and Kathryn Grayson and Howard Keel sang it in the remake called *Lovely to Look At* (MGM, 1952).

## TOYLAND
Victor Herbert (w: Glen MacDonough)
M. Witmark and Sons—New York
1903
**Show:** *Babes in Toyland*
Introduced by Bessie Wynn in the show. Corrine Morgan and the Haydn Quartet had a hit recording in 1904 (Victor 2721).

## TRAGEDY
Barry, Robin and Maurice Gibb
Brother Gibb
1978, 1979
The Bee Gees had the number 1 hit, which charted for thirteen weeks (RSO 918). It sold over two million copies.

## TRAIL OF THE LONESOME PINE, THE
Harry Carroll (w: Ballard MacDonald)
Shapiro Music—New York
1913
Introduced in vaudeville by the composer. Henry Burr and Albert Campbell scored a hit with their recording (Columbia A-1315). Spectacularly revived by Stan Laurel and Oliver Hardy in the film *Way Out West* (MGM, 1937). Popular among the cowboy vocal groups of the 1930s and 1940s.

## TRAMP! TRAMP! TRAMP!
Victor Herbert (w: Rida Johnson Young)

M. Witmark and Sons—New York

1910

**Show:** *Naughty Marietta*

Orville Harrold and a male chorus sang it in the show. Nelson Eddy and another male chorus sang it in the film version (MGM, 1935).

## TRES MOUTARDE (TOO MUCH MUSTARD)

Cecil Macklin

Cary—London

1911

A marvelous syncopated instrumental made famous by the Victor Military Band's recording (Victor 17292). It has been revived in the biopic *The Story of Vernon and Irene Castle* (RKO, 1939), and again in 1952 by Joe "Fingers" Carr on his LP *Bar Room Piano* (Capitol T-280).

## TRICKS

Zez Confrey (w & m)

Leo Feist—New York

1922

Introduced and first recorded by Paul Whiteman and His Orchestra (Victor 18939). The composer made an outstanding piano roll (QRS 2052). As a sequel to "Stumbling," it received many recordings, especially by the Country Club Orchestra (Cameo 258), Isham Jones (Brunswick 2311), Vincent Lopez (Okeh 4673), and Emil Coleman (Vocalion 14409).

## TROLLEY SONG, THE

Hugh Martin (w: Ralph Blane)

Leo Feist—New York

1944

**Film:** *Meet me in St. Louis* (MGM)

Judy Garland sang it in the film and had a number 4 hit (Decca 23361). The pop vocal group the Pied Pipers outdid her with a number 2 hit that charted for fourteen weeks (Capitol 168).

## TRUE COLORS

Billy Steinberg and Tom Kelly

Billy Steinberg Music

1986

Cyndi Lauper had the number 1 hit, which charted for twelve weeks (Portrait 06247). Used in the early 1990s as a theme song for Kodak film.

## TRUE LOVE

Cole Porter (w & m )

Buxton Hill—New York

1956

**Film:** *High Society* (MGM)

Bing Crosby and Grace Kelly sang it in the film. They had the number 3 hit that charted for twenty-two weeks and sold over one million copies (Capitol 3507).

## TRY A LITTLE TENDERNESS

Harry Woods/James Campbell/Reg Connelly

Robbins Music—New York

1932

Ted Lewis and His Band had the number 6 hit in 1933, which charted for ten weeks (Columbia 2748-D). Otis Redding revived it in 1966 in a definitive and very soulful version, which reached number 25 on the pop charts, charting for six weeks (Volt 141). Three Dog Night revived it in 1969 with a number 29 hit that charted for four weeks (Dunhill/ABC 4177). It was prominently featured in the film *The Commitments* (20th Century Fox, 1991), about an Irish group who try to make it as an R&B act.

## TRY TO REMEMBER

Harvey Schmidt (w: Tom Jones)

Chappell—New York

1960

**Show:** *The Fantastics*

Jerry Orbach sang it in the show. Has become a cabaret standard.

## TUCK ME TO SLEEP IN MY OLD 'TUCKY HOME

George W. Meyer (w: Sam Lewis and Joe Young)

Irving Berlin—New York

1921

Vernon Dalhart had the biggest hit vocally (Victor 18807) and the Benson Orchestra had it instrumentally (Victor 18820). It has become a favorite of Dixieland bands beginning with the 1954 recording by the Firehouse Five Plus Two (Good Time Jazz 90).

## TURN! TURN! TURN!

Pete Seeger (w & m)

Melody Trails—New York

1962

The Byrds had the number 1 hit in 1965 that charted for eleven weeks (Columbia 43424). The words are taken from the book of Ecclesiastes in the Bible. The Byrds's recording is notable for the prominent use of Roger McGuinn's twelve-string electric guitar, and the beautiful vocal harmonies of McGuinn, Clark, Crosby, and Hillman.

## TUTTI FRUTTI

Richard Penniman/D. LaBostroe/Joe Lubin

Venice Music

1955, 1956

Little Richard had been singing this song in nightclubs with a set of off-color lyrics. With some adjustment, the song was recorded by him and became a number 17 pop hit (Specialty 561). It introduced into the rock vocabulary "A-wop-bam-a-loo-bop, a-wop-bam-boom!" plus Richard's energetic singing and exuberant "Whooos" (later imitated by Paul McCartney in "She Loves You"). Pat Boone's much-sanitized cover version actually sold better than Richard's, reaching number 12 and charting for ten weeks (Dot 15443).

## TWEEDLEE DEE

Winfield Scott (w & m)

Progressive Music—New York

1954

LaVern Baker first recorded it, and scored a number 14 pop hit in 1955 (Atlantic 1047). It was Georgia Gibbs, however, who had the number 2 hit, which charted for nineteen weeks and sold over a million copies (Mercury 70517). The Gibbs version was a direct "copy" of Baker's disc, and for years Baker resented the fact that she was deprived of a higher chart position (and more record sales) by her imitator.

## 12TH STREET RAG

Euday L. Bowman

Euday L. Bowman—Fort Worth Texas

1914

The most recorded rag of all time. Pee Wee Hunt's 1948 number 1 hit charted for thirty-two weeks and sold more than three million records, the biggest-selling ragtime recording (Capitol 15105).

## TWILIGHT TIME

Buck Ram/Morty Nevins and Artie Dunn

Campbell-Porgie—New York

1944

The Three Suns had the number 14 hit (Hit 7092). The Platters revived it in 1958 with their million-selling number 1 hit, which charted for fourteen weeks (Mercury 71289).

## TWIST, THE

Hank Ballard (w & m)

Lois Music—London

1959

Hank Ballard originally recorded it in 1960 (King 5171), but his version was not very successful. Dick Clark of *American Bandstand* thought the song and dance had potential, and found a singer named Ernest Evans in Philadelphia to record it. Christening him Chubby Checker (a play on the name "Fats Domino"), Clark promoted the song and the singer until it became a number 1 hit in 1960, charted for fifteen weeks, and sold over one million copies (Parkway 811). The same recording hit the charts in 1961, where it again reached number 1 and stayed on the charts for eighteen weeks; only one other song has charted number 1 in two different years—Bing Crosby's "White Christmas." Meanwhile, the dance craze spread like wildfire, inspired teen exploitation flicks such as *Twist around the Clock* (Columbia, 1962) and *Don't Knock the Twist* (Columbia, 1963), both featuring Checker. Follow-up songs included "Let's Twist Again" which charted twice in the Top 10 in 1961 (Parkway 824) and "Slow Twistin'," from 1962, a duet with Dee Dee Sharp (Parkway 835). In 1978, Checker recorded a new version with the Fat Boys titled "The Twist (Yo, Twist!)," for the rap audience and it reached number 16 on the charts (Tin Pan 887571). The song continues to be the singer's best-known number, and he performs it on revival tours regularly.

## TWIST AND SHOUT

Bert Russell and Phil Medley

Robert Mellin Music—New York

1960, 1963

First recorded by the Top Notes, in a forgotten version, in 1961; a year later, the Isley Brothers cut the definitive version, which reached number 17 on the charts (Wand 124). This version was much beloved by John Lennon, who literally shouted the song at the

Beatles's first album session in 1963 (released in the United States on *Introducing...the Beatles*, Vee Jay 1062 in 1964). Released as a single in the United States a year later, the song reached number 2, a position it held for four out of nine chart weeks (Tollie 9001); it returned to the charts in 1986 for a number 23 hit (Capitol 5624).

## TWO SLEEPY PEOPLE
Hoagy Carmichael (w: Frank Loesser)
Famous Music—New York
1938
**Film:** *Thanks For the Memory* (Paramount)
Bob Hope and Shirley Ross sang it in the film and had a number 15 hit (Decca 2219). Fats Waller had the number 1 hit that charted for eleven weeks (Bluebird 10000).

## UN-BREAK MY HEART
Diane Warren (w & m)
Realsongs
1996
Toni Braxton had the number 1 hit, which held that position for eleven of the thirty-seven weeks charted and sold over one million copies (LaFace 24200).

## UNCHAINED MELODY
Alex North (w: Hy Zaret)
Frank Music—New York
1955
Film: *Unchained* (Warner Bros.)
Number 1 hit for Les Baxter, holding its position for two out of twenty-one chart weeks (Capitol 3055). Quickly covered by various singers, including a number 3 hit for Al Hibbler (Decca 29441) in 1955 and a number 6 hit for Roy Hamilton (Epic 9102). Ten years later, the Righteous Brothers recorded it in its most famous pop version, achieving a number 4 hit (Philles 129). Revived in the film *Ghost* (Paramount, 1990), the 1965 recording charted again, reaching number 11, and a new version was released, selling over a million copies, but it reached only number 19 (Curb 76842).

## UNDECIDED
Charles Shavers (w: Sid Robin)
Leeds Music—New York
1939

Ella Fitzgerald, with Chick Webb's Orchestra, had the number 8 hit, which charted for four weeks (Decca 2323). The Ames Brothers revived it in 1951 for a number 2 hit, which charted for twenty-one weeks and sold over one million copies (Coral 60566).

## UNDER THE ANHEUSER BUSH
Harry Von Tilzer (w: Andrew B. Sterling)
Harry Von Tilzer—New York
1903
Rosalie introduced it in vaudeville. Like his Wurzberger song, this was a turn-of-the-century version of a singing commercial. The popular comedy singing team of Arthur Collins and Byron Harlan recorded it (Victor 2668).

## UNDER THE BAMBOO TREE
Bob Cole (w & m)
Jos. W. Stern—New York
1902
**Show:** *Sally in Our Alley*
Introduced by Marie Cahill in the show, and by Cole and J. Rosamond Johnson in vaudeville. Arthur Collins had the hit recording (Victor 1633). Judy Garland and Margaret O'Brien sang it in the film *Meet Me in St. Louis* (MGM, 1944). T. S. Eliot quoted it in his poem, "Sweeney Agonistes."

## UNDER THE BOARDWALK
Artie Resnick and Kenny Young
T. M. Music—New York
1964
Number 4 hit for the Drifters, charting for twelve weeks (Atlantic 2237). It is a classic of early 1960s harmony.

## UNDER THE SEA
Alan Menken (w: Howard Ashman)
Walt Disney
1988
**Film:** *The Little Mermaid* (Disney)
Academy Award winner for Best Song for 1989.

## UNFORGETTABLE
Irving Gordon (w & m)
Bourne—New York
1951

Nat "King" Cole had the number 12 hit, which charted for fifteen weeks (Capitol 1808). It was revived by his daughter Natalie, who sang a "duet" with her father by dubbing in her voice onto his recording. Their version was a number 14 hit in 1991, charting for ten weeks and selling over half a million copies. It helped relaunch the younger Cole's career as a mainstream singer.

## UP ON THE ROOF
Gerry Goffin and Carole King
Aldon Muisc—New York
1962
Number 5 hit for the Drifters (Atlantic 2162) in 1963. A classic of early 1960s pop, and covered countless times since.

## UPTOWN GIRL
Billy Joel (w & m)
Joel Songs
1983
A million-seller for Joel that crested at number 3, with a total of sixteen weeks on the charts (Columbia 04149). Written for Joel's second wife, Christie Brinkley.

## UP WHERE WE BELONG
Buffy Sainte Marie and Jack Nitzsche
(w: Will Jennings)
Famous Music—New York
1982
**Film:** *An Officer and a Gentleman* (Paramount)
Academy Award winner for Best Song. Joe Cocker and Jennifer Warnes had the number 1 hit, which charted for fifteen weeks and sold over two million copies (Island 99996).

## UPSIDE DOWN
Nile Rodgers and Bernard Edwards
Chic Music
1980
Diana Ross had the number 1 hit, which charted for seventeen weeks (Motown 1494). It sold over one million copies, and was a comeback hit for Ross.

## VARSITY DRAG, THE
Ray Henderson (w: Bud DeSylva and Lew Brown)

DeSylva, Brown and Henderson—New York
1927
**Show:** *Good News*
Introduced in the show by Zelma O'Neal, accompanied by George Olsen and his Music. Olsen also recorded it (Victor 20875), as did Edna Fischer as a piano solo (Victor 21384). The song was one of three that created dance fads in the 1920s (the other two were "The Charleston" and "The Black Bottom"). Dorothy McNulty and Billy Taft sang it in the first film version (MGM, 1930) and June Allyson and Peter Lawford sang it in the second (MGM, 1947).

## VENUS
R. Van Leeuwen (w & m)
Fat Zach Music—New York
1969
Number 1 hit in 1970 for Dutch rockers Shocking Blue (Colossus 108); sixteen years later, revived as a number 1 hit by British new wavers Bananarama (London 886056). Not to be confused with the 1959 number 1 hit by Frankie Avalon (Chancellor 1031).

## VERY THOUGHT OF YOU, THE
Ray Noble (w & m)
M. Witmark and Sons—New York
1934
Ray Noble and His Orchestra not only had the number 1 hit, which charted for fourteen weeks, but used it as his theme song (Victor 24657). Ricky Nelson revived it in 1964 with a number 26 hit that charted for five weeks (Decca 31612).

## VISION OF LOVE
Mariah Carey and Ben Margulies
Vision of Love Songs
1990, 1991
Mariah Carey's first release and first number 1 hit in 1990, which charted for seventeen weeks (Columbia 73348). It sold over half a million copies.

## VOGUE
Madonna Ciccone and Shep Pettibone
WB Music
1990

Number 1 dance hit for Madonna, promoted by a clever video. It held the top spot for three out of sixteen chart weeks, and sold over three million copies (Sire 19863). Based on the short-lived dance fad, "voguing."

## VOLARE (NEL BLU DIPINTO DI BLU)
Domenico Modugno (w: Mitchell Parish)
Robbins Music—New York
1958
Number 1 hit for Italian actor/singer Domenico Modugno, holding the top spot for five out of thirteen chart weeks, and selling half a million copies (Decca 30677). Immediately covered for a number 12 hit by Dean Martin (Capitol 4028), and covered in 1960 by Bobby Rydell for a number 4 hit (Cameo 179). Al Martino scored a number 33 hit in 1975 (Capitol 4134). Has become a lounge singer's favorite; also provided the name for a Plymouth car of the 1970s.

## WABASH BLUES
Fred Meinken (w: Dave Ringle)
Leo Feist—New York
1921
Introduced and featured by Isham Jones and His Orchestra; his recording sold over a million copies (Brunswick 5065). The Benson Orchestra, with Roy Bargy at the piano, also had a hit recording (Victor 18820). It has become a jazz band favorite.

## WAIT TILL THE SUN SHINES, NELLIE
Harry Von Tilzer (w: Andrew B. Sterling)
Harry Von Tilzer—New York
1905
One of the greatest hits of this decade, it was introduced in vaudeville by Winona Winter. Byron G. Harlan had the hit recording in 1906 (Columbia 3321). Mary Martin and Bing Crosby sang it in the film *The Birth of the Blues* (Paramount, 1941) and in the film that bore the song's name (20th Century Fox, 1952). A great favorite of barbershop quartets.

## WAITING FOR THE ROBERT E. LEE
Lewis Muir (w: L. Wolfe Gilbert)
F. A. Mills—New York
1912

Introduced in vaudeville by Al Jolson. Ruth Roye helped to build sales of over a million copies of sheet music. Dolly Connolly had a hit recording (Columbia A-1197). It was revived for the film *The Story of Vernon and Irene Castle* (RKO, 1939), and used again when Judy Garland sang it in the film *Babes of Broadway* (MGM, 1941). Al Jolson came full circle when he sang it on the soundtrack for his biopic *The Jolson Story* (Columbia, 1946).

## WAKE THE TOWN AND TELL THE PEOPLE
Jerry Livingston (w: Sammy Gallop)
Joy Music—New York
1955
Les Baxter, with vocals by the Notables, had the number 5 hit that charted for twelve weeks (Capitol 3120).

## WAKE UP, LITTLE SUSIE
Boudleaux and Felice Bryant
Acuff-Rose Publications—Nashville
1957
The Everly Brothers had the number 1 hit, which charted for twenty weeks and sold over one million copies (Cadence 1337). Simon and Garfunkel's version, recorded at their Central Park reunion concert in 1979, reached number 27 in 1982 (Warner Bros. 50053).

## WALK DON'T RUN
Johnny Smith
Forshay Music—New York
1960
Originally composed by jazz guitarist Smith and recorded by him, the instrumental became a number 2 hit when it was released by the guitar-twanging group the Ventures, in 1960 (Dolton 25). Rerecorded by them four years later, it charted again, this time reaching number 8 (Dolton 96). A surf-rock perennial.

## WALK LIKE A MAN
Bob Crewe and Bob Gaudio
Bo Bob Music—New York
1963
The Four Seasons had the number 1 hit, which charted for twelve weeks (Vee-Jay 485).

## WALK RIGHT IN
Erik Darling and Willard Svanoe
Ryerson Music—New York
1962, 1963
The Rooftop Singers had the number 1 hit, which charted for eleven weeks and sold more than one million copies (Vanguard 35017). A favorite of the early 1960s folk-song movement.

## WALKIN' MY BABY BACK HOME
Fred Ahlert/Roy Turk/Harry Richman
DeSylva, Brown and Henderson—New York
1930
In 1931, two versions of this song both reached number 8 on the charts, and charted for a total of five weeks, recorded by Nick Lucas, the singing guitarist (Brunswick 6048), and Ted Weems and His Orchestra (Victor 22637). Johnny Ray revived it in 1952 with a number 4 hit that charted for twenty weeks (Columbia 39750).

## WALKIN' THE DOG
Shelton Brooks (w & m)
Will Rossiter—Chicago
1916
Introduced in vaudeville by Delta and Alpha Mudge. Revived in 1950 by Pete Daily and His Dixieland Band (Capitol 1486).

## WALLFLOWER, THE (AKA DANCE WITH ME HENRY)
James Etta Rogers and Phyliss Otis
Modern Music—New York
1955
Etta James recorded the original of this song, which she called "Roll With Me Henry" (Modern 947) as an answer song to Hank Ballard's 1954 R&B hit "Work With Me Annie" (Federal 12169); seeking to hide the sexual double entendre, the song was retitled "The Wallflower." Georgia Gibbs had the cover version, which was a number 1 hit as "Dance With Me Henry"; it charted for twenty weeks and sold over one million copies (Mercury 70572).

## WANG WANG BLUES, THE
Gus Mueller/"Buster" Johnson/Henry Busse
Leo Feist—New York
1921
Introduced in vaudeville by Paul Whiteman and His Orchestra, it was composed by his clarinetist (Mueller), trombonist (Johnson), and lead trumpeter (Busse); their recording sold over one million copies (Victor 18694). Bennie Krueger also had a hit recording (Brunswick 2083). It was revived in 1951 when Benny Goodman's 1941 sextet version was rereleased (Columbia 39478).

## WANNABE
Spice Girls/Matthew Rowebottom/
Richard Stannard
Full Keel Music
1997
The Spice Girls, a manufactured girl group from England, created tremendous publicity when they first appeared. Their first disc became number 1 and stayed on the chart for twenty-two weeks (Virgin 38579). It sold over one million copies. But the group had a short life; within two years, it had splintered and the hits had ended.

## WAR
Norman Whitfield and Barrett Strong
Jobete Music—Detroit
1970
Soulful antiwar hit—number 1 for singer Edwin Starr—that held the top spot for three out of thirteen weeks on the charts (Gordy 7101). Revived by Bruce Springsteen during his 1985-86 "Born in the U.S.A." tour. His live version reached number 8 on the charts in 1986 (Columbia 06432). Famous for its "War—Huh!—What is it good for?" chorus.

## WATERFALLS
Marqueze Etheridge/Lisa Lopes/Rico Wade/
Pat Brown/Ramon Murray
EMI April Music
1994
TLC, a female vocal trio, scored seven Top 10 hits in the 1990s. This number 1 hit charted for twenty-eight weeks and sold over one million copies (LaFace 24107).

## WATERMELON MAN
Herbie Hancock
Hancock Music—Bronx, New York
1963

Mongo Santamaria had the number 10 pop hit, which remained on the charts six weeks (Battle 45909). Hancock recorded it several times over his career, and it has become a modern jazz standard.

## WAY DOWN YONDER IN NEW ORLEANS
Turner Layton (w: Henry Creamer)
Shapiro, Bernstein—New York
1922
**Show:** *Strut Miss Lizzie*
Introduced by the composers in their revue, which quickly closed, it was then put into the show *Spice of 1922*. It was featured with great success by Blossom Seeley in vaudeville, and her recording helped establish it as a standard (Columbia A-3731); Paul Whiteman's version also helped (Victor 19030). It has become a favorite of jazz bands ever since the Cotton Pickers (Brunswick 2404) and Frankie Trumbauer with Bix Beiderbecke (Okeh 40843, 1927) made their hit recordings. It was revived in 1950 by Ray Anthony and His Orchestra, with piano solos by Lou Busch (Capitol 958), and again in 1953 by Frankie Laine and Jo Stafford, accompanied by Paul Weston and His Orchestra, with piano solo by Carl Fischer (Columbia 40116). It was revived again in 1960 by pop singer Freddie Cannon in a number 3 hit, which charted for eleven weeks and sold over one million copies (Swan 4043).

## WAY IT IS
B. R. Hornsby (w & m)
Zappo Music
1986
First single released by the jazz-flavored pianist/songwriter Bruce Hornsby, reaching number 1 and charting for fifteen weeks (RCA 5023). A light piece of social commentary, marked by Hornsby's excellent piano work.

## WAY WE WERE, THE
Marvin Hamlisch (w: Alan and Marilyn Bergman)
Colgems Music—New York
1973
**Film:** *The Way We Were* (Columbia)
Academy Award winner for Best Song. Barbra Streisand, who starred in the film, had the number 1 hit, which charted for seventeen weeks (Columbia 45944). It sold over two million copies.

## WAY YOU DO THE THINGS YOU DO, THE
William Robinson and Bobby Rogers
Jobete Music—Detroit
1964
Although only a number 11 hit—and the first charting single—for the Temptations in its original release (Gordy 7028), it remains a perennial classic. Two original members of the group, Eddie Kendricks and David Ruffin, revived it, along with pop stars Hall and Oates in 1985 for a number 20 single (RCA 14178). Oddly, the biggest hit version came from the new-wave British rock group UB40, who reached number 6 with the song in 1990 (Virgin 98978).

## WAY YOU LOOK TONIGHT, THE
Jerome Kern (w: Dorothy Fields)
Chappell—New York
1936
**Film:** *Swing Time* (RKO)
Academy Award winner for Best Song. Fred Astaire, who sang it in the film, had the number 1 hit recording that retained its position for six of the seventeen weeks on the chart (Brunswick 7717). Billie Holiday, with Teddy Wilson's Orchestra, made a number 3 hit on the charts (Brunswick 7762). The song has become a jazz and cabaret standard.

## WAY YOU MAKE ME FEEL, THE
Michael Jackson (w & m)
Mijak Music
1987
Number 1 pop hit in 1988 for Michael Jackson, charting for thirteen weeks, as well as a number 1 R&B single (Epic 07645).

## WAYWARD WIND, THE
Herb Newman and Stan Lebowsky
Warman Music—Hollywood
1956
Gogi Grant had the number 1 hit, which charted for twenty-two weeks and sold over one million copies (Era 1013).

## WE ARE THE WORLD
Michael Jackson and Lionel Richie

Mijac Music and Brockman Music—New York
1985
USA for Africa, a star-studded group of rock, R&B, and pop performers getting together to help the starving people of Africa, had the number 1 hit that charted for twelve weeks (Columbia 04839). It sold over six million copies.

## WE BUILT THIS CITY
Starship (w & m)
Little Mole Music
1985
Starship had this number 1 hit, which charted for fifteen weeks (Grunt 14170). It sold over one million copies.

## WE DIDN'T START THE FIRE
Billy Joel (w & m)
Joel Songs
1989
Four decades of U.S. history reduced to three minutes, primarily a litany of names and events. It spent two weeks at number 1 on the pop charts, out of a total of fifteen weeks (Columbia 73021).

## WE MAY NEVER LOVE LIKE THIS AGAIN
Al Kasha and Joel Kirschhorn
20th Century Fox and Warner Bros.—New York
1974
**Film:** *The Towering Inferno* (20th Century Fox)
Academy Award winner for Best Song. Maureen McGovern sang it in the film.

## WE SHALL OVERCOME
Zilphia Horton/Frank Hamilton/
Guy Carawan/Pete Seeger
Ludlow Music—New York
1960, 1963
Taken from a folk hymn (originally "I Shall Overcome"), this became the anthem for the civil rights and anti–Vietnam War movements.

## WEAK
Brian Alexander Morgan (w & m)
Warner-Tamerlane
1992, 1993

SWV (Sisters with Voices), a vocal trio, had this number 1 hit that charted for twenty-two weeks (RCA 62521). It sold over one million copies.

## WEDDING BELL BLUES
Laura Nyro (w & m)
Celestial Music—Great Neck, N.Y.
1966
A number 1 hit in 1969 for the vocal group the Fifth Dimension, holding that position for three out of fourteen weeks on the chart, and selling over a million copies (Soul City 779). Originally recorded on Laura Nyro's debut album, *More than A New Discovery* (Verve Forecast 3020) in 1967.

## WEDDING BELLS ARE BREAKING UP THAT OLD GANG OF MINE
Sammy Fain (w: Irving Kahal and
Willie Raskin)
Waterson, Berlin and Snyder—New York
1929
Johnny Perkins introduced it in vaudeville. Norman Brokenshire and His Gang introduced it on radio over WCAU, Philadelphia. Gene Austin had the hit recording (Victor 21893). The Four Aces had a number 22 hit in 1954 (Decca 29123).

## WEDDING OF THE PAINTED DOLL
Nacio Herb Brown (w: Arthur Freed)
Sherman, Clay—San Francisco
1929
**Film:** *Broadway Melody* (MGM)
Introduced in the film by Charles King, who had a hit recording (Victor 21964). Leo Reisman and His Orchestra had the hit instrumental (Columbia 1780-D). It was revived in the film *Singin' in the Rain* (MGM, 1952).

## WELL, DID YOU EVAH?
Cole Porter (w & m)
Chappell and Co.—New York
1940
**Show:** *DuBarry Was a Lady*
Betty Grable and Charles Walters sang it in the show. Bing Crosby and Frank Sinatra sang it in the film *High Society* (MGM, 1956).

## WE'RE OFF TO SEE THE WIZARD
Harold Arlen (w: E.Y. Harburg)
Leo Feist—New York
1939
**Film:** *The Wizard of Oz* (MGM)
Judy Garland, Ray Bolger, Jack Haley, and Bert Lahr sang it in the film.

## WEST END BLUES
Joe Oliver (w: Clarence Williams)
Clarence Williams Music—New York
1928
This jazz classic was made famous by Louis Armstrong and His Hot Five (Okeh 8597), with what is perhaps Armstrong's finest solo work on disc. It has become a New Orleans jazz favorite.

## WHAT A DIFF'RENCE A DAY MADE
Maria Grever (w: Stanley Adams)
Edward B. Marks Music—New York
1934
The Dorsey Brothers Orchestra, with vocals by Bob Crosby, had the number 5 hit, which charted for seven weeks (Decca 283). Andy Russell revived it in 1944 with a number 14 hit that charted for eight weeks (Capitol 167). Dinah Washington revived it again in 1959 with a number 8 hit that charted for fourteen weeks (Mercury 71435), and Esther Phillips revived it yet again in 1975 with a number 20 hit that charted for nine weeks (Kudu 925).

## WHAT A WONDERFUL WORLD
George David Weiss and Bob Thiele
Valando Music—New York
1967
Louis Armstrong recorded it in 1967 (ABC 10982). When the disc was featured in the film *Good Morning, Vietnam* (Touchstone, 1988), it was rereleased and became a number 32 hit, which charted for three weeks (A&M 3010).

## WHAT CAN I SAY AFTER I SAY I'M SORRY?
Walter Donaldson and Abe Lyman
Leo Feist—New York
1926

Introduced in vaudeville by Bee Palmer. Ruth Etting also made it popular. A hit vocal recording was made by Jane Gray, with Rube Bloom accompanying at the piano (Harmony 114-H). Abe Lyman's Orchestra did a nice instrumental version (Brunswick 3069).

## WHAT DID I DO TO BE SO BLACK AND BLUE
Thomas Waller and Harry Brooks (w: Andy Razaf)
Mills Music—New York
1929
**Show:** *Connie's Hot Chocolates*
Introduced in the show by Edith Wilson. Ethel Waters had the hit recording (Columbia 2184-D). The song is used as one of the themes of Ralph Ellison's classic novel *Invisible Man* (1952).

## WHAT DO YOU DO SUNDAYS, MARY?
Stephen Jones (w: Irving Caesar)
Harms—New York
1923
**Show:** *Poppy*
Introduced in the show by Robert Woolsey. Paul Whiteman and His Orchestra had the hit recording (Victor 19145), followed by Carl Fenton and His Orchestra, with piano interlude by Phil Ohman (Brunswick 2487), and the Ambassadors (Vocalion 14681).

## WHAT IS THIS THING CALLED LOVE?
Cole Porter (w & m)
Harms—New York
1930
**Show:** *Wake Up and Dream*
Frances Shelley sang it and Tilly Losch and Toni Birkmayer danced to it in the show. Leo Reisman and His Orchestra had the number 5 hit that charted for nine weeks (Victor 22282). Artie Shaw and His Orchestra revived it in 1939 with a number 15 hit (Bluebird 10001), and three years later, Tommy Dorsey and His Orchestra, with vocal by Connie Haines, had a number 13 hit (Victor 27782). Ginny Simms sang it in the Cole Porter biopic *Night and Day* (Warner Bros., 1946). Les Paul revived it again in 1948 with a number 11 hit (Capitol 15070).

## WHAT KIND OF FOOL AM I?
Leslie Bricusse and Anthony Newley

Essex Music—New York

1961

**Show:** *Stop the World—I Want To Get Off*

Anthony Newley sang it in the show. Sammy Davis Jr. had the number 17 hit that charted for ten weeks (Reprise 20,048). Rick Springfield revived it in 1982 with a number 21 hit that charted for nine weeks (RCA 13245).

## WHAT THE WORLD NEEDS NOW IS LOVE

Burt Bacharach (w: Hal David)

Blue Seas Music

1965

Jackie DeShannon had the number 7 hit, which charted for nine weeks (Imperial 66110). A classic of the light pop that Bacharach and David so effortlessly produced in the mid-1960s.

## WHAT YOU GOIN' TO DO WHEN THE RENT COMES ROUND?

Harry Von Tilzer (w: Andrew B. Sterling)

Harry Von Tilzer—New York

1905

A great song in syncopation by dialect singer Arthur Collins (Victor 4432). Revived in 1950 by Jimmy Durante and Eddie Jackson (MGM 30255).

## WHAT'LL I DO?

Irving Berlin (w & m)

Irving Berlin—New York

1924

**Show:** *Music Box Revue*

Grace Moore sang it in the show. It has become a standard and one of Berlin's biggest-selling ballads. Paul Whiteman and His Orchestra had the hit recording (Victor 19299). It was used in the film *Alexander's Ragtime Band* (20th Century Fox, 1938).

## WHATEVER LOLA WANTS

Richard Adler and Jerry Ross

Frank Music—New York

1955

**Show:** *Damn Yankees*

Gwen Verdon sang it in the show. Sarah Vaughan had the number 6 hit that charted for eleven weeks (Mercury 70595).

## WHATEVER WILL BE, WILL BE (QUE SERA, SERA)

Jay Livingston and Ray Evans

Artists Music—New York

1955

**Film:** *The Man Who Knew Too Much* (Paramount)

Academy Award winner for Best Song. Doris Day, who sang it in the film, had the number 2 hit, which charted for twenty-two weeks (Columbia 40704). It sold over one million copies.

## WHAT'S NEW PUSSYCAT?

Burt Bacharach (w: Hal David)

United Artists Music

1965

**Film:** *What's New Pussycat?* (United Artists)

Theme song for the film of the same name, Woody Allen's first screen comedy. A number 3 hit for Tom Jones, charting for ten weeks (Parrot 9765).

## WHAT'S GOING ON?

Marvin Gaye/Al Cleveland/Renaldo Benson

Jobete Music—Detroit

1970, 1971

Number 2 hit for Gaye, the title track from his eloquent album commenting on current events, including Vietnam, the civil rights movement, and black power. It held the number 2 spot for three out of thirteen weeks on the charts, and held the number 1 R&B spot for five weeks (Tamla 54201).

## WHAT'S LOVE GOT TO DO WITH IT?

Graham Lyle and Terry Britten

Good Single

1984

Tina Turner had the number 1 hit that charted for eighteen weeks (Capitol 5354). It sold over one million copies, and launched her 1980s-era comeback.

## WHEEL OF FORTUNE

Bennie Benjamin and George Weiss

Laurel Music—New York

1952

Kay Starr had the number 1 hit, which charted for twenty-five weeks and sold over one million copies (Capitol 1964).

## WHEN A MAN LOVES A WOMAN
Calvin Lewis and Andrew Wright
Pronto Music—New York
1966
Percy Sledge had the number 1 hit that charted for ten weeks (Atlantic 2326). It was revived in 1991 by Michael Bolton, who also had a number 1 hit, which charted for sixteen weeks (Columbia 74020). A classic R&B ballad.

## WHEN CAN I SEE YOU
Babyface (w & m)
Sony Songs
1993
Babyface, whose real name is Kenneth Edmonds, has had a dominant role in the 1990s, not only as a song-writer and solo artist, but as a record producer and co-owner of LaFace Records. This number 4 hit stayed on the charts for thirty weeks (Epic 77550). It sold over half a million copies.

## WHEN DOVES CRY
Prince (w & m)
Controversy Music
1984
Prince's biggest hit, it became number 1, a position it held for five out of sixteen chart weeks (Warner 29286). It sold over two million copies.

## WHEN I LOST YOU
Irving Berlin (w & m)
Waterson, Berlin and Snyder—New York
1912
Written on the death of his first wife, Berlin's heartbreak shows through. It sold over two million copies of sheet music. Henry Burr had the hit recording (Victor 17275).

## WHEN I TAKE MY SUGAR TO TEA
Sammy Fain/Irving Kahal/Pierre Norman
Famous Music—New York
1931
The Boswell Sisters had the number 6 hit, which charted for six weeks (Brunswick 6083).

## WHEN I'M NOT NEAR THE GIRL I LOVE
Burton Lane (w: E. Y. Harburg)
Crawford Music—New York
1946
**Show:** *Finian's Rainbow*
David Wayne sang it in the show. Tommy Steel sang it in the film (Warner Bros., 1968).

## WHEN IRISH EYES ARE SMILING
Ernest R. Ball (w: Chauncey Olcott and George Graff Jr.)
M. Witmark and Sons—New York
1912
**Show:** *The Isle O' Dreams*
Introduced in the show by colyricist Chauncey Olcott. He also had the hit record (Columbia A-1310). It was revived in the Ball biopic *Irish Eyes Are Smiling* (20th Century Fox, 1944) and in the Olcott biopic *My Wild Irish Rose* (Warner Bros., 1947). A St. Patrick's Day perennial.

## WHEN IT'S ALL GOIN' OUT AND NOTHIN' COMIN' IN
Bert Williams and George Walker (rev. w: James Weldon Johnson)
Jos. W. Stern—New York
1902
Bert Williams introduced it in vaudeville and made its recording (Victor 994). It was subsequently interpolated into the white show *Sally in Our Alley*.

## WHEN IT'S SLEEPY TIME DOWN SOUTH
Leon and Otis Rene and Clarence Muse
New Idea Man Organization
1930
Paul Whiteman and His Orchestra had the number 6 hit in 1931 that charted for ten weeks (Victor 22828). Louis Armstrong and His Orchestra recorded it first, in 1931, and it became his theme song (Okeh 41504). He revived it in 1952, backed by the Gordon Jenkins Orchestra, and he had a number 19 hit (Decca 27899).

## WHEN MY BABY SMILES AT ME
Bill Munro (w: Andrew B. Sterling and Ted Lewis)
Harry Von Tilzer—New York
1920
**Show:** *The Greenwich Village Follies of 1919*

Introduced in the show by Ted Lewis and His Jazz Band, who also had the hit recording (Columbia A-2908). It became his theme song. He rerecorded it in 1938 and it became a hit again (Decca 2054). It was used in the film of the same name (20th Century Fox, 1948).

## WHEN MY BABY WALKS DOWN THE STREET

Jimmy McHugh/Gene Austin/Irving Mills

Jack Mills—New York

1924

Introduced and recorded by lyricist Gene Austin as a duet with Aileen Stanley (Victor 19585). Other hit recordings include Warner's Seven Aces (Columbia 305-D) and Waring's Pennsylvanians (Victor 19610).

## WHEN RAGTIME ROSIE RAGGED THE ROSARY

Lewis F. Muir (w: Edgar Leslie)

F. A. Mills—New York

1911

A favorite in vaudeville, and now with Dixieland jazz bands.

## WHEN THE MIDNIGHT CHOO-CHOO LEAVES FOR ALABAM'

Irving Berlin (w & m)

Waterson, Berlin and Snyder—New York

1912

Hit recording by Arthur Collins and Byron Harlan (Victor 17246). Revived by Alice Faye in *Alexander's Ragtime Band* (20th Century Fox, 1938), by Fred Astaire and Judy Garland in *Easter Parade* (MGM, 1948) and by the cast of *There's No Business Like Show Business* (20th Century Fox, 1954).

## WHEN THE MOON COMES OVER THE MOUNTAIN

Harry Woods/Howard Johnson/Kate Smith

Robbins Music—New York

1931

Kate Smith had the number 1 hit, which charted for eight weeks (Columbia 2516-D). It became her theme song for her radio show and for personal appearances. She sang it in the film *The Big Broadcast* (Paramount, 1932).

## WHEN THE RED, RED ROBIN COMES BOB, BOB BOBBIN' ALONG

Harry Woods (w & m)

Irving Berlin—New York

1926

Al Jolson had the hit vocal recording (Brunswick 3222), and Paul Whiteman and His Orchestra the instrumental hit (Victor 20177). The song sold over one million copies of sheet music and became a standard. Doris Day revived it in 1953 (Columbia 39970) and Susan Hayward sang it in the Lillian Roth biopic *I'll Cry Tomorrow* (MGM, 1956).

## WHEN WILL I BE LOVED?

Phil Everly (w & m)

Acuff-Rose—Nashville

1960

Number 8 hit for the Everly Brothers (Cadence 1380) in its original recording. However, Linda Ronstadt had the biggest hit, with her version recorded fifteen years later. It reached number 2, a spot it held for two out of thirteen weeks on the charts, and also topped the country charts (Capitol 4050).

## WHEN YOU BELIEVE

Stephen Schwartz and Babyface

SKG Songs

1997, 1998

**Film:** *The Prince of Egypt* (DreamWorks)

Academy Award winner for Best Song. Whitney Houston and Mariah Carey had the number 15 hit that charted seven weeks (DreamWorks 59022). It sold over half a million copies.

## WHEN YOU WISH UPON A STAR

Leigh Harline (w: Ned Washington)

Irving Berlin—New York

1940

**Film:** *Pinocchio* (Disney)

The seventh Academy Award winner for Best Song. The incredibly popular Glenn Miller and His Orchestra had the number 1 hit, which charted for sixteen weeks (Bluebird 10570). Cliff Edwards, who sang it in the film, scored the number 10 hit (Victor 26477). Revived in 1960 by Dion and the Belmonts for a number 30 hit (Laurie 3052).

## WHEN YOU WORE A TULIP AND I WORE A BIG RED ROSE

Percy Wenrich (w: Jack Mahoney)

Leo Feist—New York

1914

Introduced in vaudeville by Dolly Connolly, who made it an instant hit. The American Quartet had the hit record (Victor 17652). Revived in the film *For Me and My Gal* (MGM, 1942) by Judy Garland and Gene Kelly; their recording, backed by David Rose's Orchestra, made it a number 19 hit once again (Decca 18480).

## WHEN YOU'RE GOOD YOU'RE LONESOME

Grace Doro (w & m)

Jerome H. Remick—New York

1920

Edythe Baker made an outstanding piano roll (Melodee 3749).

## WHEN YOU'RE SMILING

Mark Fisher/Joe Goodwin/Larry Shay

Harold Rossiter—Chicago

1928

Seger Ellis had the hit recording (Columbia 1494-D). Louis Armstrong had a popular version that helped make this a standard (Okeh 41298). Joe "Fingers" Carr revived it in 1951 (Capitol 1974), and Frank Sinatra sang it in the film *Meet Danny Wilson* (Universal, 1952).

## WHERE DID OUR LOVE GO?

Eddie Holland/Lamont Dozier/Brian Holland

Jobete Music—Detroit

1964

The Supremes' first number 1 pop hit, holding that position for two out of thirteen weeks on the charts (Motown 1060). It launched their three-year hit-making career with Diana Ross and established their basic sound.

## WHERE DID ROBINSON CRUSOE GO WITH FRIDAY ON SATURDAY NIGHT?

George W. Meyer (w: Sam Lewis and Joe Young)

Waterson, Berlin and Snyder—New York

1916

**Show:** *Robinson Crusoe Jr.*

Great comic song introduced in the show by Al Jolson, who also made the hit recording (Columbia A-1976).

## WHERE DID YOU GET THAT GIRL?

Harry Puck (w: Bert Kalmar)

Kalmar and Puck—New York

1913

Introduced in vaudeville by Lewis and Dody. Walter Van Brunt had the hit record (Victor 17414).

## WHERE DO BROKEN HEARTS GO?

Frank Wildhorn and Chuck Jackson

Scaramanga Music

1985, 1988

Number 1 hit in 1988 for pop chanteuse Whitney Houston, holding that position for two out of thirteen weeks on the charts; also an adult-contemporary number 1 (Arista 9674). A fine pop ballad.

## WHERE OR WHEN

Richard Rodgers (w: Lorenz Hart)

Chappell—New York

1937

**Show:** *Babes in Arms*

Mitzi Green and Ray Heatherton sang it in the show. Hal Kemp and His Orchestra with vocal by Skinnay Ennis had the number 1 hit, which charted for sixteen weeks (Brunswick 7856). Judy Garland, Douglas MacPhail, and Betty Jaynes sang it in the film version (MGM, 1939). Guy Lombardo and His Royal Canadians revived it in 1943 with a number 19 hit (Decca 18548), Lena Horne sang it in the Rodgers and Hart biopic *Words and Music* (MGM, 1948), and Dion and the Belmonts revived it yet again in 1960 with a number 3 hit that charted for eleven weeks (Laurie 3044).

## WHERE THE BLUE OF THE NIGHT MEETS THE GOLD OF THE DAY

Fred Ahlert/Roy Turk/Bing Crosby

DeSylva, Brown and Henderson—New York

1931

Bing Crosby sang it in the film *The Big Broadcast* (Paramount, 1932) and recorded it the same year, achieving a number 4 hit that charted for seven weeks (Brunswick 6226). Crosby used it as his radio theme song, and it became forever identified with him. The music is based on "Tit-Willow" from the Gilbert and Sullivan operetta *The Mikado*.

## WHIP-POOR-WILL

Jerome Kern (w: B.G. DeSylva)

T. B. Harms—New York

1920

**Show:** *Sally*

Introduced in the show by Marilyn Miller and Irving Fisher. Isham Jones and His Orchestra had the hit recording (Brunswick 5045). It was revived in the Miller biopic *Look for the Silver Lining* (Warner Bros., 1949).

## WHISPERING

John Schonberger (w: Malvin Schonberger)

Sherman, Clay—San Francisco

1920

Introduced by Paul Whiteman and His Orchestra, whose recording sold over two million copies (Victor 18690). The song became a standard. Les Paul had a number 7 hit, which charted for sixteen weeks in 1951 (Capitol 1748). Fittingly, Paul Whiteman's last hit recording was of this song in 1954, thirty-four years after his first hit (Coral 61228).

## WHISTLE WHILE YOU WORK

Frank Churchill (w: Larry Morey)

Irving Berlin—New York

1937

**Film:** *Snow White and the Seven Dwarfs* (Disney)

Adriana Caselotti sang it in the film with the dwarfs. Taken from the soundtrack, the Seven Dwarfs had the number 2 hit that charted for thirteen weeks (Victor 25736).

## WHISTLER AND HIS DOG, THE

Arthur Pryor

Carl Fischer—New York

1905

Theme song for radio's *Big Jon and Sparky* show that features the whistling of the catchy melody. Prince's Band had the original hit recording (Columbia A-64).

## WHISTLING RUFUS

Kerry Mills

F. A. Mills—New York

1899

Another cakewalk hit from the master. John Philip Sousa toured Europe the following year and played it as an encore. It was especially popular in England, where bands recorded it for the following fifty years. Banjoist Vess L. Ossman made six recordings of it in six years between 1900 and 1906. It has become a favorite of Dixieland bands.

## WHITE CHRISTMAS

Irving Berlin (w & m)

Irving Berlin—New York

1942

**Film:** *Holiday Inn* (Paramount)

Academy Award winner for Best Song. Sung by Bing Crosby and Marjorie Reynolds in film. Bing Crosby had the number 1 hit, which originally charted for eleven weeks in that position out of seventeen in the Top 40 (Decca 18429). He rerecorded it in 1947, and achieved a number 1 hit again; this later version continued to chart for the next twenty Christmas seasons (Decca 23778). Both versions combined became the best-selling single ever, eventually selling over fifty million copies. Needless to say, a holiday favorite.

## WHITE RABBITT

Grace Slick (w & m)

Copper Penny Music—Hollywood

1966, 1967

Jefferson Airplane had this number 8 hit, which charted for nine weeks (RCA Victor 9248). The song is based on *Alice's Adventures in Wonderland*, with a healthy dose of 1960s drug references thrown in.

## WHITER SHADE OF PALE

Keith Reid and Gary Brooker

Essex Music—New York

1967

Number 5 hit for art-rockers Procol Harum that took its melody from a Bach cantata (Deram 7507). A perennial FM-radio favorite.

## WHO?

Jerome Kern (w: Otto Harbach and Oscar Hammerstein)

Harms—New York

1925

**Show:** *Sunny*

Marilyn Miller and Paul Frawley sang it in the show. George Olsen and His Music had the hit recording

(Victor 19840). Marilyn Miller and Lawrence Gray sang it in the first film version (First National, 1930). Anna Neagle and John Carroll sang it in the second version (RKO, 1941). Tommy Dorsey and His Orchestra revived it with a number 5 hit that charted for ten weeks in 1937 (Victor 25693). Judy Garland sang it in the Kern biopic *Till the Clouds Roll By* (MGM, 1946). Ray Bolger sang it in the Marilyn Miller biopic *Look For the Silver Lining* (Warner Bros., 1949).

## WHO CAN IT BE NOW?
Colin Hay (w & m)
Blackwood Music
1982
Australian pop rockers Men At Work had the number 1 hit, which charted for seventeen weeks (Columbia 02888). Colin Hay was lead vocalist and guitarist for the group.

## WHO TAKES CARE OF THE CARETAKER'S DAUGHTER WHILE THE CARETAKER'S BUSY TAKING CARE?
Chick Endor (w & m)
Shapiro, Bernstein—New York
1925
Introduced in vaudeville by Cliff Edwards who had the hit vocal recording (Pathé 025128). Whitey Kaufman had the hit instrumental (Victor 19638). It was revived in an album in 1961, performed by Joe "Fingers" Carr and the Girls from Club sixteen (*The Riotous, Raucous, Red-Hot 20's*, Warner Bros. 1423).

## WHO WOULDN'T LOVE YOU?
Carl Fisher (w: Bill Carey)
Music World—Hollywood
1942
Kay Kyser and His Orchestra had the number 1 hit, which charted for twenty-three weeks and sold over one million copies (Columbia 36526).

## WHOLE LOT-TA SHAKIN' GOIN' ON
Dave Williams and Sunny David
Marlyn-Copar—New York
1957

Jerry Lee Lewis had the number 3 hit, which charted for twenty weeks and sold over one million copies (Sun 267). Along with "Great Balls of Fire," a classic performance by Lewis and a song forever associated with him.

## WHOLE LOTTA LOVING
Antoine Domino and Dave Bartholomew
Marquis Music—Hollywood
1958
Fats Domino had the number 6 hit, which charted for twelve weeks and sold over one million copies (Imperial 5553).

## WHOLE NEW WORLD, A
Alan Menken (w: Tim Rice)
Wonderland Music
1992
**Film:** *Aladdin* (Disney)
Academy Award winner for Best Song. Peabo Bryson and Regina Belle had the number 1 hit, which charted for eighteen weeks (Columbia 74751). It sold over half a million copies.

## WHO'LL TAKE MY PLACE WHEN I'M GONE?
Billy Fazioli (w: Ray Klages)
Broadway Music—New York
1922
Great song of the 1920s. Hit recordings by Bennie Krueger and His Orchestra (Brunswick 2303) and Markel's Orchestra (Okeh 4665).

## WHO'S AFRAID OF THE BIG BAD WOLF?
Frank E. Churhill and Ann Ronnell
Irving Berlin—New York
1933
**Film:** *The Three Little Pigs* (Disney)
Don Bestor and His Orchestra had the number 2 hit that charted for eight weeks (Victor 24410). The song plays a major role in Edward Albee's dark comedy, *Who's Afraid of Virginia Woolf?* (1964).

## WHO'S SORRY NOW?
Ted Snyder (w: Bert Kalmar and Harry Ruby)
Waterson, Berlin and Snyder—New York
1923

A standard that sold over one million copies of sheet music. Van and Schenck introduced it in vaudeville. The hit instrumental recording was by Isham Jones and His Orchestra (Brunswick 2438), and the hit vocal by Marion Harris (Brunswick 2443). Gloria De Haven sang it in the Kalmar-Ruby biopic *Three Little Words* (MGM, 1950). It was revived in 1958 by Connie Francis, who had a number 4 hit that charted for thirteen weeks and sold over one million copies (MGM 12588). It was revived again in 1975 by Marie Osmond in a number 40 hit (MGM/Kolob 14786).

## WHOSE BABY ARE YOU?
Jerome Kern (w: Anne Caldwell)
T. B. Harms—New York
1920
**Show:** *The Night Boat*
Introduced in the show by Louise Groody and Hal Skelly. Joseph C. Smith and His Orchestra had the hit recording (Victor 18661). Victor Arden made the hit piano roll arrangement (QRS 1132).

## WHY COULDN'T IT BE POOR LITTLE ME?
Isham Jones (w: Gus Kahn)
Jerome H. Remick—New York
1924
Introduced by the composer, who also had the hit recording conducting the Ray Miller Orchestra (Brunswick 2788). George Olsen (Victor 19573) and Ben Bernie (Vocalion 14957) also had fine arrangements, but jazz fans will always remember Muggsy Spanier's Stomp Six recording (Autograph 626).

## WHY DO FOOLS FALL IN LOVE?
Frank Lymon and George Goldner
Patricia Music—New York
1956
Frankie Lymon and the Teenagers had the number 6 hit that charted for sixteen weeks and sold over one million copies (Gee 1002). Diana Ross revived it in 1981 with the number 7 hit that charted for fourteen weeks (RCA 12349). The song was subject to a lawsuit that was finally settled, and the song's authorship was properly credited to group members Sherman Garnes and Herman Santiago.

## WHY DO I LOVE YOU?
Jerome Kern (w: Oscar Hammerstein)
T. B. Harms—New York
1927
Show: *Show Boat*
Norma Terris, Howard Marsh, Edna May Oliver, and Charles Winninger sang it in the show. Nat Shilkret and the Victor Orchestra had the hit recording (Victor 21215). Kathryn Grayson and Howard Keel sang it in the third film version (MGM, 1951).

## WHY DON'T YOU BELIEVE ME?
Lew Douglas/King Laney/Roy Rodde
Brandom Music—New York
1952
Joni James had the number 1 hit, which charted for twenty-three weeks and sold over one million copies (MGM 11333). The Duprees revived it in 1963 with their number 37 hit (Coed 584).

## WHY WAS I BORN?
Jerome Kern (w: Oscar Hammerstein)
T. B. Harms—New York
1929
**Show:** *Sweet Adeline*
Helen Morgan sang it in the show and also had the hit recording (Victor 22199), and Irene Dunne sang it in the film version (Warner Bros., 1935). Lena Horne sang it in the Kern biopic *Till the Clouds Roll By* (MGM, 1946). Vic Damone revived it in 1949 with a number 20 hit (Mercury 5326), and Gogi Grant sang it in *The Helen Morgan Story* (Warner Bros., 1957).

## WILD CHERRIES
Ted Snyder
Ted Snyder—New York
1908
Great piano rag originally recorded by the Victor Orchestra (Victor 16472) in 1910. Played in vaudeville and nightclubs by such ragtime pianists as comedian Jimmy Durante. Frank Banta later recorded it in 1921 (Gennett 4735). It sold a million copies of sheet music.

## WILD FLOWER
Vincent Youmans (w: Otto Harbach and

Oscar Hammerstein)

Harms—New York

1923

**Show:** *The Wildflower*

Introduced in the show by Guy Robertson. The hit recording was by Ben Bernie and His Orchestra (Vocalion 14555).

## WILD THING

Chip Taylor (w & m)

Blackwood Music

1965, 1966

Number 1 hit for the ultimate garage-rockers the Troggs, holding the top spot for two out of nine weeks on the chart (Atco 6415). Covered a year later by Robert Kennedy imitator "Senator Bobby" for a number 20 hit (Parkway 127). Well-loved by anyone who has ever plugged in an electric guitar.

## WILD WILD WOMEN, THE

Al Piantadosi/Al Wilson/Henry Lewis

Al Piantadosi—New York

1917

Introduced in vaudeville by singer Henry Lewis. It was revived in 1942 by Spike Jones and His City Slickers (Bluebird 30-0818).

## WILL YOU LOVE ME IN DECEMBER AS YOU DO IN MAY?

Ernest R. Ball (w: J. J. Walker)

M. Witmark and Sons—New York

1905

This was Ernest Ball's first hit. The Haydn Quartet had a hit recording in 1906 (Victor 4575). It was introduced in vaudeville by Janet Allen, who subsequently became the first wife of Mrs. J. J. Walker, who became the mayor of New York City (in 1926). It became his theme song for the rest of his life.

## WILL YOU LOVE ME TOMORROW?

Carole King and Gerry Goffin

Aldon Music—New York

1960, 1961

The Shirelles had the number 1 hit, which charted for fifteen weeks (Scepter 1211). Classic girl-group chirping.

## WILL YOU REMEMBER?

Sigmund Romberg (w: Rida Johnson Young)

G. Schirmer—New York

1917

**Show:** *Maytime*

Peggy Wood and Charles Purcell sang it in the show. Olive Kline and Lambert Murphy had the hit recording in 1918 (Victor 18399). Nelson Eddy and Jeanette MacDonald sang it in the film version (MGM, 1937). Jane Powell and Vic Damone sang it in the Romberg biopic *Deep in My Heart* (MGM, 1954).

## WILLIE THE WEEPER

Grant V. Rymal/Walter Melrose/Marty Bloom

Melrose Bros.—Chicago

1927

A jazz standard, it was first recorded by King Oliver and his Dixie Syncopators (Vocalion 1112). Cab Calloway later performed the song as part of his Cotton Club act, and it became closely associated with him thanks to the addition of the "Hi-de-ho" chorus. He called his 1931 rendition "Minnie the Moocher" (Brunswick 6074).

## WILLOW WEEP FOR ME

Ann Ronnell (w & m)

Irving Berlin—New York

1932

Paul Whiteman and His Orchestra (with vocal by Irene Taylor) had the number 2 hit, which charted for seven weeks (Victor 24187). Chad and Jeremy revived it in 1964 with a number 15 hit that charted for eight weeks (World Artists 1034).

## WINDMILLS OF YOUR MIND, THE

Michel Legrand (w: Marilyn and Alan Bergman)

United Artists Music—New York

1968

**Film:** *The Thomas Crown Affair* (Mirsch)

Academy Award winner for Best Song. Dusty Springfield had the number 31 hit (Atlantic 2623).

## WINDY

Ruthann Friedman (w & m)

Irving Music—Hollywood

1967

The Association had the number 1 hit, which charted for thirteen weeks and sold more than one million copies (Warner 7041). A classic piece of 1960s pop.

## WINTER
Albert Gumble (w: Alfred Bryan)
Jerome H. Remick—New York
1910
The Lyric Quartet had the best-selling record (Victor 5814). The song was revived in 1953 by Spike Jones and His City Slickers, with vocal by the Mello Men, for a number 23 hit (RCA Victor 20-5067).

## WINTER WONDERLAND
Felix Bernard (w: Dick Smith)
Donalsdon, Douglas and Gumble—New York
1934
Guy Lombardo and His Royal Canadians had the number 2 hit, which charted for nine weeks and launched this Christmas perennial (Decca 294). Perry Como revived it in 1946 with the Satisfiers and Russ Case's Orchestra, gaining a number 10 hit (RCA Victor 20-1968). Johnny Mercer with the Pied Pipers had the number 4 hit in 1947 (Capitol 316).

## WIPE OUT
The Surfaris (w & m)
Miraleste Music—Hollywood
1963
Number 2 surf instrumental by the aptly named Surfaris, charting for ten weeks (Dot 16479). Reissued in 1966 for a second run, reaching number 16. The popular rap group the Fat Boys united with the 1960s surf vocal group the Beach Boys to recut the song in 1987, and it reached number 12 (Tin Pan Apple 885960). A surf-rock classic.

## WISH YOU WERE HERE
Harold Rome (w & m)
Chappell—New York
1952
**Show:** *Wish You Were Here*
Jack Cassidy sang it in the show. Eddie Fisher had the number 1 hit, which charted for twenty-one weeks and sold over one million copies (RCA Victor 20-4830).

## WITCH DOCTOR
Ross Bagdasarian (w & m)
Monarch Music—Chicago
1958
Number 1 hit for David Seville (aka Ross Bagdasarian; also the voice of the Chipmunks), holding the top spot for three out of eighteen chart weeks, and selling over a million copies; also an R&B number 1, an unusual feat for a white artist singing what is little more than a novelty song (Liberty 55132). A kitsch classic, everyone loves to sing the nonsense chorus, beginning, "Oo, ee, oo, ah-ah . . ." Beloved around the campfire.

## WITH A SONG IN MY HEART
Richard Rodgers (w: Lorenz Hart)
Harms—New York
1929
**Show:** *Spring Is Here*
Lillian Taiz and John Hundley sang it in the show. Bernice Claire and Frank Albertson sang it in the film version (First National, 1930). Leo Reisman and His Orchestra had the hit recording (Victor 21923). It became so identified with Jane Froman that it became the title of her biopic, and she sang the song on its soundtrack (20th Century Fox, 1952).

## WITH PLENTY OF MONEY AND YOU
Harry Warren (w: Al Dubin)
Harms—New York
1936
**Film:** *Gold Diggers of 1937* (Warner Bros.)
Dick Powell sang it in the film. Henry Busse and His Orchestra, with vocal by Bob Hannon, had the number 1 hit that charted for nine weeks (Decca 1076).

## WITHOUT A SONG
Vincent Youmans (w: Billy Rose and Edward Eliscue)
Vincent Youmans—New York
1929
**Show:** *Great Day*
Lois Deppe and the Jubilee Singers sang it in the show. Paul Whiteman and His Orchestra had the hit recording (Columbia 2098-D).

## WOLVERINE BLUES
Ferd "Jelly Roll" Morton/Benjamin and John Spikes

Melrose Bros.—Chicago

1923

Introduced by the New Orleans Rhythm Kings (Gennett 5102) and as a piano solo by the composer (Gennett 5289). The hit recording of this jazz standard was by Gene Rodemich and His Orchestra (Brunswick 2455). Other fine versions include Albert E. Short and His Tivoli Syncopators (Vocalion 14554) and the Benson Orchestra (Victor 19140). In 1927, the Jelly Roll Morton Trio made another hit recording (Victor 21064). It was revived in 1938 by the Old Time Band (Bluebird 7816) and in 1946 by Pete Daily and His Chicagoans (Jump 12). The Spikes Brothers originally bought the tune from Jelly Roll Morton, and then added lyrics to it. Morton was annoyed when he saw their credit on the sheet music.

## WOMAN IN LOVE, A

Frank Loesser (w & m)

Frank Music—New York

1955

**Film:** *Guys and Dolls* (MGM)

Marlon Brando and Jean Simmons sang it in the film. The Four Aces had the number 14 hit that charted for twelve weeks (Decca 29725). Not to be confused with Barry Gibbs's 1980 song of the same title, a number 1 hit in 1980 by Barbra Streisand (Columbia 11364).

## WONDERFUL COPENHAGEN

Frank Loesser (w & m)

Frank Music—New York

1951

**Film:** *Hans Christian Andersen* (RKO)

Danny Kaye sang it in the film.

## WONDERFUL WORLD

Barbara Campbell/Herb Alpert/Lou Adler

Kags Music—New York

1959, 1960

Number 12 hit for Sam Cooke, charting eleven weeks (Keen 2112). This soulful ballad has become a perennial, revived in 1965 by Herman's Hermits for a number 4 hit (MGM 13354), and again in 1978 by Art Garfunkel for a number 17 hit (Columbia 10676).

## WOODMAN, WOODMAN, SPARE THAT TREE

Irving Berlin (w & m)

Waterson, Berlin and Snyder—New York

1911

**Show:** *Ziegfeld Follies of 1911*

Introduced in the show by Bert Williams, who also made a hit recording (Columbia A-1321). A sentimental favorite.

## WOODSTOCK

Joni Mitchell (w & m)

Siquomb Publishing—New York

1969

Crosby, Stills, Nash and Young had the number 11 hit, which charted for ten weeks (Atlantic 2723). Although Mitchell did not actually attend the 1969 festival, the song is considered the classic statement about it and what it mean to a generation.

## WORLD IS WAITING FOR THE SUNRISE, THE

Ernest Seitz (w: Eugene Lockhart)

Chappell-Harms—New York

1919

The first hit recording was made by Isham Jones and His Orchestra in 1922 (Brunswick 2313). It was revived in 1950 by the Firehouse Five Plus Two as a banjo feature for Harper Goff (Good Time Jazz 13). The next year, Les Paul and Mary Ford sold over a million copies with their number 2 hit version (Capitol 1748).

## WOULD YOU LIKE TO TAKE A WALK?

Harry Warren (w: Billy Rose and Mort Dixon)

Remick Music—New York

1930

**Show:** *Sweet and Low*

Hannah Williams and Hal Thompson sang it in the show. Rudy Vallee and His Connecticut Yankees had the number 4 hit in 1931 that charted for seven weeks (Victor 22611).

## WRAP YOUR TROUBLES IN DREAMS

Harry Barris (w: Ted Koehler and Billy Moll)

Shapiro, Bernstein—New York

1931

Bing Crosby had the number 4 hit, which charted for six weeks (Victor 22701). Erskine Hawkins and His Orchestra revived it in 1942 with a number 23 hit (Bluebird 11485).

## WUNDERBAR

Cole Porter (w & m)

T. B. Harms—New York

1948

**Show:** *Kiss Me Kate*

Sung by Alfred Drake and Patricia Morrison in the show.

## YAMA YAMA MAN, THE

Karl L. Hoschna (w: Otto A. Hauerbach)

M. Witmark and Sons—New York

1908

**Show:** *Three Twins*

Introduced by Bessie McCoy, it established her as a star, and forever after she was billed as "the Yama Yama Girl." Ada Jones and the Victor Light Opera Company had the hit recording in 1909 (Victor 16326).

## YANKEE DOODLE BLUES

George Gershwin (w: Irving Caesar and

Bud DeSylva)

Harms—New York

1922

**Show:** *Spice of 1922*

Georgie Price sang it in the show. A great syncopated number featured in vaudeville by Al Jolson and by jazz bands such as Jazzbo's Carolina Serenaders (Cameo 258) and Ladd's Black Aces (Gennett 4995) and by such dance bands as Isham Jones and His Orchestra (Brunswick 2286) and the Virginians (Victor 18913). Joan Leslie and Hazel Scott performed it in the Gershwin biopic *Rhapsody In Blue* (Warner Bros., 1945), while June Haver and Gloria DeHaven sang it in the film *I'll Get By* (Twentieth Century Fox, 1950).

## YANKEE DOODLE BOY, THE

George M. Cohan (w & m)

F. A. Mills—New York

1904

**Show:** *Little Johnny Jones*

A personal favorite of the composer, who identified with the song's title and sang it in his show. Billy Murray had the hit recording in 1905 (Victor 4229). James Cagney won an Academy Award for his portrayal of Cohan in the biopic *Yankee Doodle Dandy* (Warner Bros., 1942), singing this song. He reprised it in a dance in *The Seven Little Foys* (Paramount, 1955).

## YEARNING

Joe Burke (w: Benny Davis)

Irving Berlin—New York

1925

Introduced on radio by Gene Austin, who had a hit recording (Victor 19625). Instrumentally, there were Roger Wolfe Kahn's (Victor 19616), Harry Reser's (Columbia 319-D), Bennie Krueger's (Brunswick 2859) and Ben Bernie's (Vocalion 15002) versions. It was revived in 1938 by Tommy Dorsey's Orchestra with vocal by Jack Leonard in a number 3 hit (Victor 25815).

## YELLOW DOG BLUES

W. C. Handy (w & m)

Pace and Handy Music—Memphis

1914

Originally titled "Yellow Dog Rag," it didn't go anywhere until the title was changed in 1919. Then, Joseph C. Smith's Orchestra made a hit recording (Victor 18618). In 1930 Ted Lewis and His Band made a number 4 hit recording (Columbia 2217-D) and it soon became a standard played by jazz bands.

## YELLOW ROSE OF TEXAS, THE

Don George (w & m)

Planetary Music—New York

1955

Mitch Miller and His Orchestra and Chorus had the number 1 hit, which charted for nineteen weeks and sold over one million copies (Columbia 40540). It was originally published in 1853 and became a favorite in minstrel shows; it also was a popular Confederate marching song during the Civil War.

## YES SIR, THAT'S MY BABY

Walter Donaldson (w: Gus Kahn)

Irving Berlin—New York

1925

Written for and introduced by Eddie Cantor. Gene Austin had the hit vocal recording (Victor 19656) along with Margaret Young (Brunswick 2939). Ben Bernie's Orchestra (Vocalion 15080) and the Coon-Sanders Orchestra (Victor 19745) had the hit instrumental recordings. It is a standard and a favorite of jazz bands. It was revived by the Firehouse Five Plus Two in 1950 (Good Time Jazz 14).

## YES! WE HAVE NO BANANAS
Frank Silver and Irving Cohn
Shapiro, Bernstein—New York
1923
Introduced by Eddie Cantor on tour in *Make It Snappy* and thereafter in vaudeville. Billy Jones (Vocalion 14579) had the hit vocal recording and he also appeared on disc with Bennie Krueger and His Orchestra (Brunswick 2445). The Great White Way Orchestra (Victor 19068) and Selvin's Orchestra (Vocalion 14590) also had fine versions. It was revived in 1950 by Spike Jones and His City Slickers (RCA Victor 20-3912). A classic comic novelty song.

## YESTERDAY
John Lennon and Paul McCartney
Maclen Music—New York
1965
The Beatles had the number 1 hit, which held the top position for four of the nine weeks on the chart, selling over one million copies (Capitol 5498). It is alleged that it is the most covered song of this century because more than 2,500 artists have recorded it. Before writing the final lyric, McCartney sang the dummy words "scrambled eggs" to the opening notes.

## YESTERDAYS
Jerome Kern (w: Otto Harbach)
T. B. Harms—New York
1933
**Show:** *Roberta*
Fay Templeton sang it in the show. Leo Reisman and His Orchestra had the number 3 hit, which charted for eight weeks (Brunswick 6701). Irene Dunne and Helen Westley sang it in the film version (RKO, 1935). When the film was remade, it was retitled *Lovely to Look At* (MGM, 1952) and Kathryn Grayson sang it while Marge and Gower Champion danced to it.

## YIP-I-ADDY-I-AY
John H. Flynn (w: Will D. Cobb)
Will D. Cobb—New York
1908
**Show:** *The Merry Widow and the Devil*
Introduced by Blanche Ring, this novelty became part of her vaudeville act. Her rendition became so famous that she was asked by Victor to record it in the next year (Victor 60017).

## YOU
Walter Donaldson
(w: Harold Adamson)
Leo Feist—New York
1936
**Film:** *The Great Ziegfeld* (MGM)
Tommy Dorsey and His Orchestra had the number 1 hit, which charted for ten weeks (Victor 25291). Sammy Kaye and His Orchestra revived it in 1952 with a number 28 hit (Columbia 39724).

## YOU AND THE NIGHT AND THE MUSIC
Arthur Schwartz (w: Howard Dietz)
Harms—New York
1934
**Show:** *Revenge With Music*
Libby Holman and Georges Metaxa sang it in the show and Holman had the number 11 hit that charted for five weeks (Victor 24839).

## YOU ARE MY LUCKY STAR
Nacio Herb Brown (w: Arthur Freed)
Robbins Music—New York
1935
**Film:** *Broadway Melody of 1936* (MGM)
Dick Powell and Frances Langford sang it in the film. Eddy Duchin and His Orchestra, with vocals by Lew Sherwood, had the number 1 hit that charted for nine weeks (Victor 25125). Gene Kelly and Debbie Reynolds sang it in the film *Singin' in the Rain* (MGM, 1952).

## YOU ARE MY SUNSHINE
Jimmie Davis and Charles Mitchell
Southern Music—New York
1940
Bing Crosby had the number 19 hit in 1941 (Decca 3952). The composer, country blues singer Jimmie Davis, ran for governor of Louisiana and won, helped by using this as his campaign song in 1944. Ray Charles revived it in 1962 when he had the number 7 hit (ABC-Paramount 10375).

## YOU ARE THE SUNSHINE OF MY LIFE
Stevie Wonder (w & m)
Jobete Music—Hollywood
1972, 1973
Stevie Wonder had this memorable number 1 hit, which charted for thirteen weeks (Tamla 54232). A standard pop love ballad.

## YOU BELONG TO ME
Pee Wee King/Redd Stewart/Chilton Price
Ridgeway Music—Hollywood
1952
Jo Stafford had the number 1 hit, which stayed in that position for twelve of the twenty-five weeks charted and sold nearly two million copies (Columbia 39811). The Duprees revived it in 1962 with a number 7 hit, which charted for nine weeks (Coed 569).

## YOU BROUGHT A NEW KIND OF LOVE
Sammy Fain/Irving Kahal/Pierre Norman
Famous Music—New York
1930
**Film:** *The Big Pond* (Paramount)
Maurice Chevalier sang it in the film and recorded the number 12 hit (Victor 22405). Paul Whiteman and His Orchestra, with vocals by Bing Crosby, had the number 3 hit, which charted for eight weeks (Columbia 2171-D).

## YOU CAN'T DO WHAT MY LAST MAN DID
J. C. Johnson and Allie Moore
Chateau Music—New York
1923
Introduced on record by James P. Johnson in a splendid piano solo (Victor 19123).

## YOU CAN'T HURRY LOVE
Brian Holland/Lamont Dozier/
Eddie Holland
Jobete Music—Detroit
1966
Number 1 hit for the Supremes, holding the top spot for two out of eleven weeks on the charts; also a number 1 R&B hit (Motown 1097). Revived in 1983 by Phil Collins for the film soundtrack of *Buster*; his version reached number 10 (Atlantic 89933).

## YOU CAN'T KEEP A GOOD MAN DOWN
Perry Bradford (w & m)
Perry Bradford—New York
1920
Introduced in vaudeville by Sophie Tucker. Hit recording by Mamie Smith and Her Jazz Hounds (Okeh 4113). Chet Gordon made a great version on piano roll (US 39961).

## YOU DO SOMETHING TO ME
Cole Porter (w & m)
Harms—New York
1929
**Show:** *Fifty Million Frenchmen*
William Gaxton and Genevieve Tobin sang it in the show. Leo Reisman and His Orchestra had the hit recording (Victor 22244). Jane Wyman sang it in the Porter biopic *Night and Day* (Warner Bros., 1945). Mario Lanza sang it in the film *Because You're Mine* (MGM, 1952). Louis Jourdan sang it in the film *Can-Can* (20th Century Fox, 1960).

## YOU DON'T HAVE TO BE A STAR
J. Dean and J. Glover
Groovesville Music
1976
Marilyn McCoo and Billy Davis Jr. had the number 1 hit that charted for eighteen weeks (ABC 12208). It sold over one million copies.

## YOU GO TO MY HEAD
J. Fred Coots (w: Haven Gillespie)
Remick Music—New York
1938
Larry Clinton and His Orchestra, with vocal by Bea Wain, had the number 3 hit that charted for twelve weeks (Victor 25849).

## YOU KEEP ME HANGIN' ON
Eddie Holland/Lamont Dozier/Brian Holland
Jobete Music—Detroit
1966
Number 1 hit for Motowners The Supremes, noteworthy for its dramatic instrumental and vocal arrangement. It held the top position for two out of ten chart weeks, and was also an R&B number 1 hit (Motown

1101). Covered two years later by rockers Vanilla Fudge for a number 6 hit (Atco 6590), and then in 1987 by British pop-rocker Kim Wilde, who brought it back to number 1 (MCA 53024).

## YOU LIGHT UP MY LIFE

Joe Brooks (w & m)

Big Hill Music

1976, 1977

**Film:** *You Light Up My Life* (Columbia)

Academy Award winner for Best Song. Debby Boone, daughter of 1950s singing idol Pat Boone, had this number 1 hit that stayed in that position for ten of the twenty-one weeks charted (Warner/Curb 8455). It sold over two million copies, and was the best-selling record of the 1970s. A feel-good pop ballad that was tremendously popular.

## YOU MADE ME LOVE YOU

James V. Monaco (w: Joseph McCarthy)

Broadway Music—New York

1912

**Show:** *Honeymoon Express*

Al Jolson sang it in the show and had a hit recording (Columbia A-1374). It was identified with him for the rest of his career. Harry James and His Orchestra had a number 5 hit in 1941, which charted for eighteen weeks and sold over one million copies (Columbia 36296). Judy Garland sang it in the film *The Broadway Melody of 1938* (MGM, 1937). Al Jolson sang it in his biopic *The Jolson Story* (Columbia, 1946) and Doris Day sang it in the Ruth Etting biopic *Love Me or Leave Me* (MGM, 1955).

## YOU MAKE ME FEEL LIKE DANCING

Leo Sayer and Vincent Poncia

Long Manor Music

1976

Leo Sayer had this number 1 hit in 1977, when it charted for seventeen weeks (Warner 8283). It sold over one million copies. A disco favorite, propelled by Sayer's dramatic falsetto vocal.

## YOU MAKE ME FEEL SO YOUNG

Josef Myrow (w: Mack Gordon)

Bregman, Vocco and Conn—New York

1946

**Film:** *Three Little Girls in Blue* (20th Century Fox)

Del Porter and Carol Stewart sang it in the film. Dick Haymes had the number 21 hit (Decca 18914).

## YOU MUST HAVE BEEN A BEAUTIFUL BABY

Harry Warren (w: Johnny Mercer)

Remick Music—New York

1938

**Film:** *Hard to Get* (Warner Bros.)

Dick Powell sang it in the film. Bing Crosby, accompanied by the Bob Crosby Orchestra, had the number 1 hit, which charted for eleven weeks (Decca 2147). Bobby Darin revived it in 1961 with a number 5 hit, which charted for nine weeks (Atco 6206). The Dave Clark Five revived it again in 1967 for a number 35 hit (Epic 10179).

## YOU MUST LOVE ME

Andrew Lloyd Webber (w: Tim Rice)

Evita Music

1996

**Film:** *Evita* (Cinergi)

Academy Award winner for Best Song. Madonna starred in the movie and had the number 18 hit, which charted for fourteen weeks (Warner 17495). The song was written for the film version specifically for Madonna. It sold over half a million copies.

## YOU NEVER KNEW ABOUT ME

Jerome Kern (w: P. G. Wodehouse)

T. B. Harms—New York

1917

**Show:** *Oh, Boy!*

Introduced in the show by Marie Carroll and Tom Powers. The hit recording was by Edna Brown and Edward Hamilton (Victor 18259).

## YOU SAID SOMETHING

Jerome Kern (w: P. G. Wodehouse and J. Kern)

T. B. Harms—New York

1916

**Show:** *Have a Heart*

Introduced in the show by Marjorie Gateson and Donald MacDonald. The hit recording was by Alice Green and Harry MacDonough (Victor 18260).

## YOU SEND ME
L. C. Cook (w & m)
Higuera Music—Culver City, Calif.
1957
Sam Cooke had the number 1 hit that his brother wrote; it charted for seventeen weeks and sold over one million copies (Keen 3-4013). The song was Cooke's first crossover into the pop market; previously he had sung gospel as the lead singer with the group the Soul Stirrers. The song became Cooke's most famous number, and the one that is still most closely associated with him. Teresa Brewer covered the song for a number 8 hit the same year that charted for eleven weeks (Coral 61898).

## YOU TELL ME YOUR DREAM, I'LL TELL YOU MINE
Charles N. Daniels (w: Seymour Rice and Albert Brown)
Whitney Warner—Detroit
1899
Originally introduced by Ella Butler as a waltz song about children, it later became a favorite of barbershop quartets with a more robust atmosphere. Later versions feature spelling effects and an ending by James A. Leyden with embellishments. The Mills Brothers revived it in 1939 with a number 14 hit (Decca 2285).

## YOU TOOK ADVANTAGE OF ME
Richard Rodgers (w: Lorenz Hart)
Harms—New York
1928
**Show:** *Present Arms*
Joyce Barbour and Busby Berkeley sang and danced to it in the show. Paul Whiteman and His Orchestra had the hit recording (Victor 21398). Judy Garland sang it in the film *A Star Is Born* (Warner Bros., 1954).

## YOU WERE MEANT FOR ME
Nacio Herb Brown (w: Arthur Freed)
Robbins Music—New York
1929
**Film:** *Broadway Melody* (MGM)
Charles King sang it in the film. Nat Shilkret and the Victor Orchestra had the hit recording (Victor 21886). Dan Dailey sang it in the film of the same name (20th Century Fox, 1948). Connie Boswell had a number 19 hit in 1948 (Decca 25313). It was sung and danced to by Gene Kelly and Debbie Reynolds in *Singin' in the Rain* (MGM, 1952).

## YOU WERE ONLY FOOLING
Larry Fotine (w: Billy Faber and Fred Meadows)
Shapiro, Bernstein—New York
1948
The Ink Spots had the number 8 hit (Decca 24507). Vic Damone revived it in 1965 with a number 30 hit (Warner 5616).

## YOU'D BE SURPRISED
Irving Berlin (w & m)
Irving Berlin—New York
1919
**Show:** *Ziegfeld Follies of 1919*
Introduced in the show by Eddie Cantor, his recording sold over a million copies (Emerson 10102). Sheet music sales topped 750,000. Dan Dailey revived it in the film *There's No Business like Show Business* (20th Century Fox, 1954).

## YOU'LL BE IN MY HEART
Phil Collins (w & m)
Walt Disney Music
1998
**Film:** *Tarzan* (Disney)
Academy Award winner for Best Song of 1999. Phil Collins had the number 21 hit, which charted for seven weeks (Walt Disney 60025).

## YOU'LL NEVER KNOW
Harry Warren (w: Mack Gordon)
Bregman, Vocco and Conn—New York
1943
**Film:** *Hello, Frisco, Hello* (20th Century Fox)
Academy Award winner for Best Song. Alice Faye sang it in the film. Dick Haymes had the number 1 hit that charted for eighteen weeks (Decca 18556).

## YOU'LL NEVER WALK ALONE
Richard Rodgers (w: Oscar Hammerstein)
Williamson Music—New York
1945

**Show:** *Carousel*

Christine Johnson sang it in the show. Frank Sinatra had the number 9 hit (Columbia 36825). Patti LaBelle and Her Blue Belles revived it in 1964, achieving a number 34 hit (Parkway 896).

## YOUNG AT HEART

Johnny Richards (w: Carolyn Leigh)

Cheerio Music—New York

1954

Frank Sinatra had the number 2 hit, which charted for twenty-two weeks and sold over one million copies (Capitol 2703). The song became closely associated with Sinatra and the 1950s in general. It was prominently featured in the McCarthy-era film *The Front* (United Artists, 1976), starring Woody Allen.

## YOUNG LOVE

Carole Joyner and Ric Cartey

Stars—New York

1956

In 1957, both Hollywood heartthrob Tab Hunter (Dot 15533) and country-rockabilly star Sonny James (Capitol 3602) had number 1 hits with this song, both versions charting for seventeen weeks and each selling over one million copies. (The song was originally recorded by Rick Cartey, but failed to see any action.) Donny Osmond revived it in 1973 with a number 25 hit that charted for seven weeks (MGM/Kolob 14583).

## YOUNGER THAN SPRINGTIME

Richard Rodgers (w: Oscar Hammerstein)

Williamson Music—New York

1949

**Show:** *South Pacific*

William Tabbart sang this in the show. Gordon MacRae had the number 30 hit (Capitol 598).

## YOUR BOY IS ON THE COAL PILE NOW

Sam Ward (w & m)

Leo Feist—New York

1918

Outstanding piano roll version by H. Claar (Connorized 6423).

## YOUR FEET'S TOO BIG

Ada Benson and Fred Fisher

Joe Davis—New York

1936

Tommy Tucker and His Orchestra introduced it on radio, but it wasn't until Fats Waller made his number 15 hit in 1939 that he became associated with it forever (Bluebird 10500).

## (YOUR LOVE KEEPS LIFTING ME) HIGHER AND HIGHER

Gary Jackson/Carl Smith/Raynard Miner

Chevis Music

1967

Number 6 hit for Jackie Wilson, charting for nine weeks (Brunswick 55336); it was also a number 1 R&B hit. Ten years later, pop vocalist Rita Coolidge remade it for a number 2 hit, charting for seventeen weeks and selling over a million copies (A&M 1922). It remains her best-seller, and is closely associated with her.

## YOU'RE A GRAND OLD FLAG

George M. Cohan (w & m)

F. A. Mills—New York

1906

**Show:** *George Washington, Jr.*

This patriotic flag-waver was sung by the composer in his show. He also sang it in the movie *The Phantom President* (Paramount, 1932). Billy Murray had the enormous hit and biggest-selling Victor record of the first decade (Victor 4634). James Cagney sang it in the biopic *Yankee Doodle Dandy* (Warner Bros., 1942). Joel Grey sang it in the Broadway musical *George M!* (1968).

## YOU'RE AN OLD SMOOTHIE

Richard Whiting and Nacio Herb Brown

(w: Bud DeSylva)

Harms—New York

1932

**Show:** *Take a Chance*

Ethel Merman and Jack Haley sang it in the show. Paul Whiteman and His Orchestra had the number 11 hit in 1933, which charted for four weeks (Victor 24202).

## YOU'RE BREAKING MY HEART

Pat Genaro and Sunny Skylar

Algonquin Music—New York

1948

Vic Damone had the number 1 hit, which charted for twenty-six weeks and sold over one million copies (Mercury 5271).

## YOU'RE DRIVING ME CRAZY

Walter Donaldson (w & m)

Donaldson, Douglas and Gumble—New York

1930

Guy Lombardo and His Royal Canadians had the number 1 hit, which charted for twelve weeks (Columbia 2335-D).

## YOU'RE GETTING TO BE A HABIT WITH ME

Harry Warren (w: Al Dubin)

M. Witmark and Sons—New York

1932

**Film:** *Forty-Second Street* (Warner Bros.)

Dick Powell and Bebe Daniels sang it in the film. Bing Crosby, accompanied by Guy Lombardo and His Royal Canadians, had the number 1 hit that charted for fourteen weeks (Brunswick 6472). The song has become a cabaret standard.

## YOU'RE JUST IN LOVE

Irving Berlin (w & m)

Irving Berlin—New York

1950

**Show:** *Call Me Madam*

Ethel Merman and Russell Nype sang this in the show. Perry Como with the Fontane Sisters had the number 5 hit that charted for seventeen weeks (RCA Victor 20-3945).

## YOU'RE LUCKY TO ME

Eubie Blake (w: Andy Razaf)

Shapiro, Bernstein—New York

1930

**Show:** *Lew Leslie's Blackbirds of 1930*

Ethel Waters sang it in the show, accompanied by Eubie Blake at the piano.

## YOU'RE NO GOOD

Clint Ballard, Jr. (w & m)

MPL Communications—New York

1963, 1974

Number 1 hit for Linda Ronstadt in 1975, charting for ten weeks (Capitol 3990). Her first number 1 hit, and a dramatic pop-rock song.

## YOU'RE SIXTEEN

Bob Sherman and Dick Sherman

Viva Music

1960

Ringo Starr, backed by Paul McCartney on kazoo and Harry Nilsson on vocals, had this number 1 hit in 1973 that charted for twelve weeks (Apple 1870). It sold more than one million copies. The song features the memorable couplet, "She walked out of my dreams/ and into my car. . . ."

## YOU'RE SO RIGHT FOR ME

Jay Livingston and Ray Evans

Chappell—New York

1958

**Show:** *Oh Captain*

Edward Platt and Abbe Lane sang it in the show.

## YOU'RE SO VAIN

Carly Simon (w & m)

Quackenbush Music—New York

1972

Carly Simon, a top songwriter and singer, had this number 1 hit that charted for fourteen weeks (Elektra 45824). It sold over one million copies. Mick Jagger sings harmony vocals on the single, leading to speculation that the song was addressed to him. Simon finally admitted that she wrote it about Warren Beatty.

## YOU'RE THE CREAM IN MY COFFEE

Ray Henderson (w: Bud DeSylva and Lew Brown)

DeSylva, Brown and Henderson—New York

1928

**Show:** *Hold Everything*

Jack Whiting sang it in the show. Ted Weems and His Orchestra had a hit recording (Victor 21767), as did Ruth Etting (Columbia 1707-D). It was revived in the DeSylva-Brown-Henderson biopic *The Best Things in Life Are Free* (20th Century Fox, 1956).

## YOU'RE THE ONE THAT I WANT

John Farrar (w & m)

Stigwood Music

1978

**Film:** *Grease* (Paramount)

John Travolta and Olivia Newton-John, who starred in the film, had this number 1 hit that charted for sixteen weeks (RSO 891). It sold over two million copies.

## YOU'RE THE TOP

Cole Porter (w & m)

Harms—New York

1934

**Show:** *Anything Goes*

William Gaxton and Ethel Merman sang it in the show. Merman had a number 4 hit, which charted for nine weeks (Brunswick 7342). Paul Whiteman and His Orchestra had the number 2 hit, which charted for ten weeks (Victor 24769). Cole Porter, who accompanied himself at the piano, had a number 10 hit in 1935 (Victor 24766). Ethel Merman sang it in the film version (Paramount, 1936). Bing Crosby and Mitzi Gaynor sang it in the film remake (Paramount, 1956). Cary Grant and Ginny Simms sang it in the Porter biopic *Night and Day* (Warner Bros., 1946). One of Porter's best-known and wittiest lyrics.

## YOU'VE GOT A FRIEND

Carole King (w & m)

Screen Gems-Columbia Music—New York

1971

James Taylor had the number 1 hit, which charted for twelve weeks (Warner 7498). It sold over one million copies. Covered that same year in a classic duet version by Roberta Flack and Donny Hathaway, which became a number 29 pop hit (Atlantic 2808). A lovely pop-rock ballad.

## YOU'VE GOT TO SEE MAMA EVERY NIGHT (OR YOU CAN'T SEE MAMA AT ALL)

Con Conrad (w: Billy Rose)

Leo Feist—New York

1923

Dolly Kay had a hit vocal recording (Columbia A-3808), backed by Frank Westphal and His Orchestra, as did Aileen Stanley and Billy Murray (Victor 19027).

Bennie Krueger and His Orchestra (Brunswick 2390) and Gene Fosdick's Hoosiers (Vocalion 14496) had the instrumental hits.

## YOU'VE LOST THAT LOVIN' FEELIN'

Barry Mann/Cynthia Weil/Phil Spector

Screen Gems-Columbia Music—New York

1964

Number 1 hit in 1965 for the soulful Righteous Brothers, featuring their dramatic vocal interplay. It held the top spot for two out of thirteen weeks on the charts (Philles 124), and remains one of their best-loved recordings. Revived in 1969 by Dionne Warwick for a number 16 hit (Scepter 12262) and popsters Hall and Oates in 1980 for a number 12 hit (RCA 12103).

## ZIGEUNER

Noel Coward (w & m)

Harms—New York

1929

**Show:** *Bitter Sweet*

Evelyn Laye sang it in the show. Anna Neagle sang it in the first film version (United Artists, 1933) and Jeanette MacDonald sang it in the second film version (MGM, 1940).

## ZING! WENT THE STRINGS OF MY HEART

James Hanley (w & m)

Harms—New York

1935

**Show:** *Thumbs Up!*

Hal LeRoy and Eunice Healy sang it in the show. Judy Garland sang it in the film *Listen Darling* (MGM, 1938). She recorded it in 1939, but it wasn't released until 1943, when it was a number 22 hit (Decca 18543).

## ZIP-A-DEE-DO-DAH

Allie Wrubel (w: Ray Gilbert)

Santly-Joy—New York

1946

**Film:** *Song of the South* (RKO-Disney)

Academy Award winner for Best Song. James Baskett sang the song in the film. Johnny Mercer had the number 8 hit that charted for eight weeks (Capitol 323). Bob B. Soxx and the Blue Jeans had the number 8 hit that charted for nine weeks in 1962 (Philles 107).

# ACADEMY AWARD WINNERS FOR BEST SONG

1934 - The Continental

1935 - Lullaby of Broadway

1936 - The Way You Look Tonight

1937 - Sweet Leilani

1938 - Thanks for the Memory

1939 - Over the Rainbow

1940 - When You Wish upon a Star

1941 - The Last Time I Saw Paris

1942 - White Christmas

1943 - You'll Never Know

1944 - Swinging on a Star

1945 - It Might As Well Be Spring

1946 - On the Atchson, Topeka and the Santa Fe

1947 - Zip-a-Dee-Doo-Dah

1948 - Buttons and Bows

1949 - Baby, It's Cold Outside

1950 - Mona Lisa

1951 - In the Cool, Cool, Cool of the Evening

1952 - High Noon

1953 - Secret Love

1954 - Three Coins in the Fountain

1955 - Love Is a Many-Splendored Thing

1956 - Whatever Will Be

1957 - All the Way

1958 - Gigi

1959 - High Hopes

1960 - Never on Sunday

1961 - Moon River

1962 - Days of Wine and Roses

1963 - Call Me Irresponsible

1964 - Chim Chim Cheree

1965 - The Shadow of Your Smile

1966 - Born Free

1967 - Talk to the Animals

1968 - The Windmills of Your Mind

1969 - Raindrops Keep Falling on My Head

1970 - For All We Know (Karlin)

1971 - Theme from Shaft

1972 - The Morning After

1973 - The Way We Were

1974 - We May Never Love Like This Again

1975 - I'm Easy

1976 - Evergreen

1977 - You Light Up My Life

1978 - Last Dance

1979 - It Goes Like It Goes

1980 - Fame

1981 - Arthur's Theme

1982 - Up Where We Belong

1983 - Flashdance . . . What a Feeling

1984 - I Just Called to Say I Love You

1985 - Say You, Say Me

1986 - Take My Breath Away

1987 - I've Had the Time of My Life

1988 - Let the River Run

1989 - Under the Sea

1990 - Sooner or Later

1991 - Beauty and the Beast

1992 - A Whole New World

1993 - Streets of Philadelphia

1994 - Can You Feel the Love Tonight

1995 - Colors of the Wind

1996 - You Must Love Me

1997 - My Heart Will Go On

1998 - When You Believe

1999 - You'll Be in My Heart

# INDEX BY COMPOSER

Andersson, Benny / Stig Anderson /
Bjorn Ulvaeus
    DANCING QUEEN
Anka, Paul (w & m)
    LONELY BOY
    PUT YOUR HEAD ON MY SHOULDER
Applegate, Mary and Jennifer Rush
    POWER OF LOVE, THE
Archer, Harry (w: Harlan Thompson)
    I LOVE YOU
Arlen, Harold (w: Ira Gershwin)
    MAN THAT GOT AWAY, THE
Arlen, Harold (w: E. Y. Harburg)
    OVER THE RAINBOW
    WE'RE OFF TO SEE THE WIZARD
Arlen, Harold (w: Ted Koehler)
    AS LONG AS I LIVE
    BETWEEN THE DEVIL AND THE DEEP
      BLUE SEA
    GET HAPPY
    I GOTTA RIGHT TO SING THE BLUES
    I'VE GOT THE WORLD ON A STRING
    LET'S FALL IN LOVE
    STORMY WEATHER
Arlen, Harold (w: Johnny Mercer)
    AC-CENT-TCHU-ATE THE POSITIVE
    BLUES IN THE NIGHT
    COME RAIN OR COME SHINE
    HIT THE ROAD TO DREAMLAND
    ONE FOR MY BABY
    THAT OLD BLACK MAGIC
Arlen, Harold (w: Billy Rose and E. Y. Harburg)
    IT'S ONLY A PAPER MOON
Armstrong, Harry and Billy Clark
    I LOVE MY WIFE, BUT, OH, YOU KID!
    SHAKY EYES
Armstrong, Henry W. (w: Richard H. Gerard)
    SWEET ADELINE
Arndt, Felix
    NOLA
Arnheim, Gus and Abe Lyman
(w: Arthur Freed)
    I CRIED FOR YOU
Arzonia, Joe (w & m)
    PREACHER AND THE BEAR, THE
Ashford, Nicholas and Valerie Simpson
    AIN'T NO MOUNTAIN HIGH ENOUGH
Austin, Gene and Roy Bergere
    HOW COME YOU DO ME LIKE YOU DO?

Austin, Gene / Emmet O'Hara / Irving Mills
    CHARLESTON CHARLEY
Axton, Hoyt (w & m)
    JOY TO THE WORLD
Axton, Mae / Tommy Durden / Elvis Presley
    HEARTBREAK HOTEL
Ayer, Nat D. (w: A. Seymour Brown)
    GEE, I LIKE THE MUSIC WITH MY MEALS
    IF YOU TALK IN YOUR SLEEP, DON'T
      MENTION MY NAME
    KING CHANTICLEER
    OH, YOU BEAUTIFUL DOLL
Babyface (Kenny Edmonds) (w & m)
    EXHALE (SHOOP SHOOP)
    I'LL MAKE LOVE TO YOU
    WHEN CAN I SEE YOU
Babyface (Kenny Edmonds) / L.A. Reid /
Daryl Simmons
    END OF THE ROAD
Bacharach, Burt (w: Hal David)
    I'LL NEVER FALL IN LOVE AGAIN
    RAINDROPS KEEP FALLIN' ON MY HEAD
    (THEY LONG TO BE) CLOSE TO YOU
    THIS GUY'S IN LOVE WITH YOU
    WHAT THE WORLD NEEDS NOW IS LOVE
    WHAT'S NEW PUSSYCAT?
Bacharach, Burt and Carole Bayer Sager
    ON MY OWN
Bacharach, Burt / Carole Bayer Sager /
Christopher Cross / Peter Allen
    ARTHUR'S THEME
Bachman, Randy / Burton Cummings /
Jim Kale / Garry Peterson
    AMERICAN WOMAN
Baer, Abel (w: L. Wolfe Gilbert)
    LUCKY LINDY
Baer, Abel / Cliff Friend / Jack Meskill
    BLUE HOOSIER BLUES
Bagdasarian, Ross (w & m)
    WITCH DOCTOR
Baker, Gary and Frank Myers
    I SWEAR
Ball, Ernest R. (w: Chauncey Olcott and
George Graff, Jr.)
    WHEN IRISH EYES ARE SMILING
Ball, Ernest R. (w: J. Keirn Brennan)
    DEAR LITTLE BOY OF MINE
    LET THE REST OF THE WORLD GO BY
    LITTLE BIT OF HEAVEN, A

Cooke, Sam (w & m)
   CHAIN GANG
Cooper, Joe (w: Bert Kalmar)
   I'VE BEEN FLOATING DOWN THE OLD
      GREEN RIVER
Coots, J. Fred (w: Lou Davis)
   HERE COMES MY BALL AND CHAIN
   I'M CROONIN' A TUNE ABOUT JUNE
Coots, J. Fred (w: Haven Gillespie)
   SANTA CLAUS IS COMIN' TO TOWN
   YOU GO TO MY HEAD
Coots, J. Fred (w: Nick and Charles Kenny)
   LOVE LETTERS IN THE SAND
Coots, J. Fred (w: Sam Lewis)
   FOR ALL WE KNOW
Cory, George and Douglass Cross
   I LEFT MY HEART IN SAN FRANCISCO
Cosby, Henry/William "Smokey" Robinson/
Stevie Wonder
   TEARS OF A CLOWN, THE
Coslow, Sam (w & m)
   SWEEPIN' THE CLOUDS AWAY
Covay, Don and John Berry
   PONY TIME
Coward, Noel (w & m)
   I'LL SEE YOU AGAIN
   ZIGEUNER
Craig, Francis (w: Kermit Goell)
   NEAR YOU
Crane, Jimmie and Al Jacobs
   I NEED YOU NOW
Crane, Jimmie/Al Jacobs/Jimmy Brewster
(aka Milt Gabler)
   IF I GIVE MY HEART TO YOU
Crewe, Bob and Bob Gaudio
   BIG GIRLS DON'T CRY
   RAG DOLL
   WALK LIKE A MAN
Crewe, Bob/Sandy Linzer/Denny Randell
   LET'S HANG ON
Croce, Jim (w & m)
   BAD, BAD LEROY BROWN
   TIME IN A BOTTLE
Cronin, Kevin (w & m)
   KEEP ON LOVING YOU
Cropper, Steve and Otis Redding
   (SITTIN' ON) THE DOCK OF THE BAY
Cross, Christopher (w & m)
   SAILING

Crow, Sheryl/Wyn Cooper/Bill Bottrell/
David Baerwald/Kevin Gilbert
   ALL I WANNA DO
Crumit, Frank and Dave Zoob
(w: Howard Johnson)
   SWEET LADY
Culture Club (w & m)
   KARMA CHAMELEON
Dabney, Ford (w: Cecil Mack)
   THAT'S WHY THEY CALL ME "SHINE"
Dabney, Ford (w: Cecil Mack and Lew Brown)
   SHINE
Daly, Joseph M. (w & m)
   CHICKEN REEL
Dance, Leo (w: Eric Little)
   MY TIME IS YOUR TIME
Daniels, Charles N. (w: Seymour Rice and
Albert Brown)
   YOU TELL ME YOUR DREAM, I'LL TELL
      YOU MINE
Daniels, Lashawn/Rodney and Fred
Jerkins/Brandy Norwood/Japhe Tejeda
   BOY IS MINE, THE
Danoff, Bill (w & m)
   AFTERNOON DELIGHT
Darewski, Hermann E. (w: R.P. Weston)
   SISTER SUSIE'S SEWING SHIRTS FOR SOLDIERS
Darin, Bobby and Jean Murray
   SPLISH SPLASH
Darion, Joe and Mitch Leigh
   IMPOSSIBLE DREAM, THE
Darling, Erik and Willard Svance
   WALK RIGHT IN
Daugherty, Doc and Ellis Reynolds
(w: Al Neiburg)
   CONFESSIN' THAT I LOVE YOU
David, Lee (w: Billy Rose)
   TONIGHT YOU BELONG TO ME
David, Mack (w & m)
   I DON'T CARE OF THE SUN DON'T SHINE
Davis, Charlie (w: Walter Melrose)
   COPENHAGEN
Davis, Charlie (w: Fred Rose)
   JIMTOWN BLUES
Davis, Jimmie and Charles Mitchell
   YOU ARE MY SUNSHINE
Davis, Katherine/Henry Onorati/
Harry Simeone
   LITTLE DRUMMER BOY, THE

**Green, Florence and Luther Dixon**
  SOLDIER BOY
**Green, John (w: Edward Heyman)**
  BODY AND SOUL
  I COVER THE WATERFRONT
  OUT OF NOWHERE
**Green, John (w: Billy Rose and Edward Heyman)**
  I WANNA BE LOVED
**Greenberg, Steve (w & m)**
  FUNKYTOWN
**Greenfield, Howard (w: Jack Keller)**
  EVERYBODY'S SOMEBODY'S FOOL
**Greenwich, Ellie/Jeff Barry/Phil Spector**
  DA DOO RON RON
**Greer, Jesse (w: Benny Davis)**
  I'M GONNA MEET MY SWEETIE NOW
**Grever, Maria (w: Stanley Adams)**
  WHAT A DIFF'RENCE A DAY MADE
**Gross, Walter (w: Jack Lawrence)**
  TENDERLY
**Grubb, Gayle (w & m)**
  ETIQUETTE BLUES
**Guidry, Robert (w & m)**
  SEE YOU LATER, ALLIGATOR
**Gumble, Albert (w: A. Seymour Brown)**
  AT THE MISSISSIPPI CABARET
**Gumble, Albert (w: Alfred Bryan)**
  WINTER
**Guthrie, Arlo (w & m)**
  ALICE'S RESTAURANT
**Hadjidakis, Manes (w: Billy Towne)**
  NEVER ON SUNDAY
**Hall, Daryl (w: Hall/Oates/Sara Allen)**
  I CAN'T GO FOR THAT
**Hall, Daryl and Janna Allen**
  KISS ON MY LIST
**Hall, Daryl and John Oates (w: Sara Allen, Hall and Oates)**
  MANEATER
**Hall, Daryl/Warren Pash/Sara Allen/Janna Allen**
  PRIVATE EYES
**Hall, Tom T. (w & m)**
  HARPER VALLEY P.T.A.
**Hall, Wendell W. (w & m)**
  IT AIN'T GONNA RAIN NO MO'
**Hamilton, Dan (w & m)**
  FALLIN' IN LOVE

**Hamlisch, Marvin (w: Alan and Marilyn Bergman)**
  WAY WE WERE, THE
**Hamlisch, Marvin (w: Carole Bayer Sager)**
  NOBODY DOES IT BETTER
**Hamm, Fred and Dave Bennett**
  BYE BYE BLUES
**Hamm, Fred and Jack Gardner (w: Harry Harris)**
  HANGIN' AROUND
**Hammer, Jack and Otis Blackwell**
  GREAT BALLS OF FIRE
**Hammerstein, Arthur and Dudley Wilkinson**
  BECAUSE OF YOU
**Hammond, Albert and Diane Warren**
  NOTHING'S GONNA STOP US NOW
**Hancock, Herbie**
  WATERMELON MAN
**Handman, Lou (w: Grant Clarke and Edgar Leslie)**
  BLUE (AND BROKEN HEARTED)
**Handman, Lou (w: Herman Ruby and Billy Rose)**
  I CAN'T GET THE ONE I WANT
**Handman, Lou (w: Roy Turk)**
  ARE YOU LONESOME TONIGHT?
  I'M GONNA CHARLESTON BACK
    TO CHARLESTON
**Handy, W. C. (w & m)**
  BEALE STREET
  HESITATING BLUES
  JOE TURNER BLUES
  MEMPHIS BLUES
  ST. LOUIS BLUES
  YELLOW DOG BLUES
**Handy, W. C. (w: J. Tim Brymn)**
  AUNT HAGAR'S CHILDREN BLUES
**Handy, Will (pseudonym of Bob Cole and J. Rosamond Johnson)**
  OH, DIDN'T HE RAMBLE
**Hanley, James F. (w & m)**
  ZING! WENT THE STRINGS OF MY HEART
**Hanley, James F. (w: Grant Clarke)**
  SECOND HAND ROSE
**Hanley, James F. (w: B. G. DeSylva)**
  MINE
**Hanley, James F. (w: Ballard MacDonald)**
  INDIANA
  ROSE OF WASHINGTON SQUARE

MacCall, Ewan (w & m)
  FIRST TIME EVER I SAW YOUR FACE, THE
MacDermot, Galt (w: James Rado and
Gerome Ragni)
  AQUARIUS/LET THE SUNSHINE IN
MacDonald, Jimmy (w: Jack Hoffman)
  I WANNA SAY HELLO
Mack, Ronald (w & m)
  HE'S SO FINE
Macklin, Cecil
  TRES MOUTARDE (TOO MUCH MUSTARD)
Maguire, Hannibal (w & m)
  DUCK'S QUACK, THE
Malie, Tommie and Jimmy Steiger
  LOOKING AT THE WORLD THRU ROSE
    COLORED GLASSES
Malneck, Matt and Frank Signorelli
(w: Gus Kahn)
  I'LL NEVER BE THE SAME
Malneck, Matt and Frank Signorelli
(w: Mitchell Parish)
  STAIRWAY TO THE STARS
Mancini, Henry (w: Mercer, Johnny)
  DAYS OF WINE AND ROSES
  MOON RIVER
Mandel, Johnny (w: Paul F. Webster)
  SHADOW OF YOUR SMILE, THE
Mann, Barry/Cynthia Weil/Phil Spector
  YOU'VE LOST THAT LOVIN' FEELIN'
Mann, Barry/Cynthia Weil/Jerry Leiber/
Mike Stoller
  ON BROADWAY
Marks, Gerald (w: Seymour Simons)
  ALL OF ME
Marks, Gerald/Irving Caesar/Sammy Lerner
  IS IT TRUE WHAT THEY SAY ABOUT DIXIE?
Marks, Johnny (w & m)
  RUDOLPH THE RED-NOSED REINDEER
Marley, Bob (w & m)
  I SHOT THE SHERIFF
Marshall, Henry I. (w: Stanley Murphy)
  BE MY LITTLE BABY BUMBLE BEE
  I WANT TO LINGER
Martin, Hugh (w: Ralph Blane)
  TROLLEY SONG, THE
Martin, Max (w & m)
  ...BABY ONE MORE TIME
Marx, Richard (w & m)
  HOLD ON TO THE NIGHTS

Masser, Michael (w: Linda Creed)
  GREATEST LOVE OF ALL
Masser, Michael (w: Gerry Goffin)
  SAVING ALL MY LOVE FOR YOU
Masser, Michael and Will Jennings
  DIDN'T WE ALMOST HAVE IT ALL
Mayfield, Percy (w & m)
  HIT THE ROAD JACK
Mayhew, Billy (w & m)
  IT'S A SIN TO TELL A LIE
McCall, C. W./Bill Fries/Chip Davis
  CONVOY
McCartney, Paul (w & m)
  BAND ON THE RUN
  COMING UP
  EBONY AND IVORY
  SILLY LOVE SONGS
McCartney, Paul and Linda McCartney
  MY LOVE
McCartney, Paul and Michael Jackson
  SAY, SAY, SAY
McCord, Charles and Matthews
  BIRMINGHAM BLUES
McCormack, Keith and Faye Voss
  SUGAR SHACK
McCoy, Van
  HUSTLE, THE
McDaniels, Eugene (w & m)
  FEEL LIKE MAKIN' LOVE
McElroy, Thomas and Denzil Foster
  MY LOVIN' (YOU'RE NEVER GONNA
    GET IT)
McFerrin, Bobby (w & m)
  DON'T WORRY BE HAPPY
McHugh, Jimmy (w: Harold Adamson)
  IT'S A MOST UNUSUAL DAY
McHugh, Jimmy (w: Dorothy Fields)
  DIGGA-DIGGA-DO
  DOIN' THE NEW LOW-DOWN
  I CAN'T GIVE YOU ANYTHING BUT LOVE
  ON THE SUNNY SIDE OF THE STREET
McHugh, Jimmy (w: Clarence Gaskill)
  I CAN'T BELIEVE THAT YOU'RE IN LOVE
    WITH ME
McHugh, Jimmy (w: Arnold Johnson)
  GOODBYE BLUES
McHugh, Jimmy (w: Ted Koehler)
  I'M IN THE MOOD FOR LOVE
  SPREADIN' RHYTHM AROUND

McHugh, Jimmy (w: Irving Mills)
EVERYTHING IS HOTSY TOTSY NOW

McHugh, Jimmy/Gene Austin/Irving Mills
WHEN MY BABY WALKS DOWN THE STREET

McLean, Don (w & m)
AMERICAN PIE

McPhail, Lindsay and Walter Hirsch
SAN

McVie, Christine
DON'T STOP

Meinken, Fred (w: Dave Ringle)
WABASH BLUES

Mellencamp, John (w & m)
JACK AND DIANE
R.O.C.K. IN THE U.S.A.

Mencher, Murray (w: Billy Moll)
I WANT A LITTLE GIRL

Menken, Alan (w: Howard Ashman)
BEAUTY AND THE BEAST
UNDER THE SEA

Menken, Alan (w: Tim Rice)
WHOLE NEW WORLD, A

Menken, Alan (w: Stephen Schwartz)
COLORS OF THE WIND

Mercer, Johnny (w & m)
DREAM
SOMETHING'S GOTTA GIVE
TOP BANANA

Mercury, Freddie
CRAZY LITTLE THING CALLED LOVE

Merrill, Alan and Jake Hooker
I LOVE ROCK 'N ROLL

Merrill, Bob (w & m)
HOW MUCH IS THAT DOGGIE IN
THE WINDOW?
MY TRULY, TRULY FAIR

Merrill, George and Shannon Rubicam
I WANNA DANCE WITH SOMEBODY

Merrill, George/Shannon Rubicam/Narada Walden
HOW WILL I KNOW?

Messenheimer, Sam/Irving Abrahamson/Ray West
IDOLIZING

Meyer, Chuck and Biff Jones
SUDDENLY THERE'S A VALLEY

Meyer, George and Arthur Johnston
(w: Grant Clark and Roy Turk)
I'M A LITTLE BLACKBIRD LOOKING FOR
A BLUEBIRD
MANDY, MAKE UP YOUR MIND

Meyer, George W. (w: Alfred Bryan)
BROWN EYES, WHY ARE YOU BLUE?

Meyer, George W. (w: Gus Kahn)
SITTIN' IN A CORNER

Meyer, George W. (w: Edgar Leslie and
E. Ray Goetz)
FOR ME AND MY GAL

Meyer, George W. (w: Sam Lewis and Joe Young)
CRY BABY BLUES
TUCK ME TO SLEEP IN MY OLD
'TUCKY HOME
WHERE DID ROBINSON CRUSOE GO WITH
FRIDAY ON SATURDAY NIGHT?

Meyer, George W. (w: Roy Turk)
SOMEONE IS LOSIN' SUSAN

Meyer, Joseph (w: Alfred Bryan)
BLUE RIVER

Meyer, Joseph (w: Bud DeSylva)
SUGAR PLUM

Meyer, Joseph (w: Al Dubin and Billy Rose)
CUP OF COFFEE, A SANDWICH AND
YOU, A

Meyer, Joseph (w: Billy Rose and
Ballard MacDonald)
CLAP HANDS! HERE COMES CHARLEY!

Meyer, Joseph (w: Herman Ruby)
MY HONEY'S LOVIN' ARMS

Meyer, Joseph and Roger Wolfe Kahn
(w: Irving Caesar)
CRAZY RHYTHM

Meyer, Joseph/Bud DeSylva/Al Jolson
CALIFORNIA, HERE I COME

Michael, George (w & m)
FAITH

Michael, George and Andrew Ridgeley
CARELESS WHISPER

Miller, Glenn (w: Mitchell Parish)
MOONLIGHT SERENADE

Miller, Ned/Chester Cohn/Jules Stein/
Bennie Krueger
SUNDAY

Miller, Roger (w & m)
KING OF THE ROAD

Mills, Kerry
WHISTLING RUFUS

Mills, Kerry (w: Thurland Chattaway)
RED WING

Mills, Kerry (w: Andrew B. Sterling)
MEET ME IN ST. LOUIS, LOUIS

Murphy, Owen (w & m)
OH, BABY
Murphy, Walter
FIFTH OF BEETHOVEN
Myers, Sherman (w: Chester Wallace)
MOONLIGHT ON THE GANGES
Myrow, Josef (w: Mack Gordon)
YOU MAKE ME FEEL SO YOUNG
Napoleon, Phil and Frank Signorelli
GREAT WHITE WAY BLUES
Naset, C. (w: Gus Kahn)
SUSIE
Nash, Johnny
I CAN SEE CLEARLY NOW
Navarro, Esther (w & m)
SPEEDOO
Nelson, Bob/Harry Link/Al Lentz/
Irving Aaronson
BOO HOO HOO (YOU'RE GONNA CRY WHEN
I'M GONE)
Nelson, Steve and Jack Rollins
FROSTY THE SNOW MAN
Nelson, Steve and Norman Kaye
SAY IT WITH YOUR HEART
Nevin, Ethelbert (w: Frank L. Stanton)
MIGHTY LAK' A ROSE
New Orleans Rhythm Kings
(w: Walter Melrose)
TIN ROOF BLUES
Newlon, Jack
ORIENTAL BLUES
Newman, Herb and Stan Lebowsky
WAYWARD WIND, THE
Newman, Randy (w & m)
MAMA TOLD ME (NOT TO COME)
SHORT PEOPLE
Newton, Eddie (w: T. Lawrence Seibert)
CASEY JONES
Nicks, Stevie (w & m)
DREAMS
Noble, Ray (w & m)
I HADN'T ANYONE TILL YOU
VERY THOUGHT OF YOU, THE
Noble, Ray/James Campbell/Reg Connelly
GOODNIGHT SWEETHEART
North, Alex (w: Hy Zaret)
UNCHAINED MELODY
Northup, Jos. C.
CANNON BALL

Norworth, Jack and Nora Bayes
MR. MOON MAN TURN OFF YOUR LIGHT
Nowels, Rick and Ellen Shipley
HEAVEN IS A PLACE ON EARTH
Nyro, Laura (w & m)
WEDDING BELL BLUES
O'Connor, Desmond and Ray Hartley
LET'S DO IT AGAIN
O'Donnell, Charley (w: Bobby Heath)
MY PONY BOY
O'Hara, Geoffrey (w & m)
K-K-K-KATY
O'Sullivan, Raymond (w & m)
ALONE AGAIN (NATURALLY)
Oakland, Ben (w: Milton Drake)
JAVA JIVE
Olcott, Chauncey (w & m)
MY WILD IRISH ROSE
Olcott, Chauncey and Ball, Ernest R.
(w: Rida Johnson Young)
MOTHER MACHREE
Oliver, Joe (w: Walter Melrose)
DOCTOR JAZZ
SUGAR FOOT STOMP
Oliver, Joe (w: Clarence Williams)
WEST END BLUES
Olman, Abe (w: James Brockman)
DOWN AMONG THE SHELTERING PALMS
Olman, Abe (w: Ed Rose)
OH, JOHNNY, OH, JOHNNY, OH!
Olman, Abe (w: Jack Yellen)
O-HI-O (DOWN BY THE)
Orbison, Roy
CRYIN'
Orbison, Roy and Bill Dees
OH, PRETTY WOMAN
Orbison, Roy and Joe Melson
RUNNING SCARED
Orzabel, Roland/Ian Stanley/Chris Hughes
EVERYBODY WANTS TO RULE
THE WORLD
Osborne, Nat (w: Ballard MacDonald)
IN SOUDAN
Otis, Clyde and Nancy Lee
STROLL, THE
Overstreet, W. Benton (w: Billy Higgins)
THERE'LL BE SOME CHANGES MADE
Owens, Anita (w & m)
DAISIES WON'T TELL

# INDEX BY PUBLISHER

MERRY WIDOW'S GOT A SWEETIE NOW, THE

SHAKE IT AND BREAK IT

**Harman Music**

I SAW MOMMY KISSING SANTA CLAUS

**T. B. Harms**

ALL ALONE MONDAY

ALL THROUGH THE NIGHT

ALWAYS TRUE TO YOU IN MY FASHION

AND I AM ALL ALONE

ANYTHING GOES

APRIL IN PARIS

AS TIME GOES BY

AUTUMN IN NEW YORK

BAMBALINA

BEFORE I MET YOU

BEGIN THE BEGUINE

BILL

BIRTH OF THE BLUES, THE

BLACK BOTTOM

BLUE DANUBE BLUES

BLUE ROOM, THE

BODY AND SOUL

BONGO ON THE CONGO

BROTHER, CAN YOU SPARE A DIME?

BULL FROG PATROL

BUNGALOW IN QUOGUE, THE

CAN THIS BE LOVE?

CAN'T HELP LOVIN' DAT MAN

CAN'T WE BE FRIENDS?

CARIOCA

CHANSONETTE

CHARLESTON

CLAP YO' HANDS

CLEOPATTERER

CONTINENTAL, THE

CRAZY RHYTHM

CRICKETS ARE CALLING, THE

CUP OF COFFEE, A SANDWICH AND YOU, A

DANCING IN THE DARK

DEEP IN MY HEART, DEAR

DESERT SONG, THE

DIXIE MOON

DO IT AGAIN

DO-DO-DO

DON'T FENCE ME IN

FASCINATING RHYTHM

FINE AND DANDY

GIRL FRIEND, THE

HALLELUJAH!

HAS ANYBODY HERE SEEN KELLY?

HE LOVES AND SHE LOVES

HELLO! MA BABY

HOORAY FOR HOLLYWOOD

HOW'D YOU LIKE TO SPOON WITH ME?

I COVER THE WATERFRONT

I GET A KICK OUT OF YOU

I GOTTA RIGHT TO SING THE BLUES

I GUESS I'LL HAVE TO CHANGE MY PLAN

I KNOW THAT YOU KNOW

I MIGHT BE YOUR ONCE-IN-A-WHILE

I WANNA BE LOVED BY YOU

I WANT TO BE HAPPY

I'LL BUILD A STAIRWAY TO PARADISE

I'LL SEE YOU AGAIN

INDIAN LOVE CALL

IT'S ONLY A PAPER MOON

I'VE GOT RINGS ON MY FINGERS

I'VE TOLD EV'RY LITTLE STAR

JUST CROSS THE RIVER FROM QUEENS

JUST ONE OF THOSE THINGS

KA-LU-A

KATY-DID

KISS IN THE DARK, A

LAND WHERE THE GOOD SONGS GO, THE

LEAVE IT TO JANE

LEFT ALL ALONE AGAIN BLUES

LET'S DO IT

LIMEHOUSE BLUES

LIZA

LOOK FOR THE SILVER LINING

LOOKING FOR A BOY

LOVELY TO LOOK AT

LOVER, COME BACK TO ME

LUCKY DAY

MACK THE KNIFE ("MORITAT")

MAKE BELIEVE

MAN I LOVE, THE

MAYBE

MERRY-GO-ROUND BROKE DOWN, THE

MOONLIGHT ON THE GANGES

MY CASTLE IN THE AIR

MY HEART STOOD STILL

NIGHT AND DAY

OH ME! OH MY! (OH YOU!)

OH, LADY BE GOOD

OL' MAN RIVER

OLD FASHIONED LOVE

OLD-FASHIONED GARDEN

ONE ALONE

POOR BUTTERFLY

**T. B. Harms** (*continued*)

RISE 'N SHINE

SHE DIDN'T SAY "YES"

SHINE ON YOUR SHOES, A

SHOW ME THE WAY TO GO HOME

SIREN'S SONG, THE

SISTER SUSIE'S SEWING SHIRTS FOR SOLDIERS

SMOKE GETS IN YOUR EYES

SOME LITTLE BUG IS GOING TO FIND YOU

SOMEBODY LOVES ME

SOMEONE TO WATCH OVER ME

SOMETIMES I'M HAPPY

STOUT HEARTED MEN

SUGAR PLUM

SUN SHINES BRIGHTER, THE

SUNNY

SUNNY DISPOSISH

SWANEE

TEA FOR TWO

TELL ME PRETTY MAIDEN

TEN CENTS A DANCE

THEY DIDN'T BELIEVE ME

THINKING OF YOU

THOU SWELL

THREE LITTLE WORDS

TILL THE CLOUDS ROLL BY

TOO MARVELOUS FOR WORDS

TOUCH OF YOUR HAND, THE

WHAT DO YOU DO SUNDAYS, MARY?

WHAT IS THIS THING CALLED LOVE?

WHIP-POOR-WILL

WHO?

WHOSE BABY ARE YOU?

WHY DO I LOVE YOU?

WHY WAS I BORN?

WILD FLOWER

WITH A SONG IN MY HEART

WITH PLENTY OF MONEY AND YOU

WUNDERBAR

YANKEE DOODLE BLUES

YESTERDAYS

YOU AND THE NIGHT AND THE MUSIC

YOU DO SOMETHING TO ME

YOU NEVER KNEW ABOUT ME

YOU SAID SOMETHING

YOU TOOK ADVANTAGE OF ME

YOU'RE AN OLD SMOOTHIE

YOU'RE THE TOP

ZIGEUNER

ZING! WENT THE STRINGS OF MY HEART

**Charles K. Harris**

COME TAKE A TRIP IN MY AIRSHIP

GOOD BYE, MY LADY LOVE

HEAVEN WILL PROTECT THE WORKING GIRL

HELLO CENTRAL, GIVE ME HEAVEN

I WONDER WHO'S KISSING HER NOW

**Harrisongs**

GIVE ME LOVE (GIVE ME PEACE ON EARTH)

MY SWEET LORD

**Harvard Music**

PONY TIME

**Harwin Music**

MAN THAT GOT AWAY, THE

**Hastings Music**

TALK TO THE ANIMALS

**Havard Music**

TOSSIN' AND TURNIN'

**F. B. Haviland**

BLUE BELL

DOWN IN JUNGLE TOWN

**J. Fred Helf Co.**

PLAY THAT BARBERSHOP CHORD

**Helf & Hager**

EVERYBODY WORKS BUT FATHER

**Heroic Music**

GIRLS JUST WANNA HAVE FUN

**Higuera Music**

YOU SEND ME

**Hill and Range Songs**

BLUE SUEDE SHOES

FROSTY THE SNOW MAN

GREAT BALLS OF FIRE

LET ME GO, LOVER!

SH-BOOM

**Hit and Run Music**

I'M TOO SEXY

INVISIBLE TOUCH

**Carl Hoffman Music**

DILL PICKLES

**Holey Moley Music**

EYE OF THE TIGER

**Hot-Cha Music**

I CAN'T GO FOR THAT

KISS ON MY LIST

PRIVATE EYES

**P. J. Howley**

MY NAME IS MORGAN BUT IT
AIN'T J.P.

**Lost Boys Music**
TOTAL ECLIPSE OF THE HEART
**Lowal Corp.**
GIGI
NIGHT THEY INVENTED CHAMPAGNE, THE
**Lowery Music**
BE-BOP-A-LULA
ROSE GARDEN
**Low-TWI Music**
DIZZY
**LSR**
SMILES
**Ludix Music**
SOLDIER BOY
**Ludlow Music**
WE SHALL OVERCOME
**Maclen Music**
ALL YOU NEED IS LOVE
COME TOGETHER
EIGHT DAYS A WEEK
GET BACK
HARD DAY'S NIGHT, A
HELP!
HEY JUDE
LADY MADONNA
LET IT BE
LUCY IN THE SKY WITH DIAMONDS
PENNY LANE
SHE CAME IN THROUGH THE
BATHROOM WINDOW
TICKET TO RIDE
YESTERDAY
**Management Agency & Music Publishing**
ALONE AGAIN (NATURALLY)
**Maple Leaf Music**
NO MORE
**Edward B. Marks Music**
I'D DO ANYTHING FOR LOVE
LOLLIPOP
MANHATTAN
ORIGINAL DIXIELAND ONE-STEP
PAPER DOLL
PEANUT VENDOR, THE
STRANGE FRUIT
THERE'LL BE SOME CHANGES MADE
WHAT A DIFF'RENCE A DAY MADE
**Marlo Music**
I CAN DREAM, CAN'T I?
OH WHAT A BEAUTIFUL MORNIN'

OKLAHOMA
PEOPLE WILL SAY WE'RE IN LOVE
SURREY WITH THE FRINGE ON TOP, THE
**Marlyn-Copar**
WHOLE LOT-TA SHAKIN' GOIN' ON
**Marquis Music**
WHOLE LOTTA LOVING
**Marty's Music**
EL PASO
**Massey Music**
MY HEART CRIES FOR YOU
**Maurice Richmond Music**
IF I HAD MY WAY
**Mayday Music**
AMERICAN PIE
**Mayfair Music**
I'LL WALK ALONE
**MCA Music**
HOLD ON
**McCarthy & Fisher**
DARDANELLA
I'M ALWAYS CHASING RAINBOWS
I'M GOIN' TO SETTLE DOWN OUTSIDE OF
LONDON TOWN
IN THE LAND O' YAMO YAMO
THEY GO WILD SIMPLY WILD OVER ME
**McCartney Music**
SILLY LOVE SONGS
**Me Good Publishing**
ALL 4 LOVE
**Megasong Publishing**
SIGN, THE
**Mellow Music**
CRY
**Melody Trails**
TURN! TURN! TURN!
**Melrose Bros**
ALL NIGHT BLUES
BOOGIE WOOGIE
COPENHAGEN
DEEP HENDERSON
DOCTOR JAZZ
HANGIN' AROUND
IT'S TIGHT LIKE THAT
JIMTOWN BLUES
KANSAS CITY STOMP
KING PORTER STOMP
MILENBERG JOYS
MOBILE BLUES

THERE, I'VE SAID IT AGAIN
**Velvet Apple Music**
I WILL ALWAYS LOVE YOU
9 TO 5
**Venice Music**
TUTTI FRUTTI
LONG TALL SALLY
**Richard E. Vernor Pub. Co.**
SWEETHEART OF SIGMA CHI, THE
**Victoria**
LOVE NEST, THE
**Villa Moret**
CHLOE
MOONLIGHT AND ROSES
PROUD OF A BABY LIKE YOU
**Village Music**
TILL I WALTZ AGAIN WITH YOU
**Virgin Music**
COLD HEARTED
EVERYBODY WANTS TO RULE THE WORLD
FOREVER YOUR GIRL
GONNA MAKE YOU SWEAT (EVERYBODY DANCE NOW)
OPPOSITES ATTRACT
**Vision of Love Songs**
I DON'T WANNA CRY
VISION OF LOVE
**Viva Music**
YOU'RE SIXTEEN
**Vogue Music**
BLUE VELVET
**Harry Von Tilzer**
ALEXANDER, DON'T YOU LOVE YOUR BABY NO MORE?
ALL SHE'D SAY WAS UMH HUM
CUBANOLA GLIDE, THE
DOWN WHERE THE WURZBURGER FLOWS
I LOVE IT
I LOVE, I LOVE, I LOVE MY WIFE, BUT OH, YOU KID
I WANT A GIRL (JUST LIKE THE GIRL THAT MARRIED DEAR OLD DAD)
LOVIE JOE
MANSION OF ACHING HEARTS
ON A SUNDAY AFTERNOON
PLEASE LET ME SLEEP
ROW ROW ROW
UNDER THE ANHEUSER BUSH
WAIT TILL THE SUN SHINES, NELLIE

WHAT YOU GOIN' TO DO WHEN THE RENT COMES ROUND?
WHEN MY BABY SMILES AT ME
**Wand Publishing Co.**
DALLAS BLUES
**Warden Music**
BATTLE OF NEW ORLEANS, THE
**Warman Music**
SUDDENLY THERE'S A VALLEY
TO KNOW HIM IS TO LOVE HIM
WAYWARD WIND, THE
**Warner-Tamerlane**
ALL I WANNA DO
HUSTLE, THE
SLOW HAND
WEAK
**Warwick Music**
MOLASSES, MOLASSES
**Waterson Inc.**
BLUE-EYED SALLY
**Waterson, Berlin & Snyder**
AGGRAVATIN' PAPA
ALL THE QUAKERS ARE SHOULDER SHAKERS DOWN IN QUAKER TOWN
AT THE DEVIL'S BALL
BEALE STREET MAMA
BUZZIN' THE BEE
DANCING FOOL
DOES THE SPEARMINT LOSE ITS FLAVOR ON THE BEDPOST OVERNIGHT?
FOR ME AND MY GAL
HELLO CENTRAL, GIVE ME NO MAN'S LAND
HOW YA GONNA KEEP 'EM DOWN ON THE FARM?
I GAVE YOU UP JUST BEFORE YOU THREW ME DOWN
I'M ALL BOUND ROUND WITH THE MASON DIXON LINE
I'VE BEEN FLOATING DOWN THE OLD GREEN RIVER
JEAN
LET A SMILE BE YOUR UMBRELLA
MARGIE
MOONLIGHT
MY SUNNY TENNESSEE
NOW HE'S GOT A BEAUTIFUL GIRL
OH! GEE, OH! GOSH, OH! GOLLY, I'M IN LOVE
**Waterson, Berlin & Snyder** (*continued*)

I WISH I COULD SHIMMY LIKE MY
  SISTER KATE
I'VE FOUND A NEW BABY
JAIL HOUSE BLUES
JUST WAIT TILL YOU SEE MY BABY DO
  THE CHARLESTON
MAMA'S GONE, GOODBYE
MOROCCO BLUES
MY PILLOW AND ME
OH DADDY BLUES
SQUEEZE ME
'TAIN'T NOBODY'S BIZNESS IF I DO
WEST END BLUES

**Dootsie Williams**
EARTH ANGEL

**Spencer Williams Music**
COTTON BELT BLUES

**Williamson Music**
EVERYTHING'S COMING UP ROSES
GETTING TO KNOW YOU
HELLO YOUNG LOVERS
I WHISTLE A HAPPY TUNE
IF I LOVED YOU
I'LL BE SEEING YOU
IT MIGHT AS WELL BE SPRING
IT'S A GRAND NIGHT FOR SINGING
JUNE IS BUSTIN' OUT ALL OVER
MY FAVORITE THINGS
NO OTHER LOVE
SOME ENCHANTED EVENING
YOU'LL NEVER WALK ALONE
YOUNGER THAN SPRINGTIME

**Windsor Music**
GOOD MORNING, CARRIE

**Windswept Pacific Entertainment**
SAVE THE BEST FOR LAST

**Wingate Music**
CALIFORNIA DREAMIN'

**M. Witmark & Sons**
ABSENCE MAKES THE HEART GROW FONDER
ABSINTHE FRAPPE
AH! SWEET MYSTERY OF LIFE
ALL OVER NOTHING AT ALL
AM I BLUE?
ANGEL CHILD
ARE YOU FROM DIXIE?
AUNTIE SKINNER'S CHICKEN DINNER
BAKE DAT CHICKEN PIE
BANDANA DAYS

BEBE
BLOWIN' IN THE WIND
BO LA BO
CAKEWALK IN THE SKY, THE
CALIFORNIA, HERE I COME
COME DOWN MA EVENIN' STAR
CUDDLE UP A LITTLE CLOSER
DAUGHTER OF ROSIE O'GRADY, THE
DAYS OF WINE AND ROSES
DEAR LITTLE BOY OF MINE
DON'T THINK TWICE (IT'S ALL RIGHT)
EVERY DAY IS LADIES' DAY TO ME
EVERY LITTLE MOVEMENT
FORTY-SECOND STREET
GIVE ME THE SULTAN'S HAREM
GOING UP
GOODNIGHT, ANGELINE
GYPSY BLUES
HEIDELBERG (STEIN SONG)
I CAN'T DO THE SUM
I LOVE TO GO SWIMMIN' WITH WIMMEN
I'M A JONAH MAN
I'M FALLING IN LOVE WITH SOMEONE
I'M JUST WILD ABOUT HARRY
IN A SHANTY IN OLD SHANTY TOWN
IN HONEYSUCKLE TIME
IN MY MERRY OLDSMOBILE
IN OLD NEW YORK
INDIAN SUMMER
ITALIAN STREET SONG
IT'S MAGIC
JEEPERS CREEPERS
KISS ME AGAIN
LET THE REST OF THE WORLD GO BY
LIKE A ROLLING STONE
LITTLE BIT OF HEAVEN, A
LOVE WILL FIND A WAY
LULLABY OF BROADWAY
MA BLUSHIN' ROSIE
MOTHER MACHREE
MR. TAMBOURINE MAN
MY WILD IRISH ROSE
'NEATH THE SOUTHERN MOON
PAINTING THE CLOUDS WITH SUNSHINE
SHAKY EYES
SMILIN' THROUGH
SOUTH AMERICA, TAKE IT AWAY
STAY IN YOUR OWN BACKYARD

**M. Witmark & Sons** (*continued*)

# INDEX BY YEAR OF PUBLICATION

YOU CAN'T HURRY LOVE
YOU KEEP ME HANGIN' ON
**1967**
AIN'T NO MOUNTAIN HIGH ENOUGH
ALL YOU NEED IS LOVE
DAYDREAM BELIEVER
FOR ONCE IN MY LIFE
GENTLE ON MY MIND
GREEN TAMBOURINE
GROOVIN'
HARPER VALLEY P.T.A.
I SECOND THAT EMOTION
LEAVING ON A JET PLANE
LETTER, THE
LIGHT MY FIRE
LUCY IN THE SKY WITH DIAMONDS
NIGHTS IN WHITE SATIN
ODE TO BILLIE JOE
PENNY LANE
RESPECT
ROSE GARDEN
RUBY TUESDAY
SAN FRANCISCO (BE SURE TO WEAR FLOWERS
    IN YOUR HAIR)
SOUL MAN
TALK TO THE ANIMALS
TEARS OF A CLOWN, THE
TO SIR, WITH LOVE
WHAT A WONDERFUL WORLD
WHITER SHADE OF PALE
WINDY
(YOUR LOVE KEEPS LIFTING ME) HIGHER
    AND HIGHER
**1968**
ABRAHAM, MARTIN AND JOHN
BORN TO BE WILD
CRIMSON AND CLOVER
DIZZY
HEY JUDE
HONEY
HOOKED ON A FEELING
I'LL NEVER FALL IN LOVE AGAIN
IN THE YEAR 2525
JUMPIN' JACK FLASH
LADY MADONNA
LOVE CHILD
LOVE IS BLUE
MACARTHUR PARK
MRS. ROBINSON

PEOPLE GOT TO BE FREE
PROUD MARY
(SITTIN' ON) THE DOCK OF THE BAY
SUNSHINE OF YOUR LOVE
SUSPICIOUS MINDS
THIS GUY'S IN LOVE WITH YOU
TIDE IS HIGH, THE
WINDMILLS OF YOUR MIND, THE
**1969**
AMERICAN WOMAN
BAD MOON RISING
BRIDGE OVER TROUBLED WATER
COME TOGETHER
DOWN ON THE CORNER
GET BACK
GIVE PEACE A CHANCE
HE AIN'T HEAVY . . . HE'S MY BROTHER
HONKY TONK WOMEN
I CAN'T GET NEXT TO YOU
LAY, LADY, LAY
ME AND BOBBY McGEE
MY CHERIE AMOUR
PUT A LITTLE LOVE IN YOUR HEART
RAINDROPS KEEP FALLIN' ON MY HEAD
SHE CAME IN THROUGH THE
    BATHROOM WINDOW
SUGAR, SUGAR
THANK YOU (FALETTINME BE MICE ELF AGIN)
WOODSTOCK
**1970**
BEING ALIVE
CANDY MAN, THE
CRACKLIN' ROSIE
EVERYTHING IS BEAUTIFUL
FOR ALL WE KNOW
HAVE YOU EVER SEEN THE RAIN?
I THINK I LOVE YOU
I'LL BE THERE
JOY TO THE WORLD
JUST MY IMAGINATION
KNOCK THREE TIMES
LET IT BE
LONG AND WINDING ROAD, THE
MAKE IT WITH YOU
MAMA TOLD ME (NOT TO COME)
MY DING-A-LING
MY SWEET LORD
ONE BAD APPLE
VENUS

GREATEST LOVE OF ALL
HOW DEEP IS YOUR LOVE
I JUST WANT TO BE YOUR EVERYTHING
JUST THE WAY YOU ARE
LAST DANCE
NIGHT FEVER
NOBODY DOES IT BETTER
SHORT PEOPLE
TOMORROW

**1978**
BAD GIRLS
BOOGIE OOGIE OOGIE
DA YA THINK I'M SEXY?
FIRE
GOT MY MIND SET ON YOU
GREASE
HEART OF GLASS
I WILL SURVIVE
KISS YOU ALL OVER
LE FREAK
MISS YOU
MY LIFE
SAVING ALL MY LOVE FOR YOU
SHADOW DANCING
THREE TIMES A LADY
TRAGEDY
YOU'RE THE ONE THAT I WANT

**1979**
ANOTHER BRICK IN THE WALL (PART II)
CRAZY LITTLE THING CALLED LOVE
DO THAT TO ME ONE MORE TIME
GOOD TIMES
HEARTACHE TONIGHT
HOT STUFF
IT GOES LIKE IT GOES
MY SHARONA
PLEASE DON'T GO
RAINBOW CONNECTION
SAILING

**1980**
ANOTHER ONE BITES THE DUST
CALL ME
CELEBRATION
COMING UP
FAME
FUNKYTOWN
I LOVE A RAINY NIGHT
IT'S STILL ROCK AND ROLL TO ME
JESSIE'S GIRL

(JUST LIKE) STARTING OVER
KEEP ON LOVING YOU
KISS ON MY LIST
LADY
MAGIC
9 TO 5
ONE THAT YOU LOVE, THE
RAPTURE
UPSIDE DOWN

**1981**
ARTHUR'S THEME
CENTERFOLD
CHARIOTS OF FIRE
ENDLESS LOVE
I CAN'T GO FOR THAT
MEMORY
MORNING TRAIN
PHYSICAL
PRIVATE EYES
SLOW HAND

**1982**
AFRICA
BEAT IT
BILLIE JEAN
COME ON EILEEN
DOWN UNDER
EBONY AND IVORY
EYE OF THE TIGER
HARD TO SAY I'M SORRY
JACK AND DIANE
MANEATER
THAT'S WHAT FRIENDS ARE FOR
TOTAL ECLIPSE OF THE HEART
UP WHERE WE BELONG
WHO CAN IT BE NOW?

**1983**
ALL NIGHT LONG (ALL NIGHT)
ALWAYS
CRAZY FOR YOU
EVERY BREATH YOU TAKE
FLASHDANCE . . . WHAT A FEELING
ISLANDS IN THE STREAM
KARMA CHAMELEON
REFLEX, THE
SAY, SAY, SAY
SWEET DREAMS ARE MADE OF THIS
TELL HER ABOUT IT
TIME AFTER TIME
UPTOWN GIRL

WITHDRAWN